Correctio
SAPARES? A
TAPNER – a well know
schoolmaster

East Sussex Census – 1851 Index

Volume 6

RUSTED STAPLES

Please note that where staples have rusted they have been removed
and replaced. Unfortunately this has resulted in discoloration of
some pages and covers. These copies are the only ones available
and as information is unaffected I do hope that the
blemishes do not cause too much offence.

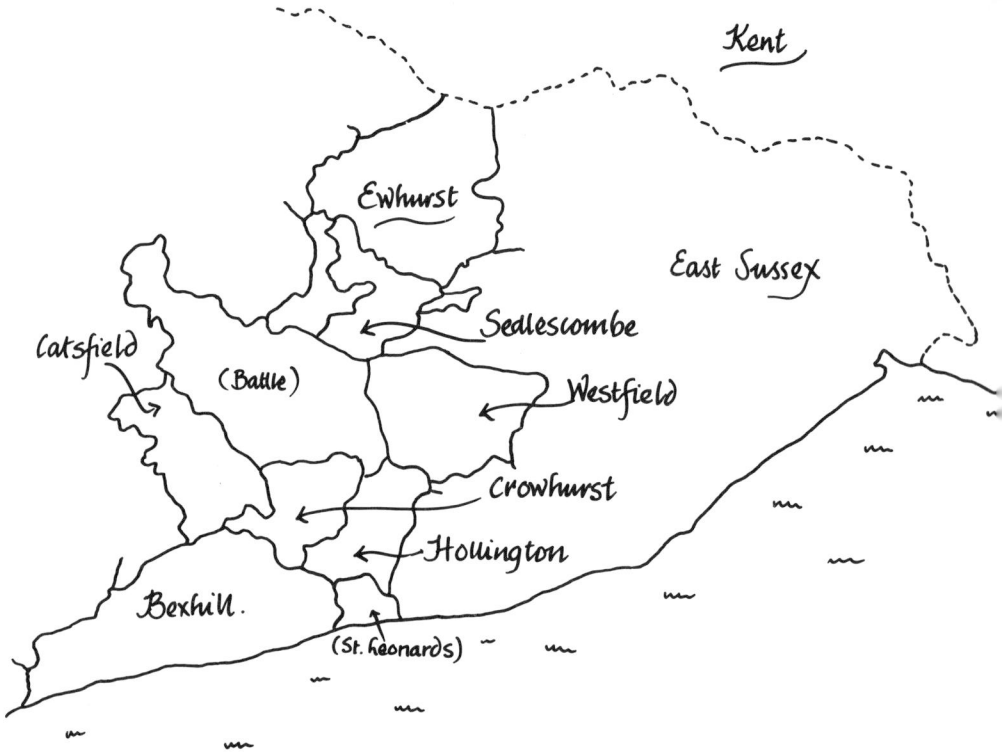

Rough Map showing location of Parishes covered.

POPULATION - 1851 Census

	Pop.	Sched.B un-named	H.H's.	Hses Inhab.	Empty	Bld.
Hollington	579	0	98	83	1	0
Bexhill	2146	2	413	405	14	0
Catsfield	549	1	112	109	3	0
Crowhurst	592	0	79	89	0	0
Westfield	890	10	172	172	1	0
Sedlescombe............	715	0	140	138	1	0
Ewhurst	1205	8	225	225	6	0
TOTALS.................	6676	21	1239	1221	26	0

Average 5.405 persons per household and 5.48 persons per house.

East Sussex County Planning Information Paper No. 43 forecast for 1986 suggested the following figures:

Hollington	5400	people	2000	Households	
Bexhill	36000	"	18800	"	
Catsfield	700	"	750	"	(sic)
Crowhurst	800	"	325	"	
Westfield	2400	"	1000	"	
Sedlescombe	1300	"	550	"	
Totals	46600	"	23425	"	= Household average of 1.989

EAST SUSSEX CENSUS - 1851 INDEX

Volume 6

Compiled by C. June Barnes

CONTENTS:-

Parishes are not named in the Index, but can be identified by checking the folio
number listed in the 9th column against the following summary:-

```
HO107 1636
Registrar's District - Bexhill
Folios   1- 20 ....... Hollington   Enumeration District No.1
        21- 33 ....... Bexhill         "          "        2a
        34- 47 .......    "            "          "        2b
        48- 60 ......     "            "          "        2c
        61- 71 .......    "            "          "        2d
        72- 85 .......    "            "          "        2e
        86-102 .......    "            "          "        2f
       103-115 ....... Catsfield       "          "        3a
       116-124 .......    "            "          "        3b
       125-138 ....... Crowhurst       "          "        4a
       139-147 .......    "            "          "        4b
       148-157 ....... Westfield       "          "        5a
       158-168 .......    "            "          "        5b
       169-182 .......    "            "          "        5c
Registrar's District - Ewhurst
Folios 183-197 ....... Sedlescombe  Enumeration District No.1a
       198-211 .......    "            "          "        1b
       212-228 ....... Ewhurst         "          "        2a
       229-245 .......    "            "          "        2b
       246-254 .......    "            "          "        2c
```

ISBN 1 870264 05 3

CHAPMAN COUNTY CODES

County Abbreviations used in the Index

AVN	Avon	NTH	Northamptonshire
BDF	Bedfordshire	NBL	Northumberland
BRK	Berkshire	NTT	Nottinghamshire
BKM	Buckinghamshire	OXF	Oxfordshire
CAM	Cambridgeshire	RUT	Rutland
CHS	Cheshire	SAL	Shropshire
CLV	Cleveland	SOM	Somersetshire
CON	Cornwall	STS	Staffordshire
CUL	Cumberland	SFK	Suffolk
DBY	Derbyshire	SRY	Surrey
DEV	Devonshire	SSX	Sussex
DOR	Dorsetshire	SXE	East Sussex
DUR	Durham	SXW	West Sussex
ESS	Essex	WAR	Warwickshire
GLS	Gloucestershire	WES	Westmorland
HAM	Hampshire	WIL	Wiltshire
HEF	Herefordshire	WMD	West Midlands
HRT	Hertfordshire	WOR	Worcestershire
HUM	Humberside	ERY	East Riding
HUN	Huntingdonshire	WRY	West Riding
IOM	Isle of Man	NRY	North Riding
IOW	Isle of Wight	EYK	East Yorkshire
KEN	Kent	NYK	North Yorkshire
LAN	Lancashire	SYK	South Yorkshire
LEI	Leicestershire	WYK	West Yorkshire
LIN	Lincolnshire	YKS	Yorkshire
LND	London		
MDX	Middlesex	IRL	Ireland
MSY	Merseyside	SCT	Scotland
NFK	Norfolk	WLS	Wales
		CO	County

- * -

STANDARD ABBREVIATIONS FOR RELATIONSHIP TO HEAD OF HOUSEHOLD

apprentice .... AP	housekeeper .... HK	servant .... SV
assistant .... AS	husband .... HU	sister CI
aunt .... AU	inmate .... IM	sister-in-law .. CL
boarder .... BO	journeyman .... JM	son .... SO
brother .... BR	lodger .... LG	son-in-law ..... SL
brother-in-law ...... BL	lodger's DA .... LD	son's wife ..... SW
clerk .... CK	lodger's SO .... LS	step brother ... SB
companion .... CM	lodger's WI .... LW	step-daughter .. SD
cousin .... CO	maidservant .... MV	step-father .... SF
daughter .... DA	matron .... MA	step-mother .... SM
daughter-in-law ..... DL	mistress .... MT	step-sister .... SC
father .... FA	mistress' DA ...... MD	step-son .... SS
father-in-law .... FL	mistress' SO ...... MS	stranger .... SG
foreman .... FM	mother .... MO	teacher .... TE
governess .... GO	mother-in-law ..... ML	traveller ...... TR
grand-daughter ...... GD	neice .... NC	uncle .... UC
grand-father .... GF	nephew .... NP	visitor .... VR
grand-mother .... GM	nurse .... NS	wife .... WI
grand-son .... GS	orphan .... OR	wife's DA ...... WD
great aunt .... GA	patient .... PT	wife's FA ...... WF
great uncle .... GU	porter .... PO	wife's GD ......WGD
groom .... GM	prisoner .... PS	wife's GS ......WGS
guest .... GT	pupil .... PP	wife's MO ...... WM
half-brother .... HB	relation .... RE	wife's CI ...... WC
half sister .... HC	relative .... RE	wife's SO ...... WS
head .... HD	scholar .... SH	wife's BR ...... WB
	school teacher .... ST	

Any of the above with G as prefix to read Great--

In addition to the above and other standard abbreviations the following have been used where necessary:

Ag.Lab ...	Agricultural Labourer	? ..	unclear/indecipherable entry
Lab	Labourer	W ..	Widow/Widower
Emp	Employed/Employing	M ..	Married
Ac	Acres	U ..	Un-married
Illeg	Illegible	W ..	Weeks
C G S	Coast Guard Service	M ..	Months
S	Service	D ..	Days
/	not given	+ ..	more information on return
*	an evaluated entry - the compiler's best interpretation. Also at times used to draw attention to an entry - e.g. Sched.B etc.		
()	bracketed words are speculation or have been erased on the returns by the registrar when checking.		

- * -

USING THE INDEX

The index is not intended to be a substitute for the original entries. Researchers are advised to use it as a finding aid only, and are urged to consult the originals for verification. All entries have been fed into a computer directly from micro-films of the original enumerator's books, and checked against these. Apologies are made for any errors or misinterpretations which may occur. As with all transcribing it is often very difficult to interpret names of people and places. Place names outside Sussex in particular fell prey to error as the enumerators were often unfamiliar with them. The very best has been done to transcribe or interpret as accurately as possible. In the event of there being an error I would appreciate it if I could be informed of such a mistake, preferably after such a discrepancy has been checked against the returns. The master index on disc will then be amended and the correction added to the sheet of notes and corrections available for each volume upon submitting a S.A.E.

I have made it my policy to reproduce what was actually entered by the enumerators, changing spelling only in very obvious instances. The spelling therefore is often a little unusual. In this particular volume many entries for Bexhill and Catsfield sadly did not have the address named on the returns. In many cases it was difficult to establish the ages because the Registrar put lines through them - in particular those for females. Much of Enumeration District No.2 - Ewhurst Registrar's District was written in a very shaky hand, whilst Enumeration District No.4b - Bexhill Registrar's District (Crowhurst) revealed some very unusual spellings. The enumerator for Enumeration District No.5a - Bexhill Registrar's District (Westfield) didn't give the birthplace for many of his entries, and where it seems likely that the birthplace was probably Westfield this has been entered as (?Westfield).

Un-named persons living in barns etc. are given as numbers on Schedule B of the returns. Some of these were also named in the returns, and where this happened I have included their names in the index. Such entries are marked with * in the first column. I included the details of Sarah Samson who was amongst the Schedule B persons named in Crowhurst, although the entry had been crossed out. There were also 5 persons known to be absent under Schedules D, and in Sedlescombe space had been left for one of these. He has been entered in the index as Smith Farmer. There were 19 persons under Schedule C, being those in the area temporarily. The population figures on page 2 have been reconciled against those on the returns. The Population figure for Bexhill mentioned by Aylwin Guilmant in her introduction were extracted from Victoria County History. Occasionally a head of household is not given due to absence, and often the next of kin, usually the wife, but in some instances a servant, is listed as the head.

The microfilms of the returns can be seen at the Census Rooms of the P.R.O. in Portugal Street, London, or locally at Hastings, Eastbourne and Brighton Reference Libraries. Copies are also held by East Sussex Record Office in Lewes. A list of addresses can be found at the back of this book. It is advisable to make appointments to use micro-film viewers.

FORMAT OF THE INDEX

There are 9 columns:
1) House number - NOT ADDRESS
2) Names, surnames followed by given names in alphabetical order
3) Relationship to head of household (See page 5)
4) Condition - whether married, un-married or widowed
5) Age
6) Occupation where given
7) County and town of birth where given (See page 4)
8) Address as and when given on return
9) Folio number on microfilm - no differentiation is made between Sides A or B. The Parish name is established by cross referencing this number against those of the Parishes listed on page 3.

INTRODUCTION

The first Census in England took place in 1801. It was little more than the counting of heads in every place at a given time. Those who were absent, as in the case of soldiers and sailors, were overlooked.

The 1851 Census returns are invaluable in that this was the first time that members of the Royal Navy based in home waters were included. Further interesting points were that the enumeration was held on one day only, the 31st March; the place of birth was included in the entry and it was made under the superintendence of the registration officers.

The places covered by this volume are all within the Rape of Hastings; Crowhurst, Hollington and Westfield are in Baldslow Hundred. Sedlescombe and Ewhurst are within Staple Hundred, while Catsfield is in Ninfield Hundred. Bexhill, still a village at this time, was considerably larger than the aforementioned places and was in the Hundred of Bexhill, but Bexhill Parish was situated partly in this Hundred and partly in Hastings Borough and Cinque Port.

The toll roads, introduced by the Turnpike Act of 1836, would have opened up certain of these areas, particularly Sedlescombe, but there was little rise in population in the decade between 1841 and 1851. It is interesting to note that the population of Catsfield actually fell from 589 to 550 during this period. The two villages with the largest rise experienced were Crowhurst and Bexhill. This could be accounted for by the addition of the railway workers. One in six persons were still employed on the land but even the porters on the railway were higher paid than the labouring class.

The Timber industry continued to grow in Sussex during the 19th century and it is thought that the large estates may have contributed to this growth, timber being an invaluable cash crop. Improved roads and the railway network would certainly have eased the transportation problem experienced during earlier centuries when Sussex roads had the reputation of being notoriously bad. There was an expansion in Hop growing and again the wood for the poles would have been produced locally.

Much of the arable land was converted into pasture, with cattle rearing, dairy farming and poultry raising. The last was particularly well suited to the small farms of the weald. Again the railway network was heavily used for the transportation of produce both to London and to the growing coastal regions. Bexhill, however, was the last of the Sussex resorts to develop as such but much of this did not take place until after the 1880s. The population rising from a mere 2026 in 1851 to over 12,000 by the end of the century.

Horsfield in his History of Sussex (1838) described Bexhill as having "many good houses and some very hansome residences" but twenty years later the Tourists Handbook was perhaps more honest when it stated that " in this small village standing on a hill overlooking the sea there was only one building of note and this was the Church...." There was also The Bell, an old posting house. This Inn was for many years the meeting place of the local community with an assembly room which at one time was used as a small theatre by touring players. The area to-day known as the Old Town would have been completely self-sufficient with its Manor House, farms, forge and family businesses. Other communities would have been at Sidley and Little Common, only reached by country lanes.

Planned expansion in Bexhill commenced as early as c.1840 with the development of the Pages estate towards the west of the town. The first portion of St.Mark's Church in Little Common was built in 1842 on land given by Sir Godfrey Webster of the Battle Abbey Estate, but the church did not become a separate parish until 1857, curates from St.Peter's Church in the Old Town had originally served it. One of the most interesting facts thrown up by this Census surprisingly showed that nearly half the population went to no place of worship.

While the population of most of the villages mentioned rose between 1841 and 1851, within the next decade the position was reversed, with a fall in population in all areas with the exception of Catsfield where it rose by 31 from 550 to 584. Bexhill by comparison fell from 2026 to 2011. The drop in population 1851-1861 may have been due to various emigration schemes to colonies, encouraged by certain of the owners of large estates in the 1850's.

7

Aylwin Guilmant 1988

DESCRIPTIONS OF ENUMERATION DISTRICTS

N.B. The following descriptions are Crown Copyright material at the Public Record Office and are reproduced by permission of H.M.S.O.

HO107 1636 folios 1-20
Enumeration District No.1 Registrar's District - Bexhill.

"The whole of the Parish of Hollington, including Hollington Street, Sir Charles Lambs, the Harrow Inn, Iron Latch, Gate and Little Wilting etc."
Enumerator - William Christopher

HO107 1636 folios 21-33
Enumeration District No.2a Registrar's District - Bexhill.

"All that part of the Parish of Bexhill which lies south of the main road leading from Glyne Gapp to Barnham Hill (as far as Braggs Lane) including the Martello Towers in this district and part of Bexhill Street."
Enumerator - Richard Barnard

HO107 1636 folios 34-47
Enumeration District No.2b Registrar's District - Bexhill.

"All that part of the Parish of Bexhill that lies South of the Main road leading from Glyne Gapp to Barnham Hill, from Braggs Lane to Barnham Hill, taking the South West Bounds of the Parish to Sluice Rockhouse Bank, down to the Sea and the Martello Towers back to Braggs Lane."
Enumerator - John Plumb

HO107 1636 folios 48-60
Enumeration District No.2c Registrar's District - Bexhill.

"All that part of the Parish of Bexhill that lies North of the Main Road from Braggs Lane to Barnham Hill taking the Bounds of the Parish to Whydown and the South of the Main road to the Gunters, Haywards Mill including Thomas Leonards, down to Braggs Lane."
Enumerator - Jesse Barrows

HO107 1636 folios 61-71
Enumeration District No.2d Registrar's District - Bexhill.

"All that part of the Parish of Bexhill that lies North of the Main road from Sidley Corner by Gunters to Whydown taking Lunsfords X Cobbs Hill and the houses south of the Main road from the Water Mill to Sidley Corner."
Enumerator - Stephen Thomas

HO107 1636 folios 72-85
Enumeration District No.2e Registrar's District - Bexhill.

"All that part of the Parish of Bexhill which lies North of the Main Road from Sidley Corner to the Water Mill taking the Bounds of the Parish to Buckholt, Coombs, Worsham, Pepston and to Glyne Gapp and all the houses North of the Main Road to Sidley Corner."
Enumerator - William Thomas

HO107 1636 folios 86-102
Enumeration District No.2f Registrar's District - Bexhill.

"All that part of the Parish of Bexhill commencing at the 2 houses adjoining Districts 1 & 5 taking the North side of Bexhill Street to Braggs Lane, the Down Farm and the Gunters and taking the Houses (to) the South of the Main road to Sidley Corner and to the 2 Houses."
Enumerator - John Thomas

8

HO107 1636 folios 103-115
Enumeration District No.3a   Registrar's District - Bexhill.

"All that part of the Parish of Catsfield which lies South and East of the Main
road from Catsfield Stream to Powder Mill Lane including Tilton, Water Mill,
Henleys Down, Place Farm to Powder Mill Lane and houses (to) the South of the
main road to Catsfield Stream."
Enumerator - Joshua Adams

HO107 1636 folios 116-124
Enumeration District No.3b   Registrar's District - Bexhill.

"All that part of the Parish of Catsfield which lies North and West of the Main
road from Catsfield Stream to Powder Mill Lane including the Stream Farm, Marl
Pits, Burnt Barns, Steven's Crouch, Keepers, Park Gate to Powder Mill Lane and
the houses on the North of the Main road to Catsfield Stream."
Enumerator - William Sheather

HO107 1636 folios 125-138
Enumeration District No.4a   Registrar,s District - Bexhill.

"All that part of the Parish of Crowhurst which lies North and East of the Main
road from Woods Gate through Crowhurst Street up the Forward Lane taking the
bounds of that part of of the Parish to the Dairy, Crowhurst Place, Pump and
farm houses, Green Street down to Woods Gate, including the line of Railway now
in progress."
Enumerator - Thomas Waters

HO107 1636 folios 139-147
Enumeration District No.4b   Registrar's District - Bexhill.

"All that part of the Parish of Crowhurst which lies South and West of the Main
road from Woods Gate to Crowhurst Street including the Church Farm up Forward
Lane to John Miller's taking the Bounds of that part of the Parish to Thomas
Sharpes at the Water Mill, Stephen Taylors, Tilden Cooks, Croucher to Woods
Gate"
Enumerator - Henry Hutchison

HO107 1636 folios 148-157
Enumeration District No.5a   Registrar's District - Bexhill.

"All that part of the Parish of Westfield which lies East of the Main road from
Cock Martins to Brede Bridge including Buckhurst, Lankhurst, Westfield moore,
the Down to Paddletoss, Dolcham, Knights to Brede Bridge to Bulls Eye Corner."
Enumerator - Thomas Noakes

HO107 1636 folios 158-168
Enumeration District No.5b   Registrar's District - Bexhill.

"All that part of the Parish of Westfield which lies West of the Main road from
Cock Martins to Bulls Eye Corner taking all the houses on the West side of the
Main road to Sprays Bridge to Sedlescombe including New England, Kent Street,
Bluemans, Rogue Fosters, the Parsonage and Church farm to Bulls Eye Corner."
Enumerator - James Selmes

HO107 1636 folios 169-182
Enumeration District No.5c   Registrar's District - Bexhill.

"All that part of the Parish of Westfield which lies North of the Main road from
Bulls Eye Corner taking the main road to Sprays, John Mawles to Sedlescombe
including all the houses within the Bounds of that part of the Parish by
H.Sharpes Esq., Lambs Cottage, Crowham, Brede Bridge and houses on the West of
the main road to Bulls Eye Corner."
Enumerator - James Catt

HO107 1636 folios 183-197
Enumeration District No.1a   Registrar's District - Ewhurst.

"All that part of the Parish (Sedlescombe) lying on the East side of the
Turnpike Road from Westfield to Cripps Corner including Swales Green back to
Austford, Brickkiln, Herst and down Brede Lane."
Enumerator - Albert Sinden

HO107 1636 folios 198-211
Enumeration District No.1b   Registrar's District - Ewhurst.

"All that part of the Parish (Sedlescombe) lying on the West side of the
Turnpike Road leading from Westfield to Cripps Corner down Popping Hole Lane
back to the Old Beech, Swales Green Farm down to Footland across the Hancox
taking the back Turnpike Road, Windmill Stream thence to Castlemans."
Enumerator - James Byner

HO107 1636 folios 212-228
Enumeration District No.2a   Registrar's District - Ewhurst.

"Ewhurst Green to Padgham to Sempsted thence to Soggs Back to Ewhurst Green then
to Ockham to Dykes and Odiam thence to Faye farm house back to Long Lees to
Brasses, Prawles and Shoreham."
Enumerator - William Coppard

HO107 1636 folios 229-245
Enumeration District No.2b   Registrar's District - Ewhurst.

"Staple Cross to Hollow Walls to Wattle Hill, to Ednix, Ellinghall to
Stockwood, Newhouse to Adams Lane, Lordine, Colliers Green to Staple Cross."
Enumaerator - William Beck

HO107 1636 folios 246-254
Enumeration District No.2c   Registrar's District - Ewhurst.

"Staple Cross to Strawberry Hill to Deadman's Wood on to Cripps Corner to Catts
Green to Brede High back to Watts Palace (sic) to Stocklands, Miles's, Beacon to
Staple Cross."
Enumerator - Charles S Beck

FURTHER READING & BIBLIOGRAPHY

I have used the following to help establish names of places and people.
   A Dictionary of British Surnames by P.H. Reaney
   Bartholomew Gazetteer of Britain
   Phillimore Atlas & Index of Parish Registers
   The Penguin Dictionary of Surnames by Basil Cottle
   The Place Names of Sussex by Judith Glover
   also Telephone directories and Ordinance Survey maps of the areas.

The following books are recommended for further reading:
   Bexhill-on-Sea A Pictorial History by Aylwin Guilmant
   Twenty Centuries in Sedlescombe by B.Lucey

Acknowledgements:
I thank all who continue to support and encourage me with this project,
especially Stuart, Anthony, Emily and Alison who have been particularly patient
and tolerant whilst learning to live with the Index.   Thanks to Stuart for
checking some of the obscure entries with me and for "proof-reading"; to Aylwin
Guilmant for her very interesting introduction, and to Pete and Marianne Smith
for their continued success in producing such lovely covers.   An especially big
thank you to all those users of the index who have written with encouragement
and good wishes.   It makes the task even more worthwhile.
                                                            June Barnes

----

		AGE		OCCUPATION	BIRTHPLACE	ADDRESS	FOL
12 ----	WILLIAM	LG U	20		NONE GIVEN	MADKITS?	130
79 ABBITT	EDWIN	SO U	4		SSX BEXHILL	POND HOUSE (LITTLE COMMON)	47
79 ABBITT	ELIZA	WI M	42	SHOE BINDER	SSX BEXHILL	POND HOUSE (LITTLE COMMON)	47
79 ABBITT	ELLEN	DA U	6		SSX BEXHILL	POND HOUSE (LITTLE COMMON)	47
79 ABBITT	EMILY	DA U	13		SSX BEXHILL	POND HOUSE (LITTLE COMMON)	47
79 ABBITT	THOMAS	SO U	10	SCHOLAR	SSX BEXHILL	POND HOUSE (LITTLE COMMON)	47
79 ABBITT	WILLIAM	HD M	45	RAIL LAB	SSX HOOE	POND HOUSE (LITTLE COMMON)	47
48 ABBOT	FRIEND?	SV U	20	GROCER'S ASSISTANT	SSX BEXHILL	LITTLE COMMON	57
5 ABBOTS	ALFRED	GS U	14	AG.LAB	SSX BEXHILL	KITES NEST	51
60 ABBOTT	EUNICE	SV U	17	HOUSE SERVANT	SSX BEXHILL	BIRCHINGTON	45
34 ADAMS	ALBERT	SO U	18	AG.LAB	SSX BEXHILL	LUNSFORDS LANE SIDLEY	70
66 ADAMS	ALFRED	LG U	16	AG.LAB	SSX BATTLE	SIDLEY GREEN	84
68 ADAMS	ALFRED	SO U	17	AG.LAB	SSX CATSFIELD	NOT GIVEN	114
34 ADAMS	ANN	DA U	6		SSX BEXHILL	LUNSFORDS LANE SIDLEY	70
52 ADAMS	ANN	DA U	7		SSX MOUNTFIELD	BEECH	208
19 ADAMS	ANN	HD U	55	GENTLEWOMAN ANNUITANT	SSX HASTINGS	BELL HILL	25
70 ADAMS	ANN	VR W	77	ANNUITANT	SSX WARTLING	POTMANS	114
69 ADAMS	ANSLEY	SO U	19		SSX CATSFIELD	NOT GIVEN	114
69 ADAMS	BETTY	WI M	47		SSX BEXHILL	NOT GIVEN	114
69 ADAMS	CHARLES	SO U	28	AG.LAB	SSX BEXHILL	NOT GIVEN	114
52 ADAMS	CLARA	DA U	7M		SSX SEDLESCOMBE	BEECH	208
83 ADAMS	CORDELIA	WI M	37		SSX BEXHILL	CHURCH STREET	99
23 ADAMS	DELIA	VR M	24		SSX BATTLE	CHARITY HOUSE	154
68 ADAMS	EDWARD	SO U	5		SSX CATSFIELD	NOT GIVEN	114
34 ADAMS	ELIZABETH	DA U	11	SCHOLAR	SSX BEXHILL	LUNSFORDS LANE SIDLEY	70
68 ADAMS	ELIZABETH	DA U	15		SSX CATSFIELD	NOT GIVEN	114
68 ADAMS	ELIZABETH	WI M	41		SSX BEXHILL	NOT GIVEN	114
27 ADAMS	ELIZABETH	WI M	54		SSX WARBLETON	NOT GIVEN	92
83 ADAMS	EMILY	DA U	3W		SSX BEXHILL	CHURCH STREET	99
52 ADAMS	EMILY	DA U	5		SSX MOUNTFIELD	BEECH	208
68 ADAMS	GEORGE	HD M	42	AG.LAB	SSX CATSFIELD	NOT GIVEN	114
27 ADAMS	GEORGE	SL U	13		SSX BEXHILL	NOT GIVEN	92
52 ADAMS	GEORGE	SO U	8		SSX MOUNTFIELD	BEECH	208
70 ADAMS	GEORGE	SV U	13	AG.LAB	SSX CATSFIELD	POTMANS	114
2 ADAMS	HENRY	SO U	14	FARMER'S SON	SSX CATSFIELD	NEW BARN FARM	106
83 ADAMS	JAMES	HD M	35	PAINTER	SSX HASTINGS	CHURCH STREET	99
69 ADAMS	JAMES	SO U	15	AG.LAB	SSX CATSFIELD	NOT GIVEN	114
2 ADAMS	JAMES	SO U	26	FARMER'S SON	SSX CATSFIELD	NEW BARN FARM	106
23 ADAMS	JAMES	VR M	25		SSX BATTLE	CHARITY HOUSE	154
4 ADAMS	JANE	WI M	21		SSX BEXHILL	SIDLEY GREEN	75
27 ADAMS	JOHN	HD M	60	AG.LAB	SSX CATSFIELD	NOT GIVEN	92
2 ADAMS	JOHN	SO U	23	FARMER'S SON	SSX CATSFIELD	NEW BARN FARM	106
11 ADAMS	JOSEPH	LG U	36	AG.LAB	OXF HENTH?	PARK HOUSE	121
5 ADAMS	JOSHUA	HD M	43	FARMER 105 AC EMP 5	SSX CATSFIELD	NOT GIVEN	106
34 ADAMS	LOUISA	DA U	14		SSX BEXHILL	LUNSFORDS LANE SIDLEY	70
5 ADAMS	LUCY	DA U	4		SSX CATSFIELD	NOT GIVEN	106
4 ADAMS	LUCY	HD W	83	ANNUITANT	SSX ASHBURNHAM	NOT GIVEN	106
5 ADAMS	LUCY	WI M	42		SSX WALDRON	NOT GIVEN	106
27 ADAMS	MARY	DA U	33		SSX CATSFIELD	NOT GIVEN	92
52 ADAMS	MARY	WI M	34		SSX CATSFIELD	BEECH	208
34 ADAMS	NAOMI	DA U	3		SSX BEXHILL	LUNSFORDS LANE SIDLEY	70
69 ADAMS	ROBERT	HD M	56	AG.LAB	SSX CATSFIELD	NOT GIVEN	114
68 ADAMS	SARAH	DA U	10		SSX CATSFIELD	NOT GIVEN	114
34 ADAMS	SARAH	WI M	46		SSX ASHBURNHAM	LUNSFORDS LANE SIDLEY	70
2 ADAMS	SARAH	WI M	52		SSX EAST GRINSTED	NEW BARN FARM	106
69 ADAMS	SARAH A	DA U	13		SSX CATSFIELD	NOT GIVEN	114
4 ADAMS	STEPHEN	HD M	22	THATCHER	SSX CATSFIELD	SIDLEY GREEN	75
34 ADAMS	STEPHEN	HD M	45	AG.LAB	SSX CATSFIELD	LUNSFORDS LANE SIDLEY	70
2 ADAMS	STEPHEN	HD M	54	FARMER 130 AC EMP 1	SSX CATSFIELD	NEW BARN FARM	106
2 ADAMS	STEPHEN	SO U	15	FARMER'S SON	SSX CATSFIELD	NEW BARN FARM	106
52 ADAMS	THOMAS	HD M	33	BRICKLAYER EMP 4	SSX SEDLESCOMBE	BEECH	208
34 ADAMS	THOMAS	SO U	9		SSX BEXHILL	LUNSFORDS LANE SIDLEY	70
69 ADAMS	THOMAS	SO U	9		SSX CATSFIELD	NOT GIVEN	114
37 ADAMS	WILLIAM	LG U	27	AG.LAB	SSX WHATLINGTON	FOOTLAND	205
23 ADAMS	WILLIAM	VR U	2		NOT GIVEN (?BATTLE)	CHARITY HOUSE	154
66 ADDS	GEORGE	SV U	26	AG.LAB	SSX HOLLINGTON	BEACH FARM	14
34 ADES	ALFRED	HD M	50	AG.LAB	SSX BREDE	MABBS	191
3 ADES	ANN	SV U	13	GENERAL SERVANT	SSX SEDLESCOMBE	BEACON MILL	249
25 ADES	ANNA MARIA	NC U	19		SSX NORTHIAM	SEDLESCOMBE STREET	204
35 ADES	CAROLINE	DA U	5	SCHOLAR	SSX SEDLESCOMBE	MABBS	191
35 ADES	CHARLOTTE	DA U	7	SCHOLAR	SSX SEDLESCOMBE	MABBS	191
72 ADES	CHARLOTTE	DA U	26		SSX HOLLINGTON	STEMPS?	15
72 ADES	EDWIN	SO U	25	BLACKSMITH	SSX HOLLINGTON	STEMPS?	15
72 ADES	GEORGE	HD M	65	AG.LAB	SSX BREDE	STEMPS?	15
35 ADES	GEORGE	SO U	11	AG.LAB	SSX SEDLESCOMBE	MABBS	191
35 ADES	HENRY	HD M	36	AG.LAB	SSX WESTFIELD	MABBS	191
35 ADES	JAMES	SO U	1		SSX SEDLESCOMBE	MABBS	191
57 ADES	JAMES	SO U	10	SCHOLAR	SSX SEDLESCOMBE	GATE HOUSE	209
57 ADES	LEONORA	DA U	2M		SSX SEDLESCOMBE	GATE HOUSE	209
35 ADES	LUCY	DA U	8		SSX SEDLESCOMBE	MABBS	191
72 ADES	LUCY	WI M	59		SSX HOLLINGTON	STEMPS?	15

Ref	Name	Rel	Cond	Age	Occupation	County	Birthplace	Address	Page
57	ADES MARTHA	WI	M	40		SSX	EWHURST	GATE HOUSE	209
35	ADES MARY	DA	U	3		SSX	SEDLESCOMBE	MABBS	191
57	ADES MARY	DA	U	8	SCHOLAR	SSX	SEDLESCOMBE	GATE HOUSE	209
14	ADES MARY	HD	W	84	ANNUITANT	SSX	TICEHURST	SEDLESCOMBE STREET	202
35	ADES MARY	WI	M	38		SSX	HASTINGS	MABBS	191
57	ADES MATILDA	DA	U	12		SSX	SEDLESCOMBE	GATE HOUSE	209
35	ADES PHILADELPHIA	DA	U	4M		SSX	SEDLESCOMBE	MABBS	191
34	ADES PHILADELPHIA	WI	M	51		SSX	GUESTLING	MABBS	191
72	ADES ROBERT	SO	U	23		SSX	HOLLINGTON	STEMPS?	15
57	ADES SALLY	DA	U	4		SSX	SEDLESCOMBE	GATE HOUSE	209
57	ADES SPENCER	HD	M	40	AG.LAB	SSX	SEDLESCOMBE	GATE HOUSE	209
57	ADES SPENCER	SO	U	6	SCHOLAR	SSX	SEDLESCOMBE	GATE HOUSE	209
36	ADES STEPHEN	SV	U	14	FARM LAB	SSX	SEDLESCOMBE	HERST	209
57	ADES WILLIAM	SO	U	14		SSX	ST.LEONARDS ON SEA	GATE HOUSE	191
13	AGTON MARGARET	NC	U	8		SRY	MORTLAKE	YEW TREES	173
33	ALDRIDGE GEORGE	LG	U	29	RAILWAY LAB	HAM		MOORS FARM	147
*71	ALDRIGE JAMES	SO	U	10		SSX	HENFIELD	IN CAMP BY ROADSIDE	60
*71	ALDRIGE LUCY	/	U	25	VAGRANT	SSX	ASHINGTON	IN CAMP BY ROADSIDE	60
81	ALLEN ANN	DA	U	5	SCHOLAR	SSX	BEXHILL	DINGAREE COTTAGE	32
81	ALLEN ELIZABETH	WI	M	30		SSX	CROWHURST	DINGAREE COTTAGE	32
81	ALLEN HARRIOTT	DA	U	10	SCHOLAR	SSX	BEXHILL	DINGAREE COTTAGE	32
81	ALLEN HENRY	HD	M	40	MASTER MARINER	SSX	HASTINGS	DINGAREE COTTAGE	32
81	ALLEN LOUSIA	DA	U	7	SCHOLAR	SSX	BEXHILL	DINGAREE COTTAGE	32
81	ALLEN MARY	DA	U	5M		SSX	BEXHILL	BELL HILL (SIC)	33
81	ALLEN SARAH	DA	U	3		SSX	BEXHILL	BELL HILL (SIC)	33
66	ALLINGHAM ALFRED	LG	U	11	GROCER/DRAPER AP	KEN	TONBRIDGE	STAPLE CROSS	241
55	ALLNUT SAMUEL HALDER?	LG	U	16	LEARNING TO FARM	BRK	SUTTON	HANCOX FARM	209
65	AMORE A R (MALE)	PP	U	3	PUPIL	SSX	HASTINGS	NOT GIVEN	96
65	AMORE P H (MALE)	PP	U	5	PUPIL	SSX	HASTINGS	NOT GIVEN	96
36	ANDERSON CHARLES	SO	U	5		SSX	BROOMHILL	49 MARTELLO TOWER	41
36	ANDERSON ELIZABETH	DA	U	9	SCHOLAR	SSX	BROOMHILL	49 MARTELLO TOWER	41
36	ANDERSON JANE	WI	M	42		COR	ST.DOMINIC	49 MARTELLO TOWER	41
36	ANDERSON JOHN	SO	U	7	SCHOLAR	SSX	BROOMHILL	49 MARTELLO TOWER	41
36	ANDERSON ROBERT	HD	M	39	COM BOATMAN COAST GUARD	DEV	DEVONPORT	49 MARTELLO TOWER	41
36	ANDERSON ROBERT	SO	U	11	SCHOLAR	SSX	BROOMHILL	49 MARTELLO TOWER	41
36	ANDERSON SARAH	DA	U	13		SSX	PETT	49 MARTELLO TOWER	41
36	ANDERSON SOPHIA	DA	U	5?		SSX	BROOMHILL	49 MARTELLO TOWER	41
34	ANDREWS ELLEN	SV	U	28	HOUSEMAID	SSX	RYE	RECTORY	205
43	ANDREWS JOHN	/	M	61	AG.LAB	SSX	LANCING	OCKHAM	221
43	ANDREWS SARAH	/	M	61	WIFE OF JOHN	SSX	NORTHIAM	OCKHAM	221
76	ANSCOMB JANE	WI	M	51?		SSX	HERSTMONCEUX	APPLE TREE	182
76	ANSCOMB WILLIAM	HD	M	61	AG.LAB	SSX	WESTFIELD	APPLE TREE	182
22	APPS ALICE	DA	U	15		SSX	CATSFIELD	NOT GIVEN	109
23	APPS ALLICE	WI	M	61		IRL		NOT GIVEN	109
11	APPS ANNE	DA	U	16		SSX	SEDLESCOMBE	BARRICKS	187
12	APPS BARBARA	DA	U	32		SSX	CATSFIELD	NOT GIVEN	108
23	APPS CHARLES	HD	M	60	AG.LAB	SSX	CATSFIELD	NOT GIVEN	109
22	APPS CHARLES	SO	U	27	AG.LAB	SSX	CATSFIELD	NOT GIVEN	109
11	APPS EDWARD	SO	U	21	AG.LAB	SSX	SEDLESCOMBE	BARRICKS	187
22	APPS ELIZABETH	WI	M	56		SSX	BEXHILL	NOT GIVEN	109
11	APPS GEORGE	HD	M	60	AG.LAB	SSX	BREDE	BARRICKS	187
11	APPS GEORGE	SO	U	12	AG.LAB	SSX	SEDLESCOMBE	BARRICKS	187
22	APPS HENRY	SO	U	9		SSX	CATSFIELD	NOT GIVEN	109
65	APPS JAMES	LG	U	26	AG.LAB	SSX	SEDLESCOMBE	CASTLEMANS	210
22	APPS JAMES	SO	U	17	AG.LAB	SSX	CATSFIELD	NOT GIVEN	109
22	APPS JOHN	HD	M	56	AG.LAB	SSX	CATSFIELD	NOT GIVEN	109
22	APPS MARY A	DA	U	13		SSX	CATSFIELD	NOT GIVEN	109
11	APPS MOSES	SO	U	17	AG.LAB	SSX	SEDLESCOMBE	BARRICKS	187
10	APPS SAMUEL	LG	U	23	AG.LAB	SSX	SEDLESCOMBE	BARRICKS	187
22	APPS SARAH	DA	U	11		SSX	CATSFIELD	NOT GIVEN	109
11	APPS SARAH	WI	M	59		SSX	EWHURST	BARRICKS	187
19	APPS THOMAS	LG	U	24	AG.LAB	SSX	SEDLESCOMBE	COTTAGE	174
12	APPS WILLIAM	HD	W	62		SSX	CATSFIELD	NOT GIVEN	107
5	ARCHER ENOS?	SO	U	12	SHOEMAKER	SSX	SEDLESCOMBE	SEDLESCOMBE STREET	201
5	ARCHER GEORGE	SO	U	22	SHOEMAKER	SSX	SEDLESCOMBE	SEDLESCOMBE STREET	201
5	ARCHER JOHN	HD	M	61	SHOEMAKER	KEN	HYTHE	SEDLESCOMBE STREET	201
5	ARCHER SARAH	WI	M	56		SSX	CROWHURST	SEDLESCOMBE STREET	201
5	ARCHER THOMAS	SO	U	18	SHOEMAKER	SSX	SEDLESCOMBE	SEDLESCOMBE STREET	201
11	ARIES EDWARD	SV	U	35	HOUSE SERVANT	BKM	STRATTON AUDLEY	PARK HOUSE	121
62	ASHBY CORDELIA	HD	U	66	INDEPENDANT LADY	SSX	HASTINGS	EWHURST GREEN	224
51	ASHBY ELENORA	WI	M	52		KEN	BROMLEY	GALLEY HILL	29
78	ASHBY HENRY	HD	U	51	MILLER	SSX	TICEHURST	DOWN	182
51	ASHBY JULIA E	DA	U	17		SSX	BEXHILL	GALLEY HILL	29
51	ASHBY MARIA	DA	U	11		SSX	BEXHILL	GALLEY HILL	29
51	ASHBY WILLIAM R	HD	M	58	LIEUT COAST GUARD	MDX	ST.MARYLEBONE	GALLEY HILL	29
21	ASHDOWN SARAH A	WI	M	55		SSX	RYE	IN THE LIBERTY	40
21	ASHDOWN WILLIAM	HD	M	62	COAST GUARD CHIEF BOATMAN	SSX	WESTFIELD	IN THE LIBERTY	40
26	ASHDOWN WILLIAM	SV	U	27	COACHMAN	SSX	BATTLE	BEXHILL STREET	26
3	ASKELL JOHN	SV	U	48	AG.LAB	SSX	WESTFIELD	DOLEHAM	152
64	ASTLEN WILLIAM	LG	W	33	RAILWAY LAB	CAM		RAILWAY HUT	137
13	ATTREALL JAMES	HD	M	43	FELLMONGER	SSX	SEAFORD	LOWER FISHPOND	153
13	ATTREALL JAMES	SO	U	22	LAB	SSX	DALLINGTON	LOWER FISHPOND	153
13	ATTREALL SARAH	WI	M	43		SSX	DALLINGTON	LOWER FISHPOND	153
31	ATTREE JAMES	HD	M	57	AG.LAB	SSX	BREDE	DOG KENNELL	9
31	ATTREE MARY	WI	M	58		SSX	HOOE	DOG KENNELL	9
5	ATTWOOD MARY	HK	U	60		SSX	WARTLING	SIDLEY	90

Age	Name	Rel	M	Age2	Occupation	County	Place	Location	No.
27	AUSTIN AMY	DA	U	20		SSX	EWHURST	SEMPSTED FARM	236
27	AUSTIN HENRY	SO	U	30		KEN	PEMBURY	SEMPSTED FARM	236
24	AUSTIN JOHN	SV	U	13		SSX	SALEHURST	ROCKS	175
27	AUSTIN SOPHIA	WI	M	61		KEN	ROLVENDEN	SEMPSTED FARM	236
27	AUSTIN THOMAS	HD	M	61	FARMER 174 AC EMP 13 LAB	SSX	BREDE	SEMPSTED FARM	236
27	AUSTIN THOMAS	SO	U	34		KEN	PEMBURY	SEMPSTED FARM	236
24	AVARD ELIZABETH	SV	U	22	HOUSE SERVANT	KEN	SANDWICH	PEBSHAM FARM SIDLEY	78
24	AVARD SARAH	SV	U	17	HOUSE SERVANT	KEN	SANDWICH	PEBSHAM FARM SIDLEY	78
21	AWARD ALFRED	NP	U	16	AG.LAB	KEN	SANDHURST	ODIAM FARM	218
21	AWARD NAOMI	VR	U	14	SERVANT	KEN	SANDHURST	ODIAM FARM	218
65	AYLING CHARLES	HD	M	35	COAST GUARD SERVICE	SSX	BOSHAM	STRAWBERRY BANK	45
65	AYLING MARY A	DA	U	4	SCHOLAR	SSX	BEXHILL	STRAWBERRY BANK	45
65	AYLING MARY A	WI	M	30		KEN	ASH	STRAWBERRY BANK	45
60	BADCOCK ELI	SO	U	20	AG.LAB	SSX	EWHURST	SEMPSTED FARM	240
60	BADCOCK GEORGE	SO	U	16	AG.LAB	SSX	EWHURST	SEMPSTED FARM	240
60	BADCOCK JOHN	SO	U	11	AG.LAB	SSX	EWHURST	SEMPSTED FARM	240
60	BADCOCK MARY	HD	W	50		SSX	EWHURST	SEMPSTED FARM	240
60	BADCOCK WALTER	SO	U	14	AG.LAB	SSX	EWHURST	SEMPSTED FARM	240
38	BAILEY HANNAH	VR	W	81		SSX	CROWHURST	MARCHANTS	237
70	BAILY DAVID	LG	U	27	POLICE CONSTABLE	SSX	BECKLEY	STAPLE CROSS	241
36	BAKER ALBERT	GS	U	17	AG.LAB	SSX	EWHURST	WATTS LANE	237
46	BAKER ALBERT	SO	U	3		SSX	EWHURST	NOT GIVEN	238
33	BAKER ALLIS	DA	U	4		SSX	EWHURST	REEVES	237
61	BAKER ANN	DA	U	37		SSX	WESTFIELD	COTTAGE	180
26	BAKER ANN	WI	M	49		SSX	BEXHILL	NOT GIVEN	54
46	BAKER BENJAMIN	HD	M	37	AG.LAB	SSX	EWHURST	NOT GIVEN	238
46	BAKER BENJAMIN	SO	U	16	AG.LAB	SSX	EWHURST	NOT GIVEN	238
22	BAKER BERTHA	DA	U	4M		NOT GIVEN (?WESTFIELD)		BAKERS	154
61	BAKER CAROLINE CHARLOTTE	DA	U	4		SSX	EWHURST	SEMPSTED FARM	240
75	BAKER CHARLES	SO	U	10		SSX	WESTFIELD	DOWN	181
33	BAKER CHARLES	SO	U	13	AG.LAB	SSX	EWHURST	REEVES	237
37	BAKER CHARLOTTE	WI	M	24		SSX	WESTFIELD	MOUNT PLEASANT	166
61	BAKER CHARLOTTE	WI	M	63		SSX	WESTFIELD	COTTAGE	180
33	BAKER CHRISTOPHER	SO	U	13	AG.LAB	SSX	EWHURST	REEVES	237
17	BAKER CORDELIA	WI	M	60		SSX	NORTHIAM	COLLIERS GREEN	234
7	BAKER DAVID	SV	U	21		SSX	WESTFIELD	PLATNIX	173
42	BAKER DELIA	HD	U	70	LODGING HOUSE KEEPER	SSX	WESTFIELD	1 DORSETT COTTAGE	28
33	BAKER EDITH	DA	U	1		SSX	EWHURST	REEVES	237
35	BAKER ELENOR	DA	U	2		SSX	EWHURST	WATTS LANE	237
57	BAKER ELIZABETH	DA	U	3		SSX	WESTFIELD	BARRACKS	179
57	BAKER ELIZABETH	LG	M	22		SSX	BATTLE	BARRACKS	179
81	BAKER ELIZABETH	SV	W	67	HOUSE KEEPER	SSX	CROWHURST	STAPLE CROSS	243
22	BAKER ELIZABETH	WI	M	29?		SSX	WESTFIELD	BAKERS	154
58	BAKER EMILA	NC	U	5		SSX	BEXHILL	NOT GIVEN	58
75	BAKER FREDERICK	SO	U	6		SSX	WESTFIELD	DOWN	182
10	BAKER GEORGE	LG	U	26	RAILWAY LAB	SSX	PATERHAM (SIC)	FORWARD LANE	129
57	BAKER GEORGE	SO	U	4		SSX	WESTFIELD	BARRACKS	179
75	BAKER GEORGE	SO	U	15		SSX	WESTFIELD	DOWN	181
78	BAKER GEORGE	SO	U	19	AG.LAB	SSX	EWHURST	EWHURST GREEN	227
13	BAKER GEORGE	SV	U	25	GROOM	SSX	SALEHURST	PARSONAGE	130
35	BAKER HARRIET	DA	U	4M		SSX	EWHURST	WATTS LANE	237
66	BAKER HARRIET	GD	U	2		SSX	BEXHILL	SIDLEY GREEN	84
35	BAKER HARRIET	WI	M	30		SSX	BECKLEY	WATTS LANE	237
36	BAKER HENRY	SO	U	26	AG.LAB	SSX	EWHURST	WATTS LANE	237
61	BAKER HENRY ELIAS	SO	U	9	SCHOLAR	SSX	EWHURST	SEMPSTED FARM	240
61	BAKER JAMES	HD	M	37	AG.LAB	SSX	EWHURST	SEMPSTED FARM	240
33	BAKER JAMES	HD	M	42	AG.LAB	SSX	NORTHIAM	REEVES	237
17	BAKER JAMES	HD	M	62	AG.LAB	SSX	EWHURST	COLLIERS GREEN	234
60	BAKER JAMES	LG	M	30	RAILWAY LAB	WIL	BRADFORD	RAILWAY HUT	136
57	BAKER JAMES	LG	U	3M		SSX	WESTFIELD	BARRACKS	179
61	BAKER JAMES	SO	U	11	AG.LAB	SSX	EWHURST	SEMPSTED FARM	240
75	BAKER JAMES	SO	U	12		SSX	WESTFIELD	DOWN	181
33	BAKER JAMES	SO	U	15	AG.LAB	SSX	EWHURST	REEVES	237
78	BAKER JAMES	SO	U	21	AG.LAB	SSX	EWHURST	EWHURST GREEN	227
37	BAKER JOHN	HD	M	23	AG.LAB	SSX	EWHURST	MOUNT PLEASANT	166
75	BAKER JOHN	HD	M	34	SHOEMAKER	SSX	WESTFIELD	DOWN	181
70	BAKER JOHN	HD	M	50	GARDENER	SSX	EWHURST	EWHURST GREEN	225
51	BAKER JOHN	SO	U	4		SSX	EWHURST	SNAGS HALL	222
75	BAKER JOHN	SO	U	8		SSX	WESTFIELD	DOWN	182
59	BAKER JOHN	SO	U	19	AG.LAB	SSX	EWHURST	SNAGS HALL	224
17	BAKER JOSEPH	SO	U	19	AG.LAB	SSX	EWHURST	COLLIERS GREEN	234
75	BAKER LEWIS	NP	U	32		SSX	WESTFIELD	DOWN	182
78	BAKER LYDIA	DA	U	17	OUT OF SERVICE	SSX	EWHURST	EWHURST GREEN	227
59	BAKER MARIA	DA	U	23		SSX	EWHURST	SNAGS HALL	224
46	BAKER MARIA	WI	M	44		KEN	FEVERSHAM	NOT GIVEN	238
59	BAKER MARIA	WI	M	46		SSX	EWHURST	SNAGS HALL	224
22	BAKER MARTHA	DA	U	5		NOT GIVEN (?WESTFIELD)		BAKERS	154
46	BAKER MARTHA	DA	U	17		SSX	EWHURST	NOT GIVEN	238
66	BAKER MARY	DA	M	26		SSX	BEXHILL	SIDLEY GREEN	84
22	BAKER MARY	DA	U	2		NOT GIVEN (?WESTFIELD)		BAKERS	154
75	BAKER MARY	WI	M	36		SSX	WESTFIELD	DOWN	181
33	BAKER MARY	WI	M	38		SSX	NORTHIAM	REEVES	237
70	BAKER MARY	WI	M	50		SSX	SEDLESCOMBE	EWHURST GREEN	225
57	BAKER MARY A	WI	M	25		SSX	HASTINGS	BARRACKS	179
9	BAKER MARY ANN	SV	U	18	GENERAL SERVANT	SSX	EWHURST	COLLIERS GREEN	233
7	BAKER MARY J	WI	M	22?		SSX	NINFIELD	SIDLEY	65

13

#	Name	Rel/Cond	Age	Occupation	County/Place of Birth	Address	Pg
7	BAKER NELSON	SO U	4?		SSX NINFIELD	SIDLEY	65
75	BAKER NONIS	SO U	1		SSX WESTFIELD	DOWN	182
7	BAKER REUBEN	HD M	26	AG.LAB	SSX WARBLETON	SIDLEY	65
61	BAKER RICHARD	SO U	28		SSX WESTFIELD	COTTAGE	180
61	BAKER SAMUEL	HD M	61	GARDENER	SSX WESTFIELD	COTTAGE	180
36	BAKER SARAH	WI M	61		SSX BECKLEY	WATTS LANE	237
57	BAKER SARAH A	DA U	1		SSX WESTFIELD	BARRACKS	179
61	BAKER SEBINA	DA U	6	SCHOLAR	SSX EWHURST	SEMPSTED FARM	240
61	BAKER SEBINA	WI M	31		SSX BREDE	SEMPSTED FARM	240
59	BAKER SERENA	DA U	17		SSX EWHURST	SNAGS HALL	224
33	BAKER SOPHIA	DA U	8		SSX EWHURST	REEVES	237
78	BAKER SUSANNAH	HD W	55		NEW BRUNSWICK AMERICA	EWHURST GREEN	227
57	BAKER THOMAS	HD M	27	AG.LAB	SSX WESTFIELD	BARRACKS	179
26	BAKER THOMAS	HD M	48	FARMER 15 AC	SSX CHIDDINGLY	NOT GIVEN	54
36	BAKER THOMAS	HD M	66	AG.LAB	KEN HAWKHURST	WATTS LANE	237
75	BAKER THOMAS	SO U	4		SSX WESTFIELD	DOWN	182
59	BAKER THOMAS	SO U	21	AG.LAB	SSX EWHURST	SNAGS HALL	224
78	BAKER THOMAS	SO U	23	AG.LAB	SSX EWHURST	EWHURST GREEN	227
17	BAKER THOMAS	SO U	26	AG.LAB	SSX EWHURST	COLLIERS GREEN	234
61	BAKER THOMAS WALTER	SO U	2		SSX EWHURST	SEMPSTED FARM	240
49	BAKER TIMOTHY	/ U	25	TWINE SPINNER	SSX EWHURST	SNAGS HALL	222
59	DAKER TIMOTHY	HD M	57	WEAVER	SSX EWHURST	SNAGS HALL	224
66	BAKER UN-NAMED INFANT BOY	GS U	1W		SSX BEXHILL	SIDLEY GREEN	84
66	BAKER WILLIAM	GS U	3		SSX BEXHILL	SIDLEY GREEN	84
22	BAKER WILLIAM	HD M	27	GROCER	SSX WESTFIELD	BAKERS	154
35	BAKER WILLIAM	HD M	29	AG.LAB	SSX WESTFIELD	WATTS LANE	237
57	BAKER WILLIAM	LG M	18	AG.LAB	SSX WESTFIELD	BARRACKS	179
46	BAKER WILLIAM	SO U	7	SCHOLAR	SSX EWHURST	NOT GIVEN	238
27	BAKER WILLIAM	SV U	12	ERRAND BOY	NOTTINGHAM	FORTLAND? HOUSE	123
59	BAKER WILLIAM AMOS	GS U	6		SSX EWHURST	SNAGS HALL	224
18	BALKHAM ANN	DA U	2		SSX BEXHILL	IN THE LIBERTY	39
16	BALKHAM EDWARD	HD W	69	AG.LAB	SSX RYE	STONE COTTAGE IN THE LIBERTY	39
18	BALKHAM ELIZABETH	DA U	12		SSX BEXHILL	IN THE LIBERTY	39
17	BALKHAM GEORGE	HD M	28	SHOEMAKER	SSX BEXHILL	IN THE LIBERTY	39
18	BALKHAM GEORGE	SO U	8	SCHOLAR	SSX BEXHILL	IN THE LIBERTY	39
18	BALKHAM JAMES	HD M	36	AG.LAB	SSX BEXHILL	IN THE LIBERTY	39
18	BALKHAM JAMES	SO U	9		SSX BEXHILL	IN THE LIBERTY	39
18	BALKHAM JOHN	SO U	2		SSX BEXHILL	IN THE LIBERTY	39
18	BALKHAM MARY	DA U	11M		SSX BEXHILL	IN THE LIBERTY	39
17	BALKHAM MARY A	WI M	24		SSX BEXHILL	IN THE LIBERTY	39
18	BALKHAM RHODA	WI M	36		SSX PEVENSEY	IN THE LIBERTY	39
18	BALKHAM SAMUEL	SO U	6		SSX BEXHILL	IN THE LIBERTY	39
9	BALL WILLIAM	SV W	32	COACHMAN	BKM NOT KNOWN	PARK GATE	120
67	BALLARD ALFRED	SO U	13		SSX ETCHINGHAM	CASTLEMANS	210
54	BALLARD ELIZABETH	SV U	19	HOUSE SERVANT	SSX HURST GREEN	CASTLEMANS	195
67	BALLARD HARRIETT	DA U	15		SSX ETCHINGHAM	CASTLEMANS	210
67	BALLARD JOHN	HD W	46	AG.LAB	SSX SEDLESCOMBE	CASTLEMANS	210
43	BALLARD MARY	NC U	12	SCHOLAR	SSX SEDLESCOMBE	POPPING HOLE LANE	206
43	BALLARD WILLIAM	FA W	69	AG.LAB	SSX BATTLE	POPPING HOLE LANE	206
27	BANG ELIZA	VR U	30		MDX SELFKET*	GREEN STREET	132
27	BANG HANNAH	VD U	5M		ISLINGTON	GREEN STREET	132
12	BANISTER CHARLOTTE	DA U	11		NOT GIVEN (?WESTFIELD)	LOWER FISHPOND	153
26	BANISTER EDWARD	SO U	30	FARRIER	SSX EWHURST	CRIPPS	252
12	BANISTER GEORGE	SO U	20		SSX WESTFIELD	LOWER FISHPOND	153
26	BANISTER JAMES	HD M	71	FARRIER	SSX PEASMARSH	CRIPPS	252
12	BANISTER JANE	DA U	13		NOT GIVEN (?WESTFIELD)	LOWER FISHPOND	153
26	BANISTER LOUISA	DA U	22		SSX EWHURST	CRIPPS	252
12	BANISTER LUCY	WI M	52		SSX WESTFIELD	LOWER FISHPOND	153
26	BANISTER MATILDA	DA U	19		SSX EWHURST	CRIPPS	252
26	BANISTER PHEBE	WI M	60		KEN BENENDEN	CRIPPS	252
12	BANISTER TILDEN	SO U	15		SSX WESTFIELD	LOWER FISHPOND	153
12	BANISTER WILLIAM	HD M	53	AG.LAB	SSX ORE	LOWER FISHPOND	153
3	BANKES EDWARD	LG U	24	BRICKMAKER	UNKNOWN	FORWARD LANE	128
22	BARBER EDWARD	HD M	39	GROCER MASTER EMP 1	LAMBETH	SEDLESCOMBE STREET	189
22	BARBER EDWARD JAMES	SO U	6	SCHOLAR	SSX SEDLESCOMBE	SEDLESCOMBE STREET	189
22	BARBER ELIZABETH	WI M	31		SSX SEDLESCOMBE	SEDLESCOMBE STREET	189
22	BARBER FANNY ELIZABETH	DA U	2		SSX SEDLESCOMBE	SEDLESCOMBE STREET	189
22	BARBER JOHN ROBERT	SO U	4	SCHOLAR	SSX SEDLESCOMBE	SEDLESCOMBE STREET	189
18	BARDEN ANN	DA U	11		SSX BEXHILL	SHORT WOOD HOUSE - SIDLEY	68
18	BARDEN CAROLINE	DA U	8	SCHOLAR	SSX BEXHILL	SHORT WOOD HOUSE - SIDLEY	68
21	BARDEN GEORGE	SV U	20	AG.LAB	SSX BEXHILL	FREEZELAND? SIDLEY	68
18	BARDEN JOSEPH	SO U	6	SCHOLAR	SSX BEXHILL	SHORT WOOD HOUSE - SIDLEY	68
18	BARDEN SOPHIA	WI M	42		SSX CATSFIELD	SHORT WOOD HOUSE - SIDLEY	68
18	BARDEN URIAH	SO U	2		SSX BEXHILL	SHORT WOOD HOUSE - SIDLEY	68
18	BARDEN WILLIAM	HD M	42	AG.LAB	SSX BEXHILL	SHORT WOOD HOUSE - SIDLEY	68
3	BARHAM ANN	DA U	28		NOT GIVEN (?WESTFIELD)	DOLEHAM	151
3	BARHAM ARTHUR	SO U	26		NOT GIVEN (?WESTFIELD)	DOLEHAM	151
3	BARHAM EDMUND	GS U	4		NOT GIVEN (?WESTFIELD)	DOLEHAM	151
3	BARHAM EDMUND	HD M	60	FARMER	SSX WESTFIELD	DOLEHAM	151
17	BARHAM ELIZABETH	DA U	24		SSX SEDLESCOMBE	SEDLESCOMBE STREET	203
3	BARHAM FANNY	DA U	15		NOT GIVEN (?WESTFIELD)	DOLEHAM	151
17	BARHAM FRANCES	WI M	59	NURSE	SSX EWHURST	SEDLESCOMBE STREET	203
17	BARHAM HANNAH	WI M	60		KEN KENNORITON?	BREDE HIGH	251
3	BARHAM MARY	DA U	23		NOT GIVEN (?WESTFIELD)	DOLEHAM	151
17	BARHAM MARY	GD U	7		MDX HAMMERSMITH*	SEDLESCOMBE STREET	203
68	BARHAM MARY	WI M	57		SSX GUESTLING	MOUNT PLEASANT	197

	Surname	Given	Rel	MS	Age	Occupation	County	Birthplace	Residence	Pg
3	BARHAM	MATILDA	DA	U	21		NOT GIVEN (?WESTFIELD)		DOLEHAM	151
3	BARHAM	PHILLIDELPHIA	WI	M	56		SSX	WESTFIELD	DOLEHAM	151
17	BARHAM	SAMUEL	HD	M	55	AG.LAB	SSX	BREDE	BREDE HIGH	251
17	BARHAM	THOMAS	HD	M	60	AG.LAB	SSX	BATTLE	SEDLESCOMBE STREET	203
68	BARHAM	TILDEN	HD	M	61	RELIEVING OFFICER	SSX	WESTFIELD	MOUNT PLEASANT	197
3	BARHAM	WILLIAM	SO	U	18		NOT GIVEN (?WESTFIELD)		DOLEHAM	151
67	BARKER	ALFRED	SO	U	13		SSX	BEXHILL	SIDLEY GREEN	84
4	BARKER	BENJAMIN	HD	M	37	BRICKLAYER	SSX	BEXHILL	SIDLEY CORNER	89
4	BARKER	BENJAMIN	SO	U	9	SCHOLAR	SSX	BEXHILL	SIDLEY CORNER	89
8	BARKER	BENJAMIN	SO	U	13		SSX	BEXHILL	SIDLEY	66
8	BARKER	CAROLINE	DA	U	2		SSX	BEXHILL	SIDLEY	66
8	BARKER	ELIZA	DA	U	19		SSX	BEXHILL	SIDLEY	66
8	BARKER	ELIZABETH	DA	U	5		SSX	BEXHILL	SIDLEY	66
8	BARKER	ELLEN	DA	U	9		SSX	BEXHILL	SIDLEY	66
22	BARKER	EMMA	SV	U	19	HOUSE SERVANT	SSX	BEXHILL	NOT GIVEN	54
4	BARKER	FREDERICK	SO	U	4	SCHOLAR	SSX	BEXHILL	SIDLEY CORNER	89
4	BARKER	GEORGE	SO	U	12		SSX	BEXHILL	SIDLEY CORNER	89
8	BARKER	HARRIET	DA	U	11		SSX	BEXHILL	SIDLEY	66
67	BARKER	HARRIET	WI	M	56		SSX	BEXHILL	SIDLEY GREEN	84
8	BARKER	HENRY	SO	U	15		SSX	BEXHILL	SIDLEY	66
67	BARKER	HENRY	SO	U	18		SSX	BEXHILL	SIDLEY GREEN	84
4	BARKER	ISABELLA	DA	U	14		SSX	BEXHILL	SIDLEY CORNER	89
4	BARKER	ISABELLA	WI	M	32		SSX	BEXHILL	SIDLEY CORNER	89
4	BARKER	JAMES	SO	U	6	SCHOLAR	SSX	BEXHILL	SIDLEY CORNER	89
8	BARKER	JANE	DA	U	7		SSX	BEXHILL	SIDLEY	66
8	BARKER	MARY	WI	M	42		SSX	BEXHILL	SIDLEY	66
8	BARKER	RICHARD	HD	M	44	CARPENTER	SSX	BEXHILL	SIDLEY	66
67	BARKER	RICHARD	HD	M	61	BRICKLAYER	SSX	BEXHILL	SIDLEY GREEN	84
4	BARKER	SARAH	DA	U	1		SSX	BEXHILL	SIDLEY CORNER	89
67	BARKER	STEPHEN	SO	U	21		SSX	BEXHILL	SIDLEY GREEN	84
86	BARNARD	ANN	DA	U	4		SSX	BEXHILL	NOT GIVEN	99
86	BARNARD	EDWARD	HD	M	34	TAILOR	SSX	BEXHILL	NOT GIVEN	99
86	BARNARD	ELLEN	DA	U	8	SCHOLAR	SSX	BEXHILL	NOT GIVEN	99
97	BARNARD	HARRIET	WI	M	39		SSX	BULVERHITHE	NOT GIVEN	100
86	BARNARD	JESSIE	DA	U	2		SSX	BEXHILL	NOT GIVEN	99
86	BARNARD	LUCY	DA	U	6	SCHOLAR	SSX	BEXHILL	NOT GIVEN	99
1	BARNARD	RICHARD	SO	U	44	SHOEMAKER	SSX	BEXHILL	BELL HILL	24
86	BARNARD	SARAH	DA	U	10	SCHOLAR	SSX	BEXHILL	NOT GIVEN	99
86	BARNARD	SARAH	WI	M	32		SSX	BEXHILL	NOT GIVEN	99
97	BARNARD	THOMAS	HD	M	42	CORDWAINER	SSX	BEXHILL	NOT GIVEN	100
1	BARNARD	THOMAS	HD	W	74	SHOEMAKER	SSX	BURWASH	BELL HILL	24
1	BARNARD	WILLIAM	SO	U	32	SHOEMAKER	SSX	BEXHILL	BELL HILL	24
97	BARNES	ANN	WI	M	24		BKM	BUCKINGHAM	HUT	20
64	BARNES	BARBARA	WI	M	61		SSX	WALBERTON	SIDLEY GREEN	83
35	BARNES	CAROLINE	DA	U	25		SSX	WESTFIELD	KENT STREET	166
64	BARNES	EDMUND	HD	M	43	AG.LAB	SSX	BEXHILL	SIDLEY GREEN	83
35	BARNES	EDMUND	SO	U	23		SSX	WESTFIELD	KENT STREET	166
97	BARNES	ELIZABETH	DA	U	10?		BRK	OFFINGTON	HUT	20
43	BARNES	ELIZABETH	HD	W	70	PAUPER SHOEMAKER'S WIFE	SSX	HELLINGLY	SIDLEY GREEN	81
35	BARNES	EMILY	DA	U	2M		SSX	WESTFIELD	KENT STREET	166
35	BARNES	HARRIETT	DA	U	20		SSX	WESTFIELD	KENT STREET	166
97	BARNES	JAMES	HD	M	36	RAILWAY LAB	SOM	STREET	HUT	20
80	BARNES	MARGARET	SV	W	51?	HOUSEKEEPER	SSX	ROBERTSBRIDGE	BEAUPORT HOUSE	16
97	BARNES	MARTHA A	DA	U	7		BKM	NEWPORT PAGNELL	HUT	20
35	BARNES	REUBEN	SO	U	15		SSX	WESTFIELD	KENT STREET	166
12	BARNES	RICHARD	LG	U	30	RAIL LAB	NOR	NORWICH	RAILWAY HUT	6
35	BARNES	SAMUEL	SO	U	18		SSX	WESTFIELD	KENT STREET	166
35	BARNES	THOMAS	HD	M	58	AG.LAB	SSX	BREDE	KENT STREET	166
62	BARNES	THOMAS	LG	U	25	RAIL LAB	KEN	GREAT CHART	PUMP HOUSE	14
35	BARNES	WILLIAM	SO	U	5		SSX	WESTFIELD	KENT STREET	166
16	BARROW	CHARLOTTE	WI	M	31		SSX	HELLINGLY	NOT GIVEN	91
16	BARROW	JAMES	SO	U	15		SSX	BEXHILL	NOT GIVEN	91
16	BARROW	JESSE	HD	M	46	RETAILER OF BEER	SSX	BEXHILL	NOT GIVEN	91
16	BARROW	SARAH	DA	U	13		SSX	BEXHILL	NOT GIVEN	90
16	BARROW	SPENCER	SO	U	4		SSX	BEXHILL	NOT GIVEN	91
16	BARROW	STEPHEN	SO	U	8		SSX	BEXHILL	NOT GIVEN	91
16	BARROW	WILLIAM	SO	U	6		SSX	BEXHILL	NOT GIVEN	91
19	BARSHELL	CHARLES	LG	U	30	RAILWAY LAB	HAM	YAPTON	CROWHURST VILLAGE	131
11	BARTHOLOMEW	SAMUEL	SV	U	70	AG.LAB	SSX	EASTBOURNE	WILTING FARM HOUSE	6
24	BARTON	ARTHUR	SO	U	34	FARMER 1100 AC EMP 30	SSX	EWHURST	PEBSHAM FARM SIDLEY	78
24	BARTON	HARRIET	HD	W	62	ANNUITANT	SSX	HAILSHAM	PEBSHAM FARM SIDLEY	78
24	BARTON	THOMAS	SO	U	29	JOINT FARMER	SSX	EWHURST	PEBSHAM FARM SIDLEY	78
6	BATES	ALFRED	SO	U	1		SSX	EWHURST	COLLIERS GREEN	233
33	BATES	BENJAMIN	LG	W	98	BLIND	SSX	NORTHIAM	KENT STREET	166
2	BATES	CAROLINE	DA	U	18		SSX	EWHURST	PADGHAM FARM	215
6	BATES	DAVID	FA	W	74	AG.LAB	SSX	EWHURST	COLLIERS GREEN	233
4	BATES	DAVID	HD	M	37	AG.LAB	SSX	EWHURST	COLLIERS GREEN	232
10	BATES	EDWIN	HD	M	32	AG.LAB	SSX	WESTFIELD	SPRING COTTAGES	153
6	BATES	ELIZABETH	WI	M	32		SSX	NORTHIAM	COLLIERS GREEN	233
2	BATES	HARRIET	DA	U	14		SSX	EWHURST	PADGHAM FARM	215
4	BATES	JAMES	SO	U	1		SSX	EWHURST	COLLIERS GREEN	233
10	BATES	JEMIMA	DA	U	2		SSX	WESTFIELD	SPRING COTTAGES	153
2	BATES	JOHN	SO	U	16	AG.LAB	SSX	EWHURST	PADGHAM FARM	215
10	BATES	JULIA	WI	M	24		SSX	ROTHERFIELD	SPRING COTTAGES	153
6	BATES	KITTY	DA	U	3		SSX	EWHURST	COLLIERS GREEN	233
21	BATES	LEWIS	LG	U	24	AG.LAB	SSX	EWHURST	ODIAM FARM	218

No.	Name	Rel	MS	Age	Occupation	County	Parish	Place	Page
15	BATES MARTHA	VR	M	62		SSX	ORE	PARKERS	153
2	BATES MARY	DA	U	14		SSX	EWHURST	PADGHAM FARM	215
2	BATES PHILADELPHIA	WI	M	47		SSX	BODIAM	PADGHAM FARM	215
2	BATES RICHARD	SO	U	8	SCHOLAR	SSX	EWHURST	PADGHAM FARM	215
4	BATES SARAH	WI	M	33		SSX	FAIRLIGHT	COLLIERS GREEN	233
2	BATES THOMAS	HD	M	41	AG.LAB	SSX	EWHURST	PADGHAM FARM	215
4	BATES THOMAS	SO	U	4		SSX	EWHURST	COLLIERS GREEN	233
2	BATES THOMAS	SO	U	10	SCHOLAR	SSX	EWHURST	PADGHAM FARM	215
60	BATES THOMAS BADCOCK	SO	U	27	AG.LAB	SSX	EWHURST	SEMPSTED FARM	240
6	BATES WALTER	HD	M	33	AG.LAB	SSX	EWHURST	COLLIERS GREEN	233
2	BATES WILLIAM	GS	U	1		SSX	EWHURST	PADGHAM FARM	215
25	BATH CHARLES	LG	/	19	RAIL LAB	NOT GIVEN		RAILWAY HUT	8
62	BAYLEY BANJAMIN	HD	M	50	SUB-CONTRACTOR RAILWAY	YKS	FIRLAKE	RAILWAY HUT	136
62	BAYLEY BENJAMIN	SO	U	16	RAILWAY LAB	WAR	SHEPHFIELD?	RAILWAY HUT	136
66	BAYLEY EMILY	CI	U	26	HOUSE KEEPER	KEN	TENTERDEN	STAPLE CROSS	241
62	BAYLEY HARRIOT	WI	M	43		YKS	HULL	RAILWAY HUT	136
66	BAYLEY HENRY	HD	M	36	GROCER & DRAPER	KEN	TENTERDEN	STAPLE CROSS	241
62	BAYLEY SUSANNA	DA	U	17		LIN	BARTON	RAILWAY HUT	136
62	BAYLEY THOMAS	SO	U	13	RAILWAY LAB	WAR	SHEPHFIELD?	RAILWAY HUT	136
63	BEAL HANNAH	WI	M	66		SSX	SEDLESCOMBE	STAPLE CROSS	241
63	BEAL WILLIAM	HD	M	78	AG.LAB RECEIVES RELIEF	SSX	EWHURST	STAPLE CROSS	241
10	BEAN ELIZABETH	DA	U	11	SCHOLAR	SSX	BEXHILL	BELL HILL	25
10	BEAN HARRIETT	WI	M	49		SSX	BODIAM	BELL HILL	25
10	BEAN JAMES	HD	M	50	AG.LAB	SSX	BEXHILL	BELL HILL	25
10	BEAN JAMES	SO	U	6	SCHOLAR	SSX	BEXHILL	BELL HILL	25
10	BEAN THOMAS	SO	U	13?		SSX	BEXHILL	BELL HILL	25
61	BEANY BENJAMIN	SV	U	17	GROOM ETC	SSX	PIDDINGHOE	HURCHINGTON	58
52	BEARD ELIZA	WI	M	35		ESS	RAMSEY	HOPPOLE CASTLE	179
52	BEARD GEORGE	HD	M	40	HORSE DEALER	KEN	CHATHAM	HOPPOLE CASTLE	179
41	BEARD MARY	VR	U	2		SSX	WESTFIELD	WALNUT TREE	156
52	BEARD THOMAS	BR	U	23		SSX	BRIGHTON	HOPPOLE CASTLE	179
84	BECK CHARLES GOODWIN	HD	M	30	BREWER	SSX	EWHURST	STAPLE CROSS	243
92	BECK JANE MARIA	DA	U	19		SSX	EWHURST	STAPLE CROSS	244
84	BECK OLIVIA	WI	M	27		HRT	NORTH MIMMS	STAPLE CROSS	243
92	BECK WILLIAM	HD	M	59	BREWER EMP 3MEN	SSX	LAUGHTON	STAPLE CROSS	244
22	BEECHAM CHARLES	LG	U	NK20	RAIL LAB	UNKNOWN		RAILWAY HUT	8
13	BEECHING ALBERT	GS	U	5	SCHOLAR	SSX	BEXHILL	MILL HOUSE - SIDLEY	66
78	BEECHING BENJAMIN	SO	U	10	SCHOLAR	SSX	BEXHILL	NOT GIVEN (LITTLE COMMON)	47
78	BEECHING CAROLINE	WI	M	41		SSX	PEVENSEY	NOT GIVEN (LITTLE COMMON)	47
78	BEECHING EMILY	DA	U	6		SSX	BEXHILL	NOT GIVEN (LITTLE COMMON)	47
78	BEECHING HENRY	SO	U	4		SSX	BEXHILL	NOT GIVEN (LITTLE COMMON)	47
28	BEECHING HENRY	SV	U	22	BUTCHER	SSX	BEXHILL	BEXHILL STREET	26
78	BEECHING JOSEPH	SO	U	8	SCHOLAR	SSX	BEXHILL	NOT GIVEN (LITTLE COMMON)	47
78	BEECHING THOMAS	SO	U	13	AG.LAB	SSX	BEXHILL	NOT GIVEN (LITTLE COMMON)	47
78	BEECHING WILLIAM	HD	M	61	COAL MERCHANT	SSX	BEXHILL	NOT GIVEN (LITTLE COMMON)	47
55	BEENEY BETSY	WI	M	23		SSX	BEXHILL	LITTLE COMMON	57
23	BEENEY CHARLOTTE	SV	U	14	HOUSE SERVANT	SSX	CROWHURST	NOT GIVEN	131
6	BEENEY HENRY	SV	U	13		SSX	BATTLE	DUKE FARM	129
29	BEENEY JAMES	HD	M	56	FARM LAB	KEN	SANDHURST	GREEN STREET	132
29	BEENEY JAMES	SO	U	21	FARM LAB	SSX	CROWHURST	GREEN STREET	132
29	BEENEY JANE	DA	U	11		SSX	CROWHURST	GREEN STREET	132
29	BEENEY RUTH	DA	U	19		SSX	CROWHURST	GREEN STREET	132
29	BEENEY RUTH	WI	M	56		SSX	SALEHURST	GREEN STREET	132
29	BEENEY SARAH	DA	U	17		SSX	CROWHURST	GREEN STREET	132
55	BEENEY WILLIAM	HD	M	21	AG.LAB	SSX	BEXHILL	LITTLE COMMON	57
55	BEENEY WILLIAM	SO	U	15		SSX	BEXHILL	LITTLE COMMON	57
28	BEENY GEORGE	LG	M	60	FARM LAB	SSX	BATTLE	FORWARD LANE	146
42	BEEVIS CAROLINE	DA	U	4		SSX	BEXHILL	NOT GIVEN	94
42	BEEVIS E J (FEMALE)	DA	U	1		SSX	BEXHILL	NOT GIVEN	94
110	BEEVIS ELIZABETH	WI	M	63		SSX	BATTLE	NOT GIVEN	101
42	BEEVIS HANNAH	WI	M	25		SSX	CROWHURST	NOT GIVEN	94
42	BEEVIS JAMES	HD	M	35	BRICKLAYER	SSX	BEXHILL	NOT GIVEN	94
110	BEEVIS JOHN	HD	M	71	BRICKLAYER	SSX	BEXHILL	NOT GIVEN	101
42	BEEVIS MARY ANN	DA	U	5		SSX	BEXHILL	NOT TIVEN	94
110	BEEVIS WILLIAM	SO	U	32	BRICKLAYER'S LAB	SSX	BEXHILL	NOT GIVEN	101
49	BEIVES? PHILLA	WI	M	39	DRESSMAKER	SSX	BEXHILL	LITTLE COMMON	57
49	BEIVES? THOMAS	HD	M	44	BRICKLAYER	SSX	BEXHILL	LITTLE COMMON	57
22	BENEY ELLEN	DA	U	12		SSX	SEDLESCOMBE	ODIAM GATE	218
47	BENEY GEORGE	SO	U	14	AG.LAB	SSX	SEDLESCOMBE	NOT GIVEN	111
5	BENEY GEORGE	SV	U	20	FARM LAB	SSX	BATTLE	NOT GIVEN	107
22	BENEY HARRIET	DA	U	4		SSX	EWHURST	ODIAM GATE	218
47	BENEY HENRY	SO	U	21	AG.LAB	SSX	PIDDINGHAM	NOT GIVEN	111
72	BENEY HORRACE	SV	U	14	AG.LAB	SSX	BEXHILL	WATERMILL HOUSE	114
22	BENEY JAMES	SO	U	6		SSX	EWHURST	ODIAM GATE	218
22	BENEY JANE	WI	M	39		SSX	EASTBOURNE	ODIAM GATE	218
47	BENEY MARIA	DA	U	11	SCHOLAR	SSX	BATTLE	NOT GIVEN	111
29	BENEY MARY	WI	M	66		SRY	LINSFIELD	BREDE BRIDGE	176
22	BENEY MATILDA	DA	U	2		SSX	EWHURST	ODIAM GATE	218
47	BENEY SUSANNAH	HD	W	41	RARISH RELIEF	SSI	FALMER	NOT GIVEN	111
22	BENEY THOMAS	HD	M	36	AG.LAB	SSX	BATTLE	ODIAM GATE	218
29	BENEY TRUST	HD	M	52	RAIL LAB	KEN	HAWKHURST	BREDE BRIDGE	176
19	BENGE DAVID	HD	M	66	AG.LAB	SSX	MOUNTFIELD	MOUNT EPHRAIM	164
3	BENGE DAVID	SV	U	21	AG.LAB	SSX	WESTFIELD	DOLEHAM	152
67	BENGE JAMES	GS	U	10	SCHOLAR	SSX	EWHURST	STAPLE CROSS	241
19	BENGE SARAH	DA	U	27		SSX	WESTFIELD	MOUNT EPHRAIM	164
19	BENGE SARAH	WI	M	62		SSX	WESTFIELD	MOUNT EPHRAIM	164

No.	Name	Rel	M	Age	Occupation	Birthplace	Address	Pg
67	BENGE WILLIAM	GS	U	9	SCHOLAR	SSX EWHURST	STAPLE CROSS	241
12	BENNETT ANN	DA	U	5		SSX BEXHILL	54 MARTELLO TOWER IN LIBERTY	38
12	BENNETT ELIZABETH	DA	U	11		SSX BEXHILL	54 MARTELLO TOWER IN LIBERTY	38
12	BENNETT GEORGE	SO	U	7		SSX BEXHILL	54 MARTELLO TOWER IN LIBERTY	38
52	BENNETT HARRIOT	WI	M	41		SSX BEXHILL	LITTLE COMMON	57
12	BENNETT HENRY	HD	M	43	COAST GUARD	DEV PLYMOUTH	54 MARTELLO TOWER IN LIBERTY	38
12	BENNETT HENRY	SO	U	9		SSX BEXHILL	54 MARTELLO TOWER IN LIBERTY	38
52	BENNETT HENRY WILLIAM	SO	U	2		SSX BEXHILL	LITTLE COMMON	57
52	BENNETT JAMES	HD	M	41	BRICKLAYER	SSX BEXHILL	LITTLE COMMON	57
53	BENNETT JAMES	HD	M	52	BRICKLAYER	SSX BEXHILL	LITTLE COMMON	57
52	BENNETT JAMES	SO	U	9	SCHOLAR	SSX BEXHILL	LITTLE COMMON	57
12	BENNETT JESSE	SO	U	2		SSX BEXHILL	54 MARTELLO TOWER IN LIBERTY	39
34	BENNETT JOHN	BD	U	50	GENTLEMAN	BRK WALLINGFORD	COURT LODGE FARM	147
12	BENNETT MARY	DA	U	4		SSX BEXHILL	54 MARTELLO TOWER IN LIBERTY	39
52	BENNETT MARY ANN	VR	U	15		SSX BEXHILL	LITTLE COMMON	57
53	BENNETT MARY ANN	WI	M	43		SSX WARTLING	LITTLE COMMON	57
12	BENNETT SARAH	WI	M	36		DOR CORFE CASTLE	54 MARTELLO TOWER IN LIBERTY	38
53	BENNETT THOMAS	BR	U	45	BRICKLAYER'S LAB	SSX BEXHILL	LITTLE COMMON	57
27	BENNETT WILLIAM	HD	W	77	BRICKLAYER	SSX BEXHILL	BEXHILL STREET	28
17	BENTLEY GEORGE	LG	U	26	RAIL LAB	HEF BUYDEN	RAILWAY HUT	7
33	BENTLY CHARLES	LG	U	19	RAILWAY LAB	LEI	MOORS FARM	147
1	BENY CHARLES	LG	U	30	AG.LAB	SSX BATTLE	CATSFIELD GREEN	119
5	BETCHLEY ABRAHAM	SV	U	21	GRINDER	SSX EAST GRINSTEAD	SIDLEY	65
48	BETTS KEZIAH	WI	M	38		SFK STONEHAM	NO.5 GALLEY HILL	29
48	BETTS SAMUEL	HD	M	39	COAST GUARD	IOW RYDE	NO.5 GALLEY HILL	29
16	BIDE JANE	WI	M	27		BIRMINGHAM	RAILWAY HUT	130
16	BIDE JOHN	SO	U	9		READING*	RAILWAY HUT	130
16	BIDE SAMUEL	HD	M	29	RAILWAY LAB	SRY FARNHAM	RAILWAY HUT	130
5	BINDER LUCY	VR	M	58	CARPENTER'S WIFE	SSX BEXHILL	NEW INN SIDLEY	76
15	BIRCHETT CAROLINE	DA	U	6	SCHOLAR	SSX BEXHILL	NOT GIVEN	90
15	BIRCHETT CAROLINE	WI	M	27		SSX BEXHILL	NOT GIVEN	90
15	BIRCHETT GEORGE	HD	M	30	AG.LAB	SSX BEXHILL	NOT GIVEN	90
15	BIRCHETT GEORGE	SO	U	11M		SSX BEXHILL	NOT GIVEN	90
15	BIRCHETT SAMUEL	SO	U	3		SSX BEXHILL	NOT GIVEN	90
2	BISHOP CHARLES	SO	U	7	SCHOLAR	SSX CATSFIELD	CATSFIELD GREEN	119
19	BISHOP FRANCES	WI	M	28		NOT GIVEN	SEDLESCOMBE STREET	188
19	BISHOP FRANCES JANE	DA	U	6	SCHOLAR	NOT GIVEN	SEDLESCOMBE STREET	188
19	BISHOP FRANK	SO	U	7	SCHOLAR	NOT GIVEN	SEDLESCOMBE STREET	188
36	BISHOP GEORGE	SO	U	8M		SSX EWHURST	FURNACE PONDS	253
36	BISHOP HARRIOT	DA	U	8		SSX SALEHURST	FURNACE PONDS	253
36	BISHOP HENRY	SO	U	4		SSX SALEHURST	FURNACE PONDS	253
2	BISHOP JAMES	SO	U	6	SCHOLAR	SSX CATSFIELD	CATSFIELD GREEN	119
2	BISHOP JAMES	SO	U	18	AG.LAB	SSX CATSFIELD	CATSFIELD GREEN	119
2	BISHOP JESSE	HD	M	41	SEALER IN MARINE STORES	UNKNOWN	CATSFIELD GREEN	119
2	BISHOP JESSE	SO	U	15	AG.LAB	SSX CATSFIELD	CATSFIELD GREEN	119
36	BISHOP MARY	WI	M	39		SSX SALEHURST	FURNACE PONDS	253
19	BISHOP MARY ANN	DA	U	4	SCHOLAR	NOT GIVEN	SEDLESCOMBE STREET	189
19	BISHOP ROBERT	HD	M	40	BUTCHER JM	NOT GIVEN	SEDLESCOMBE STREET	188
36	BISHOP SAMUEL	HD	M	44	AG.LAB	SSX SEDLESCOMBE	FURNACE PONDS	253
36	BISHOP SOPHIA	DA	U	11	SCHOLAR	SSX SALEHURST	FURNACE PONDS	253
2	BISHOP SUSSANNAH	WI	M	38		SSX HASTINGS	CATSFIELD GREEN	119
36	BISHOP THOMAS	SO	U	15	AG.LAB	SSX SALEHURST	FURNACE PONDS	253
19	BISHOP UN-NAMED INFANT BOY	SO	U	1M		NOT GIVEN	SEDLESCOMBE STREET	188
2	BISHOP UN-NAMED INFANT GIRL	DA	U	1M		SSX CATSFIELD (ASSUMED)	CATSFIELD GREEN	119
32	BISHOP WILLIAM	NP	U	11		NOT GIVEN (?WESTFIELD)	BUCKHURST	155
32	BISHOP WINIFRED	NC	U	12		NOT GIVEN (?WESTFIELD)	BUCKHURST	155
77	BISHOPP BARTEN	SO	U	12	GROCER & DRAPER	KEN LENHAM	STAPLE CROSS	243
77	BISHOPP DAVID	SO	U	5	SCHOLAR	KEN LENHAM	STAPLE CROSS	243
77	BISHOPP EDWARD	SO	U	10	SCHOLAR	KEN LENHAM	STAPLE CROSS	243
77	BISHOPP EDWARD BARTON	HD	M	39	(GROCER & DRAPER?)	KEN WOODCHURCH	STAPLE CROSS	242
77	BISHOPP MATILDA	DA	U	5M		SSX EWHURST	STAPLE CROSS	243
77	BISHOPP MATILDA	WI	M	37		SSX WADHURST	STAPLE CROSS	242
77	BISHOPP SPENCER	SO	U	5	SCHOLAR	KEN LENHAM	STAPLE CROSS	243
77	BISHOPP WELLER	SO	U	8	SCHOLAR	KEN LENHAM	STAPLE CROSS	243
5	BLACKMAN ALFRED	SO	U	16		SSX CATSFIELD	CATSFIELD GREEN	120
55	BLACKMAN BENJAMIN	LG	U	20	BRICKLAYER	SSX CATSFIELD	NOT GIVEN	112
51	BLACKMAN CATHERINE	DA	U	3		SSX CATSFIELD	NOT GIVEN	112
51	BLACKMAN CATHERINE	WI	M	23		SSX CATSFIELD	NOT GIVEN	112
5	BLACKMAN CHARLES	SO	U	6	SCHOLAR	SSX CATSFIELD	CATSFIELD GREEN	120
3	BLACKMAN DEALY	WI	M	40		SSX BREDE	WHEEL COTTAGE	172
48	BLACKMAN DELIA M	SV	U	19	HOUSE SERVANT	SSX WESTFIELD	WESTBROOK	178
4	BLACKMAN EDWARD	SO	U	11		SSX CROWHURST	FORWARD LANE	129
5	BLACKMAN ELEN	WI	M	28		SSX ORE	CATSFIELD GREEN	120
3	BLACKMAN ELIZA	6D	U	1		SSX WESTFIELD	WHEEL COTTAGE	172
50	BLACKMAN ELLEN	SD	U	10	SCHOLAR	SSX CATSFIELD	SIDLEY GREEN	82
53	BLACKMAN EMMA	DA	U	3		SSX CATSFIELD	NOT GIVEN	112
4	BLACKMAN FREDERICK	SO	U	15		SSX CROWHURST	FORWARD LANE	129
4	BLACKMAN GEORGE	SO	U	20	AG.LAB	SSX CROWHURST	FORWARD LANE	129
51	BLACKMAN HENRY	HD	M	27	BRICKLAYER	SSX CATSFIELD	NOT GIVEN	112
86	BLACKMAN ISAAC	NP	U	28	SHIP WRIGHT	SSX RYE	EWHURST GREEN	228
93	BLACKMAN JAMES	HD	M	27	AG.LAB	SSX CROWHURST	TILE KILN	19
86	BLACKMAN JAMES	NP	U	5	SCHOLAR	SSX RYE	EWHURST GREEN	228
47	BLACKMAN JAMES	SO	U	2		SSX WESTFIELD	MARTINS COTTAGE	178
4	BLACKMAN JAMES	SO	U	6	SCHOLAR	SSX CROWHURST	FORWARD LANE	129
52	BLACKMAN JAMES	VR	U	18	BRICKLAYER	SSX CATSFIELD	NOT GIVEN	112
53	BLACKMAN JANE	WI	M	22		SSX CATSFIELD	NOT GIVEN	112

53	BLACKMAN JOHN	HD M	33	PAINTER	SSX CATSFIELD	NOT GIVEN	112
53	BLACKMAN JOHN	SO U	5M		SSX CATSFIELD	NOT GIVEN	112
4	BLACKMAN JOHN	SO U	9	SCHOLAR	SSX CROWHURST	FORWARD LANE	129
4	BLACKMAN MAREY (SIC)	WI M	56?		KEN SEELE (SIC)	FORWARD LANE	129
93	BLACKMAN MARY	WI M	23		SSX HOLLINGTON	TILE KILN	19
53	BLACKMAN MARY A	DA U	5	SCHOLAR	SSX CATSFIELD	NOT GIVEN	112
13	BLACKMAN MERCY	HD W	78	PAUPER	SSX EWHURST	PRIMROSE COTTAGE	163
5	BLACKMAN ROBERT	HD M	39	BRICKLAYER	SSX CATSFIELD	CATSFIELD GREEN	120
39	BLACKMAN SABINA	SV·U	19		SSX WESTFIELD	BENSKINS	177
24	BLACKMAN SARAH	HD W	73	PAUPER	SSX WESTFIELD	NEW ENGLAND	164
50	BLACKMAN SARAH	SD U	8	SCHOLAR	SSX CATSFIELD	SIDLEY GREEN	82
47	BLACKMAN SARAH	WI M	31	AG.LAB (SIC)	SSX WESTFIELD	MARTINS COTTAGE	178
4	BLACKMAN STEPHEN	SO U	13		SSX CROWHURST	FORWARD LANE	129
3	BLACKMAN THOMAS	HD M	41	AG.LAB	SSX ASHBURNHAM	WHEEL COTTAGE	172
86	BLACKMAN THOMAS	NP U	25	SHOE MAKER	SSX RYE	EWHURST GREEN	228
47	BLACKMAN WILLIAM	HD M	36	AG.LAB	SSX WESTFIELD	MARTINS COTTAGE	178
4	BLACKMAN WILLIAM	HD M	56	UNABLE TO WORK - BLIND	SSX BATTLE	FORWARD LANE	129
47	BLACKMAN WILLIAM	SO U	1		SSX WESTFIELD	MARTINS COTTAGE	178
33	BLANCH FRANCES	WI M	42		SSX ROBERTSBRIDGE	MADDAMS	220
33	BLANCH GAINS	SO U	3		SSX EWHURST	MADDAMS	220
33	BLANCH WILLIAM	HD M	45	AG.LAB	SSX EWHURST	MADDAMS	220
33	BLANCH WILLIAM	SO U	12	SCHOLAR	SSX EWHURST	MADDAMS	220
24	BLIDE ELIZABETH	WI M	54		SSX BEXHILL	NOT GIVEN	54
24	BLIDE HARRIOT	DA U	18	(HOUSE SERVANT)	SSX BEXHILL	NOT GIVEN	54
24	BLIDE MARY ANN	GD U	4?		SSX BEXHILL	NOT GIVEN	54
24	BLIDE WILLIAM	HD M	56	AG.LAB	SSX BEXHILL	NOT GIVEN	54
24	BLIDE WILLIAM	SO U	28	AG.LAB	SSX BEXHILL	NOT GIVEN	54
65	BLOOMFIELD K C (FEMALE)	AS U	23	ASSISTANT GOVERNESS	SFK BACKSON	NOT GIVEN	96
23	BLUNDELL SARAH ANN	DA U	32	DRESSMAKER	SSX BATTLE	SEDLESCOMBE STREET	204
23	BLUNDELL THOMAS	HD W	57	CARPENTER	SSX BATTLE	SEDLESCOMBE STREET	204
3	BLUNT ELEN	WI M	20		SSX BRIGHTON	FORWARD LANE	128
3	BLUNT GEORGE	HD M	26	BRICKMAKER	SSX WINCHELSEA	FORWARD LANE	128
3	BLUNT GEORGE	SO U	3		SSX BRIGHTON	FORWARD LANE	128
64	BLUNT JOHN	LG U	26	RAILWAY LAB	SCT	RAILWAY HUT	137
3	BLUNT MARAH (SIC)	DA U	1		SRY GILFORD (SIC)	FORWARD LANE	128
15	BLYDE HARRIET	WI M	36		SSX BEXHILL	RIST WOOD SIDLEY	77
15	BLYDE JAMES	HD M	37	AG.LAB	SSX BEXHILL	RIST WOOD SIDLEY	77
23	BLYDE SARAH	SV U	25	HOUSEMAID	SSX BEXHILL	BEXHILL STREET	26
10	BODLE ELIZA	DA U	3M		SSX BEXHILL	BIGGS HILL SIDLEY	76
10	BODLE ELIZABETH ANN	DA U	3		SSX WINCHELSEA	BIGGS HILL SIDLEY	76
10	BODLE FRANK	SO U	8	SCHOLAR	SSX BATTLE	BIGGS HILL SIDLEY	76
32	BODLE GEORGE	SL U	18	AG.LAB	SSX WESTFIELD	DOWN	176
10	BODLE MARY JANE	DA U	2		SSX BEXHILL	BIGGS HILL SIDLEY	76
10	BODLE PHILADELPHIA	WI M	30		SSX WESTFIELD	BIGGS HILL SIDLEY	76
10	BODLE THOMAS	HD M	32	AG.LAB	SSX BATTLE	BIGGS HILL SIDLEY	76
32	BONES ALFRED	SO U	5		NOT GIVEN (?WESTFIELD)	BUCKHURST	155
32	BONES ELIZA	WI M	45		NOT GIVEN (?WESTFIELD)	BUCKHURST	155
32	BONES GEORGE	SO U	12		NOT GIVEN (?WESTFIELD)	BUCKHURST	155
32	BONES JOHN	SO U	15		NOT GIVEN (?WESTFIELD)	BUCKHURST	155
52	BONES PLASHA	SV U	17		SSX WESTFIELD	HOPPOLE CASTLE	179
32	BONES SPENCER	SO U	10		NOT GIVEN (?WESTFIELD)	BUCKHURST	155
32	BONES THOMAS	HD M	55	AG.LAB	SSX (?WESTFIELD)	BUCKHURST	155
32	BONES WILLIAM	SO U	7		NOT GIVEN (?WESTFIELD)	BUCKHURST	155
10	BONIFACE BENJAMIN	LG U	21	RAIL LAB	SSX BEEDING	SPRING COTTAGES	153
32	BOOTH ANN	DA U	6		SSX SLAUGHAM	WOODSGATE	93
32	BOOTH DAVID	SO U	1M		SSX BEXHILL	WOODSGATE	93
32	BOOTH E (FEMALE)	WI M	41		YKS THORNE	WOODSGATE	93
9	BOOTH EDWARD	HD M	51	ANNUITANT	NORWICH	PARK GATE	120
32	BOOTH ELIZABETH	DA U	9		YKS THORNE	WOODSGATE	93
13	BOOTH GEORGE	HD M	54	FARMER	SSX BATTLE	YEW TREES	173
9	BOOTH MARIANN	WI M	45		YKS	PARK GATE	120
5	BOOTH RICHARD	SV U	17		YKS THORNE	NEW INN SIDLEY	76
30	BOOTH SARAH	HD W	84	PARISH RELIEF	SSX PEASMARSH	BREDE LANE	190
13	BOOTH SARAH	WI M	54		SSX MOUNTFIELD	YEW TREES	173
32	BOOTH THOMAS	HD M	53	FARM BAILIFF	YKS THORNE	WOODSGATE	93
73	BOOTS ALBERT	SO U	8		SSX EWHURST	STAPLE CROSS	242
68	BOOTS ANN	CI U	55	TEA DEALER	SSX EWHURST	STAPLE CROSS	241
93	BOOTS ANNA	DA U	1		SSX EWHURST	STAPLE CROSS	244
24	BOOTS BENJAMIN	HD M	33	AG.LAB	SSX EWHURST	LORDINE FARM	235
67	BOOTS BENJAMIN	HD W	59	CARPENTER	SSX EWHURST	STAPLE CROSS	241
67	BOOTS BENJAMIN	SO U	22	CARPENTER	SSX EWHURST	STAPLE CROSS	241
66	BOOTS CHARLES G	SO U	4		SSX EWHURST	EWHURST GREEN	225
73	BOOTS EDWARD	SO U	5		SSX EWHUSRT	STAPLE CROSS	242
93	BOOTS ELIZABETH	WI M	32		SSX EWHURST	STAPLE CROSS	244
66	BOOTS ELIZABETH A	DA U	3		SSX EWHURST	EWHURST GREEN	225
63	BOOTS ELLEN	/ U	13	SCHOLAR	SSX EWHURST	RECTORY HOUSE	224
24	BOOTS ELLEN	DA U	11M		SSX EWHURST	LORDINE FARM	235
8	BOOTS ELLEN	DA U	15	SCHOLAR	SSX EWHURST	PADGHAM	216
66	BOOTS ELLEN A	DA U	26	HOUSE KEEPER	SSX EWHURST	EWHURST GREEN	225
64	BOOTS EMMA ANN	DA U	4		SSX EWHURST	EWHURST GREEN	224
66	BOOTS FREDERICK	SO U	28	CARPENTER	SSX EWHURST	EWHURST GREEN	225
73	BOOTS HELEN	DA U	7		SSX EWHURST	STAPLE CROSS	242
67	BOOTS HESTER	DA U	24		SSX EWHURST	STAPLE CROSS	241
64	BOOTS HORACE JOSIAH	HD M	32	WHEELWRIGHT	SSX EWHURST	EWHURST GREEN	224
64	BOOTS JANE	DA U	1		SSX EWHURST	EWHURST GREEN	224
24	BOOTS JANE	DA U	2		SSX EWHURST	LORDINE FARM	235

18

	Name	Rel	Cond	Age	Occupation	Birthplace	Location	Ref
24	BOOTS JANE	WI	M	32		SSX EWHURST	LORDINE FARM	235
73	BOOTS JOHN	SO	U	2		SSX EWHURST	STAPLE CROSS	242
79	BOOTS JOSEPH	HD	M	44	AG.LAB	SSX EWHURST	EWHURST GREEN	227
66	BOOTS JOSIAH	HD	W	58	CARPENTER MASTER	SSX EWHURST	EWHURST GREEN	225
79	BOOTS MARGARET	DA	U	14	SCHOLAR	SSX NORTHIAM	EWHURST GREEN	227
66	BOOTS MARY	DA	U	23		SSX EWHURST	EWHURST GREEN	225
73	BOOTS MARY	WI	M	32		SSX EWHURST	STAPLE CROSS	242
90	BOOTS MARY	WI	M	38?	DRESSMAKER	KEN GOUDHURST	NOT GIVEN	18
79	BOOTS MARY	WI	M	52		SSX NORTHIAM	EWHURST GREEN	227
73	BOOTS MARY ANN	DA	U	7M		SSX EWHURST	STAPLE CROSS	242
64	BOOTS MARY ANN	WI	M	32		SSX EWHURST	EWHURST GREEN	224
64	BOOTS MARY ANN SMITH	DA	U	3		SSX EWHURST	EWHURST GREEN	224
67	BOOTS MATILDA	DA	U	29		SSX EWHURST	STAPLE CROSS	241
93	BOOTS RICHARD	SO	U	4		SSX EWHURST	STAPLE CROSS	244
79	BOOTS SARAH	DA	U	16	SCHOLAR	SSX NORTHIAM	EWHURST GREEN	227
66	BOOTS T WALTER	SO	U	29	DRAPER	SSX EWHURST	EWHURST GREEN	225
90	BOOTS THOMAS	HD	M	49	TOLL COLLECTOR	KEN BIDDENDEN	NOT GIVEN	18
68	BOOTS THOMAS	HD	U	51	AG.LAB	SSX EWHURST	STAPLE CROSS	241
8	BOOTS THOMAS	HD	W	40	AG.LAB	SSX EWHURST	PADGHAM	216
8	BOOTS THOMAS	SO	U	13	AG.LAB	SSX EWHURST	PADGHAM	216
73	BOOTS WALTER	HD	M	36	PLUMBER	SSX EWHURST	STAPLE CROSS	242
79	BOOTS WILLIAM	SO	U	19	AG.LAB	SSX EWHURST	EWHURST GREEN	227
93	BOOTS WILLIAM HENRY	HD	M	39	WHEELWRIGHT 1AP	SSX EWHURST	STAPLE CROSS	244
80	BORARD LOUISA	SV	U	25	LADIES MAID	SWITZERLAND	BEAUPORT HOUSE	16
80	BORARD MARIA	SV	U	19	NURSE	SWITZERLAND	BEAUPORT HOUSE	16
110	BOTLE WILLIAM	VR	U	27	AG.LAB	SSX BEXHILL	NOT GIVEN	101
83	BOURNE ALFRED	SO	U	22	AG.LAB	SSX EWHURST	EWHURST GREEN	227
50	BOURNE ANN	DA	U	5	SCHOLAR	SSX EWHURST	SNAGS HALL	222
83	BOURNE EDGAR	SO	U	17	AG.LAB	SSX EWHURST	EWHURST GREEN	227
50	BOURNE EDWARD	HD	M	27	AG.LAB	SSX EWHURST	SNAGS HALL	222
50	BOURNE EDWARD	SO	U	3		SSX EWHURST	SNAGS HALL	222
50	BOURNE ELIZABETH	WI	M	27		SSX EWHURST	SNAGS HALL	222
50	BOURNE ELIZABETH MARY	DA	U	1		SSX EWHURST	SNAGS HALL	222
84	BOURNE GEORGE	SO	U	5	SCHOLAR	SSX EWHURST	EWHURST GREEN	228
84	BOURNE HENRY	HD	M	35	AG.LAB	SSX NORTHIAM	EWHURST GREEN	227
83	BOURNE HENRY	HD	M	60	AG.LAB	SSX EWHURST	EWHURST GREEN	227
84	BOURNE HENRY	SO	U	8	SCHOLAR	SSX EWHURST	EWHURST GREEN	228
75	BOURNE JAMES	HD	M	29	AG.LAB	SSX EWHURST	EWHURST GREEN	226
75	BOURNE JAMES	SO	U	2M		SSX EWHURST	EWHURST GREEN	226
84	BOURNE JANE	DA	U	3		SSX EWHURST	EWHURST GREEN	228
84	BOURNE JANE	WI	M	31		KEN WHITERSHAM	EWHURST GREEN	227
84	BOURNE JOHN	SO	U	1		SSX EWHURST	EWHURST GREEN	228
83	BOURNE JOHN	SO	U	19	AG.LAB	SSX EWHURST	EWHURST GREEN	227
75	BOURNE JULIA	WI	M	23		SSX MOUNTFIELD	EWHURST GREEN	226
83	BOURNE MARTHA	WI	M	58		SSX SEDLESCOMBE	EWHURST GREEN	227
50	BOURNE THOMAS	SO	U	7	SCHOLAR	SSX EWHURST	SNAGS HALL	222
84	BOURNE THOMAS	SO	U	10	AG.LAB	SSX EWHURST	EWHURST GREEN	228
75	BOURNE WILLIAM	SO	U	2		SSX EWHURST	EWHURST GREEN	226
35	BOUTER? ROBERT	HD	M	73	ANNUITANT	SSX CATSFIELD	NOT GIVEN	110
35	BOUTER? SARAH	WI	M	75		SSX WADHURST	NOT GIVEN	110
105	BOWER SARAH A	CO	M	52		CITY OF LONDON	ROSE COTTAGE	101
38	BOWLES ANN	DA	U	3	SCHOLAR	SSX EWHURST	MARCHANTS	237
38	BOWLES GEORGE	SO	U	7	SCHOLAR	SSX EWHURST	MARCHANTS	237
38	BOWLES JAMES	SO	U	21		SSX NORTHIAM	MARCHANTS	237
38	BOWLES MAHALAH	NC	U	17	SERVANT	SSX BURWASH	MARCHANTS	237
38	BOWLES ROBERT	HD	M	51	BLACKSMITH	SSX BURWASH	MARCHANTS	237
38	BOWLES SERENA	WI	M	39		SSX BECKLEY	MARCHANTS	237
38	BOWLES THOMAS	SO	U	10	SCHOLAR	SSX EWHURST	MARCHANTS	237
38	BOWLES TRAM	SO	U	5	SCHOLAR	SSX EWHURST	MARCHANTS	237
33	BOWLEY ESTHER	DA	U	17		HRT BOURINS* SHEEPS HILL	CROWHURST PLACE	133
33	BOWLEY GEORGE HENRY	HD	M	46	GAME KEEPER	HRT WILMORE GREEN	CROWHURST PLACE	133
33	BOWLEY MARY	WI	M	45		HRT HICKING	CROWHURST PLACE	133
39	BRANDHERT ANN	WI	M	22		KEN LITTLE MONGEHAM	RAILWAY HUT	133
39	BRANDHERT JAMES	HD	M	25	BRICKMAKER'S LAB	SILCHESTER?*	RAILWAY HUT	133
39	BRANDHERT MARY ANN	DA	U	2		KEN LITTLE MONGEHAM	RAILWAY HUT	133
41	BRATT JOSIAH	HD	M	45	FARMER 160 AC EMP 6	ST. JOHN'S HORSLEYDOWN	PRESTON FARM SIDLEY	81
96	BRAUNT? THOMAS	LG	W	38	RAIL LAB	BRK	HUT	19
53	BRAY DAVID	SO	U	3		ESS HENFIELD	RAILWAY HUT	135
53	BRAY ELIZABETH	WI	M	34		BONEY	RAILWAY HUT	135
53	BRAY LEWCEY	DA	U	3M		SSX CROWHURST	RAILWAY HUT	135
59	BRAY MARGARET	HK	W	59	HOUSE KEEPER	SSX RINGMER	SIDLEY GREEN	83
53	BRAY WILLIAM	HD	M	30	RAILWAY LAB	ESS HENFIELD	RAILWAY HUT	135
*68	BRAYNE DAVID	SO	U	12		CORK	BARN (SCHED.B)	138
*68	BRAYNE JOHN	HD	M	40	TRAVELLER	CORK	BARN (SCHED.B)	138
*68	BRAYNE JOHN	SO	U	10		CORK	BARN (SCHED.B)	138
*68	BRAYNE MAREY	WI	M	32		CORK	BARN (SCHED.B)	138
*68	BRAYNE PATRICK	SO	U	6		CORK	BARN (SCHED.B)	138
1	BRETT ANNA	SV	U	16	HOUSE SERVANT	SSX NINFIELD	VICARAGE HOUSE	161
20	BRETT DELIA	WI	M	53		SSX BEXHILL	NOT GIVEN	53
20	BRETT JOHN	HD	M	58	AG.LAB	SSX BEXHILL	NOT GIVEN	53
20	BRETT MARY	DA	U	14		SSX BEXHILL	NOT GIVEN	53
20	BRETT WILLIAM	SO	U	12	AG.LAB	SSX BEXHILL	NOT GIVEN	53
33	BRIDGEHEAD HARRY	SV	U	15	PLOUGH BOY	SSX CATSFIELD	BROOMHAM HOUSE	124
19	BRIDGLAND BARBARA	WI	M	46		SSX BATTLE	NOT GIVEN	108
19	BRIDGLAND JAMES	SO	U	11	SCHOLAR SUNDAY	SSX CATSFIELD	NOT GIVEN	109
19	BRIDGLAND JANE	DA	U	6	SCHOLAR SUNDAY	SSX CATSFIELD	NOT GIVEN	109

19	BRIDGLAND JOHN	HD M	56	AG.LAB	KEN SPELDHURST	NOT GIVEN	108
19	BRIDGLAND ROBERT	SO U	20	AG.LAB	SSX CATSFIELD	NOT GIVEN	109
19	BRIDGLAND SARAH	DA U	8	SCHOLAR SUNDAY	SSX CATSFIELD	NOT GIVEN	108
25	BRIDGLAND THOMAS	LG U	24	BAVIN MAKER	SSX CATSFIELD	CATSFIELD STREAM	122
19	BRIDGLAND WILLIAM	SO U	13	SCHOLAR SUNDAY	SSX CATSFIELD	NOT GIVEN	109
19	BRISTOW ANN	SV U	17	HOUSE SERVANT	SSX BEXHILL	NOT GIVEN	53
23	BRISTOW ANN	WI M	42		SSX BEXHILL	NOT GIVEN	54
23	BRISTOW ELIZABETH	DA U	12		SSX BEXHILL	NOT GIVEN	54
23	BRISTOW MARY JANE	DA U	2		SSX BEXHILL	NOT GIVEN	54
23	BRISTOW ROBERT	SO U	8	SCHOLAR	SSX BEXHILL	NOT GIVEN	54
23	BRISTOW THOMAS	HD M	42	AG.LAB	SSX BEXHILL	NOT GIVEN	54
3	BRISTOW THOMAS	SV U	19	AG.LAB	SSX BEXHILL	BARNHORN HILL	37
69	BRITT AARON	SO U	16	AG.LAB	SSX HOLLINGTON	YEW TREE	15
91	BRITT ALFRED	SO U	15?	AGE UNKNOWN	NOT GIVEN	STREET	19
3	BRITT ALFRED	SO U	17	AG.LAB	SSX BEXHILL	SIDLEY GREEN	75
30	BRITT CAROLINE	GD U	6		SSX HASTINGS	FORWARD LANE	146
43	BRITT CAROLINE	WI M	30		SSX HOLLINGTON	HOLLINGTON STREET	11
35	BRITT CATHRINE	DA U	6		SSX BEXHILL	NOT GIVEN	93
55	BRITT CHARLES	BR U	23	AG.LAB	SSX BEXHILL	NOT GIVEN	95
34	BRITT CHARLES THOMAS	SO U	2		SSX HOLLINGTON	PARSONAGE	9
3	BRITT CHARLOTTE	DA U	15		SSX BEXHILL	SIDLEY GREEN	75
69	BRITT EDMUND	SO U	20	AG.LAB	SSX HOLLINGTON	YEW TREE	15
30	BRITT ELIZABETH	DA U	21		SSX CROWHURST	FORWARD LANE	146
54	BRITT ELLEN	DA U	4		SSX BEXHILL	NOT GIVEN	95
30	BRITT ELLEN	DA U	12	DUMB	SSX CROWHURST	FORWARD LANE	146
43	BRITT FRANCES	DA U	3		SSX HOLLINGTON	HOLLINGTON STREET	11
3	BRITT FREDERIC	SO U	9	SCHOLAR	SSX BEXHILL	SIDLEY GREEN	75
35	BRITT GEORGE	HD M	37	AG.LAB	SSX BEXHILL	NOT GIVEN	93
55	BRITT GEORGE	HD U	26	AG.LAB	SSX BEXHILL	NOT GIVEN	95
43	BRITT GEORGE	SO U	1		SSX HOLLINGTON	HOLLINGTON STREET	11
91	BRITT GEORGE	SO U	20		NOT GIVEN	STREET	19
3	BRITT GEORGE	SO U	20	AG.LAB	SSX BEXHILL	SIDLEY GREEN	75
34	BRITT GEORGE WILLIAM	SO U	3		SSX HOLLINGTON	PARSONAGE	9
33	BRITT HANNAH	WI M	62		SSX BEXHILL	BEXHILL STREET	27
91	BRITT HARRIET	DA U	18?	AGE UNKNOWN	NOT GIVEN	STREET	19
87	BRITT HARRIETT	SV U	16?		SSX BEXHILL	HAYWARDS	18
30	BRITT HARRIETT	WI M	51		SSX WARTLING	FORWARD LANE	146
13	BRITT HARRIOTT	HD W	58	GROCER	SSX BURWASH	BELL HILL	25
35	BRITT HENRY	SO U	9M		SSX BEXHILL	NOT GIVEN	93
13	BRITT HENRY	SO U	17	GROCER	SSX BEXHILL	BELL HILL	25
30	BRITT JAMES	HD M	54	FARM LAB	SSX HOLLINGTON	FORWARD LANE	146
35	BRITT JANE	DA U	7		SSX BEXHILL	NOT GIVEN	93
3	BRITT JANE	WI M	48		SSX BEXHILL	SIDLEY GREEN	75
34	BRITT JOHN	HD M	28	AG.LAB	SSX BEXHILL	PARSONAGE	9
40	BRITT JOHN	LG W	78	PAUPER AG.LAB	SSX BEXHILL	BRAGGS LANE	42
34	BRITT JOHN ALFRED	SO U	7		SSX HOLLINGTON	PARSONAGE	9
54	BRITT MARY	HD W	37	PAUPER	SSX BATTLE	NOT GIVEN	95
35	BRITT MARY	WI M	29		SSX BEXHILL	NOT GIVEN	93
69	BRITT MARY	WI M	53		SSX ORE	YEW TREE	15
40	BRITT MARY A	DL U	11	SCHOLAR	SSX BEXHILL	BRAGGS LANE	42
54	BRITT MARY HARRIET?	DA U	8		SSX BEXHILL	NOT GIVEN	95
69	BRITT MOSES	SO U	9		SSX HOLLINGTON	YEW TREE	15
33	BRITT SAMUEL	HD M	70	WHEELWRIGHT	SSX BEXHILL	BEXHILL STREET	27
1	BRITT SARAH	SV U	60?		SSX BATTLE	BELL HILL	24
34	BRITT SARAH	WI M	26		SSX HOLLINGTON	PARSONAGE	9
40	BRITT SARAH A	DL U	7		SSX BEXHILL	BRAGGS LANE	42
91	BRITT SOPHIA	WI M	52		NOT GIVEN	STREET	19
33	BRITT STEPHEN	SO U	34	AG.LAB	SSX BEXHILL	BEXHILL STREET	27
3	BRITT THOMAS	HD M	50	AG.LAB	SSX BEXHILL	SIDLEY GREEN	75
43	BRITT WILLIAM	HD M	32	AG.LAB	SSX HOLLINGTON	HOLLINGTON STREET	11
91	BRITT WILLIAM	HD M	55	AG.LAB	NOT GIVEN	STREET	19
69	BRITT WILLIAM	HD M	60	AG.LAB	SSX HOLLINGTON	YEW TREE	15
54	BRITT WILLIAM HENRY	SO U	10		SSX BEXHILL	NOT GIVEN	95
93	BRITTEN HANNAH	WI M	58		SSX NINFIELD	NOT GIVEN	100
93	BRITTEN WILLIAM	HD M	66	AG.LAB	SSX CROWHURST	NOT GIVEN	100
38	BROOK AARON	/ M	30	AG.LAB	NOT GIVEN	WORK-HOUSE	156
37	BROOK ARTHUR J	SO U	6	SCHOLAR AT HOME	SSX BEXHILL	BEXHILL STREET	27
37	BROOK ARTHUR S?	HD M	40	FARMER 1000 ACRES EMP 30	SSX BEXHILL	BEXHILL STREET	27
38	BROOK CHARLOTTE	/ /	20		NOT GIVEN	WORK HOUSE	156
37	BROOK ELLEN	DA U	9	SCHOLAR AT HOME	SSX BEXHILL	BEXHILL STREET	27
37	BROOK ELLEN	WI M	35		SSX HASTINGS	BEXHILL STREET	27
25	BROOK ISAAC	LG U	39	RAIL LAB	SSX WINCHELSEA	QUEENS HEAD SEDLESCOMBE ST	189
39	BROOK JAMES	HD M	57	AG.LAB	SSX WESTFIELD	WORK-HOUSE	156
20	BROOK JOHN	HD M	33	GAME KEEPER	SSX WESTFIELD	REDLEYS	174
20	BROOK JOHN	SO U	4		SSX WESTFIELD	REDLEYS	174
19	BROOK LUCY	WI M	56		SSX FAIRLIGHT	COTTAGE	174
38	BROOK MARTHA	/ U	7M		NOT GIVEN	WORK-HOUSE	156
19	BROOK MOSES	HD M	60	AG.LAB	SSX WESTFIELD	COTTAGE	174
20	BROOK PHILADELPHIA	DA U	2		SSX WESTFIELD	REDLEYS	174
20	BROOK RACHAEL	WI M	31		SSX BEXHILL	REDLEYS	174
39	BROOK SARAH	WI M	66		NOT GIVEN (?WESTFIELD)	WORK-HOUSE	156
19	BROOK SUSANNA	GD U	5		SSX WESTFIELD	COTTAGE	174
25	BROWN GEORGE	LG U	33	RAILWAY LAB	HAM WOLVERSTON	RANSOM'S HOUSE	145
95	BROWN JAMES	LG U	51	RAIL LAB	SSX CATSFIELD	HUT	19
11	BROWN JOHN	SV U	19	AG.LAB	SSX FRAMFIELD	WILTING FARM HOUSE	6
8	BROWN THOMAS	LG W	50	RAIL LAB	SRY EGHAM	RAILWAY HUT	5

Age	Name	Status	No.	Occupation	County/Birthplace	Residence	No.
10	BROWNE JAMES	LG U	19	RAILWAY LAB	BRK READING	FORWARD LANE	129
49	BROWNE JOSEPH	VR U	22	RAILWAY LAB	SSX HASTINGS	RAILWAY HUT	135
77	BRUCE ISABELLA	VR U	19	DRESSMAKER	YKS HULL	STEMPS? LODGE	16
81	BRUCKLY SARAH	SV U	28	LAUNDRY MAID	HRT DOLCHURCH*	BEAUPORT HOUSE	17
29	BRYANT ANN	DA U	9	SCHOLAR	SSX BATTLE	BRICKWALL	190
56	BRYANT ANNE	DA U	12		SSX SEDLESCOMBE	SEDLESCOMBE STREET	195
6	BRYANT ELIZA	DA U	6		SSX SEDLESCOMBE	SPRAYS BRIDGE	173
42	BRYANT ELIZA	WI M	36		SSX SEDLESCOMBE	POPPING HOLE LANE	206
42	BRYANT ELIZABETH	DA U	5		SSX SEDLESCOMBE	POPPING HOLE LANE	206
68	BRYANT ELIZABETH	DA U	7	SCHOLAR	SSX SEDLESCOMBE	IN THE VILLAGE	211
19	BRYANT GEORGE	HD M	30	AG.LAB	SSX SEDLESCOMBE	ODIAM FARM	218
19	BRYANT GEORGE	SO U	7	SCHOLAR	SSX SEDLESCOMBE	ODIAM FARM	218
68	BRYANT GEORGE	SO U	12		SSX SEDLESCOMBE	IN THE VILLAGE	211
29	BRYANT HARRIET	WI M	29		SSX NINFIELD	BRICKWALL	190
6	BRYANT HARRIET	DA U	10		SSX SEDLESCOMBE	SPRAYS BRIDGE	172
6	BRYANT HARRIETT	WI M	33		SSX SEDLESCOMBE	SPRAYS BRIDGE	172
68	BRYANT HENRY	SO U	7M		SSX SEDLESCOMBE	IN THE VILLAGE	211
42	BRYANT HENRY	SO U	8		SSX SEDLESCOMBE	POPPING HOLE LANE	206
56	BRYANT HENRY	SO U	14	AG.LAB	SSX SEDLESCOMBE	SEDLESCOMBE STREET	195
19	BRYANT HERBERT	SO U	5		SSX SEDLESCOMBE	ODIAM FARM	218
68	BRYANT JAMES	HD M	38	AG.LAB	SSX SEDLESCOMBE	IN THE VILLAGE	211
63	BRYANT JAMES	LG U	23	RAILWAY LAB	SSX	RAILWAY HUT	137
19	BRYANT JAMES	SO U	3		SSX EWHURST	ODIAM FARM	218
56	BRYANT JANE	DA U	2		SSX SEDLESCOMBE	SEDLESCOMBE STREET	195
56	BRYANT JANE	WI M	36		SSX WESTFIELD	SEDLESCOMBE STREET	195
56	BRYANT JOHN	HD M	33	AG.LAB	SSX SEDLESCOMBE	SEDLESCOMBE STREET	195
56	BRYANT JONATHAN	SO U	7	SCHOLAR	SSX SEDLESCOMBE	SEDLESCOMBE STREET	195
56	BRYANT JOSEPH	SO U	5	SCHOLAR	SSX SEDLESCOMBE	SEDLESCOMBE STREET	195
62	BRYANT JOSHUA	GS U	9		SSX SEDLESCOMBE	AT THE STREAM	210
6	BRYANT MARY	DA U	7		SSX SEDLESCOMBE	SPRAYS BRIDGE	172
68	BRYANT MARY	DA U	9	SCHOLAR	SSX SEDLESCOMBE	IN THE VILLAGE	211
62	BRYANT MARY	WI M	60		SSX UDIMORE	AT THE STREAM	210
34	BRYANT PHILADELPHIA	SV U	17	GENERAL SERVANT	SSX SEDLESCOMBE	RECTORY	205
68	BRYANT REBECCA	WI M	37		SSX SEDLESCOMBE	IN THE VILLAGE	211
6	BRYANT SAMUEL	HD M	32	AG.LAB	SSX SEDLESCOMBE	SPRAYS BRIDGE	172
54	BRYANT SAMUEL	LG U	60	AG.LAB	SSX SEDLESCOMBE	BEECH	208
6	BRYANT SAMUEL	SO U	9M		SSX SEDLESCOMBE	SPRAYS BRIDGE	173
19	BRYANT SARAH	DA U	1		SSX EWHURST	ODIAM FARM	218
19	BRYANT SARAH	WI M	27		SSX SEDLESCOMBE	ODIAM FARM	218
29	BRYANT THOMAS	LG M	27	AG.LAB	SSX BATTLE	BRICKWALL	190
42	BRYANT UN-NAMED INFANT BOY	SO U	2D		SSX SEDLESCOMBE	POPPING HOLE LANE	206
42	BRYANT WILLAIM	SO U	13		SSX SEDLESCOMBE	POPPING HOLE LANE	206
42	BRYANT WILLIAM	HD M	41	AG.LAB	SSX SEDLESCOMBE	POPPING HOLE LANE	206
62	BRYANT WILLIAM	HD M	61	AG.LAB	SSX SEDLESCOMBE	AT THE STREAM	210
6	BRYANT WILLIAM	SO U	12		SSX SEDLESCOMBE	SPRAYS BRIDGE	172
58	BUCKE CHARLES	LG U	23	RAILWAY LAB	SSX SANDHURST	RAILWAY HUT	136
58	BUCKE JAMES	SO U	2M		SSX CROWHURST	RAILWAY HUT	136
58	BUCKE PHILADELPHIA	WI M	31		SSX SANDHURST	RAILWAY HUT	136
58	BUCKE STEPHEN	SO U	2		SSX WADHURST	RAILWAY HUT	136
58	BUCKE THOMAS	HD M	25	RAILWAY LAB	SSX SANDHURST	RAILWAY HUT	136
43	BUCKLAND ELLEN	GD U	14	SCHOLAR	SSX WARBLETON	2 DORSETT COTTAGE	28
38	BUCKLAND JOHN	HD M	63	FARMER 60 AC EMP 3 MEN	SSX BODIAM	BUCKLANDS	10
38	BUCKLAND SARAH MUNN	WI M	57		SSX PEASMARSH	BUCKLANDS	10
13	BURCHETT FRANCES	SV U	20	HOUSE SERVANT	SSX WARTLING	OFFICERS COTTAGE IN LIBERTY	39
71	BURCHETT WILLIAM	SV U	22	BLACKSMITH	SSX HEATHFIELD	WOODS FARM SIDLEY	85
23	BURCHETT WILLIAM	VR U	50	BOOT MERCHANT	SSX STORRINGTON	GLINE FARM SIDLEY	78
72	BURDEN SOPHIA	SV U	14	DOMESTIC DUTIES	SSX BEXHILL	WATERMILL HOUSE	115
65	BURFIELD C R (MALE)	PP U	8	PUPIL	SSX ST.MARY'S	NOT GIVEN	96
65	BURFIELD E (MALE)	PP U	7	PUPIL	SSX ST.MARY'S	NOT GIVEN	96
65	BURFIELD W M (MALE)	PP U	7	PUPIL	SSX ST.MARY'S	NOT GIVEN	96
49	BURGESS ALFRED	HD M	30	AG.LAB	SSX BURWASH	BADCOX	178
49	BURGESS CORDELIA	WI M	24		SSX WESTFIELD	BADCOX	178
39	BURGESS ELIZABETH	HD M	37	FARMER'S WIFE	SSX HEATHFIELD	PRAWLES FARM	221
49	BURGESS ISABELLA	NC U	5		SSX BURWASH	BADCOX	178
35	BURGESS JOHN	SV /	34	WAGGONER	SSX WESTFIELD	MILWARDS	10
21	BURGESS MARY	WI M	70		SSX BATTLE	BELL HILL	25
37	BURGESS SAMUEL	SO U	20	AG.LAB	SSX ORE	EMMARYS	10
37	BURGESS THOMAS	WI M	62		LONDON	EMMARYS	10
7	BURGESS TREYTON	LG U	25	WAGGONER	SSX PENHURST	WILTING	5
37	BURGESS WILLIAM	HD M	64	AG.LAB	SSX WESTFIELD	EMMARYS	10
21	BURGESS WILLIAM	HD M	74	AG.LAB	SSX BEXHILL	BELL HILL	25
22	BURT ANN	VR U	23	MILLINER	SSX HOOE	NOT GIVEN	54
54	BURT ELIZABETH	WI M	53		SSX BURWASH	HOLLINGTON STREET	12
31	BURT EMILY	DA U	11		SSX (?WESTFIELD)	HOLE FARM	155
59	BURT JAMES	HD W	47	AG.LAB	SSX HOOE	SIDLEY GREEN	83
47	BURT JAMES	SO U	1		SSX HOLLINGTON	HOLLINGTON STREET	11
31	BURT JOHN	HD M	62	AG.LAB	SSX WESTFIELD	HOLE FARM	155
54	BURT JOHN	SO U	22		SSX BATTLE	HOLLINGTON STREET	12
31	BURT MARY	WI M	62		SSX WESTFIELD	HOLE FARM	155
54	BURT MARY ANN	DA U	12		SSX BATTLE	HOLLINGTON STREET	12
47	BURT PETER	SO U	4		SSX CROWHURST	HOLLINGTON STREET	11
54	BURT ROBERT	HD M	53	AG.LAB	SSX CATSFIELD	HOLLINGTON STREET	12
47	BURT SPENCER	SO U	2		SSX HOLLINGTON	HOLLINGTON STREET	11
47	BURT THOMAS	HD M	28	AG.LAB	SSX BATTLE	HOLLINGTON STREET	11
54	BURT WILLIAM	SO U	15		SSX BATTLE	HOLLINGTON STREET	12
47	BURT WINIFRED	WI M	25		SSX CROWHURST	HOLLINGTON STREET	11

	Name				Occupation	Birthplace	Address	
81	BURTON CHARLES	SV	M	28	COACHMAN	SSX HASTINGS	BEAUPORT HOUSE	17
51	BURTON SUSAN	SV	U	22	HOUSE SERVANT	ESS PURFLEET	GALLEY HILL	29
25	BUTCHER HANNAH	SV	U	14	HOUSE SERVANT	SSX BEXHILL	NOT GIVEN	54
12	BUTCHER JANE	HD	W	69		SSX HOLLINGTON	SEDLESCOMBE STREET	202
25	BUTCHER JOHN	SV	U	18	AG.LAB	SSX BEXHILL	NOT GIVEN	54
25	BUTCHER MARTHA	SV	M	50	HOUSEKEEPER	SSX BEXHILL	NOT GIVEN	54
12	BUTCHER SPENCER	SO	U	6		SSX SEDLESCOMBE	SEDLESCOMBE STREET	202
57	BUTCHERS ALBERT WILLIAM	SO	U	6		SSX BEXHILL	WHITE HILL COTTAGE	58
28	BUTCHERS BENNEY	WI	M	28		SSX SEDLESCOMBE	SEDLESCOMBE STREET	204
40	BUTCHERS CAROLINE	DA	U	7	SCHOLAR	SSX BEXHILL	NOT GIVEN	56
28	BUTCHERS CHARLES	SO	U	7	SCHOLAR	SSX BATTLE	SEDLESCOMBE STREET	204
57	BUTCHERS CHARLOTTE	WI	M	27		SSX BEXHILL	WHITE HILL COTTAGE	58
28	BUTCHERS DANIEL	HD	M	34	AG.LAB	SSX MOUNTFIELD	SEDLESCOMBE STREET	204
40	BUTCHERS GEORGE	HD	M	28	AG.LAB	SSX NINFIELD	NOT GIVEN	56
9	BUTCHERS GEORGE	SO	U	12		NOT GIVEN (?WESTFIELD)	SPRING COTTAGE	152
45	BUTCHERS HENRY	HD	M	25	AG.LAB	SSX BEXHILL	LITTLE COMMON	57
57	BUTCHERS HENRY THOMAS	SO	U	8		SSX BEXHILL	WHITE HILL COTTAGE	58
9	BUTCHERS ISAAC	HD	M	55	AG.LAB	SSX WESTFIELD	SPRING COTTAGE	152
28	BUTCHERS JANE	DA	U	5	SCHOLAR	SSX SEDLESCOMBE	SEDLESCOMBE STREET	204
9	BUTCHERS PHILIDELPHIA	WI	M	56		SSX WESTFIELD	SPRING COTTAGE	152
57	BUTCHERS SAMUEL JAMES	SO	U	1		SSX BEXHILL	WHITE HILL COTTAGE	57
57	BUTCHERS SARAH	DA	U	4		SSX BEXHILL	WHITE HILL COTTAGE	58
40	BUTCHERS SARAH	WI	M	26		SSX BEXHILL	NOT GIVEN	56
40	BUTCHERS THOMAS	SO	U	1		SSX BEXHILL	NOT GIVEN	56
57	BUTCHERS WILLIAM	HD	M	31	AG.LAB	SSX BEXHILL	WHITE HILL COTTAGE	58
37	BUTCHERS WILLIAM	LG	M	60	AG.LAB	SSX NINFIELD	NOT GIVEN	56
72	BUTLER EDWARD	HD	U	36	AG.LAB	SSX SEDLECOMBE	SEDLESCOMBE STREET	211
13	BUTLER HARRIETT	WI	M	51		SSX SALEHURST	SEDLESCOMBE STREET	202
63	BUTLER JOHN	LG	U	29	RAILWAY LAB	HAM	RAILWAY HUT	137
13	BUTLER PHILIP	HD	M	64	TAILOR EMP 1	SSX SEDLESCOMBE	SEDLESCOMBE STREET	202
22	BUTLER THANKFUL	VR	U	72	ANNUITANT	SSX SEDLESCOMBE	GATE FARM	235
18	BUTLER THOMAS	LG	U	33	RAIL LAB	WIL UNKNOWN	SEDLESCOMBE STREET	203
79	BUTLER WILLIAM	SV	U	19	SERVANT	SSX BRIGHTLING	STAPLE CROSS	242
36	BUTTON EMILY	DA	U	15	HOUSE SERVANT	SSX BEXHILL	NOT GIVEN	55
17	BUTTON JESSE	SV	U	18	FARM SERVANT	SSX CROWHURST	HILL FARM	144
36	BUTTON JOHN	HD	W	54	AG.LAB	SSX BEXHILL	NOT GIVEN	55
36	BUTTON JOHN	SO	U	9		SSX BEXHILL	NOT GIVEN	55
18	BUTTON REBECCA	DA	U	16		SSX CROWHURST	FORDLAND	144
18	BUTTON THOMAS	HD	W	56	FARM LAB	SSX CROWHURST	FORDLAND	144
36	BUTTON WILLIAM	SO	U	21	AG.LAB	SSX BEXHILL	NOT GIVEN	55
58	BYNE DELIA	DA	U	10		SSX WESTFIELD	BARRACKS	180
58	BYNE FANNY	DA	U	7		SSX WESTFIELD	BARRACKS	180
21	BYNE GEORGE	LG	U	45	AG.LAB	SSX WESTFIELD	SAW PIT COTTAGE	154
58	BYNE SALLY	DA	U	5		SSX WESTFIELD	BARRACKS	180
58	BYNE SARAH	WI	M	38		SSX HAILSHAM	BARRACKS	180
38	BYNE STEPHEN	LG	M	57	CARPENTER	SSX	WORK-HOUSE	156
58	BYNE WILLIAM	HD	M	50	AG.LAB	SSX WESTFIELD	BARRACKS	180
15	BYNER ALBERT HENRY	SO	U	6	SCHOLAR	SSX SEDLESCOMBE	SEDLESCOMBE STREET	203
15	BYNER CAROLINE H	WI	M	39		SSX SEDLESCOMBE	SEDLESCOMBE STREET	203
15	BYNER ELLEN C	DA	U	14		SSX SEDLESCOMBE	SEDLESCOMBE STREET	203
15	BYNER JAMES	HD	M	37	GROCER	SSX SEDLESCOMBE	SEDLESCOMBE STREET	203
15	BYNER JAMES	SO	U	12	SCHOLAR	SSX SEDLESCOMBE	SEDLESCOMBE STREET	203
15	BYNER THOMAS WILLIAM	SO	U	11	SCHOLAR	SSX SEDLESCOMBE	SEDLESCOMBE STREET	203
10	CALLINGHAM HENRY	LG	U	23	RAIL LAB	SRY NORMANDY	RAILWAY HUT	5
10	CALLINGHAM WILLIAM	LG	U	21	RAIL LAB	SRY HOLLYSHOT	RAILWAY HUT	5
34	CAMMERON KATE	BD	W	56	LADY	BRK BEEDING	COURT LODGE FARM	147
22	CANDY HENRY	LG	U	NK45	RAIL LAB	UNKNOWN	RAILWAY HUT	8
61	CAREY MARY	SV	U	23	HOUSE MAID	SSX HOOE	HURCHINGTON	58
54	CARLEY CHARLES	SO	U	12	SCHOLAR	SSX HERSTMONCEUX	NOT GIVEN	112
54	CARLEY CORNELIUS	HD	M	38	SHOEMAKER	SSX BRIGHTLING	NOT GIVEN	112
39	CARLEY ELIZA	LG	U	17		SSX RYE	FORGE LANE	254
54	CARLEY ELIZABETH	DA	U	14		SSX HERSTMONCEUX	NOT GIVEN	112
54	CARLEY ELLEN	DA	U	11	SCHOLAR	SSX CATSFIELD	NOT GIVEN	112
54	CARLEY HANNAH	DA	U	8		SSX CATSFIELD	NOT GIVEN	112
54	CARLEY MARY	WI	M	50		SSX HERSTMONCEUX	NOT GIVEN	112
31	CARLY MARY	VR	U	54		SSX EAST HOATHLY	LUNSFORDS LANE SIDLEY	70
40	CARPENTER ANN	WI	M	25		HAM EASTMON	RAILWAY HUT	134
40	CARPENTER ANN	WI	M	35		YKS SHEFFIELD	RAILWAY HUT	134
40	CARPENTER HARRIOT	DA	U	2		SRY WANTON	RAILWAY HUT	134
40	CARPENTER JANE	DA	U	3M		SSX CROWHURST	RAILWAY HUT	134
40	CARPENTER JOHN	HD	M	21	RAILWAY LAB	HAM SHEET	RAILWAY HUT	134
40	CARPENTER WILLIAM	HD	M	25	RAILWAY LAB	HAM BURCHAM	RAILWAY HUT	134
19	CARR ALEXANDER	HD	M	27	RAIL LAB	SSX MARESFIELD	RAILWAY HUT	7
71	CARR ANNE	DA	U	4		SSX ST.LEONARDS	47 MARTELLO TOWER	31
19	CARR BARBARY	WI	M	26		SSX FLETCHING	RAILWAY HUT	7
19	CARR HARRIETT	DA	U	3		SSX WADHURST	RAILWAY HUT	7
71	CARR JOHN	HD	M	40	COAST GUARD	IRELAND	47 MARTELLO TOWER	31
71	CARR JOHN	SO	U	10	SCHOLAR	SSX ST.LEONARDS	47 MARTELLO TOWER	31
71	CARR MARGARET	WI	M	43		IRELAND	47 MARTELLO TOWER	31
71	CARR MARY	DA	U	11	SCHOLAR	SSX WINCHELSEA	47 MARTELLO TOWER	31
71	CARR RICHARD	SO	U	8	SCHOLAR	SSX ST.LEONARDS	47 MARTELLO TOWER	31
23	CARRICK ABIGAIL	WI	M	43		SSX BATTLE	NEW ENGLAND	164
23	CARRICK ANN	DA	U	8	SCHOLAR	SSX WESTFIELD	NEW ENGLAND	164
2	CARRICK ANN	WI	M	64		SSX NINFIELD	CHERRY TREE	172
23	CARRICK CHARLES	SO	U	10	SCHOLAR	SSX WESTFIELD	NEW ENGLAND	164
23	CARRICK GEORGE	HD	M	39	BRICK MAKER	SSX NINFIELD	NEW ENGLAND	164

Ref	Name	Rel	MS	Age	Occupation	Birthplace	Address	Page
23	CARRICK JANE	DA	U	5	SCHOLAR	SSX WESTFIELD	NEW ENGLAND	164
32	CARRICK MARY	/	U	10	NURSE CHILD SCHOLAR	SSX NINFIELD	SEDLESCOMBE STREET	205
23	CARRICK RAYMOND	SO	U	1		SSX WESTFIELD	NEW ENGLAND	164
2	CARRICK THOMAS	HD	M	76	GARDENER	SSX NINFIELD	CHERRY TREE	172
23	CARRICK THOMAS	SO	U	6	SCHOLAR	SSX WESTFIELD	NEW ENGLAND	164
32	CARROLE HENRY	SV	U	21	GROOM	SSI TICEHURST	BEXHILL STREET	27
31	CARTER BETSY	DA	U	7	SCHOLAR	SSX FLETCHING	BUCKHOLT SIDLEY	79
31	CARTER CHARLES	SO	U	11	SCHOLAR	SSX FLETCHING	BUCKHOLT SIDLEY	79
24	CARTER CHARLES	SO	U	16		SSX HARTLING	RAILWAY HUT	8
6	CARTER GEORGE	SV	U	13	MILLER & BAKER	SSX FLETCHING	ROSE COTTAGE - SIDLEY	65
24	CARTER LUCY	WI	M	37		SSX HARTLING	RAILWAY HUT	8
31	CARTER MARY JANE	DA	U	16	EMPLOYED AT HOME	SSX MAYFIELD	BUCKHOLT SIDLEY	79
31	CARTER OWEN	SO	U	9	SCHOLAR	SSX FLETCHING	BUCKHOLT SIDLEY	79
31	CARTER SALLY	DA	U	5		SSX FLETCHING	BUCKHOLT SIDLEY	79
1	CARTER THOMAS	LG	U	25	RAIL LAB	CHS CALDICOT	RAILWAY HUT	4
24	CARTER WILLIAM	HD	M	39	RAIL LAB	BRK HINGLEY*	RAILWAY HUT	8
31	CARTER WILLIAM	HD	W	50	FARMER 350 AC EMP 8	SSX MAYFIELD	BUCKHOLT SIDLEY	79
69	CASS CHARLES WILLIAM	HD	U	24	CURATE	MDX EDMONTON	NOT GIVEN	97
16	CATT ALBERT	SO	U	15		SSX WESTFIELD	BLUMANS	163
62	CATT ALFRED	GS	U	8		SSX WESTFIELD	INMANS	180
16	CATT ANN	WI	M	55		SSX WESTFIELD	BLUMANS	163
60	CATT BENJAMIN	HD	M	76	AG.LAB	SSX WESTFIELD	YEW TREES	180
25	CATT DAVID	HD	M	37	BAILIFF	SSX HURSTMONMCEUX	SAMPSONS SIDLEY	69
4	CATT ELIZA	DA	U	7		NOT GIVEN (?WESTFIELD)	PADDLESTONS	152
18	CATT ELIZA	WI	M	36		SSX NORTHIAM	BELL VILLA	153
27	CATT ELIZA	WI	M	39		SSX WESTFIELD	CATTS	155
4	CATT ELIZABETH	DA	U	29		NOT GIVEN (?WESTFIELD)	PADDLESTONS	152
62	CATT ELIZABETH	HD	W	75	FARMER	SSX SEDLESCOMBE	INMANS	180
52	CATT ELLEN	SV	U	17	SERVANT	SSX UDIMORE	STOCKWOOD FARM	239
36	CATT EMMA	DA	U	14		NOT GIVEN (?WESTFIELD)	SEVEN OAKS	156
4	CATT ESTHER	DA	U	23		NOT GIVEN (?WESTFIELD)	PADDLESTONS	152
69	CATT FANNY	GD	U	28		SSX WESTFIELD	MOUNT PLEASANT	181
29	CATT FRANCES	WI	M	55		SSX SEDLESCOMBE	LANKHURST	155
16	CATT FRANCIS	HD	M	57	AG.LAB	SSX WESTFIELD	BLUMANS	163
60	CATT GEORGE	SO	U	21	AG.LAB	SSX WESTFIELD	YEW TREES	180
39	CATT GEORGE	SV	U	23		SSX WESTFIELD	BENSKINS	177
25	CATT HANNAH	WI	M	37		SSX WARBLETON	SAMPSONS SIDLEY	69
25	CATT HARRIET	DA	U	7		SSX HURSTMONCEUX	SAMPSONS SIDLEY	69
36	CATT HENRY	SO	U	6		NOT GIVEN (?WESTFIELD)	SEVEN OAKS	156
36	CATT HERBERT	SO	U	10		NOT GIVEN (?WESTFIELD)	SEVEN OAKS	156
60	CATT ISABELLA	WI	M	67		SSX WESTFIELD	YEW TREES	180
62	CATT JAMES	GS	U	6		SSX WESTFIELD	INMANS	180
4	CATT JAMES	SO	U	15		NOT GIVEN (?WESTFIELD)	PADDLESTONS	152
16	CATT JAMES	SO	U	30		SSX WESTFIELD	BLUMANS	163
62	CATT JAMES	SO	W	42		SSX WESTFIELD	INMANS	180
36	CATT JANE	WI	M	49		SSX ICKLESHAM	SEVEN OAKS	156
29	CATT JOHN	HD	M	58	FARMER	SSX WESTFIELD	LANKHURST	155
71	CATT JOHN	HD	M	65	SCHOOLMASTER	SSX SEDLESCOMBE	SEDLESCOMBE STREET	211
20	CATT JOHN	HD	U	31	BUILDER EMP 8	SSX WESTFIELD	SEDLESCOMBE STREET	203
4	CATT JOHN	HD	W	53	FARMER	SSX WESTFIELD	PADDLESTONS	152
36	CATT LESTER	SO	U	20		SSX WESTFIELD	SEVEN OAKS	156
20	CATT MARIA	SV	U	18		SSX WESTFIELD	SEDLESCOMBE STREET	203
25	CATT MARTHA	DA	U	12		SSX HURSTMONCEUX	SAMPSONS SIDLEY	69
16	CATT MARY	DA	U	19		SSX WESTFIELD	BLUMANS	163
71	CATT MARY	WI	M	64		SSX WESTFIELD	SEDLESCOMBE STREET	211
33	CATT MARY ANN	SV	U	14		SSX WESTFIELD	MOOR FARM	155
4	CATT MATILDA	DA	U	14		NOT GIVEN (?WESTFIELD)	PADDLESTONS	152
37	CATT MERCY	LG	U	1		NOT GIVEN (?BREDE)	WALNUT TREE	156
25	CATT PETER	SO	U	11		SSX HURSTMONCEUX	SAMPSONS SIDLEY	69
29	CATT PHEBE	SV	U	19		NOT GIVEN (?WESTFIELD)	LANKHURST	155
37	CATT PHILA	LG	/	22		NOT GIVEN (?BREDE)	WALNUT TREE	156
29	CATT RICHARD	BR	U	61		SSX WESTFIELD	LANKHURST	155
16	CATT SAMUEL	SO	U	17		SSX WESTFIELD	BLUMANS	163
37	CATT SPENCER	LG	M	32		NOT GIVEN (?BREDE)	WALNUT TREE	156
18	CATT STEPHEN	HD	M	36	AG.LAB	SSX GUESTLING	BELL VILLA	153
36	CATT STEPHEN	HD	M	58	AG.LAB	SSX WESTFIELD	SEVEN OAKS	156
12	CATT SUSAN	SV	U	15		SSX WARBLETON	SPRAYS BRIDGE	163
27	CATT WILLIAM	HD	M	55	RETIRED SCHOOLMASTER	SSX WESTFIELD	CATTS	155
69	CATT WILLIAM	HD	W	78	FARMER	SSX WESTFIELD	MOUNT PLEASANT	181
60	CATT WILLIAM	SO	U	41	CORDWAINER	SSX WESTFIELD	YEW TREES	180
19	CATT WILLIAM	SV	U	22	LAB	SSX WESTFIELD	ROSE VILLA	153
29	CHALK ELIZABETH	WI	M	43?		NOT GIVEN	BAGGERS HOLE	9
29	CHALK SARAH JANE	DA	U	4		NOR GIVEN	BAGGERS HOLE	9
29	CHALK URIAH	HD	M	43	RAIL LAB	NOT GIVEN	BAGGERS HOLE	9
68	CHALLEN JANE	NC	U	19		SSX BRIGHTON	NOT GIVEN	97
26	CHAMPION THOMAS	SV	U	46	BUTLER	KEN EASTRY	CATSFIELD PLACE CHURCH HSE	110
24	CHAPMAN CHARLOTTE	DA	U	7	SCHOLAR	SSX BEXHILL	IN THE LIBERTY	40
44	CHAPMAN EDWARD	HD	M	51	AG.LAB	SSX EWHURST	ADAMS LANE	238
24	CHAPMAN ELIZABETH	DA	U	3		SSX BEXHILL	IN THE LIBERTY	40
13	CHAPMAN FRANCES	DA	U	16		SSX EWHURST	WATTS HOLE	251
13	CHAPMAN FRANCES	WI	M	38		SSX BREDE	WATTS HOLE	251
44	CHAPMAN HARRIET	WI	M	48		SSX EWHURST	ADAMS LANE	238
44	CHAPMAN HARRIET ANN	DA	U	14		SSX EWHURST	ADAMS LANE	238
23	CHAPMAN HENRY	VR	W	80		SSX BATTLE	RANSOM'S HOUSE	145
24	CHAPMAN JOHN	HD	M	32	CARPENTER JM	SSX WARTLING	IN THE LIBERTY	40
24	CHAPMAN JOHN T B	SO	U	9M		SSX BEXHILL	IN THE LIBERTY	40

No.	Name	Rel	Cond	Age	Occupation	Birthplace	Address	Page
13	CHAPMAN JONATHAN	SO	U	11		SSX EWHURST	WATTS HOLE	251
24	CHAPMAN MARY	DA	U	8	SCHOLAR	SSX PEVENSEY	IN THE LIBERTY	40
24	CHAPMAN MARY	WI	M	29		SSX PEVENSEY	IN THE LIBERTY	40
13	CHAPMAN THOMAS	HD	M	41	AG.LAB	SSX EWHURST	WATTS HOLE	251
45	CHARTER ANN	WI	M	37		LEICESTERSHIRE#?	RAILWAY HUT	134
45	CHARTER WILLIAM	HD	M	32	RAILWAY LAB	WAR WOOLSTON	RAILWAY HUT	134
48	CHATFIELD ABRAHAM	HD	M	57	AG.LAB	SSX BEXHILL	COLLINGTON LANE	43
49	CHATFIELD CAROLINE	VR	U	16		SSX BEXHILL	COLLINGTON COTTAGE	43
43	CHATFIELD HARRIETT	DA	U	11	SCHOLAR	SSX BEXHILL	NOT GIVEN	42
48	CHATFIELD LUCY	DA	U	12		SSX BEXHILL	COLLINGTON LANE	43
43	CHATFIELD MARIA	HD	W	57	PAUPER AG.LAB'S WIFE	SSX BEXHILL	NOT GIVEN	42
31	CHATFIELD MARY	SV	U	20	HOUSE SERVANT	SSX BEXHILL	BEXHILL STREET	27
48	CHATFIELD MARY	WI	M	42		SSX BEXHILL	COLLINGTON LANE	43
17	CHATFIELD ROBERT	LG	U	26	RAIL LAB	SSX PULBOROUGH	RAILWAY HUT	7
41	CHEAL ANN	DA	U	1		SSX BEXHILL	DOWN COTTAGE	42
41	CHEAL ANN	WI	M	26		SSX BEXHILL	DOWN COTTAGE	42
41	CHEAL ELIZA	DA	U	3		SSX BEXHILL	DOWN COTTAGE	42
41	CHEAL GEORGE	SO	U	7		SSX BEXHILL	DOWN COTTAGE	42
41	CHEAL JAMES	HD	M	26	AG.LAB	SSX HOOE	DOWN COTTAGE	42
41	CHEAL JAMES	SO	U	1		SSX BEXHILL	DOWN COTTAGE	42
37	CHEESMAN ISABEL	6D	U	10	SCHOLAR	SSX SALEHURST	STRAWBERRY HILL	253
41	CHESTER CHARLES	HD	M	57	AG.LAB	SSX BEXHILL	NOT GIVEN	56
41	CHESTER CHARLES	SO	U	29	AG.LAB	SSX BEXHILL	NOT GIVEN	56
41	CHESTER CORNELIUS	SO	U	11	AG.LAB	SSX BEXHILL	NOT GIVEN	56
41	CHESTER PHOEBA (SIC)	WI	M	55		KEN SANDHURST	NOT GIVEN	56
41	CHESTER THOMAS	SO	U	10	AG.LAB	SSX BEXHILL	NOT GIVEN	56
1	CHILD ANN	AU	U	85		SSX EWHURST	CASTLE INN	215
6	CHITTENDEN CHARLES	SO	U	17	COOPER	SSX HERSTMONCEUX	SIDLEY	90
6	CHITTENDEN JOHN	SO	U	24	COOPER	SSX HERSTMONCEUX	SIDLEY	90
6	CHITTENDEN MARY	DA	U	15		SSX HERSTMONCEUX	SIDLEY	90
6	CHITTENDEN RICHARD	HD	M	52	COOPER	SSX HERSTMONCEUX	SIDLEY	90
6	CHITTENDEN SARAH	WI	M	54		SSX WESTHAM	SIDLEY	90
6	CHITTENDEN WALKER	SO	U	30	COOPER	SSX HERSTMONCEUX	SIDLEY	90
38	CHRISMAS ANN	DA	U	2		SSX SALEHURST	PRAWLES	220
3	CHRISMAS CHARLES	BR	U	40	OCCUPIER 230 AC EMP 10	SSX HEATHFIELD	BARNHORN HILL	37
25	CHRISMAS EDWARD	LG	M	51	AG.LAB	SSX BREDE	SAMPSONS SIDLEY	69
38	CHRISMAS EMILY	DA	U	4		SSX MOUNTFIELD	PRAWLES	220
38	CHRISMAS REBACCA	HD	M	26		SSX WHATLINGTON	PRAWLES	220
3	CHRISMAS STEPHEN	BR	U	44	ICCUPIER 671.2 AC	SSX HEATHFIELD	BARNHORN HILL	37
3	CHRISMAS THOMAS	HD	M	52	OCCUPIER 671.2 AC EMP 55	SSX HEATHFIELD	BARNHORN HILL	37
35	CHRISTIAN ANN	WI	M	25		DEV	NOT GIVEN	41
76	CHRISTIAN ELIZABETH	DA	U	3	SCHOLAR	SSX BEXHILL	NOT GIVEN	98
61	CHRISTIAN ELLEN H	DA	U	13		SSX BEXHILL	SIDLEY GREEN	83
37	CHRISTIAN GEORGE	SV	U	36	AG.LAB	SSX BEXHILL	BEXHILL STREET	27
42	CHRISTIAN HANNAH	SV	U	17	HOUSE SERVANT	SSX BEXHILL	1 DORSETT COTTAGE	28
76	CHRISTIAN HANNAH	WI	M	38		SSX HOOE	NOT GIVEN	98
18	CHRISTIAN HENRY	VR	U	21	AG.LAB	SSX PEVENSEY	IN THE LIBERTY	39
20	CHRISTIAN JAMES	LG	U	20	AG.LAB	SSX BEXHILL	TWO HOUSES SIDLEY	77
76	CHRISTIAN JOHN	HD	M	43	AG.LAB	SSX BEXHILL	NOT GIVEN	98
76	CHRISTIAN JOHN	SO	U	13	AG.LAB	SSX BEXHILL	NOT GIVEN	98
35	CHRISTIAN JOSHUA	HD	M	29	AG.LAB	SSX BEXHILL	NOT GIVEN	41
35	CHRISTIAN MARY J	DA	U	2		SSX BEXHILL	NOT GIVEN	41
36	CHRISTIAN NATHANIEL	HD	U	33	AG.LAB	SSX BEXHILL	NOT GIVEN	93
6	CHRISTIAN PHILLY	HD	W	75?	PAUPER	SSX BEXHILL	BELL HILL	24
76	CHRISTIAN SARAH	DA	U	10		SSX BEXHILL	NOT GIVEN	98
61	CHRISTIAN SOPHIA	HD	W	47		SSX BEXHILL	SIDLEY GREEN	83
76	CHRISTIAN STEPHEN	SO	U	6	SCHOLAR	SSX BEXHILL	NOT GIVEN	98
20	CHRISTIAN THOMAS	LG	U	24	AG.LAB	SSX BEXHILL	TWO HOUSES SIDLEY	77
76	CHRISTIAN WALTER	SO	U	8		SSX BEXHILL	NOT GIVEN	98
94	CHRISTOPHER CHARLOTTE	WI	M	20?		SSX CROWHURST	TILE KILN	19
94	CHRISTOPHER DAVID	HD	M	26	FARMER	SSX CATSFIELD	TILE KILN	19
31	CHRISTOPHER HANNAH	HD	W	69	HOUSEKEEPER	SSX HELLINGLY	STONE HOUSE FARM	132
31	CHRISTOPHER WILLIAM	SO	U	45	FARMER 150 AC EMP 3	SSX CATSFIELD	STONE HOUSE FARM	132
36	CLARK ANN	DA	U	1		SSX SEDLESCOMBE	BYSETTERS	176
26	CLARK ANNE	WI	M	49		SSX HERSTMONCEUX	SEMPSTED FARM	235
6	CLARK CHARLES	LG	W	50	SHOEMAKER	HAM CHRISTCHURCH	COACH & HORSES	187
26	CLARK DAVID	SO	U	10		SSX EWHURST	SEMPSTED FARM	236
26	CLARK EDWARD	HD	M	55	AG.LAB	SSX WARTLING	SEMPSTED FARM	235
55	CLARK ELIZABETH	WI	M	20		DOR WAREHAM	RAILWAY HUT	135
36	CLARK ELLEN	DA	U	11		SSX ICKLESHAM	BYSETTERS	176
26	CLARK FRANCES JANE	6D	U	4		SSX BATTLE	SEMPSTED FARM	236
36	CLARK GEORGE	HD	W	50	FARMER	SSX ICKLESHAM	BYSETTERS	176
26	CLARK GEORGE	SO	U	6		SSX EWHURST	SEMPSTED FARM	236
36	CLARK GEORGE	SO	U	8		SSX ICKLESHAM	BYSETTERS	176
36	CLARK HARRIETT	DA	U	21		SSX ICKLESHAM	BYSETTERS	176
2	CLARK HENRY	SO	U	3		SRY DORKING	RAILWAY HUT	4
26	CLARK HENRY	SO	U	15	AG.LAB	SSX EWHURST	SEMPSTED FARM	235
34	CLARK JOHN	LG	U	26	RAILWAY LAB	STS	DAIRY HOUSE	133
26	CLARK MARY	DA	U	13		SSX EWHURST	SEMPSTED FARM	236
2	CLARK MARY ANN	DA	U	7		SRY FARNHAM	RAILWAY HUT	4
2	CLARK RACHEL	WI	M	26		SRY FARNHAM	RAILWAY HUT	4
2	CLARK WILLIAM	HD	M	30	RAIL LAB	HAM ALTON	RAILWAY HUT	4
55	CLARK WILLIAM	HD	M	37	RAILWAY LAB	DOR BLANDFORD	RAILWAY HUT	136
2	CLARK WILLIAM	SO	U	9M		SSX GUESTLING	RAILWAY HUT	4
25	CLARKE JANE	WI	M	40		SSX LEWES	RAILWAY HUT	131
25	CLARKE JOSEPH	HD	M	43	RAILWAY LAB	OXF BURFORD	RAILWAY HUT	131

	Name		Age	Occupation	Birthplace	Residence	Pg
27	CLARKE LOUISA	SV U	21	GOVERNESS	SRY WANDSWORTH	LITTLE WORSHAM SIDLEY	79
14	CLARKE MARIA	SV U	19		SSX ICKLESHAM	TAN YARD	153
25	CLARKE ROBERT	SO U	14		SSX LEWES	RAILWAY HUT	131
28	CLIFTON BENJAMIN	SO U	2M		SSX BEXHILL	COOMBS SIDLEY	79
28	CLIFTON CHARLOTTE	DA U	2		SSX BEXHILL	COOMBS SIDLEY	79
53	CLIFTON CHARLOTTE	DA U	16		SSX BEXHILL	ALM'S HOUSE SIDLEY	82
21	CLIFTON ELIZABETH	WI M	62		SSX BEXHILL	TWO HOUSES SIDLEY	78
72	CLIFTON GEORGE	SV U	20	AG.LAB	SSX BEXHILL	GLOVERS FARM SIDLEY	85
53	CLIFTON HARRIET	DA U	18		SSX BEXHILL	ALM'S HOUSE SIDLEY	82
15	CLIFTON JAMES	LG /	23	AG.LAB	SSX BEXHILL	MAYFIELDS HOUSE	7
53	CLIFTON JAMES	SO U	12		SSX BEXHILL	ALM'S HOUSE SIDLEY	82
53	CLIFTON JANE	DA U	4		SSX BEXHILL	ALM'S HOUSE SIDLEY	82
53	CLIFTON JOHN	HD M	46	AG.LAB	SSX HOLLINGTON	ALM'S HOUSE SIDLEY	82
53	CLIFTON JOHN	SO U	9		SSX BEXHILL	ALM'S HOUSE SIDLEY	82
28	CLIFTON JOSEPH	HD M	27	AG.LAB	SSX BEXHILL	COOMBS SIDLEY	79
28	CLIFTON JOSEPH	SO U	4		SSX BEXHILL	COOMBS SIDLEY	79
53	CLIFTON JOSEPH	SO U	6	SCHOLAR	SSX BEXHILL	ALM'S HOUSE SIDLEY	82
28	CLIFTON LUCY	WI M	31		SSX HEATON	COOMBS SIDLEY	79
53	CLIFTON LUCY	WI M	42		SSX BEXHILL	ALM'S HOUSE SIDLEY	82
53	CLIFTON LUCY ANN	DA U	10M		SSX BEXHILL	ALM'S HOUSE SIDLEY	82
53	CLIFTON SARAH	DA U	22		SSX BEXHILL	ALM'S HOUSE SIDLEY	82
21	CLIFTON WILLIAM	HD M	76	PAUPER AG.LAB	SSX HASTINGS	TWO HOUSES SIDLEY	78
10	CLINTON HENRY	HD M	47	COAST GUARD	MEATH MORNING TOWN	55 MARTELLO TOWER IN LIBERTY	38
10	CLINTON JAMES	SO U	7		SSI RYE	55 MARTELLO TOWER IN LIBERTY	38
10	CLINTON JOHN	SO U	11		HAM IOW	55 MARTELLO TOWER IN LIBERTY	38
10	CLINTON MARGARET	DA U	5		SSI RYE	55 MARTELLO TOWER IN LIBERTY	38
10	CLINTON MARGARET	WI M	46		CLARE CLAUNEY	55 MARTELLO TOWER IN LIBERTY	38
10	CLINTON MARY	DA U	3		SSI RYE	55 MARTELLO TOWER IN LIBERTY	38
10	CLINTON RICHARD	SO U	14		DOR POOLE	55 MARTELLO TOWER IN LIBERTY	38
10	CLINTON WILLIAM	SO U	8		GALWAY BREUMORE	55 MARTELLO TOWER IN LIBERTY	38
3	CLOKE AARON	HD M	38	MILLER	SSX GUESTLING	BEACON MILL	249
3	CLOKE BETSY B	WI M	30		KEN TUNBRIDGE WELLS	BEACON MILL	249
3	CLOKE MARY A	DA U	2		SSX EWHURST	BEACON MILL	249
3	CLOKE WILLIAM N	SO U	1		SSX EWHURST	BEACON MILL	249
70	CLOUT WILLIAM	LG U	19	AG.LAB	KEN SANDHURST	STAPLE CROSS	241
10	COCKET ALFRED	SO U	13		SSX BEXHILL	MOUNT IDOL - SIDLEY	66
10	COCKET DAVID	HD M	43	VETINARY SURGEON	SSX BATTLE	MOUNT IDOL - SIDLEY	66
10	COCKET DAVID	SO U	16		SSX BEXHILL	MOUNT IDOL - SIDLEY	66
10	COCKET FREDERICK	SO U	3		SSX BEXHILL	MOUNT IDOL - SIDLEY	66
10	COCKET UNICE	DA U	10		SSX BEXHILL	MOUNT IDOL - SIDLEY	66
10	COCKET UNICE	WI M	36		SSX BEXHILL	MOUNT IDOL - SIDLEY	66
56	COCKRELL JULIA M	AS U	17	TEACHER	MDX UNKNOWN	NOT GIVEN	95
56	COCKRELL MARGARET L	SH U	15		MDX UNKNOWN	NOT GIVEN	95
10	COLE CHARLOTTE	WI M	39		ESS CLACTON	FORWARD LANE	129
10	COLE EMMA	DA U	20		ESS BRAUNTON	FORWARD LANE	129
3	COLE STEPHEN	LG U	20	BRICKMAKER'S LAB	HAM BENTLEY	FORWARD LANE	128
10	COLE WILLIAM	HD M	44	RAILWAY CONTRACTOR	ESS BRAUNTON	FORWARD LANE	129
40	COLEMAN ANN	/ U	14		NOT GIVEN (?WESTFIELD)	WORK-HOUSE?	156
13	COLEMAN ANN	DA W	35		SSX WESTFIELD	PRIMROSE COTTAGE	163
12	COLEMAN ANN	SV U	17		SSX SEDLESCOMBE	ASHDOWNS	173
36	COLEMAN ANN	WI M	38		KEN CRANBROOK	MOUNT PLEASANT	166
13	COLEMAN CAROLINE	6D U	3		SSX NINFIELD	PRIMROSE COTTAGE	163
13	COLEMAN EDWIN	6S U	4		SSX NINFIELD	PRIMROSE COTTAGE	163
35	COLEMAN GEORGE	SV U	19	AG.LAB	SSX BATTLE	CROWHAM	176
2	COLEMAN HANNAH	WI M	54		SSX BEXHILL	WAKEHAMS	89
13	COLEMAN HARRIETT	6D U	6	SCHOLAR	SSX BATTLE	PRIMROSE COTTAGE	163
40	COLEMAN HENRY	HD W	63		NOT GIVEN (?WESTFIELD)	WORK-HOUSE?	156
40	COLEMAN JANE	/ U	12		NOT GIVEN (?WESTFIELD)	WORK-HOUSE?	156
27	COLEMAN JOHN	6S U	12		SSX BREDE	SEMPSTED FARM	236
40	COLEMAN MARTHA	CI W	51		NOT GIVEN (?WESTFIELD)	WORK-HOUSE?	156
40	COLEMAN ROBERT	/ U	16		NOT GIVEN (?WESTFIELD)	WORK-HOUSE?	156
2	COLEMAN SAMUEL	HD M	50	FARMER 17 AC EMP 1	SSX EASTBOURNE	WAKEHAMS	89
36	COLEMAN SARAH	DA U	15		SSX WESTFIELD	MOUNT PLEASANT	166
36	COLEMAN SPENCER	HD M	38	AG.LAB	SSX EWHURST	MOUNT PLEASANT	166
36	COLEMAN SPENCER	SO U	10		SSX BATTLE	MOUNT PLEASANT	166
38	COLEMAN WILLIAM	LG U	23	CARPENTER	NOT GIVEN	WORK-HOUSE	156
24	COLLINS ALFRED	SV U	16	AG.LAB	SSX HASTINGS ALL SAINTS	PEBSHAM FARM SIDLEY	78
18	COLLINS ANN	DA U	14		SSX BEXHILL	SIDLEY	77
46	COLLINS ANN	WI M	84		KEN WITTERSHAM	NOT GIVEN	94
18	COLLINS BENJAMIN	HD M	55	AG.LAB	SSX BEXHILL	SIDLEY	77
18	COLLINS BENJAMIN	SO U	10	SCHOLAR	SSX BEXHILL	SIDLEY	77
18	COLLINS CATHERINE	DA U	3		SSX BEXHILL	SIDLEY	77
21	COLLINS CHARLES	SL U	30	CORWAINER DEAF & DUMB	SSX BEXHILL	NOT GIVEN	91
18	COLLINS GEORGE STEPHEN	SO U	8	SCHOLAR	SSX BEXHILL	SIDLEY	77
18	COLLINS HARRIET	WI M	45		SSX BEXHILL	SIDLEY	77
18	COLLINS NEWMAN	SO U	23	SAILOR	SSX BEXHILL	SIDLEY	77
46	COLLINS THOMAS	HD M	83	PAUPER SHOEMAKER	SSX HODE	NOT GIVEN	94
*71	COLLISON JOHN	HD U	25	BASKET MAKER	SSX BRIGHTON	IN CAMP BY ROADSIDE	60
10	COLLYER JAMES	HD M	36	RAIL LAB	SRY WOKING	RAILWAY HUT	5
10	COLLYER SOPHIA	WI M	23		SSX WEST FIRLE	RAILWAY HUT	5
80	COLMAN ALFRED	SV U	16	SERVANT	SSX BEXHILL	QUEENS HEAD	32
34	COLMAN GEORGE	SO U	18	AG.LAB	SSX BEXHILL	NOT GIVEN	55
34	COLMAN HENRY	HD W	52	AG.LAB	SSX WORTHING	NOT GIVEN	55
34	COLMAN JAMES	SO U	26	AG.LAB	SSX HODE	NOT GIVEN	55
34	COLMAN JESSE	SO U	11	AG.LAB	SSX BEXHILL	NOT GIVEN	55
25	COLMAN JOHN	HD W	82	FARMER 40 AC EMP 2	KEN IVYCHURCH	NOT GIVEN	54

Ref	Name	Rel	MS	Age	Occupation	County	Birth Parish	Address	Folio
44	COLYER HENRY	HD	M	22	RAILWAY LAB	SRY	PURBRIGHT	RAILWAY HUT	134
44	COLYER JANE	WI	M	28		SRY	WORPLESDON	RAILWAY HUT	134
28	COMFORT LYDIA	MO	M	53		SSX	PENHURST	BEXHILL STREET	26
36	COOK CHARLOTTE	WI	M	23		SSX	SEDLESCOMBE	MADDAMS	220
36	COOK FRANCES	DA	U	4		SSX	EWHURST	MADDAMS	220
37	COOK JAMES	HD	M	23	AG.LAB	SSX	EWHURST	MADDAMS	220
37	COOK JANE	WI	M	19		SSX	EWHURST	MADDAMS	220
36	COOK JOHN	HD	M	26	AG.LAB	SSX	EWHURST	MADDAMS	220
36	COOK JOHN	SO	U	6	SCHOLAR	SSX	EWHURST	MADDAMS	220
12	COOK MARTHA	WI	M	51		SSX	BREDE	SPRAYS BRIDGE	163
36	COOK MARY	DA	U	3		SSX	EWHURST	MADDAMS	220
40	COOK PHILADELPHIA	HD	W	65	PAUPER	SSX	CATSFIELD	CARPENTER'S COTTAGE	166
12	COOK SAMUEL	HD	M	56	FARMER	SSX	SEDLESCOMBE	SPRAYS BRIDGE	163
37	COOK SARAH	DA	U	3		SSX	EWHURST	MADDAMS	220
62	COOK THOMAS	LG	U	21	RAIL LAB	SSX	NUTLEY	PUMP HOUSE	14
32	COOKE ELIZABETH	CL	M	43		SSX	FOURINGTON*	FARM HOUSE	133
32	COOKE GABRIL	BR	M	62	PARTNER WITH TILDEN COOKE	SSX	ASHBURNHAM	FARM HOUSE	133
35	COOKE GEORGE	SO	U	15	AG.LAB	SSX	EWHURST	MADDAMS	220
35	COOKE HARRIET	DA	U	12	SCHOLAR	SSX	EWHURST	MADDAMS	220
14	COOKE JAMES	SO	U	3		SSX	EWHURST	DAGGS LANE	217
35	COOKE JOHN	HD	M	51	AG.LAB	SSX	EWHURST	MADDAMS	220
15	COOKE LAVINIA	DA	U	24		SSX	CROWHURST	HIGH HOUSE	144
15	COOKE REBECCA	HD	W	54	FARMER 211 AC EMP 9	SSX	HASTINGS	HIGH HOUSE	144
14	COOKE SARAH	WI	M	23		SSX	EWHURST	DAGG LANE	217
35	COOKE SARAH	WI	M	50		SSX	EWHURST	MADDAMS	220
14	COOKE THOMAS	HD	M	25	AG.LAB	SSX	EWHURST	DAGG LANE	217
14	COOKE THOMAS	SO	U	4		SSX	EWHURST	DAGG LANE	217
32	COOKE TILDEN	HD	U	62	FARMER 600 AC EMP 16	SSX	ASHBURNHAM	FARM HOUSE	133
15	COOKE TILDEN	SO	U	30		SSX	CROWHURST	HIGH HOUSE	144
14	COOKE WILLIAM	SO	U	1		SSX	EWHURST	DAGGS LANE	217
91	COOMBES EMILY	LW	M	22		SSX	EWHURST	STAPLE CROSS	244
91	COOMBES MARY ELIZBETH	LD	U	4M?		SSX	EWHURST	STAPLE CROSS	244
91	COOMBES THOMAS	LG	M	25	AG.LAB	SSX	NORTHIAM	STAPLE CROSS	244
86	COPPARD ANNE	DA	U	24	SCHOOL TEACHER	SSX	EWHURST	EWHURST GREEN	228
86	COPPARD ELIZABETH	WI	M	55		ESS	NORTH WIELD	EWHURST GREEN	228
86	COPPARD WILLIAM	HD	M	54	PARISH CLERK	SSX	NORTHIAM	EWHURST GREEN	228
42	COPPER HANNAH	WI	M	35		SSX	EWHURST	MARCHANTS	238
42	COPPER THOMAS	HD	M	61	AG.LAB	SSX	NORTHIAM	MARCHANTS	238
2	COREY EMILY	DA	U	8M		SSX	BEXHILL	SIDLEY	64
2	COREY HENRY	SO	U	6	SCHOLAR	SSX	NINFIELD	SIDLEY	64
2	COREY JOSEPH	SO	U	3		SSX	BEXHILL	SIDLEY	64
2	COREY MARIA E	DA	U	5	SCHOLAR	SSX	NINFIELD	SIDLEY	64
2	COREY MARY A	DA	U	2		SSX	BEXHILL	SIDLEY	64
2	COREY SOPHIA	WI	M	35		SSX	DALLINGTON	SIDLEY	64
2	COREY WILLIAM	HD	M	45	AG.LAB	SSX	EWHURST	SIDLEY	64
2	COREY WILLIAM	SO	U	8	SCHOLAR	SSX	BATTLE	SIDLEY	64
39	CORKS MARY	GM	W	75		UNKNOWN		MARCHANTS	238
30	CORNFORD CHARLES	SO	U	18	BAKER	SSX	BEXHILL	BEXHILL STREET	27
58	CORNFORD EDWIN	SO	U	18	AG.LAB	SSX	BEXHILL	KEWHURST COTTAGE	44
30	CORNFORD HANNAH	WI	M	62		SSX	RYE	BEXHILL STREET	27
27	CORNFORD HARRIET	SV	U	15	HOUSE SERVANT	SSX	BEXHILL	LITTLE WORSHAM SIDLEY	79
30	CORNFORD HARRIOTT	DA	U	24	SERVANT	SSX	BEXHILL	BEXHILL STREET	27
58	CORNFORD JOHN	HD	M	54	AG.LAB	SSX	BEXHILL	KEWHURST COTTAGE	44
50	CORNFORD JOHN	HD	W	78	PARISH ANNUITANT	SSX	BEXHILL	LITTLE COMMON	57
58	CORNFORD JOHN	SO	U	24	AG.LAB	SSX	BEXHILL	KEWHURST COTTAGE	44
58	CORNFORD MARTHA	DA	U	13		SSX	BEXHILL	KEWHURST COTTAGE	44
58	CORNFORD MARY ANN	WI	M	43		SSX	WESTFIELD	KEWHURST COTTAGE	44
30	CORNFORD SAMUEL	HD	M	56	BAKER	SSX	BEXHILL	BEXHILL STREET	27
58	CORNFORD SARAH	DA	U	6		SSX	BEXHILL	KEWHURST COTTAGE	45
58	CORNFORD STEPHEN	SO	U	9		SSX	BEXHILL	KEWHURST COTTAGE	44
50	CORNFORD STEPHEN	SO	U	42	FARMER 7 ACRES	SSX	BEXHILL	LITTLE COMMON	57
30	CORNFORD WILLIAM	GS	U	3		SSX	BEXHILL	BEXHILL STREET	27
40	CORNS ELIZA	DA	U	5		SSX	EWHURST	MARCHANTS	238
40	CORNS HANNAH	DA	U	11		SSX	EWHURST	MARCHANTS	238
40	CORNS HARRIET	DA	U	20		SSX	EWHURST	MARCHANTS	238
40	CORNS HENRY	SO	U	13		SSX	EWHURST	MARCHANTS	238
40	CORNS JAMES	SO	U	3		SSX	EWHURST	MARCHANTS	238
40	CORNS SARAH	HD	W	39	AG.LAB'S WIDOW	KEN	WITTERSHAM	MARCHANTS	238
40	CORNS WILLIAM	GS	U	6M		SSX	EWHURST	MARCHANTS	238
49	CORNTON? EDWARD	VR	U	34	RAILWAY LAB	SSX	HASTINGS	RAILWAY HUT	135
59	CORNWELL FANNY SUSANNAH	DA	U	5		SSX	HOLLINGTON	HOLLINGTON STREET	13
59	CORNWELL HARRIETT	DA	U	2		SSX	HOLLINGTON	HOLLINGTON STREET	13
59	CORNWELL HARRIETT	WI	M	28		SSX	MOUNTFIELD	HOLLINGTON STREET	13
59	CORNWELL MICHAEL	HD	M	28	FOREMAN OF LABOURERS	SSX	BATTLE	HOLLINGTON STREET	13
59	CORNWELL MICHAEL	SO	U	3		SSX	HOLLINGTON	HOLLINGTON STREET	13
59	CORNWELL SAMUEL	SO	U	7M		SSX	HOLLINGTON	HOLLINGTON STREET	13
59	CORNWELL SUSANNAH	LG	W	68		SSX	EASTBOURNE	HOLLINGTON STREET	13
56	COSTER ELIZABETH L	SH	U	9		SOM	CASTLE CARY	NOT GIVEN	95
56	COSTER ELLEN H	SH	U	13		DEV	EXETER	NOT GIVEN	95
56	COSTER EVA JANE	SH	U	11		SOM	WELLS	NOT GIVEN	95
11	COTERELL WILLIAM	/	U	23		SRY	DARKIN	MADKETS?	129
28	COUSINS CHARLOTTE	WI	M	30		SSX	EWHURST	LONG LEES	219
28	COUSINS ELLEN	DA	U	1		SSX	EWHURST	LONG LEES	219
28	COUSINS GEORGE	HD	M	23	AG.LAB	SSX	SALEHURST	LONG LEES	219
5	COUSSINS RICHARD	HD	M	60	VICTUALLER	SSX	HASTINGS ALL SAINTS	NEW INN SIDLEY	76
3	COX ELIZA	DA	U	11		KEN	LYMPINE	COLLIERS GREEN	232

	Name		Age	Occupation	County	Birthplace	Residence	Ref
30	COX ELIZA	WI M	24		KEN	WAREHORN	STONE HOUSE	132
3	COX ELIZABETH	DA U	14		KEN	ALDINGTON	COLLIERS GREEN	232
30	COX FREDERICK CHAPMAN	SO U	2		SSX	RYE	STONE HOUSE	132
3	COX GEORGE	HD M	41	AG.LAB	SSX	EWHURST	COLLIERS GREEN	232
3	COX GEORGE	SO U	9		KEN	LYMPINE	COLLIERS GREEN	232
30	COX GEORGE HORATIO	SO U	11M		SSX	MOUNTFIELD	STONE HOUSE	132
3	COX HARRIET	DA U	16		KEN	ST.MARYS	COLLIERS GREEN	232
3	COX HARRIET	WI M	44		KEN	MONKS HORTON	COLLIERS GREEN	232
30	COX JAMES	HD M	25	SUPERINTENDANT R'WY WORKS	SOM	LANGPORT*	STONE HOUSE	132
49	COX MARY ANN	VR U	22	SERVANT	SSX	NORTHIAM	SNAGS HALL	222
37	CRAMP ALFRED	HD M	28	AG.LAB	SSX	BEXHILL	NOT GIVEN	56
5	CRAMP AMELIA	WI M	61		SSX	BATTLE	KITES NEST	51
37	CRAMP CAROLINE	DA U	1M		SSX	BEXHILL	NOT GIVEN	56
37	CRAMP CHARLOTTE	WI M	29		SSX	BEXHILL	NOT GIVEN	56
65	CRAMP EDWARD D	SO U	4M		SSX	BEXHILL	SIDLEY GREEN	84
65	CRAMP EDWIN	HD M	29	SHOEMAKER	SSX	BEXHILL	SIDLEY GREEN	84
65	CRAMP ELIZABETH	WI M	30		SSX	SEAFORD	SIDLEY GREEN	84
58	CRAMP FRANCES	DA U	8		SSX	BEXHILL	SIDLEY GREEN	83
5	CRAMP FRANCES	DA U	24	HOUSE SERVANT	SSX	BEXHILL	KITES NEST	51
5	CRAMP FREDERICK	SO U	20	AG.LAB	SSX	BEXHILL	KITES NEST	51
58	CRAMP GEORGE	HD M	38	AG.LAB	SSX	BEXHILL	SIDLEY GREEN	83
58	CRAMP GEORGE	SO U	5		SSX	BEXHILL	SIDLEY GREEN	83
37	CRAMP HARRIOT	DA U	3		SSX	BEXHILL	NOT GIVEN	56
58	CRAMP JOSEPH S	SO U	1		SSX	BEXHILL	SIDLEY GREEN	83
37	CRAMP MARGARET	DA U	1		SSX	BEXHILL	NOT GIVEN	56
58	CRAMP RHODA	DA U	4		SSX	BEXHILL	SIDLEY GREEN	83
5	CRAMP SAMUEL	HD M	71	FARMER 55 AC EMP 2 SONS	SSX	BEXHILL	KITES NEST	51
1	CRAMP SARAH	SV M	54		SSX	MOUNTFIELD	POWDERMILLS	201
58	CRAMP SARAH	WI M	35		SSX	BEXHILL	SIDLEY GREEN	83
65	CRAMP SARAH M	DA U	4		SSX	BEXHILL	SIDLEY GREEN	84
65	CRAMP THOMAS S	SO U	2		SSX	BEXHILL	SIDLEY GREEN	84
71	CREASY EDWARD	HD W	53	AG.LAB	SSX	ASHBURNHAM	SCHOOL HOUSE	15
69	CREASY ELIJAH	LG U	24	AG.LAB	SSX	HOLLINGTON	YEW TREE	15
37	CRIER ELIZA	DL U	9		SSX	BEXHILL	NOT GIVEN	93
4	CRIER GEORGE	SV U	20	AG.SERVANT	SSX	BEXHILL	GUNSES?	51
37	CRIER HARRIET	DL U	13		SSX	BEXHILL	NOT GIVEN	93
39	CRISFORD ANN	WI M	62		SSX	FAIRLIGHT	BENSKINS	177
5	CRISFORD CHARLOTTE	DA U	21		NOT GIVEN (?WESTFIELD)		SOUTHINGS	152
5	CRISFORD CHARLOTTE	WI M	46		SSX	WESTFIELD	SOUTHINGS	152
40	CRISFORD ELIZABETH	WI M	30		SSX	BREDE	MILL	177
35	CRISFORD ELLEN	DA U	10	SCHOLAR	SSX	SEDLESCOMBE	NEAR THE CHURCH	205
35	CRISFORD FRANCES	DA U	16		SSX	SEDLESCOMBE	NEAR THE CHURCH	205
40	CRISFORD GEORGE	HD M	33	MILLER	SSX	WESTFIELD	MILL	177
5	CRISFORD HARRIETT	DA U	24		NOT GIVEN (?WESTFIELD)		SOUTHINGS	152
5	CRISFORD JAMES	HD M	51	FARMER	SSX	WESTFIELD	SOUTHINGS	152
5	CRISFORD JAMES	SO U	26		NOT GIVEN (?WESTFIELD)		SOUTHINGS	152
35	CRISFORD MARTHA	DA U	18	SCHOOLMISTRESS	SSX	SEDLESCOMBE	NEAR THE CHURCH	205
14	CRISFORD MARY	WI M	26		KEN	COWDEN	BREDE HIGH	251
35	CRISFORD SPENCER	HD W	61	FARMER	SSX	SEDLESCOMBE	NEAR THE CHURCH	205
39	CRISFORD STEPHEN	HD M	63	FARMER	SSX	WESTFIELD	BENSKINS	177
14	CRISFORD THOMAS	HD M	24	FARMER 267 AC EMP 7	SSX	SEDLESCOMBE	BREDE HIGH	251
14	CRISFORD THOMAS	SO U	2		SSX	EWHURST	BREDE HIGH	251
22	CRISFORD WALTER	SV U	15	BAKER'S SERVANT	NOT GIVEN (?WESTFIELD)		BAKERS	154
72	CRITTENDEN GEORGE	HD W	74	BLACKSMITH EMP 2 MEN	KEN	CRANBROOK	STAPLE CROSS	242
72	CRITTENDEN JOSEPH	SO M	39	BLACKSMITH	SSX	EWHURST	STAPLE CROSS	242
72	CRITTENDEN LYDIA	DL M	21		SSX	SALEHURST	STAPLE CROSS	242
28	CROFT EDWARD	LG W	64	BRICKLAYER	SSX	SEDLESCOMBE	ADAMS LANE	236
82	CROFT GEORGE	SO U	7	SCHOLAR	SSX	EWHURST	EWHURST GREEN	227
76	CROFT GEORGE	SO U	19	AG.LAB	SSX	EWHURST	STAPLE CROSS	242
76	CROFT HANNAH	WI M	66		KEN	HAWKHURST	STAPLE CROSS	242
82	CROFT JAMES	SO U	4		SSX	EWHURST	EWHURST GREEN	227
82	CROFT JOHN	HD M	37	AG.LAB	SSX	EWHURST	EWHURST GREEN	227
76	CROFT JOHN	HD M	66	AG.LAB	SSX	SALEHURST	STAPLE CROSS	242
82	CROFT JOHN	SO U	15	AG.LAB	SSX	EWHURST	EWHURST GREEN	227
89	CROFT MATHEW	SV U	16	AG.LAB	SSX	BRIGHTLING	EVERSFIELDS	18
82	CROFT PHILADELPHIA	WI M	41		SSX	EWHURST	EWHURST GREEN	227
76	CROFT SARAH ANN	GD U	6	SCHOLAR	SSX	BATTLE	STAPLE CROSS	242
31	CROFT WILLIAM	LG U	23	BRICKLAYER	SSX	(?SEDLESCOMBE)	SEDLESCOMBE STREET	204
82	CROFT WILLIAM	SO U	10	SCHOLAR	SSX	EWHURST	EWHURST GREEN	227
63	CROOKE CHARLES	LG U	26	RAILWAY LAB	DOR		RAILWAY HUT	137
84	CROSSWELL CHARLES	SO U	13	AG.LAB	SSX	HOLLINGTON	GATE HOUSE	17
84	CROSSWELL FANNY	DA U	10?		SSX	HOLLINGTON	GATE HOUSE	17
84	CROSSWELL HENRY	HD M	60	AG.LAB	KEN	HADLOW	GATE HOUSE	17
84	CROSSWELL JAMES	SO U	19	AG.LAB	SSX	HOLLINGTON	GATE HOUSE	17
84	CROSSWELL JOHN	SO U	28	AG.LAB	SSX	HOLLINGTON	GATE HOUSE	17
58	CROSSWELL JOHN	SV U	28	WATCHMAN	SSX	HOLLINGTON	HOLLINGTON LODGE	13
84	CROSSWELL SARAH	WI M	54		SSX	CATSFIELD	GATE HOUSE	17
24	CROUCH (CHROUCH SIC) JAMES	SV U	23		SSX	NINFIELD	SAMPSON'S FARM	131
7	CROUCH AMELIA	DA U	16		SSX	SALEHURST	HIRNS? LODGE	120
65	CROUCH ANN	DA U	2		SSX	CATSFIELD	NOT GIVEN	113
42	CROUCH ANN	WI M	47		SSX	SALEHURST	NOT GIVEN	111
65	CROUCH BERRY	WI M	39		SSX	CATSFIELD	NOT GIVEN	113
88	CROUCH CHARLES	HD M	28	AG.LAB	SSX	EWHURST	MILL PLATT	228
65	CROUCH CHARLES	SO U	9	SCHOLAR	SSX	CATSFIELD	NOT GIVEN	113
36	CROUCH CHARLES	SO U	20	AG.LAB	SSX	CATSFIELD	SKINNERS LANE	124
88	CROUCH CHARLOTTE	WI M	38		KEN	SITINGBOURNE	MILL PLATT	228

	Name				Occupation	County	Parish	Address	Ref
75	CROUCH EDGAR	LG	U	17	AG.LAB	SSX	EWHURST	EWHURST GREEN	226
22	CROUCH EDMUND	SV	U	20	AG.LAB	SSX	EWHURST	HOPHOUSE	122
15	CROUCH EDWARD	SO	U	7		SSX	EWHURST	COLLIERS GREEN	234
36	CROUCH EDWIN	GS	U	7	SCHOLAR	SSX	CATSFIELD	SKINNERS LANE	124
36	CROUCH EDWIN	SO	U	27	SAWYER	SSX	ASHBURNHAM	SKINNERS LANE	124
15	CROUCH ELIZABETH	DA	U	9		SSX	EWHURST	COLLIERS GREEN	234
7	CROUCH ELIZABETH	WI	M	60		SSX	SALEHURST	HIRNS? LODGE	120
15	CROUCH FRANCES	DA	U	4		SSX	EWHURST	COLLIERS GREEN	234
15	CROUCH FRANCES	WI	M	38		SSX	EWHURST	COLLIERS GREEN	234
14	CROUCH GEORGE	HD	M	46	AG.LAB	SSX	BURWASH	COLLIERS GREEN	234
14	CROUCH GEORGE	SO	U	25	AG.LAB	SSX	BODIAM	COLLIERS GREEN	234
24	CROUCH GEORGE	SV	U	22	GROOM	SSX	CATSFIELD	CATSFIELD RECTORY	109
65	CROUCH HARRIET	DA	U	16		SSX	CATSFIELD	NOT GIVEN	113
14	CROUCH HENRY J	SO	U	12	AG.LAB	SSX	EWHURST	COLLIERS GREEN	234
42	CROUCH ISAAC	HD	M	43	PARISH RELIEF AG.LAB	SSX	CATSFIELD	NOT GIVEN	111
11	CROUCH JAMES	GS	U	12	SCHOLAR	SSX	EWHURST	DAGG LANE	217
58	CROUCH JAMES	LG	U	22	SERVANT	SSX	EWHURST	ELLINGHALL	240
42	CROUCH JAMES	SO	U	17	CORDWAINER'S AP	SSX	CATSFIELD	NOT GIVEN	111
36	CROUCH JAMES	SO	U	23	AG.LAB	SSX	CATSFIELD	SKINNERS LANE	124
65	CROUCH JANE	DA	U	13	SCHOLAR	SSX	CATSFIELD	NOT GIVEN	113
7	CROUCH JANE	DA	U	21		SSX	SALEHURST	HIRNS? LODGE	120
2	CROUCH JANE	LG	M	30	NURSE	SSX	CROWHURST	CATSFIELD GREEN	119
26	CROUCH JANE	WI	M	30		SSX	MOUNTFIELD	RANSOM'S COTTAGE	145
37	CROUCH JOHN	HD	M	80	AG.LAB	SSX	NINFIELD	CATSFIELD GREEN	124
16	CROUCH LUCY	WI	M	37		SSX	HEATHFIELD	DYKES FARM	217
57	CROUCH MARY	/	W	84	VISITOR	SSX	TICEHURST	SNAGS HALL	223
65	CROUCH MARY	DA	U	5		SSX	CATSFIELD	NOT GIVEN	113
14	CROUCH MARY	WI	M	40		SSX	BODIAM	COLLIERS GREEN	234
36	CROUCH MARY	WI	M	56		SSX	ASHBURNHAM	SKINNERS LANE	124
42	CROUCH MARY A	DA	U	17		SSX	CATSFIELD	NOT GIVEN	111
15	CROUCH MARY ANN	DA	U	15		SSX	EWHURST	COLLIERS GREEN	234
55	CROUCH MRS	ML	W	73	VISITOR	KEN	WITTERSHAM	HANCOX FARM	209
15	CROUCH OLIVER	HD	M	40	AG.LAB	SSX	EWHURST	COLLIERS GREEN	234
15	CROUCH OLIVER	SO	U	13	AG.LAB	SSX	EWHURST	COLLIERS GREEN	234
36	CROUCH RICHARD	HD	M	56	TIMBER MERCHANT	SSX	CATSFIELD	SKINNERS LANE	124
38	CROUCH ROBERT	SL	U	25	BLACKSMITH	SSX	EWHURST	MARCHANTS	237
3	CROUCH SARAH	SV	U	14	HOUSE SERVANT	SSX	ASHBURNHAM	NOT GIVEN	51
37	CROUCH SARAH	WI	M	75		SSX	NINFIELD	CATSFIELD GREEN	124
14	CROUCH SARAH ANN	DA	U	15		SSX	EWHURST	COLLIERS GREEN	234
65	CROUCH SPENCER	HD	M	50	AG.LAB	SSX	CATSFIELD	NOT GIVEN	113
26	CROUCH STEPHEN	HD	M	28	FARM LAB	SSX	CATSFIELD	RANSOM'S COTTAGE	145
16	CROUCH THOMAS	HD	M	43	AG.LAB	SSX	EWHYRST	DYKES FARM	217
7	CROUCH WILLIAM	HD	M	55	AG.LAB	SSX	DALLINGTON	HIRNS? LODGE	120
65	CROUCH WILLIAM	SO	U	7		SSX	CATSFIELD	NOT GIVEN	113
15	CROUCH WILLIAM	SO	U	18	AG.LAB	SSX	EWHURST	COLLIERS GREEN	234
28	CROWDER FRANCES	GD	U	6		SSX	BATTLE	PLOUGH INN	155
12	CROWDER FRANK	SO	U	3		SSX	BATTLE	STEVEN'S CROUCH	121
12	CROWDER FRED	SO	U	6		SSX	BATTLE	STEVEN'S CROUCH	121
12	CROWDER HARRIOT	WI	M	35		SSX	WESTFIELD	STEVEN'S CROUCH	121
12	CROWDER HARRY	SO	U	1		SSX	CATSFIELD	STEVEN'S CROUCH	121
12	CROWDER HENRY	HD	M	32	GAMEKEEPER	SSX	BATTLE	STEVEN'S CROUCH	121
94	CROWHURST ALFRED	HD	M	45	PAINTER & BRICKLAYER	SSX	BEXHILL	NOT GIVEN	100
94	CROWHURST ELIZA	DA	U	17		SSX	BEXHILL	NOT GIVEN	100
94	CROWHURST HARRIET	DA	U	6		SSX	BEXHILL	NOT GIVEN	100
94	CROWHURST HARRIET	WI	M	46		SSX	BEXHILL	NOT GIVEN	100
20	CROWHURST HENRY	SV	U	15	FARM SERVANT	SSX	BATTLE	WATER MILL HOUSE	145
94	CROWHURST MARY A	DA	U	16		SSX	BEXHILL	NOT GIVEN	100
94	CROWHURST SAMUEL	SO	U	3		SSX	BEXHILL	NOT GIVEN	100
10	CROWHURST WILLIAM	LG	U	22	RAILWAY LAB	SSX	HELLINGLY	FORWARD LANE	129
52	CRUSE MARY ELIZABETH	/	U	16	GOVERNESS	SOM	FROME	GREAT SANDERS	194
28	CRUSWELL JESSE	SV	U	15		SSX	HOLLINGTON	LANKHURST	155
20	CRUTTENDEN ALBERT	SO	U	8		SSX	WILLINGDON	BELL HILL	25
68	CRUTTENDEN ANN	HD	W	50	ANNUITANT	SSX	BATTLE	NOT GIVEN	97
24	CRUTTENDEN ANN	HD	W	71	ANNUITANT	SSX	SEDLESCOMBE	SEDLESCOMBE STREET	189
64	CRUTTENDEN CHARLOTTE	DA	U	10	SCHOLAR	SSX	BEXHILL	NOT GIVEN	58
24	CRUTTENDEN CHARLOTTE	DA	U	28	DRESSMAKER	SSX	BATTLE	SEDLESCOMBE STREET	189
46	CRUTTENDEN DELIA	DA	U	9	SCHOLAR	SSX	SEDLESCOMBE	MARTINS COTTAGE	178
46	CRUTTENDEN DULCEY	DA	U	2		SSX	WESTFIELD	MARTINS COTTAGE	178
20	CRUTTENDEN ELIZABETH	DA	U	7		SSX	WILLINGDON	BELL HILL	25
64	CRUTTENDEN ELIZABETH	WI	M	56		SSX	BEXHILL	NOT GIVEN	58
3	CRUTTENDEN EVERDEN (MALE)	HD	W	84	SUPERANNUATED OFFICER	SSX	BEXHILL	WAKEHAMS	89
46	CRUTTENDEN FRANCES	DA	U	7		SSX	WESTFIELD	MARTINS COTTAGE	178
80	CRUTTENDEN FREDERICK	SV	U	19	WAITER	SSX	BEXHILL	BELL HOTEL	99
20	CRUTTENDEN GEORGE	HD	M	43	AG.LAB	SSX	PEVENSEY	BELL HILL	25
46	CRUTTENDEN GEORGE	SO	U	4		SSX	WESTFIELD	MARTINS COTTAGE	178
64	CRUTTENDEN GEORGE	SO	U	13		SSX	BEXHILL	NOT GIVEN	58
115	CRUTTENDEN HANNAH	WI	M	41		SSX	BEXHILL	NOT GIVEN	102
20	CRUTTENDEN HARRIETT	DA	U	11	SCHOLAR	SSX	WESTFIELD	HARTS GREEN	164
20	CRUTTENDEN HARRIETT	WI	M	37		SSX	ASHBURNHAM	HARTS GREEN	164
115	CRUTTENDEN HENRY	HD	M	47	GARDENER	SSX	PEVENSEY	NOT GIVEN	102
50	CRUTTENDEN HENRY	SO	U	13		SSX	HOLLINGTON	HOLLINGTON STREET	11
115	CRUTTENDEN HENRY	SO	U	20		SSX	BEXHILL	NOT GIVEN	102
33	CRUTTENDEN JAMES	HD	M	33	FARMER	SSX	BEXHILL	MOOR FARM	155
33	CRUTTENDEN JAMES	SO	U	1M		SSX	BEXHILL	MOOR FARM	155
50	CRUTTENDEN JAMES	SO	U	12		SSX	HOLLINGTON	HOLLINGTON STREET	11
24	CRUTTENDEN JANE	DA	U	35		SSX	WESTFIELD	SEDLESCOMBE STREET	189

No.	Name	Rel	MS	Age	Occupation	County	Parish	Location	Folio
33	CRUTTENDEN JOHN	SV	U	16		SSX	BEXHILL	MOOR FARM	155
16	CRUTTENDEN JOSEPH	LG	W	80		KEN	SANDHURST	BLUMANS	163
20	CRUTTENDEN JOSEPH	SO	U	17		SSX	ORE	HARTS GREEN	164
33	CRUTTENDEN LUCY	WI	M	33		SSX	BEXHILL	MOOR FARM	155
64	CRUTTENDEN MARGARET	GD	U	3		SSX	BEXHILL	NOT GIVEN	58
20	CRUTTENDEN MARY	DA	U	1		SSX	WESTFIELD	HARTS GREEN	164
38	CRUTTENDEN MARY	WI	M	35		SSX	BREDE	SHOP HOUSES	124
20	CRUTTENDEN MARY A	DA	U	17		SSX	PEVENSEY	BELL HILL	25
38	CRUTTENDEN NELSON	HD	M	35	GROCER	SSX	WESTFIELD	SHOP HOUSES	124
20	CRUTTENDEN PHILADELPHIA	DA	U	9	SCHOLAR	SSX	WESTFIELD	HARTS GREEN	164
33	CRUTTENDEN PHILIS	DA	U	1		SSX	WESTFIELD	MOOR FARM	155
64	CRUTTENDEN SABINA	DA	U	26		SSX	BEXHILL	NOT GIVEN	58
20	CRUTTENDEN SAMUEL	HD	M	42	AG.LAB	SSX	WESTFIELD	HARTS GREEN	164
64	CRUTTENDEN SAMUEL	HD	M	66	AG.LAB	SSX	CROWHURST	NOT GIVEN	58
20	CRUTTENDEN SAMUEL	SO	U	13		SSX	BATTLE	HARTS GREEN	164
46	CRUTTENDEN SARAH E	WI	M	37		KEN	TENTERDEN	MARTINS COTTAGE	178
64	CRUTTENDEN SELINA	GD	U	4M		SSX	BEXHILL	NOT GIVEN	58
20	CRUTTENDEN SPENCER	SO	U	19		SSX	ORE	HARTS GREEN	164
38	CRUTTENDEN SPENCER WILLIAM	SO	U	6	SCHOLAR	SSX	CATSFIELD	SHOP HOUSES	124
20	CRUTTENDEN STEPHEN	SO	U	5		SSX	WESTFIELD	HARTS GREEN	164
46	CRUTTENDEN THOMAS	HD	M	37	CARPENTER	SSX	BATTLE	MARTINS COTTAGE	178
46	CRUTTENDEN THOMAS	SO	U	11	SCHOLAR	SSX	SEDLESCOMBE	MARTINS COTTAGE	178
20	CRUTTENDEN TILDEN	SO	U	3		SSX	WESTFIELD	HARTS GREEN	164
20	CRUTTENDEN TIMOTHY	SO	U	15		SSX	ORE	HARTS GREEN	164
50	CRUTTENDEN WILLIAM	HD	W	50	AG.LAB	SSX	HOLLINGTON	HOLLINGTON STREET	11
50	CRUTTENDEN WILLIAM	SO	U	19		SSX	HOLLINGTON	HOLLINGTON STREET	11
31	CRUTTENDEN WILLIAM	SV	U	15	FARM SERVANT	SSX	HOLLINGTON	STONE HOUSE FARM	133
102	CRYER ANN	SV	U	21		SSX	BEXHILL	NOT GIVEN	101
60	CRYER HENRY	SV	U	17	AG.LAB	SSX	BEXHILL	BIRCHINGTON	45
47	CUCKNEY MARY	WI	M	37		SSX	EWHURST	SHOREHAM	221
47	CUCKNEY WILLIAM	HD	M	34	AG.LAB	SSX	EWHURST	SHOREHAM	221
62	CULOEN? HENRY	LG	U	24	RAILWAY LAB	KEN	BOUGHTON LEES?	RAILWAY HUT	136
51	CURLEY ELIZABETH	SD	U	11	SCHOLAR	KEN	WOOLWICH	SIDLEY GREEN	82
23	CURTIS WILLIAM	HD	U	59	AG.LAB	SSX	PEVENSEY	IN THE LIBERTY	40
70	DALLAWAY ELIZABETH	DA	U	27	DRESSMAKER	SSX	BEXHILL	NOT GIVEN	97
70	DALLAWAY HARRIET	WI	M	59		SSX	BEXHILL	NOT GIVEN	97
70	DALLAWAY JAMES	SO	U	17	TAILOR'S AP	SSX	BEXHILL	NOT GIVEN	97
70	DALLAWAY THOMAS	HD	M	58	WATCHMAKER	SSX	WARBLETON	NOT GIVEN	97
43	DANIEL ANNA M	HD	W	73	HOUSE PROPRIETOR	NOR	WELLS	2 DORSETT COTTAGE	28
43	DANIEL ELIZABETH	DA	U	47	HOUSE PROPRIETOR	SSZX	BEXHILL	2 DORSETT COTTAGE	28
43	DANIEL LOUIS A	SO	U	29	HOUSE PROPRIETOR	SSX	HASTINGS	2 DORSETT COTTAGE	28
26	DANIELS CAROLINE	VR	U	21	DRESS MAKER	SSX	SALEHURST	FORGE FARM	219
39	DANN HARRIET	SV	U	30	SERVANT	SSX	HEATHFIELD	PRAWLES FARM	221
4	DANN JAMES	AP	U	18	WHEELWRIGHT AP	SSX	TICEHURST	SIDLEY	65
14	DANN JOHN	LG	U	32	GAMEKEEPER	SSX	BATTLE	MAYFIELDS HOUSE	6
4	DANN JOHN	LS	U	5	SCHOLAR	SSX	HEATHFIELD	COLLIERS GREEN	233
4	DANN LEONORA	DL	U	12		SSX	HEATHFIELD	COLLIERS GREEN	233
4	DANN MARY	LG	U	24	DRESSMAKER	SSX	HEATHFIELD	COLLIERS GREEN	233
4	DANN WILLIAM	LS	U	7M		SSX	HELLINGLY	COLLIERS GREEN	233
8	DARE EMMA	WI	M	30		SRY	WORPLESDON*	RAILWAY HUT	129
35	DARE GEORGE	RE	U	23	RAILWAY LAB	SRY	PERBRIGHT	COURT LODGE FARM	147
8	DARE GEORGE	SO	U	6M		SRY	CROWHURST	RAILWAY HUT	129
35	DARE HENRY	RE	U	18	RAILWAY LAB	SRY	PERBRIGHT	COURT LODGE FARM	147
20	DARE ISAAC	LG	U	28	RAILWAY LAB	SRY	PERBRITE	CROWHURST VILLAGE	131
35	DARE MARY	WI	M	33		SRY	FARNHAM	COURT LODGE FARM	147
8	DARE WILLIAM	HD	M	25	RAILWAY LAB	SRY	GUILFORD	RAILWAY HUT	129
35	DARE WILLIAM	HD	M	32	RAILWAY CONTRACTOR	SRY	PERBRIGHT	COURT LODGE FARM	147
35	DARE WILLIAM	SO	U	2		SRY	FARNHAM	COURT LODGE FARM	147
24	DARYMAN ANN	SV	U	33	NURSE	SOM	UNCLEAR ?ILMINSTER*	CATSFIELD RECTORY	109
45	DAVIS ANN	DA	U	8	SCHOLAR	SSX	SEDLESCOMBE	POPPING HOLE LANE	207
3	DAVIS ANN	NS	W	28	GENERAL NURSE	SSX	BATTLE	BEACON MILL	249
22	DAVIS ANN	SV	U	16	SERVANT	SSX	EWHURST	GATE FARM	235
41	DAVIS ANN	SV	U	21		SSX	UDIMORE	MILL COTTAGE	177
75	DAVIS ANN	WI	M	35		SSX	EWHURST	STAPLE CROSS	242
45	DAVIS BENJAMIN	HD	M	33	AG.LAB	SSX	MOUNTFIELD	POPPING HOLE LANE	207
45	DAVIS CHARLES	SO	U	6	SCHOLAR	SSX	SEDLESCOMBE	POPPING HOLE LANE	207
14	DAVIS CHARLOTTE	SV	U	33		SSX	GUESTLING	SEDLESCOMBE STREET	202
52	DAVIS ELLEN	SV	U	14	UNDER NURSE	SSX	WHATLINGTON	GREAT SANDERS	194
45	DAVIS EMILY	DA	U	9	SCHOLAR	SSX	SEDLESCOMBE	POPPING HOLE LANE	207
75	DAVIS EMILY JANE	DA	U	2		SSX	EWHURST	STAPLE CROSS	242
75	DAVIS GEORGE	SO	U	11	AG.LAB	SSX	EWHURST	STAPLE CROSS	242
45	DAVIS GILBERT	SO	U	4	SCHOLAR	SSX	MOUNTFIELD	POPPING HOLE LANE	207
42	DAVIS HANNAH	WI	M	57		SSX	BEXHILL	SIDLEY	81
32	DAVIS HARRIOT	HD	U	46		SSX	GUESTLING	CRIPPS COTTAGE	253
75	DAVIS JAMES HENRY	SO	U	14	AG.LAB	SSX	EWHURST	STAPLE CROSS	242
1	DAVIS JOYCE	ML	W	76	RETIRED VICTUALLER	UNKNOWN		CATSFIELD GREEN	119
25	DAVIS LEONORA E	HD	U	39		SSX	GUESTLING	SEDLESCOMBE STREET	204
14	DAVIS MARIA	VR	U	16		SSX	GUESTLING	SEDLESCOMBE STREET	202
45	DAVIS MARY JANE	DA	U	2	SCHOLAR	SSX	MOUNTFIELD	POPPING HOLE LANE	207
45	DAVIS MERCY	DA	U	11	SCHOLAR	SSX	SEDLESCOMBE	POPPING HOLE LANE	207
45	DAVIS MERCY	WI	M	30		SSX	WHATLINGTON	POPPING HOLE LANE	207
75	DAVIS STEPHEN	SO	U	7		SSX	EWHURST	STAPLE CROSS	242
75	DAVIS WILLIAM	HD	M	35	AG.LAB	SSX	BODIAM	STAPLE CROSS	242
42	DAVIS WILLIAM	HD	M	60	AG.LAB	SSX	BEXHILL	SIDLEY	81
23	DAW ANN	NS	M	62	NURSE	SSX	WARTLING	BEXHILL STREET	26
35	DAW HARRIOT	WI	M	60		SSX	WESTFIELD	DAIRY HOUSE	133

	Name	Status	Age	Occupation	County	Birthplace	Address	No.
2	DAW HENRY	HD M	63	SHEPHERD	SSX	BEXHILL	SIDLEY GREEN	75
2	DAW HENRY	SO U	38	AG.LAB	SSX	BEXHILL	SIDLEY GREEN	75
2	DAW MARY	DA U	35		SSX	BEXHILL	SIDLEY GREEN	75
40	DAW MARY	HD W	75		SSX	HOOE	BEXHILL STREET	28
35	DAW WILLIAM	HD M	60	LAB	SSX	CROWHURST	DAIRY HOUSE	133
30	DAWE MARY	VR U	23		SSX	WARBLETON	STREAM HILL	123
23	DAWS ANN	WI M	27		KEN	DEPTFORD	LORDINE	235
23	DAWS ANNIE	DA U	4		SSX	EWHURST	LORDINE	235
23	DAWS ELIZABETH	DA U	1M		SSX	EWHURST	LORDINE	235
87	DAWS ELIZABETH MARY	CI U	36	HOUSE KEEPER	SSX	EWHURST	SOGGS FARM	228
23	DAWS MARY	DA U	1		SSX	EWHURST	LORDINE	235
24	DAWS MATILDA H	VR U	27		SSX	WHATLINGTON	ROCKS	175
23	DAWS THOMAS	SO U	3		SSX	EWHURST	LORDINE	235
87	DAWS THOMAS CHESTER	HD U	37	FARMER 510 AC EMP 45	SSX	EWHURST	SOGGS FARM	228
23	DAWS WALTER WILLIAM	HD M	36	FARMER 1283 AC EMP 43	SSX	EWHURST	LORDINE	235
19	DAWSON ANN	WI M	39		SSX	SALEHURST	CATTS GREEN	251
21	DAWSON CHARLOTTE	WI M	21		SSX	WESTFIELD	SEDLESCOMBE STREET	204
19	DAWSON DAVID	SO U	2M		SSX	EWHURST	CATTS GREEN	251
13	DAWSON EDWARD	HD M	67	AG.LAB	SSX	EWHURST	COLLIERS GREEN	234
19	DAWSON EDWARD	SO U	18	AG.LAB	SSX	SALEHURST	CATTS GREEN	251
19	DAWSON GEORGE	SO U	9	SCHOLAR	SSX	EWHURST	CATTS GREEN	251
21	DAWSON HARRIETT	DA U	9	SCHOLAR	SSX	WESTFIELD	HARTS GREEN	164
19	DAWSON HENRY	SO U	3		SSX	EWHURST	CATTS GREEN	251
21	DAWSON JAMES	SO U	4		SSX	WESTFIELD	HARTS GREEN	164
19	DAWSON JAMES	SO U	20	AG.LAB	SSX	SALEHURST	CATTS GREEN	251
21	DAWSON JANE	DA U	7		SSX	WESTFIELD	HARTS GREEN	164
21	DAWSON JANE	WI M	34		SSX	SEDLESCOMBE	HARTS GREEN	164
2	DAWSON JOHN	SV U	15	FARM LAB	SSX	EWHURST	WATTLE HILL	249
83	DAWSON MARTHA	LG M	64	HOUSE KEEPER	SSX	BODIAM	STAPLE CROSS	243
43	DAWSON MARTHA	WI M	35		SSX	EWHURST	ADAMS LANE	238
13	DAWSON MARY	WI M	68		SSX	BREDE	COLLIERS GREEN	234
21	DAWSON MARY A	DA U	11		SSX	WESTFIELD	HARTS GREEN	164
21	DAWSON SARAH	DA U	1		SSX	SEDLESCOMBE	SEDLESCOMBE STREET	204
19	DAWSON STEPHEN	HD M	40	AG.LAB	SSX	EWHURST	CATTS GREEN	251
19	DAWSON THOMAS	SO U	5		SSX	EWHURST	CATTS GREEN	251
21	DAWSON WILLIAM	HD M	23	AG.LAB	SSX	WESTFIELD	SEDLESCOMBE STREET	204
43	DAWSON WILLIAM	HD M	32	AG.LAB	SSX	EWHURST	ADAMS LANE	238
21	DAWSON WILLIAM	HD M	46	AG.LAB	SSX	WESTFIELD	HARTS GREEN	164
19	DAWSON WILLIAM	SO U	7	SCHOLAR	SSX	EWHURST	CATTS GREEN	251
43	DAWSON WILLIAM	SO U	12	AG.LAB	SSX	EWHURST	ADAMS LANE	238
54	DAY ANN	DA U	8		SSX	WALDRON	RAILWAY HUT	135
26	DAY AUGUSTUS R	SO U	17	SCHOLAR AT HOME	SSX	BEXHILL	BEXHILL STREET	26
54	DAY ELI	SO U	4		DOR	MUILFORD?	RAILWAY HUT	135
54	DAY ELLEN	DA U	1		SSX	MOUNTFIELD	RAILWAY HUT	135
54	DAY FRANK	SO U	9		KEN	TUNBRIDGE	RAILWAY HUT	135
54	DAY GEORGE	HD M	32	RAILWAY LAB	SOM	BANTON	RAILWAY HUT	135
26	DAY JANE	HD W	42	GENTLEWOMAN ANNUITANT	SSX	BATTLE	BEXHILL STREET	26
88	DAY MARY	VR U	23		SSX	CHALEY	MILL PLATT	228
54	DAY MARY	WI M	33	LAUNDRESS	WIL	CHIPPENHAM	RAILWAY HUT	135
26	DAY MARY J	DA U	18	SCHOLAR AT HOME	SSX	BEXHILL	BEXHILL STREET	26
49	DAY RICHARD	VR U	24	RAILWAY LAB	SSX	HASTINGS	RAILWAY HUT	135
88	DAY WILLIAM	VR U	3		SSX	CHALEY	MILL PLATT	228
63	DEALY EMMA	PP U	10		HAM	SOUTHAMPTON	BEXHILL STREET	96
36	DEDMAN WILLIAM	LG U	27	SHEPHERD	SSX	RODWELL	NOT GIVEN	133
14	DEMER WILLIAM	LG U	25	RAILWAY LAB	YKS		NOT GIVEN	130
25	DENALE? WILLIAM	LG /	20	RAIL LAB	NOT GIVEN		RAILWAY HUT	8
1	DENGATE ELIZABETH	HD U	26	DRESSMAKER	SSX	NORTHIAM	SEDLESCOMBE STREET	186
49	DENGATE HANNAH	WI M	58		SSX	ASHBURNHAM	NOT GIVEN	239
6	DENGATE HARRIET	WI M	27		SSX	SEDLESCOMBE	COACH & HORSES	187
6	DENGATE JAMES	HD M	30	INN KEEPER	SSX	NORTHIAM	COACH & HORSES	187
58	DENGATE JAMES	HD M	62	MILLER & GRINDER	KEN	WITTERSHAM	WINDMILL	209
6	DENGATE JAMES	SO U	6M		SSX	SEDLESCOMBE	COACH & HORSES	187
49	DENGATE JANE	DA U	28		SSX	CROWHURST	NOT GIVEN	239
58	DENGATE SARAH	WI M	60?		SSX	SEAFORD	WINDMILL	209
49	DENGATE THOMAS	HD M	61	AG.LAB	SSX	CROWHURST	NOT GIVEN	239
21	DENGATTE DAVID	SO U	21	AG.LAB	SSX	CROWHURST	NOT GIVEN	131
21	DENGATTE JAMES	HD M	50	FARMER	SSX	CROWHURST	NOT GIVEN	131
24	DENGATTE MARY	SV U	17	HOUSE SERVANT	SSX	CROWHURST	SAMPSON'S FARM	131
21	DENGATTE MERCEY	WI M	55		SSX	SEDLESCOMBE	NOT GIVEN	131
29	DENNETT ALFRED	SO U	14	AG.LAB	SSX	SEDLESCOMBE	SEDLESCOMBE STREET	204
24	DENNETT DINAH	CI U	60	HOUSEKEEPER	SSX	SEDLESCOMBE	SEDLESCOMBE STREET	204
29	DENNETT EDWIN	SO U	6	SCHOLAR	SSX	SEDLESCOMBE	SEDLESCOMBE STREET	204
17	DENNETT ELLEN	DA U	14		SSX	MOUNTFIELD	SEDLESCOMBE STREET	188
29	DENNETT EMILY	DA U	3		SSX	SEDLESCOMBE	SEDLESCOMBE STREET	204
16	DENNETT FRANCES	DA U	1		SSX	SEDLESCOMBE	SEDLESCOMBE STREET	188
29	DENNETT GEORGE	SO U	10	SCHOLAR	SSX	SEDLESCOMBE	SEDLESCOMBE STREET	204
17	DENNETT HANNAH	DA U	17		SSX	MOUNTFIELD	SEDLESCOMBE STREET	188
29	DENNETT HARRIET	WI M	42		SSX	CATSFIELD	SEDLESCOMBE STREET	204
16	DENNETT JAMES	HD M	26	HUNTSMAN	SSX	MOUNTFIELD	SEDLESCOMBE STREET	188
17	DENNETT JAMES	HD M	61	BLACKSMITH MASTER EMP 1	SSX	EWHURST	SEDLESCOMBE STREET	188
24	DENNETT JAMES	HD U	72	GARDENER	SSX	WHATLINGTON	SEDLESCOMBE STREET	204
16	DENNETT JAMES	SO U	3		SSX	SEDLESCOMBE	SEDLESCOMBE STREET	188
24	DENNETT JOHN	BR U	77	GARDENER	SSX	WHATLINGTON	SEDLESCOMBE STREET	204
17	DENNETT MARY ANN	WI M	54		SSX	HAILSHAM	SEDLESCOMBE STREET	188
16	DENNETT SARAH	WI M	22		SSX	SEDLESCOMBE	SEDLESCOMBE STREET	188
29	DENNETT THOMAS	SO U	23	BRICKLAYER'S LAB	SSX	SEDLESCOMBE	SEDLESCOMBE STREET	204

	Name	Rel	M	Age	Occupation	Birth County	Birthplace	Address	No
29	DENNETT WILLIAM	HD	M	47	AG.LAB	SSX	SEDLESCOMBE	SEDLESCOMBE STREET	204
21	DENNETT WILLIAM	LG	U	23	AG.LAB	SSX	SEDLESCOMBE	ODIAM FARM	218
73	DENNIS EDWIN	SO	U	9M		SSX	BEXHILL	NOT GIVEN (LITTLE COMMON)	46
73	DENNIS ELIZABETH	WI	M	33		SSX	HAILSHAM	NOT GIVEN (LITTLE COMMON)	46
73	DENNIS HARRIETT	DA	U	4		SSX	HAILSHAM	NOT GIVEN (LITTLE COMMON)	46
73	DENNIS HENRY	HD	M	33	RAIL LAB	SSX	FOLKINGTON	NOT GIVEN (LITTLE COMMON)	46
73	DENNIS JOHN	SO	U	7	SCHOLAR	SSX	HAILSHAM	NOT GIVEN (LITTLE COMMON)	46
73	DENNIS HARRIETT	DA	U	10	SCHOLAR	SSX	HAILSHAM	NOT GIVEN (LITTLE COMMON)	46
73	DENNIS THOMAS	SO	U	2		SSX	WESTHAM	NOT GIVEN (LITTLE COMMON)	46
65	DEUDNEY ALBERT	PP	U	11	PUPIL	SSX	ST.LEONARDS	NOT GIVEN	96
80	DEUDNEY JAMES	HD	M	48	INN KEEPER	SSX	BEXHILL	BELL HOTEL	99
80	DEUDNEY MARY ANN	DA	U	20		SSX	HELLINGLY	BELL HOTEL	99
80	DEUDNEY MARY ANN	WI	M	50		SSX	WESTHAM	BELL HOTEL	99
68	DEUDNEY SARAH	VR	W	77	ANNUITANT	SSX	ST.LEONARDS	NOT GIVEN	97
61	DEVALL THOMAS	HD	U	76	FARMER 30 AC EMP 1	SSX	BEXHILL	PINNIERS (LITTLE COMMON)	45
9	DEW MARIANN	SV	W	40	LADIES MAID	YKS		PARK GATE	120
70	DINEEN CATHERINE	WI	M	30		IRELAND		47 MARTELLO TOWER	31
70	DINEEN CHARLES	HD	M	38	COAST GUARD	IRELAND		47 MARTELLO TOWER	31
70	DINEEN HANNAH	DA	U	2		SSX	BEXHILL	47 MARTELLO TOWER	31
70	DINEEN JAMES	SO	U	7	SCHOLAR AT HOME	SSX	BEXHILL	47 MARTELLO TOWER	31
70	DINEEN MARY	DA	U	5	SCHOLAR AT HOME	SSX	BEXHILL	47 MARTELLO TOWER	31
70	DINEEN THOMAS	SO	U	3M		SSX	BEXHILL	47 MARTELLO TOWER	31
36	DIPROSE ANN	WI	M	25		SSX	NINFIELD	WHYDOWN SIDLEY	71
36	DIPROSE FRANCES	DA	U	4		SSX	NINFIELD	WHYDOWN SIDLEY	71
36	DIPROSE GEORGE	SO	U	1		SSX	NINFIELD	WHYDOWN SIDLEY	71
36	DIPROSE JAMES	HD	M	26	AG.LAB	SSX	NINFIELD	WHYDOWN SIDLEY	71
57	DITON ELIZABETH	GM	W	78		SSX	WESTFIELD	BARRACKS	179
69	DIVINE CELIA	DA	U	6	SCHOLAR	SSX	WILLINGDON	(46 MARTELLO TOWER?)	31
69	DIVINE DENIS	HD	M	38	COAST GUARD	IRELAND		(46 MARTELLO TOWER?)	31
69	DIVINE ELLEN	DA	U	1		SSX	BEXHILL	(46 MARTELLO TOWER?)	31
69	DIVINE ISABELL	WI	M	34		IRELAND		(46 MARTELLO TOWER?)	31
69	DIVINE JOHN	SO	U	12	SCHOLAR	IRELAND		(46 MARTELLO TOWER?)	31
69	DIVINE MARY	DA	U	10	SCHOLAR	SSX	WILLINGDON	(46 MARTELLO TOWER?)	31
69	DIVINE SUSAN	DA	U	4		SSX	BEXHILL	(46 MARTELLO TOWER?)	31
44	DOUCH ANN	WI	M	49		SSX	WADHURST	NOT GIVEN	56
44	DOUCH HENRY	HD	M	54	AG.LAB	SSX	ASHBURNHAM	NOT GIVEN	56
39	DOWLING HARRIETT	SV	U	20	HOUSE SERVANT	SSX	BATTLE	HAILSFORD	192
27	DRAPER JAMES	LG	U	23	RAIL LAB	BRK	SANDHURST	RAILWAY HUT	8
57	DREDGE FANNY	DA	U	10		SSX	BRIGHTON	NOT GIVEN	95
57	DREDGE FANNY	WI	M	31		SSX	BRIGHTON	NOT GIVEN	95
57	DREDGE FLORA	DA	U	6		NORMANDY		NOT GIVEN	95
57	DREDGE MARTHA	DA	U	2M		SSX	BEXHILL	NOT GIVEN	95
57	DREDGE MATILDA	DA	U	4		NORMANDY		NOT GIVEN	95
57	DREDGE STEPHEN	HD	M	37	SHOEMAKER	SSX	BRIGHTON	NOT GIVEN	95
25	DRISCOLL ANN	WI	M	23		AUSTRIA BUSHMILES		53 MARTELLO TOWER IN LIBERTY	40
25	DRISCOLL HANNAH	DA	U	2		SSX	BEXHILL	53 MARTELLO TOWER IN LIBERTY	40
25	DRISCOLL JOHN	HD	M	31	COAST GUARD BOATMAN	IRL	CORK BALTIMORE	53 MARTELLO TOWER IN LIBERTY	40
25	DRISCOLL JOHN	SO	U	4	SCHOLAR	SSX	BEXHILL	53 MARTELLO TOWER IN LIBERTY	40
25	DRISCOLL MARY A	DA	U	6	SCHOLAR	SSX	BEXHILL	53 MARTELLO TOWER IN LIBERTY	40
53	DUDLEY EDWARD	HD	M	36	ENGINE CLEANER	MDX	ST.PANCRAS	1 STONE HOUSE	44
66	DUFF CHARLOTTE	DL	U	12	HAWKER	SSX	CUCKFIELD	TENT HOUSE (LITTLE COMMON)	46
66	DUFF ELIZABETH	DL	U	8	HAWKER	KEN	DOVER	TENT HOUSE (LITTLE COMMON)	46
76	DUFFY JAMES	LG	U	37	RAIL LAB	MDX	MARLEBONE (SIC)	APPLE TREE	182
25	DUGGINS DANIEL	HD	W	31	AG.LAB	UNKNOWN		NOT GIVEN	92
25	DUGGINS SARAH	DA	U	2		SSX	BEXHILL	NOT GIVEN	92
58	DUKE ALFRED	SO	U	17	AG.LAB	SSX	EWHURST	SNAGS HALL	224
38	DUKE ANN	DA	U	10		SSX	BATTLE	NOT GIVEN	56
54	DUKE ANN	DA	U	13	SCHOLAR	SSX	EWHURST	SNAGS HALL	223
58	DUKE ANN	HD	M	36	LAUNDRESS	SSX	EWHURST	SNAGS HALL	224
60	DUKE BENJAMIN	BR	U	22	AG.LAB	SSX	BEXHILL	BIRCHINGTON	45
54	DUKE FRANCES	WI	M	44		SSX	NORTHIAM	SNAGS HALL	223
54	DUKE FRANCES ANN	DA	U	8	SCHOLAR	SSX	EWHURST	SNAGS HALL	223
58	DUKE GEORGE	SO	U	9	SCHOLAR	SSX	EWHURST	SNAGS HALL	224
38	DUKE HARRIOT	HD	W	39	AG.LAB'S WIDOW	SSX	NINFIELD	NOT GIVEN	56
38	DUKE HENRY	SO	U	9		SSX	BEXHILL	NOT GIVEN	56
44	DUKE HENRY	SO	U	19	AG.LAB	SSX	EWHURST	SHOREHAM	221
44	DUKE JAMES	HD	M	51	AG.LAB	SSX	EWHURST	SHOREHAM	221
54	DUKE JOHN	SO	U	15	AG.LAB	SSX	EWHURST	SNAGS HALL	223
44	DUKE JOHN	SO	U	16	AG.LAB	SSX	EWHURST	SHOREHAM	221
60	DUKE JOHN W	SO	U	2		SSX	BEXHILL	BIRCHINGTON	45
60	DUKE LUCY B	WI	M	34		SSX	HOOE	BIRCHINGTON	45
54	DUKE MARIA ANN	DA	U	18	SERVANT AT HOME	SSX	EWHURST	SNAGS HALL	223
44	DUKE SUSAN	WI	M	49		SSX	NORTHIAM	SHOREHAM	221
60	DUKE THOMAS	HD	M	33	FARMER 38 AC EMP 2	SSX	BEXHILL	BIRCHINGTON	45
44	DUKE THOMAS	SO	U	8		SSX	EWHURST	SHOREHAM	221
54	DUKE THOMAS	SO	U	10	SCHOLAR	SSX	EWHURST	SNAGS HALL	223
54	DUKE WILLIAM	HD	M	46	AG.LAB	SSX	EWHURST	SNAGS HALL	223
32	DUKE WILLIAM	SL	U	7		SSX	BREDE	MADDAMS	220
31	DUKE WILLIAM	SO	U	10	AG.LAB	SSX	BEXHILL	(LITTLE COMMON)	55
54	DUKE WILLIAM H	SO	U	4		SSX	EWHURST	SNAGS HALL	223
5	DUNK EDGAR	SO	U	16		SSX	BEXHILL	BARNHORN HILL	38
5	DUNK EDWARD	HD	M	54	AG.LAB	SSX	NINFIELD	BARNHORN HILL	38
46	DUNK ELIZABETH	HD	W	72	PARISH RELIEF	SSX	SALEHURST	NOT GIVEN	111
5	DUNK HARRIETT	WI	M	46		KEN	SEVENOAKS	BARNHORN HILL	38
67	DUNK JAMES THOMAS	/	U	23	AG.LAB	SSX	ETCHINGHAM	CASTLEMANS	210
67	DUNK MARY	SV	W	56?	HOUSE KEEPER	SFK	LOWESTOFT	CASTLEMANS	210

	Name				Occupation	County/Parish	Location	
27	DUNK NAOMA	DA	U	13		SSX CROWHURST	FORWARD LANE	145
27	DUNK SARAH	WI	M	49		SSX SEDLESCOMBE	FORWARD LANE	145
27	DUNK WILLIAM	HD	M	48	CORDWAINER	SSX BEXHILL	FORWARD LANE	145
1	DUNK WILLIAM	LG	U	18	AG.LAB	SSX BEXHILL	SIDLEY CORNER	64
27	DUNK WILLIAM	SO	U	17	CORWAINER	SSX CROWHURST	FORWARD LANE	145
33	DUNSTALL FANNY	HD	M	32	SHEPHERD'S WIFE	SSX BEXHILL	NOT GIVEN	55
37	DUNSTALL WILLIAM	SV	M	36	SHEPHERD	SSX BEXHILL	BEXHILL STREET	28
28	DURRANT THOMAS	SV	U	18		SSX PEASMARSH	PLOUGH INN	155
69	DYER ANN	WI	M	24		SSX BEXHILL	SIDLEY	84
49	DYER CHARLOTTE	DA	U	6		SSX BEXHILL	SIDLEY GREEN	82
69	DYER EDMOND	SO	U	2		SSX BEXHILL	SIDLEY	84
70	DYER ELIZA	DA	U	9	SCHOLAR	SSX BEXHILL	SIDLEY	84
70	DYER ELIZABETH	DA	U	6	SCHOLAR	SSX BEXHILL	SIDLEY	84
9	DYER ELIZABETH	WI	M	64		SSX BEXHILL	BIGGS HILL SIDLEY	76
49	DYER EMILY	DA	U	1		SSX BEXHILL	SIDLEY GREEN	82
69	DYER GEORGE	HD	M	26	AG.LAB	SSX BEXHILL	SIDLEY	84
69	DYER GEORGE	SO	U	7		SSX BEXHILL	SIDLEY	84
49	DYER JOHN	HD	M	43	AG.LAB	SSX BEXHILL	SIDLEY GREEN	82
9	DYER MICHAEL	HD	M	66	AG.LAB	SSX EASTBOURNE	BIGGS HILL SIDLEY	76
49	DYER ROSINA	DA	U	4		SSX BEXHILL	SIDLEY GREEN	82
70	DYER SARAH	WI	M	33		SSX BEXHILL	SIDLEY	84
49	DYER SARAH ANN	DA	U	9		SSX BEXHILL	SIDLEY GREEN	82
49	DYER SARAH ANN	WI	M	31		SSX BEXHILL	SIDLEY GREEN	82
70	DYER STEPHEN	HD	M	32	AG.LAB	SSX BEXHILL	SIDLEY	84
9	DYER THOMAS	SO	U	19	AG.LAB	SSX BEXHILL	BIGGS HILL SIDLEY	76
91	DYER WILLIAM	HD	W	70	AG.LAB	SSX EASTBOURNE	NOT GIVEN	100
70	DYER WILLIAM	SO	U	8	SCHOLAR	SSX BEXHILL	SIDLEY	84
55	DYKE THOMAS	LG	M	26	RAILWAY LAB	WIL FISHERTON WOESTBURN?	RAILWAY HUT	136
29	EARL ANN	WI	M	34		SSX SEAFORD	IN THE LIBERTY	41
29	EARL EDWARD	SO	U	4		SSX BEXHILL	IN THE LIBERTY	41
29	EARL ESTHER A	DA	U	10		SSX BEXHILL	IN THE LIBERTY	41
46	EARL GEORGE	SO	M	43		SSX BEXHILL	MOAT	167
56	EARL JAMES	LG	U	59	AG.LAB	SSX BEXHILL	VICTORIA INN	12
46	EARL JEMIMA	GD	U	13		SSX HOLLINGTON	MOAT	167
29	EARL JOHN B	SO	U	2		SSX BEXHILL	IN THE LIBERTY	41
46	EARL MAHALA	GD	U	15		SSX HOLLINGTON	MOAT	167
29	EARL OFFINGTON B	HD	M	36	COAST GUARD SERVICE	SSX SEAFORD	IN THE LIBERTY	41
29	EARL OFFINGTON B	SO	U	11	SCHOLAR	SSX BEXHILL	IN THE LIBERTY	41
46	EARL RACHEL	DL	M	39		SSX HOLLINGTON	MOAT	167
29	EARL WILLIAM J	SO	U	6	SCHOLAR	SSX BEXHILL	IN THE LIBERTY	41
74	EAST CHARLES	HD	M	38	BLACKSMITH JM	KEN MARDEN	STAPLE CROSS	242
74	EAST DEBORAH	DA	U	14		KEN GOUDHURST	STAPLE CROSS	242
74	EAST ELIZABETH	DA	U	3		SSX SALEHURST	STAPLE CROSS	242
74	EAST FRANCES	DA	U	18		KEN GOUDHURST	STAPLE CROSS	242
74	EAST MARY	WI	M	37		KEN GOUDHURST	STAPLE CROSS	242
74	EAST SARAH	DA	U	7		KEN GOUDHURST	STAPLE CROSS	242
46	EASTON ANN	VR	W	78		SSX WESTFIELD	HOLLINGTON STREET	11
71	EASTON ANN	WI	M	51		SSX WESTFIELD	DOWN	181
70	EASTON EDGAR	SL	M	31	AG.LAB	SSX WESTFIELD	DOWN	181
37	EASTON ELIZA	DA	U	3		SSX BEXHILL	COCKERELLS SIDLEY	80
45	EASTON ELIZA	SV	U	23		SSX WESTFIELD	BOWERS COTTAGE	178
81	EASTON ELIZABETH	CI	U	16		SSX WESTFIELD	BULLS EYE CORNER	182
20	EASTON ELIZABETH	NS	W	59		SSX HOLLINGTON	REDLEYS	174
20	EASTON ELIZABETH	WI	M	62?		SSX HOOE	SIDLEY	68
25	EASTON EMILY	NC	U	2		SSX BEXHILL	RANSOM'S HOUSE	145
71	EASTON FREDERICK	SO	U	13		SSX WESTFIELD	DOWN	181
112	EASTON GEORGE	HD	M	55	AG.LAB	SSX BEXHILL	NOT GIVEN	102
112	EASTON HANNAH	DA	U	10		SSX BEXHILL	NOT GIVEN	102
112	EASTON HANNAH	WI	M	53		SSX ASHBURNHAM	NOT GIVEN	102
37	EASTON HARRIET	DA	U	11	SCHOLAR	SSX BEXHILL	COCKERELLS SIDLEY	80
47	EASTON HARRIET	DA	U	15		SSX BEXHILL	NOT GIVEN	94
34	EASTON HENRY	SV	U	50	SERVANT	SSX NINFIELD	COURT LODGE FARM	147
44	EASTON JESSEE	HD	M	27	RAIL LAB	SSX BEXHILL	SIDLEY GREEN	81
37	EASTON JOHN	HD	M	39	AG.LAB	SSX BEXHILL	COCKERELLS SIDLEY	80
81	EASTON JOSEPH	BR	U	23	JM (GROCER & DRAPER)	SSX WESTFIELD	BULLS EYE CORNER	182
37	EASTON LOUISA	DA	U	11M		SSX BEXHILL	COCKERELLS SIDLEY	80
112	EASTON MARY	DA	U	13		SSX BEXHILL	NOT GIVEN	102
47	EASTON MARY	HD	W	52	PAUPER	KEN BIDDENDEN	NOT GIVEN	94
40	EASTON MARY	LG	U	35	DRESSMAKER	SSX BEXHILL	BRAGGS LANE	42
37	EASTON MARY ANN	DA	U	13		SSX BEXHILL	COCKERELLS SIDLEY	80
70	EASTON PHILADELPHIA	DA	M	40		SSX WESTFIELD	DOWN	181
43	EASTON RUBEN	LG	U	26	AG.LAB	SSX WESTFIELD	BROOKS	177
39	EASTON SAMUEL	LG	U	36	RAIL LAB	SSX BEXHILL	NOT GIVEN	56
37	EASTON SOPHIA	DA	U	6	SCHOLAR	SSX BEXHILL	COCKERELLS SIDLEY	80
44	EASTON SOPHIA	WI	M	21		SSX CATSFIELD	SIDLEY GREEN	81
37	EASTON SOPHIA	WI	M	37		SSX CROWHURST	COCKERELLS SIDLEY	80
71	EASTON STEPHEN	HD	M	58	BUTCHER	SSX NINFIELD	DOWN	181
81	EASTON STEPHEN	HD	W	29	GROCER & DRAPER	SSX WESTFIELD	BULLS EYE CORNER	182
37	EASTON STEPHEN	SO	U	9	SCHOLAR	SSX BEXHILL	COCKERELLS SIDLEY	80
47	EASTON SUSANNAH	DA	U	13		SSX BEXHILL	NOT GIVEN	94
20	EASTON WILLIAM	HD	M	67	AG.LAB	SSX BEXHILL	SIDLEY	68
44	EASTON WILLIAM	SO	U	2		SSX CATSFIELD	SIDLEY GREEN	81
47	EASTON WILLIAM	SO	U	18	AG.LAB	SSX BEXHILL	NOT GIVEN	94
42	EASTWOOD ALFRED	HD	M	36	AG.LAB	SSX BEXHILL	NOT GIVEN	56
71	EASTWOOD ALLIS	GD	U	10M		NOR LYNN	NOT GIVEN	97
71	EASTWOOD ANN	WI	M	50		SSX BEXHILL	NOT GIVEN	97

	Name	Rel	MS	Age	Occupation	Co.	Parish	Address	No.
40	EASTWOOD BENJAMIN	SO	U	5		SSX	BEXHILL	BRAGGS LANE	42
40	EASTWOOD CAROLINE	WI	M	32		SSX	BEXHILL	BRAGGS LANE	42
40	EASTWOOD EDMUND	HD	M	30	AG.LAB	SSX	BEXHILL	BRAGGS LANE	42
71	EASTWOOD ELIZABETH	DA	U	18		SSX	CROWHURST	NOT GIVEN	97
18	EASTWOOD ELIZABETH	WI	M	65		SSX	BEXHILL	NOT GIVEN	91
42	EASTWOOD ELLEN	DA	U	7		SSX	BEXHILL	NOT GIVEN	56
85	EASTWOOD FRANCES	WI	M	25		SSX	HERSTMONCEUX	NOT GIVEN	99
18	EASTWOOD FREDERICK	SO	U	32	AG.LAB	SSX	BEXHILL	NOT GIVEN	91
71	EASTWOOD GEORGE	HD	M	59	BLACKSMITH	SSX	BEXHILL	NOT GIVEN	97
42	EASTWOOD GEORGE	SO	U	5		SSX	BEXHILL	NOT GIVEN	56
85	EASTWOOD HARRIET	DA	U	1		SSX	BEXHILL	NOT GIVEN	99
6	EASTWOOD HENRY	SV	U	17	BAKER	SSX	BEXHILL	ROSE COTTAGE - SIDLEY	65
71	EASTWOOD JAMES	SO	M	26	SEAMAN	SSX	BEXHILL	NOT GIVEN	97
71	EASTWOOD JANE	DL	M	30		NOR	LYNN	NOT GIVEN	97
71	EASTWOOD JOSEPH	SO	U	10		SSX	BEXHILL	NOT GIVEN	97
71	EASTWOOD M A (FEMALE)	DA	U	30		SSX	BEXHILL	NOT GIVEN	97
42	EASTWOOD MARY	MO	W	67	FARMER'S WIDOW	SSX	HOOE	NOT GIVEN	56
42	EASTWOOD MARY	WI	M	31		SSX	BEXHILL	NOT GIVEN	56
30	EASTWOOD NAOMI	WI	M	20		SSX	BEXHILL	NOT GIVEN	92
30	EASTWOOD SOENCER	HD	M	34	BRICKMAKER	SSX	BEXHILL	NOT GIVEN	92
12	EASTWOOD SPENCER	SV	M	37	FARM LAB	SSX	MAYFIELD	BINES FARM	144
18	EASTWOOD THOMAS	HD	M	69	AG.LAB	SSX	BEXHILL	NOT GIVEN	91
42	EASTWOOD THOMAS	SO	U	9		SSX	BEXHILL	NOT GIVEN	56
30	EASTWOOD UN-NAMED INFANT GIRL	DA	U	3D		SSX	BEXHILL	NOT GIVEN	92
85	EASTWOOD WILLIAM	HD	M	30	RAIL LAB	SSX	ORE	NOT GIVEN	99
17	EATON THOMAS	HD	U	24	BLACKSMITH	SSX	GUESTLING	BELL VILLA	153
25	EDMONDS ALFRED	SO	U	16	AG.LAB	SSX	BECKLEY	ODIAM	219
31	EDMONDS ANN	DL	U	16		SSX	EWHURST	MADDAMS	220
4	EDMONDS ANN	WI	M	42?		SSX	BEXHILL	SIDLEY	65
25	EDMONDS CAROLINE	WI	M	49		SSX	BECKLEY	ODIAM	219
25	EDMONDS EDWARD	SO	U	12	AG.LAB	SSX	EWHURST	ODIAM	219
25	EDMONDS FRANCES	DA	U	7	SCHOLAR	SSX	EWHURST	ODIAM	219
4	EDMONDS GEORGE	HD	M	42	WHEELWRIGHT MASTER EMP 1	SSX	BEXHILL	SIDLEY	65
65	EDMONDS GEORGE	LG	W	70	WHEELWRIGHT	SSX	WARTLING	SIDLEY GREEN	84
14	EDMONDS GEORGE	SO	U	4	SCHOLAR	SSX	BEXHILL	NOT GIVEN	90
14	EDMONDS HARRIET	WI	M	33		SSX	BEXHILL	NOT GIVEN	90
14	EDMONDS JAMES	HD	M	31	WHEELWRIGHT	SSX	BEXHILL	NOT GIVEN	90
25	EDMONDS JAMES	SO	U	14	AG.LAB	SSX	EWHURST	ODIAM	219
25	EDMONDS JANE	GD	U	7	SCHOLAR	SSX	EWHURST	ODIAM	219
25	EDMONDS JOHN	HD	M	48	AG.LAB	SSX	PEASMARSH	ODIAM	219
31	EDMONDS JOHN	SL	U	14	AG.LAB	SSX	EWHURST	MADDAMS	220
14	EDMONDS M A (FEMALE)	DA	U	2		SSX	BEXHILL	NOT GIVEN	90
14	EDMONDS THOMAS	SO	U	2M		SSX	BEXHILL	NOT GIVEN	90
14	EDMONDS WILLIAM	SO	U	6	SCHOLAR	SSX	BEXHILL	NOT GIVEN	90
25	EDMONDS WILLIAM	SO	U	10	SCHOLAR	SSX	EWHURST	ODIAM	219
20	EDWARDS EDGAR	SO	M	30	AG.LAB	SSX	WESTFIELD	SEDLESCOMBE STREET	189
66	EDWARDS GEORGE	LG	U	22	GROCER & DRAPER	KEN	NEWENDEN	EWHURST GREEN	225
20	EDWARDS SOPHIA	HD	U	56	INFIRM PARISH RELIEF	SSX	SEDLESCOMBE	SEDLESCOMBE STREET	189
57	ELDRIDGE AARON	HD	M	41	CARPENTER JM	SSX	SEDLESCOMBE	SEDLESCOMBE STREET	195
57	ELDRIDGE AARON	SO	U	14	SCHOLAR	SSX	SEDLESCOMBE	SEDLESCOMBE STREET	195
77	ELDRIDGE ABIGAIL	DA	U	9	SCHOLAR	SSX	EWHURST	EWHURST GREEN	227
10	ELDRIDGE ALBERT	GS	U	12	SCHOLAR	SSX	BATTLE	ALLENHALL LANE	250
19	ELDRIDGE ALBERT	SO	U	2		SSX	SEDLESCOMBE	SEDLESCOMBE STREET	203
14	ELDRIDGE ALFRED	SO	U	1		SSX	HOLLINGTON	MAYFIELDS HOUSE	6
19	ELDRIDGE ALFRED	SO	U	13	BAKER'S BOY	SSX	WHATLINGTON	SEDLESCOMBE STREET	203
65	ELDRIDGE ALICE	DA	U	6		SSX	SEDLESCOMBE	SEDLESCOMBE STREET	197
54	ELDRIDGE ALICE	VR	U	6M		SSX	ST.MARY IN THE CASTLE	LODGE	179
11	ELDRIDGE ANN	SV	U	21	HOUSE MAID	SSX	BATTLE	WILTING FARM HOUSE	6
57	ELDRIDGE ANN MARIA	WI	M	46		KEN	BENENDEN	SEDLESCOMBE STREET	195
32	ELDRIDGE BETSY	LG	W	64		SSX	BATTLE	STONE HOUSE	9
72	ELDRIDGE CAROLINE S	VR	U	22		SSX	BATTLE	GLOVERS FARM SIDLEY	85
65	ELDRIDGE CATHERINE	DA	U	2		SSX	SEDLESCOMBE	SEDLESCOMBE STREET	197
1	ELDRIDGE CHARLES	SO	U	17	EMPLOYED BY FATHER	SSX	CROWHURST	POWDERMILLS	128
19	ELDRIDGE CHARLOTTE	DA	U	7	SCHOLAR	SSX	WHATLINGTON	SEDLESCOMBE STREET	203
1	ELDRIDGE CHARLOTTE	DA	U	20		SSX	CROWHURST	POWDERMILLS	128
49	ELDRIDGE CHARLOTTE	HD	W	30	PARISH RELIEF AG.LAB'S WI	SSX	WESTFIELD	SWALES GREEN	193
36	ELDRIDGE CHARLOTTE	SV	U	12	HOUSE SERVANT	SSX	SEDLESCOMBE	HERST	191
14	ELDRIDGE CHARLOTTE ANN	DA	U	4		SSX	HOLLINGTON	MAYFIELDS HOUSE	6
77	ELDRIDGE EDGAR	SO	U	3		SSX	EWHURST	EWHURST GREEN	227
60	ELDRIDGE EDGAR ALBERT	SO	U	1		SSX	EWHURST	SNAGS HALL	224
50	ELDRIDGE EDWARD	SO	U	1		SSX	SEDLESCOMBE	COMPASSES	193
65	ELDRIDGE EDWIN	SO	U	9	SCHOLAR	SSX	SEDLESCOMBE	SEDLSECOMBE STREET	197
62	ELDRIDGE ELEAZER	SO	U	4		SSX	EWHURST	STAPLE CROSS	240
62	ELDRIDGE ELIJAH	SO	U	15	AG.LAB	SSX	EWHURST	STAPLE CROSS	240
2	ELDRIDGE ELIZA	DA	U	9		SSX	SEDLESCOMBE	SEDLESCOMBE STREET	186
50	ELDRIDGE ELIZABETH	DA	U	6	SCHOLAR	SSX	SEDLESCOMBE	COMPASSES	193
19	ELDRIDGE ELIZABETH	DA	U	9	SCHOLAR	SSX	WHATLINGTON	SEDLESCOMBE STREET	203
10	ELDRIDGE ELIZABETH	DL	M	38		KEN	LINTON	ALLENHALL LANE	250
19	ELDRIDGE ELIZABETH	WI	M	41		SSX	WESTFIELD	SEDLESCOMBE STREET	203
28	ELDRIDGE ELIZABETH MARIA	DA	U	8		MDX	ISLINGTON	ADAMS LANE	236
31	ELDRIDGE ELLEN	/	U	8	NURSE CHILD	SSX	ST.LEONARDS	DOG KENNELL	9
77	ELDRIDGE ELLEN	DA	U	11	SCHOLAR	SSX	EWHURST	EWHURST GREEN	226
57	ELDRIDGE EMILY ANN	DA	U	16		SSX	SEDLESCOMBE	SEDLESCOMBE STREET	195
65	ELDRIDGE FANNY	DA	U	7	SCHOLAR	SSX	SEDLESCOMBE	SEDLESCOMBE STREET	197
10	ELDRIDGE GEORGE	GS	U	5		SSX	BATTLE	ALLENHALL LANE	250
77	ELDRIDGE GEORGE	SO	U	5	SCHOLAR	SSX	EWHURST	EWHURST GREEN	227

	Name		Rel	St	Age	Occupation	County	Parish	Address	Folio
14	ELDRIDGE	GEORGE	SO	U	8		SSX	HOLLINGTON	MAYFIELDS HOUSE	6
49	ELDRIDGE	GEORGE	SO	U	10	SCHOLAR	SSX	SEDLESCOMBE	SWALES GREEN	193
50	ELDRIDGE	HARRIETT	DA	U	7	SCHOLAR	SSX	SEDLESCOMBE	COMPASSES	193
2	ELDRIDGE	HARRIETT	DA	U	11		SSX	SEDLESCOMBE	SEDLESCOMBE STREET	186
65	ELDRIDGE	HARRIETT	WI	M	40		SSX	EWHURST	SEDLESCOMBE STREET	197
2	ELDRIDGE	HENRY	HD	M	40	AG.LAB	SSX	SEDLESCOMBE	SEDLESCOMBE STREET	186
20	ELDRIDGE	HENRY	SO	U	6M		SSX	CROWHURST	CROWHURST VILLAGE	131
2	ELDRIDGE	HENRY	SO	U	5	SCHOLAR	SSX	SEDLESCOMBE	SEDLESCOMBE STREET	186
62	ELDRIDGE	HENRY	SO	U	6		SSX	EWHURST	STAPLE CROSS	240
20	ELDRIDGE	ISAAC	SO	U	1		SSX	CROWHURST	CROWHURST VILLAGE	131
20	ELDRIDGE	JAMES	HD	M	27	POWDER MAKER	SSX	CROWHURST	CROWHURST VILLAGE	131
26	ELDRIDGE	JAMES	HD	M	55	AG.LAB	SSX	BATTLE	BRICKWALL	189
9	ELDRIDGE	JAMES	HD	M	68	FARMER	SSX	ETCHINGHAM	COLLIERS GREEN	233
49	ELDRIDGE	JAMES	SO	U	2		SSX	SEDLESCOMBE	SWALES GREEN	193
62	ELDRIDGE	JAMES	SO	U	8		SSX	EWHURST	STAPLE CROSS	240
14	ELDRIDGE	JAMES	SO	U	13		SSX	HOLLINGTON	MAYFIELDS HOUSE	6
77	ELDRIDGE	JAMES	SO	U	13	AG.LAB	SSX	EWHURST	EWHURST GREEN	226
4	ELDRIDGE	JAMES	SV	U	23	AG.LAB	NOT GIVEN (?WESTFIELD)		PADDLESTONS	152
2	ELDRIDGE	JANE	DA	U	2		SSX	SEDLESCOMBE	SEDLESCOMBE STREET	186
26	ELDRIDGE	JANE	DA	U	9	SCHOLAR	SSX	SEDLESCOMBE	BRICKWALL	189
50	ELDRIDGE	JANE	DA	U	10		SSX	SEDLESCOMBE	COMPASSES	193
77	ELDRIDGE	JANE	DA	U	16	SERVANT	SSX	EWHURST	EWHURST GREEN	226
9	ELDRIDGE	JANE	WI	M	80		SSX	WESTFIELD	COLLIERS GREEN	233
60	ELDRIDGE	JANE LAURA	DA	U	8	SCHOLAR	SSX	EWHURST	SNAGS HALL	224
62	ELDRIDGE	JESSE	SO	U	13	AG.LAB	SSX	EWHURST	STAPLE CROSS	240
50	ELDRIDGE	JOHN	HD	M	41	AG.LAB	SSX	CATSFIELD	COMPASSES	193
28	ELDRIDGE	JOHN	SO	U	3		SSX	EWHURST	ADAMS LANE	236
19	ELDRIDGE	JOHN	SO	U	11		SSX	WHATLINGTON	SEDLESCOMBE STREET	203
50	ELDRIDGE	JOHN	SO	U	14	AG.LAB	SSX	SEDLESCOMBE	COMPASSES	193
77	ELDRIDGE	JOHN	SO	U	21	AG.LAB	SSX	EWHURST	EWHURST GREEN	226
10	ELDRIDGE	JOHN HENRY	SO	M	38	CARPENTER	SSX	SEDLESCOMBE	ALLENHALL LANE	250
65	ELDRIDGE	JOSEPH	HD	M	42	CARPENTER MASTER EMP 16	SSX	SEDLESCOMBE	SEDLESCOMBE STREET	197
65	ELDRIDGE	JOSEPH	SO	U	15	CARPENTER AP	SSX	SEDLESCOMBE	SEDLESCOMBE STREET	197
60	ELDRIDGE	LOIS	HD	U	30	DRESSMAKER	SSX	EWHURST	SNAGS HALL	224
28	ELDRIDGE	MARGARET	DA	U	15		SSX	EWHURST	ADAMS LANE	236
28	ELDRIDGE	MARIA	WI	M	40		KEN	ROLVENDEN	ADAMS LANE	236
77	ELDRIDGE	MARIA	WI	M	43		SSX	SALEHURST	EWHURST GREEN	226
65	ELDRIDGE	MARY	DA	U	11M		SSX	SEDLESCOMBE	SEDLESCOMBE STREET	197
50	ELDRIDGE	MARY	DA	U	4		SSX	SEDLESCOMBE	COMPASSES	193
20	ELDRIDGE	MARY	WI	M	23		SSX	BEXHILL	CROWHURST VILLAGE	131
2	ELDRIDGE	MARY	WI	M	34		SSX	WHATLINGTON	SEDLESCOMBE STREET	186
62	ELDRIDGE	MARY	WI	M	40		SSX	EWHURST	STAPLE CROSS	240
26	ELDRIDGE	MARY	WI	M	46		SSX	SEDLESCOMBE	BRICKWALL	189
14	ELDRIDGE	MARY ANN	DA	U	6		SSX	HOLLINGTON	MAYFIELDS HOUSE	6
22	ELDRIDGE	MARY HESTER?	SV	U	15	HOUSE SERVANT	SSX	SEDLESCOMBE	SEDLESCOMBE STREET	189
1	ELDRIDGE	PHILLIS	WI	M	56		SSX	ASHBURNHAM	POWDERMILLS	128
10	ELDRIDGE	REBACCA	WI	M	67		KEN	STAPLEHURST	ALLENHALL LANE	250
10	ELDRIDGE	RICHARD	HD	M	64	CARPENTER	SSX	SEDLESCOMBE	ALLENHALL LANE	250
14	ELDRIDGE	SAMUEL	HD	M	42	AG.LAB	SSX	BATTLE	MAYFIELDS HOUSE	6
28	ELDRIDGE	SAMUEL	HD	M	56	BRICKLAYER EMP 2MEN	SSX	EWHURST	ADAMS LANE	236
14	ELDRIDGE	SAMUEL	SO	U	11		SSX	HOLLINGTON	MAYFIELDS HOUSE	6
28	ELDRIDGE	SAMUEL	SO	U	22	BRICKLAYER	SSX	EWHURST	ADAMS LANE	236
28	ELDRIDGE	SARAH	DA	U	17		SSX	EWHURST	ADAMS LANE	236
62	ELDRIDGE	SARAH	DA	U	18		SSX	EWHURST	STAPLE CROSS	240
77	ELDRIDGE	SARAH	DA	U	18	SERVANT	SSX	EWHURST	EWHURST GREEN	226
71	ELDRIDGE	SARAH	SV	U	13	HOUSE SERVANT	SSX	BATTLE	WOODS FARM SIDLEY	85
14	ELDRIDGE	SARAH	WI	M	40		KEN	APPLEDORE	MAYFIELDS HOUSE	6
50	ELDRIDGE	SARAH	WI	M	40		SSX	SEDLESCOMBE	COMPASSES	193
65	ELDRIDGE	SOPHIA	DA	U	13	SCHOLAR	SSX	SEDLESCOMBE	SEDLESCOMBE STREET	197
54	ELDRIDGE	SOPHIA	VR	U	19		SSX	BATTLE	LODGE	179
62	ELDRIDGE	THOMAS	HD	M	40	TIMBER HEWER	SSX	EWHURST	STAPLE CROSS	240
77	ELDRIDGE	THOMAS	HD	M	44	AG.LAB	SSX	EWHURST	EWHURST GREEN	226
62	ELDRIDGE	THOMAS	SO	U	10		SSX	EWHURST	STAPLE CROSS	240
19	ELDRIDGE	THOMAS	SO	U	17	BRICKLAYER'S LAB	SSX	EWHURST	SEDLESCOMBE STREET	203
21	ELDRIDGE	THOMAS	WS	U	13		SSX	EWHURST	CRIPPS	252
1	ELDRIDGE	TILDEN	GS	U	4		SSX	CROWHURST	POWDERMILLS	128
2	ELDRIDGE	WALTER	GS	U	3		SSX	CROWHURST	PLOUGH INN	142
19	ELDRIDGE	WILLIAM	HD	M	44	CARPENTER	SSX	SEDLESCOMBE	SEDLESCOMBE STREET	203
1	ELDRIDGE	WILLIAM	HD	M	63	POWDER MANUFACTURER	SSX	BATTLE	POWDERMILLS	128
20	ELDRIDGE	WILLIAM	NP	M	16	APPRENTICE BUILDER	SSX	SEDLESCOMBE	SEDLESCOMBE STREET	203
2	ELDRIDGE	WILLIAM	SO	U	3		SSX	SEDLESCOMBE	SEDLESCOMBE STREET	186
77	ELDRIDGE	WILLIAM	SO	U	7	SCHOLAR	SSX	EWHURST	EWHURST GREEN	227
65	ELDRIDGE	WILLIAM	SO	U	11	SCHOLAR	SSX	SEDLESCOMBE	SEDLESCOMBE STREET	197
50	ELDRIDGE	WILLIAM	SO	U	13	AG.LAB	SSX	SEDLESCOMBE	COMPASSES	193
49	ELDRIDGE	WILLIAM	SO	U	13	AG.LAB	SSX	WESTFIELD	SWALES GREEN	193
14	ELDRIDGE	WILLIAM	SO	U	16	AG.LAB	SSX	HOLLINGTON	MAYFIELDS HOUSE	6
19	ELDRIDGE	WILLIAM	SV	U	22	BRICK MAKER'S LAB	SSX	BATTLE	SIDLEY	77
57	ELDRIDGE	WILLIAM HENRY	SO	U	18	CARPENTER AP	SSX	SEDLESCOMBE	SEDLESCOMBE STREET	195
54	ELDRIDGES	THOMAS	SV	U	23	FARM LAB	SSX	WHATLINGTON	CASTLEMANS	195
58	ELEMES	JABES	HD	M	35	RAILWAY LAB	NTH	ASHTON	RAILWAY COTTAGE	30
58	ELEMES	MARIA	WI	M	30		NTH	ASHTON	RAILWAY COTTAGE	30
48	ELLIOT	ALFRED	HD	M	40	GROCER	SSX	HOOE	LITTLE COMMON	57
48	ELLIOT	ANNE	DA	U	11M		SSX	BEXHILL	LITTLE COMMON	57
48	ELLIOT	MARTHA	DA	U	4	SCHOLAR	SSX	BEXHILL	LITTLE COMMON	57
48	ELLIOT	MARTHA	MO	W	74	GARDENER'S WIDOW	SSX	BURWASH	LITTLE COMMON	57
48	ELLIOT	MARY	DA	U	6	SCHOLAR	SSX	BEXHILL	LITTLE COMMON	57

No.	Name	Rel	St	Age	Occupation	County	Birthplace	Address	Page
48	ELLIOT SARAH ANN	WI	M	36		SSX	BEXHILL	LITTLE COMMON	57
22	ELLIOTT RICHARD	SV	U	18	GROCER'S SHOPMAN	KEN	TUNBRIDGE	SEDLESCOMBE STREET	189
52	ELLTON? JAMES (BLOTTED)	LG	U	22	RAILWAY LAB	SAL		RAILWAY HUT	135
21	ELPHICK ANN	DA	U	1		SSX	BEXHILL	NOT GIVEN	54
17	ELPHICK CAROLINE	WI	M	33		SSX	BEXHILL	GREAT WORSHAM SIDLEY	77
21	ELPHICK ELIZABETH	MO	/	52		SSX	NINFIELD	NOT GIVEN	54
24	ELPHICK EMILY	WI	M	30		SSX	EWHURST	ODIAM	219
21	ELPHICK ESTHER	WI	M	21		SSX	CATSFIELD	NOT GIVEN	54
21	ELPHICK GEORGE	HD	M	30	AG.LAB	SSX	HOOE	NOT GIVEN	54
24	ELPHICK GEORGE	SO	U	1		SSX	EWHURST	ODIAM	219
17	ELPHICK JAMES	HD	M	32	AG.LAB	SSX	BEXHILL	GREAT WORSHAM SIDLEY	77
26	ELPHICK JOHN	HD	W	63	AG.LAB	SSX	HERSTMONCEUX	SIDLEY	78
26	ELPHICK MARY	GD	U	14	HOUSEKEEPER	SSX	BEXHILL	SIDLEY	78
24	ELPHICK THOMAS	HD	M	30	AG.LAB	SSX	EWHURST	ODIAM	219
21	ELPHICK UN-NAMED BOY	SO	U	2W		SSX	BEXHILL	NOT GIVEN	54
63	ELTON ANN ROSITA	WI	M	41		HAM	NEW ALRESFORD	RAILWAY HUT	136
63	ELTON ELIZA JANE	DA	U	11	SCHOLAR	SSX	BRIGHTON	RAILWAY HUT	137
63	ELTON FREDERICK	HD	M	41	HORSE KEEPER ON LINE		WABLAVINGTON	RAILWAY HUT	136
63	ELTON FREDERICK	SO	U	15			WABLAVINGTON	RAILWAY HUT	137
63	ELTON HARRIOT ROSITA	DA	U	14	SCHOLAR		PERBRIGHT	RAILWAY HUT	137
63	ELTON LAWES ANN	DA	U	6		WOR		RAILWAY HUT	137
63	ELTON SARAH MARIA	DA	U	9	SCHOLAR	LND		RAILWAY HUT	137
63	ELTON WILLIAM	SO	U	19			WABLAVINGTON	RAILWAY HUT	136
58	ENGLISH GEORGE	SV	W	67	AG.LAB	SSX	CROWHURST	HOLLINGTON LODGE	13
58	ENGLISH GEORGE	VR	M	44	WHITESMITH	SSX	HOLLINGTON	HOLLINGTON LODGE	13
38	ENGLISH JOHN	SV	U	21	AG.LAB	SSX	HOLLINGTON	BUCKLANDS	10
32	ERREY AMOS	SO	U	2		SSX	NINFIELD	LUNSFORDS LANE SIDLEY	70
32	ERREY ANN	DA	U	8M		SSX	BEXHILL	LUNSFORDS LANE SIDLEY	70
32	ERREY ANN	WI	M	27		SSX	BEXHILL	LUNSFORDS LANE SIDLEY	70
32	ERREY EDWARD	HD	M	26	AG.LAB	SSX	WARBLETON	LUNSFORDS LANE SIDLEY	70
29	ERREY EDWARD G	SO	U	1		KEN	HAWKHURST	SIDLEY	70
29	ERREY JAMES	SO	U	1		SSX	BEXHILL	COOMBS SIDLEY	79
29	ERREY JOSEPH	SO	U	6		SSX	BEXHILL	COOMBS SIDLEY	79
29	ERREY MARY	WI	M	29		SSX	BEXHILL	COOMBS SIDLEY	79
29	ERREY MARY A	DA	U	2		KEN	HAWKHURST	SIDLEY	70
29	ERREY MARY ANN	DA	U	3		SSX	BEXHILL	COOMBS SIDLEY	79
29	ERREY RICHARD	HD	M	28	BLACKSMITH	SSX	WARBLETON	SIDLEY	70
29	ERREY THOMAS	HD	M	30	AG.LAB	SSX	WALBERTON	COOMBS SIDLEY	79
28	ERREY THOMAS	SO	U	7		SSX	BEXHILL	COOMBS SIDLEY	79
29	ERREY TRYPHENA	WI	M	23		KEN	TUNBRIDGE	SIDLEY	70
29	ERREY UN-NAMED BOY	SO	U	1M		SSX	BEXHILL	COOMBS SIDLEY	79
32	ERREY WILLIAM	SO	U	6		SSX	BEXHILL	LUNSFORDS LANE SIDLEY	70
57	EVENDEN CAROLINE	DA	U	9		SSX	HOLLINGTON	HOLLINGTON STREET	12
57	EVENDEN CHARLES	SO	U	7M		SSX	HOLLINGTON	HOLLINGTON STREET	12
18	EVENDEN EDWARD	HD	M	66	WHEELWRIGHT EMP 2	SSX	CATSFIELD	STEPHEN'S CROUCH	121
18	EVENDEN EDWARD	SO	U	22	WHEELWRIGHT	SSX	BATTLE	STEPHEN'S CROUCH	121
57	EVENDEN ELIZA	DA	U	15		SSX	ST.LEONARDS	HOLLINGTON STREET	12
57	EVENDEN FANNY	DA	U	11		SSX	ST.LEONARDS	HOLLINGTON STREET	12
57	EVENDEN GEORGE	SO	U	7		SSX	HOLLINGTON	HOLLINGTON STREET	12
18	EVENDEN HANNAH	WI	M	56		SSX	HERSTMONCEUX	STEPHEN'S CROUCH	121
18	EVENDEN HERBERT	SO	U	13	SCHOLAR	SSX	BATTLE	STEPHEN'S CROUCH	121
18	EVENDEN JAMES	LG	Y	55	AG.LAB	SSX	WINCHELSEA	BUCKHURST	164
57	EVENDEN JAMES	SO	U	16		SSX	WHATLINGTON	HOLLINGTON STREET	12
57	EVENDEN JOHN	HD	M	58	GROCER	SSX	ORE	HOLLINGTON STREET	12
57	EVENDEN JULIA	WI	M	45		SSX	WESTFIELD	HOLLINGTON STREET	12
57	EVENDEN RACHEL ANN	DA	U	5		SSX	HOLLINGTON	HOLLINGTON STREET	12
57	EVENDEN SARAH	DA	U	3		SSX	HOLLINGTON	HOLLINGTON STREET	12
10	EVENDEN WILLIAM	LG	U	21	RAILWAY LAB	MDI		FORWARD LANE	129
18	EVENDEN WILLIAM	SO	U	28	WHEELWRIGHT	SSX	HERSTMONCEUX	STEPHEN'S CROUCH	121
52	EVENS THOMAS	LG	U	30	RAILWAY LAB	HAM		RAILWAY HUT	135
29	EVERES ELIZA	GD	U	4		SSX	BATTLE	GREEN STREET	132
35	EWENS MAY	WI	M	51		SSX	BURWASH	NOT GIVEN	124
35	EWENS RICHARD	HD	M	46	GENERAL DEALER	SSX	HAILSHAM	NOT GIVEN	124
11	FAIRALL ELIZABETH	DA	U	13		SSX	WESTFIELD	YEW TREE	163
14	FAIRALL ELIZABETH	WI	M	51		SSX	WESTFIELD	RIVER HALL	163
11	FAIRALL HARRIETT	HD	W	34	PAUPER	SSX	BATTLE	YEW TREE	163
11	FAIRALL PHILADELPHIA	DA	U	7	SCHOLAR	SSX	WESTFIELD	RIVER HALL	163
14	FAIRALL SAMUEL	HD	M	56	AG.LAB	SSX	WESTFIELD	YEW TREE	163
11	FAIRALL WILLIAM	SO	U	5	SCHOLAR	SSX	BECKLEY	NEWHAVEN FARM	237
37	FAIRHALL MARTHA	SV	U	13		SSX	HASTINGS	STRAWBERRY BANK	45
65	FAREY MARY	ML	M	71	PAUPER AG.LAB	KEN	ASH	STRAWBERRY BANK	45
65	FAREY SACKET	FL	M	73	PAUPER AG.LAB	SSX	BEXHILL	(BARNHORN HILL?)	37
4	FARMER ALFRED	HD	M	31	AG.LAB	SSX	BEXHILL	SIDLEY	78
25	FARMER CAROLINE	WI	M	39		SSX	BEXHILL	(BARNHORN HILL?)	37
4	FARMER EDWARD	SO	U	3		SSX	BEXHILL	SIDLEY	78
25	FARMER GEORGE	SO	U	15	AG.LAB	SSX	BEXHILL	(BARNHORN HILL?)	37
4	FARMER HARRIETT	DA	U	2		SSX	BEXHILL	NOT GIVEN	53
16	FARMER HARRIOT	DA	U	18	HOUSE SERVANT	SSX	PENHURST	NOT GIVEN	53
16	FARMER JOHN	HD	W	61	AG.LAB	SSX	BEXHILL	SIDLEY	78
25	FARMER LUCY ANN	DA	U	18		SSX	BEXHILL	NOT GIVEN	53
16	FARMER MARY	DA	U	28	HOUSE SERVANT	SSX	RYE	(BARNHORN HILL?)	37
4	FARMER MARY	WI	M	36		SSX	BEXHILL	SIDLEY	78
25	FARMER WILLIAM	HD	M	40	AG.LAB	SSX	BEXHILL	(BARNHORN HILL?)	37
4	FARMER WILLIAM	SO	U	2M		UNKNOWN		NOT GIVEN	96
65	FARN A B (MALE)	PP	U	10	PUPIL	SSX	BRIGHTON	CHURCH STREET	99
81	FARNCOMB GEORGE	GS	U	8	SCHOLAR				

#	Name	Code	St	Age	Occupation	County	Birthplace	Residence	Pg
1	FARNCOMB GEORGE	HD	M	27	RAILROAD LAB	SSX	PYECOMB	RAILWAY HUT	4
87	FARNCOMB JANE	WI	M	36	SCHOOLMISTRESS	WAR	FOLESHILL	STAPLE CROSS	243
1	FARNCOMB MARY	DA	U	6M			NOT GIVEN	RAILWAY HUT	4
1	FARNCOMB MARY	WI	M	22			NOT GIVEN	RAILWAY HUT	4
87	FARNCOMB WILLIAM	HD	M	36	SCHOOLMASTER	WAR	FOLESHILL	STAPLE CROSS	243
52	FARRANCE CORDELIA	WI	M	46		SSX	EWHURST	STOCKWOOD FARM	239
52	FARRANCE JAMES	HD	M	43	FARMER 160 AC 5 LAB	SSX	ETCHINGHAM	STOCKWOOD FARM	239
32	FAVERD SARAH	SV	U	20	SERVANT	SSX	NINFIELD	FARM HOUSE	133
19	FEARS GEORGE	SV	U	21	AG.LAB	SSX	HAILSHAM	NOT GIVEN	53
19	FELLEY JOHN	LG	U	34	RAILWAY LAB	SRY	FRIMLEY	CROWHURST VILLAGE	131
57	FELLICKE HARRIOTT	WI	M	28		IOW	KYDE?	RAILWAY HUT	136
57	FELLICKE HENRY	HD	M	33	WAGGONER ON THE LINE	IOW	NEWPORT?	RAILWAY HUT	136
32	FIELD DRICILLA	DA	U	2		SSX	WILLINGDON	SIDLEY	79
32	FIELD ESTHER	DA	U	9M		SSX	BEXHILL	SIDLEY	79
32	FIELD SARAH	DA	U	5		SSX	MAYFIELD	SIDLEY	79
32	FIELD SILVA JONES	WI	M	28		SSX	ROTHERFIELD	SIDLEY	79
32	FIELD THOMAS	HD	M	30	AG.LAB	SSX	MAYFIELD	SIDLEY	79
31	FIELD THOMAS	SV	W	68	AG.LAB	SSX	MAYFIELD	BUCKHOLT SIDLEY	79
80	FIELDER DUGLAS	SO	U	14	AG.LAB/SARAH MEPHAM'S SO?	SSX	BECKLEY	EWHURST GREEN	227
80	FIELDER WILLIAM	SO	U	10	SCHOLAR/SARAH MEPHAM'S SO?	SSX	BREDE	EWHURST GREEN	227
52	FILDER FRANCOISE	WI	M	37		FRANCE	BRITISH SUBJECT	PAGES COTTAGE	44
52	FILDER JAMES M	HD	M	38	OCCUPIER 119 AC EMP 23	SSX		PAGES COTTAGE	44
7	FIRBY FANNY	HD	U	63	PAUPER	SSX	BEXHILL	BELL HILL	24
29	FIRMINGER AGNES F	DA	U	8M		SSX	WESTFIELD	KENT STREET	165
29	FIRMINGER ANN M	WI	M	29		SSX	BREDE	KENT STREET	165
29	FIRMINGER HARRIETT	DA	U	9		SSX	BREDE	KENT STREET	165
29	FIRMINGER SARAH A	DA	U	6		SSX	BREDE	KENT STREET	165
29	FIRMINGER THOMAS	HD	M	35	AG.LAB	SSX	BREDE	KENT STREET	165
29	FIRMINGER THOMAS E	SO	U	3		SSX	BREDE	KENT STREET	165
71	FISHER CHARLOTTE	DA	U	25		SSX	EWHURST	STAPLE CROSS	242
71	FISHER CHARLOTTE	WI	M	63?		SSX	EWHURST	STAPLE CROSS	241
71	FISHER EDWARD	HD	M	63	AG.LAB	SSX	EWHURST	STAPLE CROSS	241
71	FISHER EDWARD	SO	U	28	AG.LAB	SSX	EWHURST	STAPLE CROSS	241
5	FISHER ELIJAH	SO	U	23		SSX	EWHURST	MILISES	250
23	FISHER ELLEN	SV	U	20	SERVANT COOK	SSX	EWHURST	LORDINE	235
71	FISHER JOHN	SO	U	14	AG.LAB	SSX	EWHURST	STAPLE CROSS	242
5	FISHER JOSHUA	SO	U	20		SSX	EWHURST	MILISES	250
23	FISHER MARTHA	SV	U	15	NURSERY MAID	SSX	EWHURST	LORDINE	235
5	FISHER MARY ANN	GD	U	4		SSX	EWHURST	MILISES	250
71	FISHER PHILLIP	SO	U	18	AG.LAB	SSX	EWHURST	STAPLE CROSS	242
5	FISHER ROBERT	HD	W	55	CARRIER/FARMER 22AC EMP 3	SSX	EWHURST	MILISES	250
71	FISHER ROBERT	SO	U	10	SCHOLAR	SSX	EWHURST	STAPLE CROSS	241
5	FISHER STEPHEN	SO	U	27		SSX	EWHURST	MILISES	250
5	FISHER THOMAS	GS	U	10	SCHOLAR	SSX	EWHURST	MILISES	250
71	FISHER WILLIAM	SO	U	22	AG.LAB	SSX	EWHURST	STAPLE CROSS	242
41	FLEMING FANNY	DA	U	6		SSX	BEXHILL	BEXHILL STREET	28
41	FLEMMING CHARLES	SO	U	9		SSX	BEXHILL	BEXHILL STREET	28
41	FLEMMING HARRIOTT	DA	U	12		SSX	BEXHILL	BEXHILL STREET	28
41	FLEMMING HENRY	SO	U	17		SSX	BEXHILL	BEXHILL STREET	28
41	FLEMMING JANE	DA	U	19		SSX	BEXHILL	BEXHILL STREET	28
41	FLEMMING JOHN	HD	W	55	BOOKBINDER	SSX	BURWASH	BEXHILL STREET	28
41	FLEMMING SARAH	DA	U	15		SSX	BEXHILL	BEXHILL STREET	28
42	FOLLINGTON SPENCER	VR	M	25	SHOESMITH	SSX	HELLINGLY	FORGE LANE	254
18	FOORD CHARLOTTE	LW	M	44?		SSX	BEXHILL	SEDLESCOMBE STREET	203
38	FOORD GEORGE	HD	M	39	BRICKMAKER	SSX	FRANTFIELD	RAILWAY HUT	133
22	FOORD GEORGE	LG	U	32	AG.LAB	SSX	BEXHILL	LAND MARES? - SIDLEY	68
34	FOORD GEORGE	SV	U	21	SERVANT	SSX	NINFIELD	COURT LODGE FARM	147
23	FOORD HANNAH	/	U	1	NURSE CHILD	SSX	NINFIELD	RANSOM'S HOUSE	145
50	FOORD HENRY	HD	M	53	RAILWAY LAB	SSX		RAILWAY HUT	135
13	FOORD JOHN	HD	M	68	AG.LAB	SSX	NINFIELD	NOT GIVEN	90
9	FOORD JUDITH	HD	W	78	FORMERLY LAB'S WIFE	SSX	DALLINGTON	NOT GIVEN	52
7	FOORD MARY	HD	U	26	DRESSMAKER	SSX	FAIRLIGHT	OAK COTTAGE	152
38	FOORD MARY ANN	WI	M	40		KEN	TENTERDEN	RAILWAY HUT	133
13	FOORD PHILADELPHIA	WI	M	68		SSX	SEDLESCOMBE	NOT GIVEN	90
50	FOORD PHILLADELPHIA	WI	M	53		SSX	FRANTFORD	RAILWAY HUT	135
18	FOORD THOMAS	LG	M	42	RAIL LAB	SSX	BATTLE	SEDLESCOMBE STREET	203
18	FOORD THOMAS RICHARD	LS	U	12		SSX	BEXHILL	SEDLESCOMBE STREET	203
24	FOOTS ANN	HD	W	64	PAUPER	SFK	ICKSWORTH	NOT GIVEN	92
20	FORD CHARLES	HD	M	42	AG.LAB	SSX	NINFIELD	BURNT BARNS	122
20	FORD HARIOT	WI	M	46?		SSX	BATTLE	BURNT BARNS	122
20	FORD JAMES	SO	U	9		SSX	CATSFIELD	BURNT BARNS	122
20	FORD JOHN	SO	U	13	AG.LAB	SSX	CATSFIELD	BURNT BARNS	122
8	FOSTER ALFRED	SO	U	8		SSX	WESTFIELD	SCHOOL HOUSE	162
8	FOSTER ALFRED	SO	U	18		SSX	WESTFIELD	KIDDS	173
37	FOSTER ANN	LG	W	66	PAUPER	SSX	HEATHFIELD	MOUNT PLEASANT	166
8	FOSTER BENJAMIN	HD	M	55	BAILIFF	SSX	CATSFIELD	PARK GATE	120
39	FOSTER CAROLINE	SV	U	13		SSX	PETT	BENSKINS	177
8	FOSTER CAROLINE	WI	M	53		SSX	BATTLE	KIDDS	173
83	FOSTER CHARLOTTE	DA	U	27		SSX	HOLLINGTON	GATE HOUSE	17
14	FOSTER EDWIN	SO	U	21	AG.LAB	SSX	CROWHURST	NOT GIVEN	130
83	FOSTER ELIZABETH	DA	U	18		SSX	HOLLINGTON	GATE HOUSE	17
8	FOSTER ELIZABETH	WI	M	51		SSX	BATTLE	PARK GATE	120
83	FOSTER EMILY A	GD	U	1		SSX	HOLLINGTON	GATE HOUSE	17
5	FOSTER FREDERICK	SV	U	18	ERRAND BOY	SSX	PETT	SOUTHINGS	152
8	FOSTER GEORGE	SO	U	3		SSX	WESTFIELD	SCHOOL HOUSE	162
33	FOSTER GEORGE	SO	U	16		SSX	WESTFIELD	KENT STREET	166

No.	Name	Rel	Cond	Age	Occupation	County/Parish	Address	Pg
33	FOSTER HARRIETT	WI	M	25		SSX MOUNTFIELD	KENT STREET	166
83	FOSTER HENRY	SO	U	23	GARDENER	SSX HOLLINGTON	GATE HOUSE	17
8	FOSTER HORACE	SO	U	14		SSX CATSFIELD	PARK GATE	120
6	FOSTER JAMES	SV	U	12		NOT GIVEN (?WESTFIELD)	DOWN OAKS	152
24	FOSTER JAMES	SV	U	12		SSX SALEHURST	ROCKS	175
8	FOSTER JANE	DA	U	16		SSX CATSFIELD	PARK GATE	120
8	FOSTER JOHN	SO	U	15		SSX WESTFIELD	SCHOOL HOUSE	162
83	FOSTER JOHN	SO	U	26	AG.LAB	SSX HOLLINGTON	GATE HOUSE	17
8	FOSTER MARY	WI	M	44		SSX WESTFIELD	SCHOOL HOUSE	162
25	FOSTER ROBERT	HD	M	49	GARDENER	SSX FAIRLIGHT	BEXHILL STREET	26
8	FOSTER ROBERT	SO	U	13		SSX WESTFIELD	SCHOOL HOUSE	162
14	FOSTER SAMUEL	HD	M	67	PARISH CLERK	SSX CATSFIELD	NOT GIVEN	130
33	FOSTER SAMUEL	SO	U	1		SSX WESTFIELD	KENT STREET	166
8	FOSTER SAMUEL	SO	U	25		SSX BATTLE	KIDDS	173
14	FOSTER SARAH	WI	M	63		COUNTY OF DURHAM	NOT GIVEN	130
6	FOSTER SILAS	SV	U	22	CARTER	SSX HAILSHAM	ROSE COTTAGE - SIDLEY	65
8	FOSTER SIMEON	HD	M	48	AG.LAB	SSX WESTFIELD	SCHOOL HOUSE	162
83	FOSTER SOPHIA	DA	U	18		SSX HOLLINGTON	GATE HOUSE	17
8	FOSTER SPENCER	SO	U	17		SSX WESTFIELD	SCHOOL HOUSE	162
58	FOSTER SPENCER	SV	U	21	GROOM	SSX HOLLINGTON	HOLLINGTON LODGE	13
33	FOSTER STEPHEN	HD	M	47	AG.LAB	SSX WESTFIELD	KENT STREET	166
8	FOSTER STEPHEN	NP	U	20	AG.LAB	SSX WESTFIELD	SCHOOL HOUSE	162
13	FOSTER THOMAS	SV	U	20	FOOTMAN	SSX MOUNTFIELD	PARSONAGE	130
8	FOSTER WILLIAM	HD	M	48	AG.LAB	SSX BATTLE	KIDDS	173
83	FOSTER WILLIAM	HD	W	71	AG.LAB	SSX BATTLE	GATE HOUSE	17
8	FOSTER WILLIAM	SO	U	19		SSX WESTFIELD	SCHOOL HOUSE	162
24	FOWLER CAROLINE	VR	U	24		SSX PEASMARSH	LORDINE FARM	235
41	FOWLER EDWARD N	SV	U	14	HOUSE SERVANT	SSX PEVENSEY	PRESTON FARM SIDLEY	81
58	FRANKLIN CHARLES	LG	M	38	GARDENER	MDX KENSINGTON	SEDLESCOMBE STREET	195
58	FRANKLIN SARAH	LW	M	39		KEN BECKENHAM	SEDLESCOMBE STREET	195
49	FREELAND ALFRED	SO	U	10	SCHOLAR	SSX SEDLESCOMBE	SWALES GREEN	207
47	FREELAND CHARLES	SO	U	2		SSX SEDLESCOMBE	POPPING HOLE LANE	207
49	FREELAND EDWIN	SO	U	15	SCHOLAR	SSX SEDLESCOMBE	SWALES GREEN	207
17	FREELAND ELIZA	SV	W	60		SSX WHATLINGTON	OAKLANDS	174
47	FREELAND ELIZABETH	WI	M	26		SSX MOUNTFIELD	POPPING HOLE LANE	207
56	FREELAND ELIZABETH M	DA	U	9		SSX SEDLESCOMBE	GATE HOUSE	209
56	FREELAND GODFREY	SO	U	5		SSX SEDLESCOMBE	GATE HOUSE	209
40	FREELAND HARRIETT	DA	U	19	AG.LAB	SSX SEDLESCOMBE	HAILSFORD	192
49	FREELAND HENRY	HD	M	49	FARM BAILIFF	SSX SEDLESCOMBE	SWALES GREEN	207
37	FREELAND HENRY	LG	U	19	AG.LAB	SSX SEDLESCOMBE	FOOTLAND	205
40	FREELAND HESTER	DA	U	3		SSX SEDLESCOMBE	HAILSFORD	192
40	FREELAND HORACE	SO	U	14	AG.LAB	SSX SEDLESCOMBE	HAILSFORD	192
47	FREELAND JAMES	LG	W	65	AG.LAB	SSX BATTLE	SWALES GREEN	193
40	FREELAND MARY ANN	DA	U	1M		SSX SEDLESCOMBE	HAILSFORD	192
24	FREELAND MARY ANN	SV	U	22	HOUSE MAID	SSX BRIGHTLING	CATSFIELD RECTORY	109
56	FREELAND MARY ANN	WI	M	28		SSX EWHURST	GATE HOUSE	209
49	FREELAND SAMUEL	SO	U	12	SCHOLAR	SSX SEDLESCOMBE	SWALES GREEN	207
40	FREELAND SARAH	WI	M	36		SSX WHATLINGTON	HAILSFORD	192
49	FREELAND SARAH	WI	M	56		SSX SEDLESCOMBE	SWALES GREEN	207
23	FREELAND SARAH A	SV	U	13	HOUSE SERVANT	SSX WHATLINGTON	CRIPPS	252
40	FREELAND SARAH ANN	DA	U	5		SSX WHATLINGTON	HAILSFORD	192
47	FREELAND SPENCER	HD	M	26	AG.LAB	SSX SEDLESCOMBE	POPPING HOLE LANE	207
40	FREELAND SPENCER	HD	M	45	FARM BAILIFF	SSX SEDLESCOMBE	HAILSFORD	192
40	FREELAND SPENCER	SO	U	15	AG.LAB	SSX SEDLESCOMBE	HAILSFORD	192
56	FREELAND STEPHEN H	SO	U	3		SSX SEDLESCOMBE	GATE HOUSE	209
56	FREELAND WILLIAM	HD	M	32	AG.LAB	SSX SEDLESCOMBE	GATE HOUSE	209
40	FREELAND WILLIAM	SO	U	23	AG.LAB	SSX SEDLESCOMBE	HAILSFORD	192
56	FREELAND WILLIAM H	SO	U	7		SSX SEDLESCOMBE	GATE HOUSE	209
3	FREEMAN ALFRED	LG	U	20	AG.LAB	SSX BEXHILL	SIDLEY CORNER	65
56	FREEMAN ANDREW	SO	U	14	AG.LAB	SSX BEXHILL	KEWHURST	44
31	FREEMAN ANN	DA	U	3M		SSX HOOE	NOT GIVEN	93
15	FREEMAN ANN	DA	U	1		SSX BEXHILL	CONEYBERRY	53
22	FREEMAN ANN	DA	U	20		SSX BEXHILL	NOT GIVEN	91
66	FREEMAN ANN	WI	M	63?		SSX BEXHILL	SIDLEY GREEN	84
40	FREEMAN CAROLINE	DA	U	17		SSX BEXHILL	PRESTON COTTAGE SIDLEY	81
22	FREEMAN CHARLES	SO	U	6		SSX BEXHILL	NOT GIVEN	92
31	FREEMAN CHARLES	SV	U	19	AG.LAB	SSX BEXHILL	BUCKHOLT SIDLEY	79
22	FREEMAN CHARLOTTE	DA	U	7M		SSX BEXHILL	NOT GIVEN	92
40	FREEMAN DELIA	DA	U	10	SCHOLAR	SSX BEXHILL	PRESTON COTTAGE SIDLEY	81
26	FREEMAN EDWIN	LG	U	43	RAILWAY MAN	SSX HELLINGLY	GREEN STREET	132
57	FREEMAN EDWIN	SO	U	7M		SSX BEXHILL	ALMS HOUSE SIDLEY	83
7	FREEMAN EDWIN	SO	U	2		SSX BEXHILL	BIGGS HILL SIDLEY	76
40	FREEMAN ELENDER	DA	U	5	SCHOLAR	SSX BEXHILL	PRESTON COTTAGE SIDLEY	81
61	FREEMAN ELISA	WI	M	39		SSX BEXHILL	LANES END	30
57	FREEMAN ELIZA	DA	U	12		SSX BEXHILL	ALMS HOUSE SIDLEY	83
21	FREEMAN ELLEN	GD	U	4M		SSX BEXHILL	NOT GIVEN	91
40	FREEMAN EMILY	DA	U	12		SSX BEXHILL	PRESTON COTTAGE SIDLEY	81
1	FREEMAN FREDERICK	HD	M	28	AG.LAB	SSX BEXHILL	SIDLEY CORNER	64
57	FREEMAN FREDERICK	SO	U	5		SSX BEXHILL	ALMS HOUSE SIDLEY	83
3	FREEMAN GEORGE	LG	U	17	AG.LAB	SSX BEXHILL	SIDLEY CORNER	65
56	FREEMAN GEORGE	SO	U	6	SCHOLAR	SSX BEXHILL	KEWHURST	44
22	FREEMAN GEORGE	SO	U	13		SSX BEXHILL	NOT GIVEN	91
40	FREEMAN GEORGE	SO	U	15	AG.LAB	SSX BEXHILL	PRESTON COTTAGE SIDLEY	81
21	FREEMAN GEORGE	SO	U	22	AG.LAB	SSX BEXHILL	NOT GIVEN	91
56	FREEMAN HANNAH	DA	U	10	SCHOLAR	SSX BEXHILL	KEWHURST	44
22	FREEMAN HANNAH	WI	M	42		SSX HOLLINGTON	NOT GIVEN	91

Ref	Surname	Forename	Rel	Cond	Age	Occupation	County	Parish	Place	No.
56	FREEMAN	HANNAH	WI	M	48		SSX	BEXHILL	KEWHURST	44
21	FREEMAN	HANNAH	WI	M	53		SSX	BEXHILL	NOT GIVEN	91
75	FREEMAN	HARRIET	SV	U	20		SSX	BEXHILL	NOT GIVEN	98
63	FREEMAN	HARRIOTT	SV	U	20		SSX	BEXHILL	COAST GUARD STATION	30
40	FREEMAN	HENRY	HD	M	48	AG.LAB	SSX	BEXHILL	PRESTON COTTAGE SIDLEY	81
20	FREEMAN	HENRY	LG	U	21	AG.LAB	SSX	BEXHILL	TWO HOUSES SIDLEY	77
22	FREEMAN	HENRY	SO	U	4		SSX	BEXHILL	NOT GIVEN	92
15	FREEMAN	JAMES	HD	M	29	AG.LAB	SSX	BEXHILL	CONEYBERRY	53
61	FREEMAN	JAMES	HD	M	34	AG.LAB	SSX	BULVERHITHE	LANES END	30
56	FREEMAN	JAMES	HD	M	55	AG.LAB	SSX	BEXHILL	KEWHURST	44
61	FREEMAN	JAMES	SO	U	9	SCHOLAR	SSX	BEXHILL	LANES END	30
56	FREEMAN	JANE	DA	U	8	SCHOLAR	SSX	BEXHILL	KEWHURST	44
22	FREEMAN	JANE	DA	U	15		SSX	BEXHILL	NOT GIVEN	91
21	FREEMAN	JANE	DA	U	17		SSX	BEXHILL	NOT GIVEN	91
58	FREEMAN	JANE	WI	M	22		KEN	CRANBROOK	NOT GIVEN	58
66	FREEMAN	JOHN	HD	M	65	AG.LAB	SSX	BEXHILL	SIDLEY GREEN	84
40	FREEMAN	JOHN	SO	U	8	SCHOLAR	SSX	BEXHILL	PRESTON COTTAGE SIDLEY	81
22	FREEMAN	JOHN	SO	U	11		SSX	BEXHILL	NOT GIVEN	91
66	FREEMAN	JOHN	SO	U	29	AG.LAB	SSX	BEXHILL	SIDLEY GREEN	84
15	FREEMAN	LUCY ANN	WI	M	29		SSX	BEXHILL	CONEYBERRY	53
31	FREEMAN	MARIA	WI	M	24		SSX	HOOE	NOT GIVEN	92
56	FREEMAN	MARTHA	DA	U	6M		SSX	BEXHILL	KEWHURST	44
56	FREEMAN	MARY	DA	U	12		SSX	BEXHILL	KEWHURST	44
57	FREEMAN	MARY	WI	M	42		SSX	BEXHILL	ALMS HOUSE SIDLEY	83
40	FREEMAN	MARY	WI	M	45		SSX	BEXHILL	PRESTON COTTAGE SIDLEY	81
70	FREEMAN	MARY ANN	SV	U	14	HOUSE SERVANT	SSX	BEXHILL	NOT GIVEN	59
7	FREEMAN	MARY ANN	WI	M	35		SSX	TICEHURST	BIGGS HILL SIDLEY	76
56	FREEMAN	MOSES	SO	U	16	AG.LAB	SSX	BEXHILL	KEWHURST	44
21	FREEMAN	RACHAEL	DA	U	20		SSX	BEXHILL	NOT GIVEN	91
7	FREEMAN	SAMUEL	HD	M	67	AG.LAB	SSX	BEXHILL	BIGGS HILL SIDLEY	76
1	FREEMAN	SARAH	DA	U	3M		SSX	BEXHILL	SIDLEY CORNER	64
56	FREEMAN	SARAH	DA	U	4		SSX	BEXHILL	KEWHURST	44
22	FREEMAN	SARAH	DA	U	7		SSX	BEXHILL	NOT GIVEN	92
21	FREEMAN	SARAH	DA	U	16		SSX	BEXHILL	NOT GIVEN	91
40	FREEMAN	STEPHEN	SO	U	3		SSX	BEXHILL	PRESTON COTTAGE SIDLEY	81
7	FREEMAN	STEPHEN	SO	U	6	SCHOLAR	SSX	BEXHILL	BIGGS HILL SIDLEY 76	76
22	FREEMAN	THOMAS	HD	M	43	AG.LAB	SSX	BEXHILL	NOT GIVEN	91
21	FREEMAN	THOMAS	HD	M	46	AG.LAB	SSX	BEXHILL	NOT GIVEN	91
54	FREEMAN	THOMAS	LG	U	21	AG.LAB	SSX	BEXHILL	2 STONE HOUSE	44
2	FREEMAN	THOMAS	LG	W	72	AG.LAB	SSX	BEXHILL	LOWER BARNHORN	37
1	FREEMAN	THOMAS	SO	U	1		SSX	BEXHILL	SIDLEY CORNER	64
22	FREEMAN	THOMAS	SO	U	18	AG.LAB	SSX	BEXHILL	NOT GIVEN	91
31	FREEMAN	WILLIAM	HD	M	24	AG.LAB	SSX	BEXHILL	NOT GIVEN	92
58	FREEMAN	WILLIAM	HD	M	28	AG.LAB	SSX	BEXHILL	NOT GIVEN	58
57	FREEMAN	WILLIAM	HD	M	42	AG.LAB	SSX	BEXHILL	ALMS HOUSE SIDLEY	83
31	FREEMAN	WILLIAM	SO	U	2		SSX	HOOE	NOT GIVEN	92
57	FREEMAN	WILLIAM	SO	U	9		SSX	BEXHILL	ALMS HOUSE SIDLEY	83
22	FREEMAN	WILLIAM	SO	U	9		SSX	BEXHILL	NOT GIVEN	91
1	FREEMAN	WINIFRED	WI	M	24		SSX	BEXHILL	SIDLEY CORNER	64
23	FRENCH	EDWARD	HD	M	62	AG.LAB	SSX	BURWASH	NOT GIVEN	92
20	FRENCH	ELIZABETH	VR	U	22	SERVANT	SSX	BECKLEY	ODIAM FARM	218
23	FRENCH	ELIZABETH	WI	M	66		SSX	CROWHURST	NOT GIVEN	92
27	FRENCH	EMMILY	DA	U	4		SSX	BEXHILL	SIDLEY	69
27	FRENCH	HENRY	HD	M	26	AG.LAB	SSX	BUXTED	SIDLEY	69
27	FRENCH	MARY	DA	U	1		SSX	BEXHILL	SIDLEY	69
27	FRENCH	REBACA	WI	M	35		SSX	ASHBURNHAM	SIDLEY	69
60	FRENCH	ROSINA	WI	M	27		SSX	BEXHILL	SIDLEY GREEN	83
27	FRENCH	SAMPSON	SO	U	1M		SSX	BEXHILL	SIDLEY	69
20	FRENCH	SPENCER	VR	U	36	AG.LAB	SSX	BEXHILL	NOT GIVEN	91
60	FRENCH	WILLIAM	HD	M	28	AG.LAB	SSX	BEXHILL	SIDLEY GREEN	83
64	FUGE	JAMES	LG	U	28	RAILWAY LAB	SOM	TAUNTON	RAILWAY HUT	137
81	FULLER	ADELAIDE	SV	U	17	KITCHEN MAID	SSX	WARTLING	BEAUPORT HOUSE	17
22	FULLER	ALFRED	HD	M	36	AG.LAB	SSX	BEXHILL	LAND MARES? - SIDLEY	68
50	FULLER	ANN	DA	U	11	SCHOLAR	SSX	BATTLE	SWALES GREEN	208
15	FULLER	ARTHUR	HD	W	73	FARMER 17 AC EMP 1	SSX	BEXHILL	SIDLEY	67
22	FULLER	DELIA	WI	M	37		SSX	WESTFIELD	LAND MARES? - SIDLEY	68
34	FULLER	ELIZA	DA	U	8	SCHOLAR	SSX	EWHURST	REEVES	237
34	FULLER	ELIZA	WI	M	44		SSX	SALEHURST	REEVES	237
39	FULLER	ELIZABETH	WI	M	32		SSX	BEXHILL	PRESTON SIDLEY	80
50	FULLER	EMILY	DA	U	5		SSX	BATTLE	SWALES GREEN	208
26	FULLER	FRANCES	NC	U	27	SERVANT	SSX	BRIGHTLING	FORGE FARM	219
50	FULLER	FREDERICK	SO	U	15	AG.LAB	SSX	PETT	SWALES GREEN	208
18	FULLER	HANNAH	WI	M	59		SSX	SALEHURST	CATTS GREEN	251
22	FULLER	HARRIET	DA	U	1		SSX	BEXHILL	LAND MARES? - SIDLEY	68
15	FULLER	HARRIET	DA	U	43		SSX	ASHBURNHAM	SIDLEY	67
50	FULLER	HARRIETT	DA	U	8	SCHOLAR	SSX	BATTLE	SWALES GREEN	208
39	FULLER	HENRY	HD	M	41	AG.LAB	SSX	EWHURST	PRESTON SIDLEY	80
18	FULLER	HENRY	HD	M	43	AG.LAB	SSX	EWHURST	CATTS GREEN	251
39	FULLER	HENRY	SO	U	4		SSX	BEXHILL	PRESTON SIDLEY	80
50	FULLER	JAMES	HD	W	49	AG.LAB	SSX	WHATLINGTON	SWALES GREEN	208
81	FULLER	JAMES	SV	U	20	GROOM	SSX	BATTLE	BEAUPORT HOUSE	17
34	FULLER	JOHN	SO	U	10	SCHOLAR	SSX	EWHURST	REEVES	237
4	FULLER	JOHN	SV	M	41	FARM LAB	SSX	EWHURST	BEACON HOUSE	249
34	FULLER	JOSEPH	LG	M	77	AG.LAB	SSX	EWHURST	REEVES	237
22	FULLER	MARY	DA	U	4		SSX	BEXHILL	LAND MARES? - SIDLEY	68
34	FULLER	MARY	LW	M	74		SSX	BERWICK	REEVES	237

	Name	Rel		Age	Occupation	County	Parish	Place	No.
50	FULLER RICHARD	SO	U	13		SSX	BATTLE	SWALES GREEN	208
4	FULLER SARAH ANN	SV	M	42	HOUSE SERVANT	SSX	RYE	BEACON HOUSE	250
68	FULLER STEPHEN	FL	W	78	PAUPER AG.LAB	SSX	BATTLE	SIDLEY GREEN	84
18	FULLER STEPHEN	SO	U	14	AG.LAB	SSX	EWHURST	CATTS GREEN	251
63	FULLER WILLIAM	/	M	46	AG.LAB	SSX	EWHURST	RECTORY HOUSE	224
54	FUNNEL GEORGE	NP	U	4		SSX	MOUNTFIELD	STOCKWOOD	239
54	FUNNEL HARRIET	WI	M	38		KEN	TENTERDEN	STOCKWOOD	239
54	FUNNEL WILLIAM	HD	M	37	AG.LAB	SSX	MOUNTFIELD	STOCKWOOD	239
27	FUNNELL ANN	WI	M	49		SSX	EWHURST	CRIPPS	252
27	FUNNELL ELIZA	DA	U	24		SSX	SEDLESCOMBE	CRIPPS	252
27	FUNNELL ELLEN	DA	U	4		SSX	EWHURST	CRIPPS	252
4	FUNNELL HARRIET	SV	U	18	HOUSE SERVANT	SSX	SEDLESCOMBE	BEACON HOUSE	250
27	FUNNELL JOHN	HD	M	61	BLACKSMITH	SSX	LINDFIELD	CRIPPS	252
27	FUNNELL JOHN	SO	U	22	BLACKSMITH	SSX	SEDLESCOMBE	CRIPPS	252
27	FUNNELL MARY ANN	DA	U	6	SCHOLAR	SSX	EWHURST	CRIPPS	252
27	FUNNELL WILLIAM	SO	U	14	FARMER'S LAB	SSX	SEDLESCOMBE	CRIPPS	252
6	FURBY HANNAH	WI	M	58		SSX	BEXHILL	SLUICE HSE (IN THE LIBERTY)	38
6	FURBY JOHN	HD	M	60	LOOKER SHIP	SSX	BEXHILL	SLUICE HSE (IN THE LIBERTY)	38
16	FURMINGER AARON JAMES	SO	U	1		SSX	EWHURST	BREDE HIGH	251
16	FURMINGER ALFRED	SO	U	7		SSX	BREDE	BREDE HIGH	251
16	FURMINGER AMOS	SO	U	5		SSX	EWHURST	BREDE HIGH	251
16	FURMINGER CHARLOTTE	MO	U	66	NURSE	SSX	BREDE	BREDE HIGH	251
86	FURMINGER ELIZABETH	SV	U	19		SSX	BREDE	HARROW INN	18
30	FURMINGER HARRIET	NC	U	11	SERVANT	SSX	BREDE	RENS	220
16	FURMINGER JAMES	HD	M	38	AG.LAB	SSX	BREDE	BREDE HIGH	251
16	FURMINGER MARY ANN	DA	U	3		SSX	EWHURST	BREDE HIGH	251
16	FURMINGER SARAH	WI	M	28		SSX	EAST HOTHLY	BREDE HIGH	251
33	FURNER GEORGE	LG	U	17	AG.LAB	SSX	BREDE	MADDAMS	220
59	GAIN CAROLINE	DA	U	7M		SSX	WESTFIELD	BAKEHOUSE	180
59	GAIN CAROLINE	HK	M	30		SSX	WESTFIELD	BAKEHOUSE	180
50	GAIN CHARLES	SO	U	7		SSX	WESTFIELD	RANSOMS	178
38	GAIN FRANCES	WI	M	30		SSX	FAIRLIGHT	OWLS CASTLE	177
50	GAIN GEORGE	HD	M	30	AG.LAB	SSX	WESTFIELD	RANSOMS	178
31	GAIN GEORGE	HD	M	67	AG.LAB	SSX	ORE	DOWN	176
59	GAIN HARRIETT	DA	U	9		SSX	WESTFIELD	BAKEHOUSE	180
50	GAIN HARRIETT	WI	M	31		SSX	RYE	RANSOMS	178
59	GAIN HENRY	SO	U	11		SSX	WESTFIELD	BAKEHOUSE	180
38	GAIN JAMES	HD	M	43	AG.LAB	SSX	WESTFIELD	OWLS CASTLE	177
31	GAIN MARY	GD	U	7		SSX	WESTFIELD	DOWN	176
31	GAIN MARY	WI	M	63		SSX	ICKLESHAM	DOWN	176
29	GAIN SARAH	VR	U	63	FORMERLY SERVANT	SSX	BREDE	CRIPPS	253
29	GAIN STEPHEN	VR	U	3		SSX	SALEHURST	CRIPPS	253
59	GAIN THOMAS	SO	U	3		SSX	WESTFIELD	BAKEHOUSE	180
50	GAIN WILLIAM	SO	U	3		SSX	WESTFIELD	RANSOMS	178
33	GAINS JOHN	LG	U	29		SSX	GUESTLING	MOOR FARM	155
45	GANDER ANN MARIA	GD	U	5	SCHOLAR	SSX	BEXHILL	NOT GIVEN	94
45	GANDER ELIZABETH	HD	W	55	CARRIER	KEN	HAWKHURST	NOT GIVEN	94
12	GANDER EMMA	WI	M	27		SSX	BEXHILL	BELL HILL	25
12	GANDER GEORGE T	SO	U	4		SSX	BEXHILL	BELL HILL	25
118	GANDER HANNAH	WI	M	68		SSX	BEXHILL	NOT GIVEN	102
66	GANDER JAMES	SV	U	30	BLACKSMITH JM	SSX	WHARTLING (SIC)	MOUNT PLEASANT	197
118	GANDER JOHN	HD	M	78	PAUPER AG.LAB	SSX	HODE	NOT GIVEN	102
12	GANDER LOUIS H	SO	U	1		SSX	BEXHILL	BELL HILL	25
45	GANDER MARY ANN	DA	U	35		SSX	BEXHILL	NOT GIVEN	94
12	GANDER PETER N	SO	U	2M		SSX	BEXHILL	BELL HILL	25
12	GANDER WALTER	HD	M	28	CARRIER	SSX	BEXHILL	BELL HILL	25
11	GARDENER MARIA	WI	M	78		SSX	BATTLE	DAGG LANE	217
11	GARDENER SHADRACH	HD	M	79	AG.LAB	SSX	SEDLESCOMBE	DAGG LANE	217
63	GARDNER CHARLES	LG	U	21	RAILWAY LAB	SSX		RAILWAY HUT	137
65	GARRAD ANN	SV	U	16	HOUSE SERVANT	KEN	LYDD	NOT GIVEN	97
47	GARRETT MARTHA	GD	U	4		SSX	BREDE	WHYBORNES	167
48	GASCOYNE ELIZA	WI	M	27		KEN	CANTERBURY	RAILWAY HUT	135
48	GASCOYNE ISAC	HD	M	33	RAILWAY LAB	ESS	COLCHESTER	RAILWAY HUT	135
48	GASCOYNE SARAH	DA	U	5		UNKNOWN		RAILWAY HUT	135
48	GASCOYNE WILLIAM	SO	U	1		SSX	ST.LEONARDS	RAILWAY HUT	135
27	GATES CHARITY	WI	M	62		SSX	HELLINGLY	FORTLAND? HOUSE	123
14	GATES CHARLOTTE	DA	U	11		SSX	BEXHILL	NOT GIVEN	53
6	GATES GEORGE	SV	U	46	LOOKER'S SERVANT	SSX	BEXHILL	SLUICE HSE (IN THE LIBERTY)	38
14	GATES HARRIOT	DA	U	13		SSX	BEXHILL	NOT GIVEN	53
14	GATES HARRIOT	WI	M	40		SSX	HELLINGLY	NOT GIVEN	53
27	GATES JAMES	HD	M	66	FARMER 53 ACRES 1 LAB	SSX	NINFIELD	FORTLAND? HOUSE	123
27	GATES JANE	SV	U	17	HOUSE SERVANT	SSX	BEXHILL	LITTLE WORSHAM SIDLEY	79
14	GATES JOHN	HD	M	43	AG.LAB	SSX	BEXHILL	NOT GIVEN	53
62	GATES MARY	WI	M	66		SSX	BEXHILL	PINNIERS (LITTLE COMMON)	45
14	GATES RICHARD	SO	U	6M		SSX	BEXHILL	NOT GIVEN	53
27	GATES SARAH	DA	U	17		SSX	NINFIELD	FORTLAND? HOUSE	123
27	GATES TRAYTON	GS	U	16	AG.LAB	SSX	NINFIELD	FORTLAND? HOUSE	123
62	GATES WILLIAM	HD	M	76	AG.LAB	SSX	NINFIELD	PINNIERS (LITTLE COMMON)	45
44	GERRAD EDWARD H	SO	U	8	SCHOLAR	SSX	BEXHILL	NO.1 GALLEY HILL	28
44	GERRAD ELIZABETH	WI	M	39		SFK	CHELMONDISTON*	NO.1 GALLEY HILL	28
44	GERRAD JOHN T	SO	U	11	SCHOLAR	DOR	LULWORTH	NO.1 GALLEY HILL	28
44	GERRAD MARY A	DA	U	13	SCHOLAR	KEN	LYDD	NO.1 GALLEY HILL	28
44	GERRAD RICHARD	SO	U	6	SCHOLAR	SSX	BEXHILL	NO.1 GALLEY HILL	28
44	GERRAD THOMAS	HD	M	39	COASTGUARD	LIN	BOSTON	NO.1 GALLEY HILL	28
44	GERRAD WILLIAM R	SO	U	3		SSX	BEXHILL	NO.1 GALLEY HILL	28
15	GIBBENS THOMAS	VR	U	26	ABLE SEAMAN	COR	GWENNAP*	IN THE LIBERTY	39

39	GIBBS ELIZA	WI M	17		SSX SEDLESCOMBE	NEAR FOOTLAND	206
39	GIBBS GEORGE	HD M	22	AG.LAB	SSX BREDE	NEAR FOOTLAND	206
81	GIBBS JAMES	SV U	19	FOOTMAN	SSX BATTLE	BEAUPORT HOUSE	17
30	GIBBS SARAH	LW M	35		SSX SEDLESCOMBE	BREDE LANE	190
27	GIBBS THOMAS	LG U	40	RAILWAY LAB	WIL SALISBURY	FORWARD LANE	145
30	GIBBS WILLIAM	LG M	38	AG.LAB	SSX WESTFIELD	BREDE LANE	190
39	GIBBS WILLIAM H T	SO U	7M		SSX SEDLESCOMBE	NEAR FOOTLAND	206
44	GILES ELIZABETH	WI M	63		SSX HERSTMONMCEUX	NOT GIVEN	111
44	GILES WILLIAM	HD M	64	AG.LAB	SSX BURWASH	NOT GIVEN	111
21	GILFIN ALBERT	SO U	9		SSX EWHURST	BOYCES FARM	235
21	GILFIN JOHN A	SO U	14	SCHOLAR	SSX GUESTLING	BOYCES FARM	234
21	GILFIN MARY ANN	WI M	47		SSX BREDE	BOYCES FARM	234
21	GILFIN THOMAS R	SO U	12		SSX EWHURST	BOYCES FARM	235
21	GILFIN WILLIAM	HD M	52	FARMER 140AC EMP 7	SSX ICKLESHAM	BOYCES FARM	234
54	GILHAM ELIZA	WI M	28		SSX BEXHILL	LITTLE COMMON	57
54	GILHAM ELIZA FRANCES	DA U	9		SSX BEXHILL	LITTLE COMMON	57
51	GILHAM ELIZABETH	VR U	15	DRESSMAKER	SSX ST.LEONARDS	LITTLE COMMON	57
51	GILHAM FRANCES	HD W	76	HOUSEKEEPER	SSX BEXHILL	LITTLE COMMON	57
29	GILHAM FRANCES	WI M	25		WIL SALISBURY	WHEAT SHEAF INN	55
29	GILHAM GEORGE	SO U	10M		SSX BEXHILL	WHEAT SHEAF INN	55
54	GILHAM GEORGE THOMAS	SO U	1		SSX BEXHILL	LITTLE COMMON	57
51	GILHAM JAMES	SO U	52	CARPENTER EMP 1 MAN	SSX WARTLING	LITTLE COMMON	57
54	GILHAM MARY ANN	DA U	5		SSX BEXHILL	LITTLE COMMON	57
54	GILHAM THOMAS	HD M	43	CARPENTER JM	SSX BEXHILL	LITTLE COMMON	57
29	GILHAM WILLIAM	HD M	23	CARPENTER JM	SSX BEXHILL	WHEAT SHEAF INN	55
38	GILL ELIZABETH	SV U	64	HOUSEKEEPER	SSX WESTFIELD	NOT GIVEN	93
12	GILL GEORGE	HD M	27	AG.LAB	SSX WESTFIELD	ASHDOWNS	173
53	GILL GIDEON	LG U	68	CARPENTER	SSX WESTFIELD	SPRING HILL	179
23	GILL JOSEPH	VR U	27	GENERAL POST OFFICE	WIL MELKSHAM	LORDINE	235
12	GILL LUCY	WI M	24		SSX WESTFIELD	ASHDOWNS	173
25	GILL MARY	GD U	2		SSX WESTFIELD	FORGE	175
30	GILLHAM ALFRED	AP U	18	BLACKSMITH AP	SSX BEXHILL	LITTLE COMMON	55
59	GILLHAM ELIZA	WI M	42		SSX BEXHILL	NOT GIVEN	45
59	GILLHAM FRANCIS	DA U	5		SSX BEXHILL	NOT GIVEN	45
59	GILLHAM GEORGE	HD M	46	AG.LAB	SSX BEXHILL	NOT GIVEN	45
80	GILLHAM GEORGE	SO U	36	AG.LAB	SSX BEXHILL	POND HOUSE (LITTLE COMMON)	47
59	GILLHAM HENRY	SO U	8		SSX BEXHILL	NOT GIVEN	45
59	GILLHAM RICHARD	SO U	13		SSX BEXHILL	NOT GIVEN	45
59	GILLHAM SAMUEL	SO U	16		SSX BEXHILL	NOT GIVEN	45
80	GILLHAM THOMAS	HD W	73	SHOE REPAIRER	SSX BEXHILL	POND HOUSE (LITTLE COMMON)	47
59	GILLHAM WALTER	SO U	10		SSX BEXHILL	NOT GIVEN	45
10	GLADMAN JAMES	SO U	2		SSX WEST FIRLE	RAILWAY HUT	5
76	GLADWISH SUSAN	WI M	64		SSX BATTLE	STEMPS?	16
76	GLADWISH THOMAS	HD M	67	AG.LAB	SSX NORTHIAM	STEMPS?	16
23	GLAIZER ELIZABETH	NS M	54	MONTHLY NURSE	SSX MAYFIELD	LORDINE	235
31	GLANVILLE JOHN	HD M	43	COAST GUARD	DEV TAVISTOCK	51 MARTELLO TOWER	41
31	GLANVILLE JOHN M	SO U	6		SSX BEXHILL	51 MARTELLO TOWER	41
31	GLANVILLE MARY M	DA U	4		SSX BEXHILL	51 MARTELLO TOWER	41
31	GLANVILLE SARAH	WI M	33		GLAMORGAN PENRICE	51 MARTELLO TOWER	41
31	GLANVILLE SARAH J	DA U	3		SSX BEXHILL	51 MARTELLO TOWER	41
31	GLANVILLE WILLIAM T	SO U	1		SSX BEXHILL	51 MARTELLO TOWER	41
2	GLASPOLLE ELIZABETH	WI M	32		HAM	MARLPIT COTTAGE	151
2	GLASPOLLE GEORGE	HD M	34	BRICKMAKER	HAM	MARLPIT COTTAGE	151
2	GLASPOLLE JAMES	SO U	8		FRANCE	MARLPIT COTTAGE	151
2	GLASPOLLE WILLIAM	SO U	12		HAM	MARLPIT COTTAGE	151
18	GLAZIER ANN	WI M	32		SSX WESTFIELD	BUCKHURST	164
5	GLAZIER EDWARD	SO U	14	AG.LAB	SSX HOLLINGTON	(WILTING?)	5
5	GLAZIER ELIZABETH	DA U	4		SSX HOLLINGTON	(WILTING?)	5
18	GLAZIER GEORGE	SO U	4		SSX WESTFIELD	BUCKHURST	164
5	GLAZIER GEORGE	SO U	10		SSX HOLLINGTON	(WILTING?)	5
5	GLAZIER HARRIETT	DA U	2		SSX HOLLINGTON	(WILTING?)	5
18	GLAZIER HARRIETT	DA U	10	SCHOLAR	SSX WESTFIELD	BUCKHURST	164
5	GLAZIER HARRIETT	WI M	45		SSX PENHURST	(WILTING?)	5
5	GLAZIER HENRY	SO U	15	AG.LAB	SSX HOLLINGTON	(WILTING?)	5
18	GLAZIER JAMES	SO U	13		SSX WESTFIELD	BUCKHURST	164
18	GLAZIER JOHN	HD M	36	AG.LAB	SSX BATTLE	BUCKHURST	164
5	GLAZIER JOHN	HD M	48	AG.LAB	SSX HOLLINGTON	(WILTING?)	5
5	GLAZIER MERCY	DA U	6	SCHOLAR	SSX HOLLINGTON	(WILTING?)	5
33	GLAZIER SAMUEL	/ W	64	AG.LAB	KEN MUNDEN	PARSONAGE	9
33	GLAZIER SAMUEL	LG U	34	AG.LAB	SSX ST.MARY IN THE CASTLE	PARSONAGE	9
5	GLAZIER SAMUEL	SO U	8	SCHOLAR	SSX HOLLINGTON	(WILTING?)	5
89	GLAZIER THOMAS	SV U	35	AG.LAB	SSX CROWHURST	EVERSFIELDS	18
18	GLAZIER WILLIAM	SO U	7	SCHOLAR	SSX WESTFIELD	BUCKHURST	164
46	GLOVER ELIZABETH	WI M	67		SSX EWHURST	SHOREHAM	221
46	GLOVER WILLIAM	HD M	70	AG.LAB	SSX EWHURST	SHOREHAM	221
91	GLYDE SOLOMON	LG U	26		NOT GIVEN	STREET	19
8	GOBEY ANNE	DA U	3M		SSX SEDLESCOMBE	BARRICKS	187
7	GOBEY CORNELIUS	HD M	69	SWEEP	SSX SEDLESCOMBE	BARRICKS	187
8	GOBEY GEORGE	SO U	2		SSX SEDLESCOMBE	BARRICKS	187
8	GOBEY JAMES	HD M	30	AG.LAB	SSX SEDLESCOMBE	BARRICKS	187
8	GOBEY JOHN	SO U	8	SCHOLAR	SSX SEDLESCOMBE	BARRICKS	187
7	GOBEY PRESSELLA	WI M	78		KEN SPELDHURST	BARRICKS	187
8	GOBEY SARAH	DA U	6	SCHOLAR	SSX SEDLESCOMBE	BARRICKS	187
8	GOBEY SARAH	WI M	32		SSX SALEHURST	BARRICKS	187
8	GOBEY WILLIAM	SO U	4	SCHOLAR	SSX SEDLESCOMBE	BARRICKS	187

ID	Name	Rel	MS	Age	Occupation	Birthplace	Location	Page
40	GOBLE ALFRED	SV	U	20		KEN ROLVENDEN	MILL	177
40	GOBLE CAROLINE	DA	U	12	SCHOLAR	SSX HERSTMONCEUX	PRAWLES FARM	221
40	GOBLE RICHARD	SV	M	36	MILLER JM	KEN ROLVENDEN	MILL	177
43	GOBLE SARAH	WI	M	59	DRESSMAKER	SSX HERSTMONCEUX	NOT GIVEN	111
43	GOBLE THEOPHILUS	HD	M	74	RETIRED WEAVER	SSX STOPHAM	NOT GIVEN	111
17	GODDEN AGNES	DA	U	2		SSX EWHURST	ROCKS FARM	217
17	GODDEN BERTHA	DA	U	4		SSX EWHURST	ROCKS FARM	217
17	GODDEN HANNAH	DA	U	13		SSX EWHURST	ROCKS FARM	217
17	GODDEN HENRY	SO	U	21	AG.LAB	SSX EWHURST	ROCKS FARM	217
17	GODDEN JOSHUA	SO	U	10	SCHOLAR	SSX EWHURST	ROCKS FARM	217
17	GODDEN RAYMAN	SO	U	8	SCHOLAR	SSX EWHURST	ROCKS FARM	217
17	GODDEN THOMAS	HD	M	51	AG.LAB	SSX EWHURST	ROCKS FARM	217
17	GODDEN WILLIAM	SO	U	11	SCHOLAR	SSX EWHURST	ROCKS FARM	217
17	GODDEN WINNIFRED	WI	M	41		SSX EWHURST	ROCKS FARM	217
61	GODFREY ALFRED	HD	U	40	RAILWAY LAB	LND	RAILWAY HUT	136
9	GODFREY ELIZABETH	DA	U	19		NTH KINGSMORTON	RAILWAY HUT	5
9	GODFREY MARY	WI	M	46		DEV ---TCHAM	RAILWAY HUT	5
9	GODFREY WILLIAM	HD	M	67	RAIL LAB	MDX HAYS	RAILWAY HUT	5
18	GODFREY WILLIAM	LG	U	16	RAIL LAB	SRY PECKHAM RYE	PIGLANDS	7
51	GODWIN ANN	WI	M	40?		SSX BEXHILL	SIDLEY GREEN	82
44	GODWIN CHARLOTTE	DA	U	6	SCHOLAR	SSX EWHURST	SWALES GREEN	192
44	GODWIN ELIZA	WI	M	36		SSX GUESTLING	SWALES GREEN	192
51	GODWIN ELIZABETH	DA	U	5		SSX BEXHILL	SIDLEY GREEN	82
111	GODWIN ELLEN	DA	U	4		SSX BEXHILL	NOT GIVEN	102
54	GODWIN HANNAH	HD	W	56	PAUPER	NTH WELTON*	3 MARINE COTTAGES	29
44	GODWIN JAMES	HD	M	36	AG.LAB	SSX EWHURST	SWALES GREEN	192
111	GODWIN JAMES	SO	U	3M		SSX BEXHILL	NOT GIVEN	102
44	GODWIN JAMES	SO	U	8	SCHOLAR	SSX EWHURST	SWALES GREEN	192
54	GODWIN JOHN G	NP	U	10		SSX BEXHILL	3 MARINE COTTAGES	29
51	GODWIN JOSEPH	HD	M	36	CARPENTER	SSX BEXHILL	SIDLEY GREEN	82
51	GODWIN JOSEPH	SO	U	2		SSX BEXHILL	SIDLEY GREEN	82
111	GODWIN MARY	WI	M	31		SSX BEXHILL	NOT GIVEN	102
111	GODWIN PETER	HD	M	36	CARPENTER	SSX BEXHILL	NOT GIVEN	102
54	GODWIN STEPHEN	SO	U	21	CARPENTER	SSX BEXHILL	3 MARINE COTTAGES	29
44	GODWIN THOMAS	SO	U	3		SSX SEDLESCOMBE	SWALES GREEN	192
29	GOLDEN GEORGE	LG	U	24	RAILWAY LAB	HAM RINGWOOD	GREEN STREET	132
26	GOLDEN JULIA MARY	SV	U	18	HOUSE MAID	FRANCE BRITISH SUBJECT	CATSFIELD PLACE CHURCH HSE	110
49	GOLDSMITH ANN	HD	W	73	ANNUITANT	SSX CATSFIELD	NOT GIVEN	94
7	GOLDSMITH CAROLINE	WI	M	25		SSX WARBLETON	SEDLESCOMBE STREET	202
62	GOLDSMITH EDWARD	HD	M	80	PAUPER	SSX CATSFIELD	NOT GIVEN	95
34	GOLDSMITH EMMA E	SV	U	35	COOK	SSX NINFIELD	RECTORY	205
7	GOLDSMITH GEORGE	HD	M	26	WHEELWRIGHT	SSX NORTHIAM	SEDLESCOMBE STREET	202
7	GOLDSMITH HENRY WILLIAM	SO	U	2		KEN APPLEDORE	SEDLESCOMBE STREET	202
7	GOLDSMITH JANE	DA	U	2M		SSX SEDLESCOMBE	SEDLESCOMBE STREET	202
62	GOLDSMITH MARY	WI	M	78		KEN FAVERSHAM	NOT GIVEN	95
67	GOODSELL ALBERT	SO	U	12		SSX WESTFIELD	CASTLEMANS	211
5	GOODSELL ALBERT	SO	U	12	AG.LAB	SSX EWHURST	PADGHAM	216
5	GOODSELL ALFRED	SO	U	16	AG.LAB	SSX EWHURST	PADGHAM	216
76	GOODSELL ALICE	DA	U	2		SSX EWHURST	EWHURST GREEN	226
48	GOODSELL ALICE	DA	U	12		SSX EWHURST	SHOREHAM	222
67	GOODSELL ALLEN	SO	U	7		SSX WESTFIELD	CASTLEMANS	211
12	GOODSELL ANN	WI	M	48		KEN BORDEN*	DAGG LANE	217
67	GOODSELL ANNA	DA	U	2		SSX WESTFIELD	CASTLEMANS	211
34	GOODSELL CAROLINE	DA	U	4	SCHOLAR	SSX EWHURST	MADDAMS	220
9	GOODSELL CHARLES	SO	U	6	SCHOLAR	SSX EWHURST	PADGHAM	216
76	GOODSELL CHARLES	SO	U	9	SCHOLAR	SSX EWHURST	EWHURST GREEN	226
10	GOODSELL CHARLOTTE	DA	U	9	SCHOLAR	SSX BATTLE	BARRICKS	187
10	GOODSELL CHARLOTTE	HD	W	37	PARISH RELIEF	SSX SEDLESCOMBE	BARRICKS	187
48	GOODSELL CHARLOTTE	WI	M	41		SSX EWHURST	SHOREHAM	221
54	GOODSELL CLARA	SV	U	14	HOUSE SERVANT	SSX EWHURST	CASTLEMANS	195
76	GOODSELL EDITH	DA	U	1M		SSX EWHURST	EWHURST GREEN	226
48	GOODSELL EDMOND	HD	M	42	AG.LAB	SSX EWHURST	SHOREHAM	221
48	GOODSELL EDMOND	SO	U	18	AG.LAB	SSX EWHURST	SHOREHAM	221
31	GOODSELL ELENOR	WI	M	42		SSX EWHURST	MADDAMS	220
61	GOODSELL ELIAS	LG	U	13	AG.LAB	SSX EWHURST	SEMPSTED FARM	240
2	GOODSELL ELIZA	SV	U	17	HOUSE SERVANT	SSX EWHURST	WATTLE HILL	249
68	GOODSELL ELIZA	WI	M	24		SSX EWHURST	EWHURST GREEN	225
3	GOODSELL ELIZABETH	DA	U	5		SSX EWHURST	PADGHAM FARM	216
6	GOODSELL ELIZABETH	DA	U	7	SCHOLAR	SSX EWHURST	PADGHAM	216
56	GOODSELL EMILY	DA	U	1		SSX EWHURST	ELLINGHOURNE	239
76	GOODSELL FANNY	DA	U	6	SCHOLAR	SSX EWHURST	EWHURST GREEN	226
76	GOODSELL FRANCES	WI	M	34		KEN HERSMONDEN	EWHURST GREEN	226
67	GOODSELL FRANCES	WI	M	49		KEN SANDHURST	CASTLEMANS	211
85	GOODSELL FREDERICK	SO	U	11M		SSX EWHURST	EWHURST GREEN	228
48	GOODSELL FREDERICK	SO	U	3		SSX EWHURST	SHOREHAM	222
85	GOODSELL GEORGE	BR	U	26	AG.LAB	SSX EWHURST	EWHURST GREEN	228
48	GOODSELL GEORGE	FA	M	76	LETTER CARRIER	SSX EWHURST	SHOREHAM	222
34	GOODSELL GEORGE	HD	M	40	SAWYER	SSX EWHURST	MADDAMS	220
60	GOODSELL GEORGE	LG	U	18	AG.LAB	SSX EWHURST	SEMPSTED FARM	240
9	GOODSELL GEORGE	SO	U	15	AG.LAB	SSX EWHURST	PADGHAM	216
34	GOODSELL GODFEEY THOMAS	SO	U	1M		SSX EWHURST	MADDAMS	220
68	GOODSELL H WALTER	SO	U			SSX EWHURST	EWHURST GREEN	225
38	GOODSELL HANNAH	DA	U	5		SSX EWHURST	FORGE LANE	254
28	GOODSELL HANNAH	WI	M	73		SSX BECKLEY	CRIPPS	252
12	GOODSELL HARRIET	DA	U	15	SCHOLAR	SSX EWHURST	DAGG LANE	217
6	GOODSELL HARRIET	HD	M	38	HUSBAND TRANSPORTED	SSX BURWASH	PADGHAM	216

Ref	Name	Rel	MS	Age	Occupation	County	Parish	Place	No.
27	GOODSELL HARRIET	SV	U	16		SSX	EWHURST	SEMPSTED FARM	236
58	GOODSELL HARRIET	SV	U	17	SERVANT	SSX	EWHURST	ELLINGHALL	240
67	GOODSELL HARRIETT	DA	U	10	SCHOLAR	SSX	WESTFIELD	CASTLEMANS	210
5	GOODSELL HEATHER	DA	U	2M		SSX	EWHURST	PADGHAM	216
31	GOODSELL HENRY	HD	M	31	AG.LAB	SSX	EWHURST	MADDAMS	220
12	GOODSELL HENRY	HD	M	38	AG.LAB	SSX	EWHURST	DAGG LANE	217
67	GOODSELL HENRY	HD	M	50	AG.LAB	SSX	WESTFIELD	CASTLEMANS	211
3	GOODSELL HENRY	HD	M	54?	AG.LAB	SSX	EWHURST	PADGHAM FARM	215
34	GOODSELL HENRY	SO	U	6	SCHOLAR	SSX	EWHURST	MADDAMS	220
48	GOODSELL HENRY	SO	U	6	SCHOLAR	SSX	EWHURST	SHOREHAM	222
5	GOODSELL HENRY	SO	U	8		SSX	EWHURST	PADGHAM	216
56	GOODSELL HENRY	SO	U	12	AG.LAB	SSX	EWHURST	ELLINGHOURNE	239
12	GOODSELL HENRY	SO	U	17	AG.LAB	SSX	EWHURST	DAGG LANE	217
48	GOODSELL ISAAC	SO	U	1M		SSX	EWHURST	SHOREHAM	222
85	GOODSELL JAMES	HD	M	29	AG.LAB	SSX	EWHURST	EWHURST GREEN	228
85	GOODSELL JAMES	SO	U	5	SCHOLAR	SSX	EWHURST	EWHURST GREEN	228
3	GOODSELL JAMES	SO	U	7	SCHOLAR	SSX	EWHURST	PADGHAM FARM	215
56	GOODSELL JAMES	SO	U	8	SCHOLAR	SSX	EWHURST	ELLINGHOURNE	239
10	GOODSELL JAMES	SO	U	17	AG.LAB	SSX	SEDLESCOMBE	BARRICKS	187
5	GOODSELL JANE	DA	U	6	SCHOLAR	SSX	EWHURST	PADGHAM	216
85	GOODSELL JANE	DA	U	7	SCHOLAR	SSX	EWHURST	EWHURST GREEN	228
10	GOODSELL JERREY	SO	U	14	AG.LAB	SSX	SEDLESCOMBE	BARRICKS	187
86	GOODSELL JESSE	HD	M	28	AG.LAB	SSX	EWHURST	STAPLE CROSS	243
28	GOODSELL JESSE	HD	M	74	SHOEMAKER	SSX	EWHURST	CRIPPS	252
80	GOODSELL JESSE	SO	U	8		SSX	EWHURST	EWHURST GREEN	227
76	GOODSELL JOHN	HD	M	32	GROOM	SSX	EWHURST	EWHURST GREEN	226
56	GOODSELL JOHN	HD	M	40	AG.LAB	SSX	EWHURST	ELLINGHOURNE	239
80	GOODSELL JOHN	HD	W	44	AG.LAB	SSX	EWHURST	EWHURST GREEN	227
76	GOODSELL JOHN	SO	U	11	SCHOLAR	SSX	EWHURST	EWHURST GREEN	226
80	GOODSELL JOHN	SO	U	13	AG.LAB	SSX	BATTLE	EWHURST GREEN	227
34	GOODSELL JOSEPH	SO	U	2		SSX	EWHURST	MADDAMS	220
3	GOODSELL JOSEPH	SO	U	15	AG.LAB	SSX	EWHURST	PADGHAM FARM	215
85	GOODSELL JULIA	DA	U	3		SSX	EWHURST	EWHURST GREEN	228
85	GOODSELL JULIA	WI	M	32		KEN	HAWKHURST	EWHURST GREEN	228
5	GOODSELL MARGARET HANNAH	DA	U	2		SSX	EWHURST	[ADGHAM	216
38	GOODSELL MARTHA	DA	U	7		SSX	EWHURST	FORGE LANE	254
38	GOODSELL MARTHA	MO	M	73		SSX	WESTFIELD	FORGE LANE	254
6	GOODSELL MARY	DA	U	9	SCHOLAR	SSX	EWHURST	PADGHAM	216
56	GOODSELL MARY	WI	M	39		SSX	EWHURST	ELLINGHOURNE	239
3	GOODSELL MARY	WI	M	42		SSX	NORTHIAM	PADGHAM FARM	215
38	GOODSELL MARY	WI	M	43		SSX	SEDLESCOMBE	FORGE LANE	254
34	GOODSELL MARY ANN	DA	U	4		SSX	EWHURST	MADDAMS	220
5	GOODSELL MARY ANN	DA	U	10	SCHOLAR	SSX	EWHURST	PADGHAM	215
38	GOODSELL MARY ANN	GD	U	1		SSX	BATTLE	FORGE LANE	254
5	GOODSELL MARY ANN	WI	M	40		SSX	MOUNTFIELD	PADGHAM	216
34	GOODSELL MATILDA	DA	U	5	SCHOLAR	SSX	EWHURST	MADDAMS	220
34	GOODSELL MATILDA	WI	M	39		SSX	BREDE	MADDAMS	220
67	GOODSELL PHILADELPHIA	DA	U	4		SSX	WESTFIELD	CASTLEMANS	211
38	GOODSELL PHILADELPHIA	DA	U	9		SSX	EWHURST	FORGE LANE	254
50	GOODSELL RICHARD	HD	M	54	AG.LAB	SSX	HOLLINGTON	NOT GIVEN	239
3	GOODSELL RICHARD	SO	U	2		SSX	EWHURST	PADGHAM FARM	216
56	GOODSELL RICHARD	SO	U	10	SCHOLAR	SSX	EWHURST	ELLINGHOURNE	239
56	GOODSELL SAMUEL	SO	U	3		SSX	EWHURST	ELLINGHOURNE	239
86	GOODSELL SARAH	WI	M	26		SSX	EWHURST	STAPLE CROSS	243
38	GOODSELL SARAH ANN	DA	U	11		SSX	EWHURST	FORGE LANE	254
12	GOODSELL SARAH ANN	DA	U	11?	SCHOLAR	SSX	EWHURST	DAGG LANE	217
3	GOODSELL SOPHIA	DA	U	10	SCHOLAR	SSX	EWHURST	PADGHAM FARM	215
85	GOODSELL STEPHEN	BR	U	20	SERVANT	SSX	EWHURST	EWHURST GREEN	228
85	GOODSELL STEPHEN	FA	W	63	AG.LAB	SSX	SEDLESCOMBE	EWHURST GREEN	228
5	GOODSELL STEPHEN	HD	M	42	AG.LAB	SSX	EWHURST	PADGHAM	216
38	GOODSELL STEPHEN	HD	M	44	FARMER'S LAB	SSX	EWHURST	FORGE LANE	254
50	GOODSELL SUSAN	WI	M	41		SSX	TICEHURST	NOY GIVEN	239
9	GOODSELL THOMAS	HD	W	40	AG.LAB	SSX	EWHURST	PADGHAM	216
48	GOODSELL THOMAS	SO	U	9	SCHOLAR	SSX	EWHURST	SHOREHAM	222
6	GOODSELL THOMAS	SO	U	18	AG.LAB	SSX	EWHURST	PADGHAM	216
3	GOODSELL THOMAS	SO	U	23	AG.LAB	SSX	EWHURST	PADGHAM FARM	215
37	GOODSELL THOMAS	VR	U	16	AG.LAB	SSX	EWHURST	STRAWBERRY HILL	253
68	GOODSELL WALTER	HD	M	26	AG,LAB	SSX	EWHURST	EWHURST GREEN	225
68	GOODSELL WILLIAM	SO	U	1M		SSX	EWHURST	EWHURST GREEN	225
12	GOODSELL WILLIAM	SO	U	5		SSX	EWHURST	DAGG LANE	217
31	GOODSELL WILLIAM	SO	U	8		SSX	EWHURST	MADDAMS	220
80	GOODSELL WILLIAM	SO	U	10		SSX	EWHURST	EWHURST GREEN	227
48	GOODSELL WILLIAM	SO	U	11	SCHOLAR	SSX	EWHURST	SHOREHAM	222
10	GOODSELL WILLIAM	SO	U	12	SCHOLAR	SSX	SEDLESCOMBE	BARRICKS	187
9	GOODSELL WILLIAM	SO	U	13	AG.LAB	SSX	EWHURST	PADGHAM	216
56	GOODSELL WILLIAM	SO	U	15	AG.LAB	SSX	NORTHIAM	ELLINGHOURNE	239
5	GOODSELL WILLIAM	SO	U	19	AG.LAB	SSX	EWHURST	PADGHAM	216
86	GOODSELL WILLIAM HENRY	SO	U	4M		SSX	EWHURST	STAPLE CROSS	243
77	GOODWIN ARTHUR	SO	U	6	SCHOLAR	SSX	BEXHILL	NOT GIVEN	98
77	GOODWIN CHARLES A	FA	M	67	RETIRED BREWER	KEN	SUTTON VALANCE	NOT GIVEN	98
77	GOODWIN F E (MALE)	SO	U	10	SCHOLAR	SSX	BATTLE	NOT GIVEN	98
77	GOODWIN FRANCES	DA	U	2		SSX	BEXHILL	NOT GIVEN	98
3	GOODWIN HENRY	LG	U	31	BRICKMAKER	WAR		FORWARD LANE	128
77	GOODWIN HERBERT	SO	U	8	SCHOLAR	SSX	BATTLE	NOT GIVEN	98
77	GOODWIN JANE E?	DA	U	4	SCHOLAR	SSX	BEXHILL	NOT GIVEN	98
77	GOODWIN KATE	DA	U	7M		SSX	BEXHILL	NOT GIVEN	98

	Name		Status	Age	Occupation	County	Town	Place	No.
77	GOODWIN MARTHA	WI	M	33		SSX	BEXHILL	NOT GIVEN	98
77	GOODWIN WILLIAM F	HD	M	33	TAILOR	SSX	BATTLE	NOT GIVEN	98
62	GOUGH SOLOMON	LG	U	24	RAIL LAB	HAM	SKUES*	PUMP HOUSE	14
31	GOWER BENJAMIN	SO	U	1		SSX	BATTLE	(LITTLE COMMON)	55
7	GOWER CHARLES	SS	U	9	SCHOLAR	SSX	HAILSHAM	BIGGS HILL SIDLEY	76
92	GOWER EDWIN	SO	U	1		SSX	HOLLINGTON	TILE KILN	19
32	GOWER ELBERT	NP	U	5	SCHOLAR	SSX	HASTINGS	STREAM HILL	123
37	GOWER ELENOR	DA	U	8M		SSX	BEXHILL	CLINCH GREEN SIDLEY	71
92	GOWER ELIZA	DA	U	7		SSX	HOLLINGTON	TILE KILN	19
92	GOWER ELLEN	DA	U	12		SSX	BATTLE	TILE KILN	19
92	GOWER EMILY	DA	U	10		SSX	BATTLE	TILE KILN	19
31	GOWER GEORGE	HD	M	34	AG.LAB	KEN	CHATHAM	(LITTLE COMMON)	55
37	GOWER HANNAH	DA	U	8		SSX	BEXHILL	CLINCH GREEN SIDLEY	71
92	GOWER HANNAH	DA	U	14		SSX	CROWHURST	TILE KILN	19
31	GOWER HARRIOT	WI	M	27		SSX	BEXHILL	(LITTLE COMMON)	55
92	GOWER JAMES	HD	W	40?		SSX	WARTLING	TILE KILN	19
31	GOWER JAMES	SO	U	5		SSX	BEXHILL	(LITTLE COMMON)	55
92	GOWER JAMES	SO	U	13		SSX	CROWHURST	TILE KILN	19
6	GOWER JANE	NC	U	15	HOUSE SERVANT	SSX	BATTLE	DUKE FARM	129
37	GOWER JOHN	HD	M	40	AG.LAB	KEN	CANTERBURY	CLINCH GREEN SIDLEY	71
31	GOWER JOHN	SO	U	7		SSX	BEXHILL	(LITTLE COMMON)	55
37	GOWER JOHN W	SO	U	2		SSX	BEXHILL	CLINCH GREEN SIDLEY	71
72	GOWER JUDY	WI	M	50		SSX	BEXHILL	BRAGS LANE	32
37	GOWER MARY	DA	U	10		SSX	BEXHILL	CLINCH GREEN SIDLEY	71
38	GOWER MARY	SV	U	21	HOUSE MAID	KEN	MAIDSTONE	BUCKLANDS	10
72	GOWER MARY A	DA	U	13		SSX	BEXHILL	BRAGS LANE	32
37	GOWER SARAH	DA	U	6		SSX	BEXHILL	CLINCH GREEN SIDLEY	71
37	GOWER SARAH	WI	M	32		SSX	ASHBURNHAM	CLINCH GREEN SUDLEY	71
11	GOWER WALTER	SV	U	19	AG.LAB	SSX	EASTBOURNE	WILTING FARM HOUSE	6
72	GOWER WILLIAM	HD	M	39	AG.LAB	KEN	CANTERBURY	BRAGS LANE	32
22	GRACE*? DINAH	WI	M	49		SSX	GUESTLING	GATE FARM	235
22	GRACE*? HENRY	HD	M	49	FARMER 157 AC EMP 25	SSX	SEDLESCOMBE	GATE FARM	235
22	GRACE*? THOMAS JOHN	SO	U	15		SSX	SEDLESCOMBE	GATE FARM	235
22	GRACE*? WILLIAM HENRY	SO	U	17		SSX	SEDLESCOMBE	GATE FARM	235
25	GRANT ALEXANDER	HD	M	44	RAIL LAB	NOT GIVEN		RAILWAY HUT	8
40	GRANT CAROLINE	WI	M	38		SSX	HERSTMONCEUX	PRAWLES FARM	221
25	GRANT CHARLES	SO	U	6		KEN	FOLKESTONE	RAILWAY HUT	8
40	GRANT DAVID	SO	U	1		SSX	EWHURST	PRAWLES FARM	221
67	GRANT ELLEN STARE?	WI	M	26		KEN	MARDEN	EWHURST GREEN	225
40	GRANT JAMES	SO	U	4		SSX	EWHURST	PRAWLES FARM	221
87	GRANT JANE	NC	U	8	SCHOLAR	DBY	SAWLEY	STAPLE CROSS	243
67	GRANT JANE MILLER	DA	U	7	SCHOLAR	KEN	MARDEN	EWHURST GREEN	225
40	GRANT JOHN	HD	M	44	AG.LAB	SSX	BRIGHTLING	PRAWLES FARM	221
25	GRANT REBECCA	DA	U	2		NORTHAMPTON		RAILWAY HUT	8
25	GRANT REBECCA	WI	M	42		BKM	CASTLE THORPE	RAILWAY HUT	8
40	GRANT SARAH	DA	U	6	SCHOLAR	SSX	ROBERTSBRIDGE	PRAWLES FARM	221
25	GRANT THOMAS	SO	U	4		NOT GIVEN		RAILWAY HUT	8
67	GRANT WILLIAM	HD	M	34	FARM BAILIFF	KEN	MAIDSTONE	EWHURST GREEN	225
67	GRANT WILLIAM	SO	U	10	SCHOLAR	KEN	AYLESFORD	EWHURST GREEN	225
39	GRANT WILLIAM	SV	U	18	AG.SERVANT	SSX	BRIGHTLING	PRAWLES FARM	221
32	GRAY ELIZABETH	VR	U	28	GENTELWOMAN ANNUITANT	MDX		BEXHILL STREET	27
67	GREEN GRACE	WI	M	51		COR	ST.STEPHENS	COAST GUARD STATION	31
67	GREEN SARAH	DA	U	15		SSX	NEWHAVEN	COAST GUARD STATION	31
65	GREEN THOMAS	FL	W	75	SHOEMAKER	SSX	SEAFORD	SIDLEY GREEN	84
67	GREEN THOMAS	HD	M	44	COAST GUARD	SSX	SEAFORD	COAST GUARD STATION	31
67	GREEN THOMAS	SO	U	14	ERRAND BOY	SSX	NEWHAVEN	COAST GUARD STATION	31
10	GREEN WILLIAM	LG	U	21	RAILWAY LAB	SRY	CAMBERWELL	FORWARD LANE	129
16	GREEN WILLIAM	VR	U	27	RAILWAY LAB	YKS		RAILWAY HUT	130
45	GREENE JOHN	LG	U	31	RAILWAY LAB	LIN	BOSTON	RAILWAY HUT	134
22	GREENWOOD JAMES	LG	U	NK25	RAIL LAB	UNKNOWN		RAILWAY HUT	8
16	GRESTWOOD ALICE AUGUSTA	DA	U	4		SSX	ST.LEONARDS	RAILWAY HUT	7
16	GRESTWOOD ELIZA ELLEN	DA	U	4M		SSX	HOLLINGTON	RAILWAY HUT	7
17	GRESTWOOD FRANCIS	LG	U	47	RAIL LAB	MDX	HARROW	RAILWAY HUT	7
16	GRESTWOOD FRANCIS G	SO	U	2		SSX	ST.LEONARDS	RAILWAY HUT	7
16	GRESTWOOD GEORGE	HD	M	36	RAIL LAB	MDX	HARROW	RAILWAY HUT	7
16	GRESTWOOD SOPHIA JANE	WI	M	42		MDX	PADDINGTON	RAILWAY HUT	7
80	GREY ELIZABETH	CL	U	18		SSX	CHICHESTER	BEAUPORT HOUSE	16
80	GREY KATHERINE	CL	U	16?		SSX	CHICHESTER	BEAUPORT HOUSE	16
57	GRIFFEN EMMILY	VR	U	12		SSX	UDIMORE	ELLINGBOURNE	240
14	GRIFFIN ANN	SV	U	15	GENERAL SERVANT	SSX	BREDE	BREDE HIGH	251
17	GRIFFITH ANN	SV	U	30		WLS	ABERGELE	OAKLANDS	174
23	GROOM HANNAH	WI	M	30		NTH	FINDON	RAILWAY HUT	8
23	GROOM ISAAC	HD	M	31	RAIL LAB	NTH	EARTHLINGBOROUGH	RAILWAY HUT	8
23	GROOM JOHN	SO	U	3		DOR	MAIDEN NEWTON	RAILWAY HUT	8
23	GROOM WILLIAM	SO	U	1		SSX	ST.LEONARDS	RAILWAY HUT	8
2	GROVES CHARLES	HD	M	32	AG.LAB	SSX	EWHURST	STOCKWOOD FARM	232
2	GROVES ELIZABETH MARY	DA	U	12		SSX	EWHURST	STOCKWOOD FARM	232
2	GROVES ELLEN	DA	U	8		SSX	EWHURST	STOCKWOOD FARM	232
2	GROVES GEORGE	SO	U	2		SSX	EWHURST	STOCKWOOD FARM	232
8	GROVES MARY ANN	DA	U	9	SCHOLAR	SSX	EWHURST	COLLIERS GREEN	233
8	GROVES NORMAN	SO	U	11	SCHOLAR	SSX	EWHURST	COLLIERS GREEN	233
75	GROVES SARAH	ML	W	73	PARISH RELIEF	KEN	SANDHURST	STAPLE CROSS	242
2	GROVES SARAH	WI	M	34		SSX	EWHURST	STOCKWOOD FARM	232
8	GROVES THOMAS	HD	W	37	CARPENTER	SSX	EWHURST	COLLIERS GREEN	233
91	GUILDFORD CHARLES	LG	U	37		NOT GIVEN		STREET	19
55	GURR EDWARD	SO	U	13	ERRAND BOY	SSX	EWHURST	SNAGS HALL	223

55	GURR ELIZA	DA	U	9	SCHOLAR	SSX EWHURST	SNAGS HALL	223
55	GURR ELIZA	WI	M	39		SSX EWHURST	SNAGS HALL	223
55	GURR ELLEN	DA	U	21		SSX EWHURST	SNAGS HALL	223
55	GURR EMMA	DA	U	1		SSX EWHURST	SNAGS HALL	223
55	GURR FRANCES	DA	U	2		SSX EWHURST	SNAGS HALL	223
55	GURR GEORGE	HD	M	47	WATCH MAKER	SSX SALEHURST	SNAGS HALL	223
55	GURR ISABELLA	DA	U	17		SSX EWHURST	SNAGS HALL	223
55	GURR JOSEPH	SO	U	7	SCHOLAR	SSX EWHURST	SNAGS HALL	223
55	GURR MARY ANN	DA	U	6	SCHOLAR	SSX EWHURST	SNAGS HALL	223
53	GUTSELL ALFRED	SO	U	14	AG.LAB	SSX WESTFIELD	SPRING HILL	179
1	GUTSELL CHARLOTTE	WI	M	48		SSX WESTFIELD	BISHOPS	172
53	GUTSELL DEBORAH	WI	M	44		SSX WESTFIELD	SPRING HILL	179
23	GUTSELL EDWIN	SO	U	20		NOT GIVEN (?WESTFIELD)	CHARITY HOUSE	154
74	GUTSELL ESTHER	DA	U	2		SSX WESTFIELD	PEAR TREE	181
1	GUTSELL GEORGE	HD	M	46	AG.LAB	SSX WESTFIELD	BISHOPS	172
53	GUTSELL GEORGE	HD	M	49	AG.LAB	SSX WESTFIELD	SPRING HILL	179
81	GUTSELL GEORGE	SV	U	17	WAREHOUSE BOY	SSX WESTFIELD	BULLS EYE CORNER	182
74	GUTSELL HANNAH	WI	M	24		SSX WESTFIELD	PEAR TREE	181
34	GUTSELL HANNAH	WI	M	58		SSX WESTFIELD	KENT STREET	166
74	GUTSELL HARRIETT	DA	U	5		SSX WESTFIELD	PEAR TREE	181
27	GUTSELL HARRIETT	DA	U	17		SSX BREDE	BREDE BRIDGE	175
34	GUTSELL HARRIETT	DA	U	22		SSX WESTFIELD	KENT STREET	166
6	GUTSELL HENRY	LG	U	25	AG.LAB	SSX WESTFIELD	SPRAYS BRIDGE	173
53	GUTSELL HENRY W	SO	U	6		SSX WESTFIELD	SPRING HILL	179
34	GUTSELL JAMES	HD	M	59	AG.LAB	SSX WESTFIELD	KENT STREET	166
12	GUTSELL JAMES	SV	U	17		SSX WESTFIELD	SPRAYS BRIDGE	163
28	GUTSELL JAMES	SV	W	34		SSX WESTFIELD	PLOUGH INN	155
74	GUTSELL JOHN	SO	U	3M		SSX WESTFIELD	PEAR TREE	181
23	GUTSELL JOHN	SO	U	33	AG.LAB	SSX WESTFIELD	CHARITY HOUSE	154
74	GUTSELL LEWIS	HD	M	29	AG.LAB	SSX WESTFIELD	PEAR TREE	181
1	GUTSELL MARY	LG	W	84		SSX ROBERTSBRIDGE	BISHOPS	172
38	GUTSELL MARY A	DA	U	13		SSX ORE	MOUNT PLEASANT	166
53	GUTSELL MATTHEW	SO	U	12	SCHOLAR	SSX WESTFIELD	SPRING HILL	179
27	GUTSELL MERCY	DA	U	11		SSX BREDE	BREDE BRIDGE	175
27	GUTSELL PHEBE	DA	U	7		SSX BREDE	BREDE BRIDGE	175
27	GUTSELL PHEBE	WI	M	51		SSX CASTLE	BREDE BRIDGE	175
53	GUTSELL PHILADELPHIA	DA	U	9	SCHOLAR	SSX WESTFIELD	SPRING HILL	179
23	GUTSELL PHILIDELPHIA	WI	M	65		SSX WESTFIELD	CHARITY HOUSE	154
27	GUTSELL PHILLY	DA	U	19		SSX BREDE	BREDE BRIDGE	175
1	GUTSELL PRECELLA	DA	U	17		SSX WESTFIELD	BISHOPS	172
27	GUTSELL ROBERT	HD	M	47	AG.LAB	SSX WESTFIELD	BREDE BRIDGE	175
37	GUTSELL ROBERT	HD	M	61	AG.LAB	NOT GIVEN (?WESTFIELD)	WALNUT TREE	156
53	GUTSELL ROBERT	SO	U	23	GLOVER JM	SSX WESTFIELD	SPRING HILL	179
43	GUTSELL ROBERT	SV	U	16		SSX WESTFIELD	IRELAND	167
23	GUTSELL SAMUEL	SO	U	18		NOT GIVEN (?WESTFIELD)	CHARITY HOUSE	154
60	GUTSELL SAMUEL	SV	U	15	AG.LAB	SSX SEDLESCOMBE	YEW TREES	180
38	GUTSELL SARAH	WI	M	45		SSX BEXHILL	MOUNT PLEASANT	166
37	GUTSELL SARAH	WI	M	62		SSX BREDE	WALNUT TREE	156
1	GUTSELL STEPHEN	SO	U	2		SSX WESTFIELD	BISHOPS	172
38	GUTSELL WILLIAM	HD	M	44	AG.LAB	SSX WESTFIELD	MOUNT PLEASANT	166
23	GUTSELL WILLIAM	HD	M	74	LAB	SSX WESTFIELD	CHARITY HOUSE	154
46	GUTSELL WILLIAM	SV	U	13		SSX WESTFIELD	MOAT	167
22	GUY ELIZA	WI	M	27		SSX BATTLE	SEDLESCOMBE STREET	204
22	GUY GEORGE	HD	M	27	AG.LAB	SSX SEDLESCOMBE	SEDLESCOMBE STREET	204
22	GUY HENRY	SO	U	10M		SSX SEDLESCOMBE	SEDLESCOMBE STREET	204
69	GUY PHILADELPHIA	HD	W	71	PAUPER	SSX MOUNTFIELD	IN THE VILLAGE	211
22	GUY WILLIAM	SO	U	4		SSX BATTLE	SEDLESCOMBE STREET	204
56	HACK JESSE	HD	M	58	INNKEEPER	SSX DALLINGTON	VICTORIA INN	12
56	HACK MARIA	WI	M	59		SSX HOLLINGTON	VICTORIA INN	12
56	HACK MARY ANN	DA	U	19		SSX HOLLINGTON	VICTORIA INN	12
56	HACK ROBERT	SO	U	23		SSX HOLLINGTON	VICTORIA INN	12
56	HACK VICTORIA	DA	U	15		SSX HOLLINGTON	VICTORIA INN	12
80	HACKETT JAMES	HD	W	41	INLAND REVENUE OFFICER	HAM BEDHAMPTON	STAPLE CROSS	243
95	HALL JOSEPH	LG	U	27	RAIL LAB	DOR WIMBORNE	HUT	19
64	HAMILTON HANNAH	WI	M	37	RAILWAY LAB (SIC)	SCT	RAILWAY HUT	137
64	HAMILTON JAMES	SO	U	8		FRANCE BRITISH SUBJECT	RAILWAY HUT	137
64	HAMILTON MARGRET	DA	U	2		HRT	RAILWAY HUT	137
64	HAMILTON MARY	DA	U	6		FRANCE BRITISH SUBJECT	RAILWAY HUT	137
64	HAMILTON ROBERT	HD	M	42	RAILWAY LAB	IRL	RAILWAY HUT	137
2	HAMMOND ANN	DA	U	10		SSX CROWHURST	NOT GIVEN	128
2	HAMMOND ANN	WI	M	53		SSX BATTLE	NOT GIVEN	128
52	HAMMOND CAROLINE	WI	M	29		SSX BEXHILL	SIDLEY GREEN	82
2	HAMMOND EDWIN	SO	U	21	AG.LAB	SSX CROWHURST	NOT GIVEN	128
15	HAMMOND ELIZA	SV	U	26	HOUSE SERVANT	SSX CROWHURST	HIGH HOUSE	144
17	HAMMOND ELIZA JANE	DL	U	9		SSX CROWHURST	CROWHURST VILLAGE	130
26	HAMMOND GEORGE	SO	U	17	AG.LAB	SSX BEXHILL	NOT GIVEN	92
21	HAMMOND GEORGE	SO	U	21		SSX BEXHILL	FREEZELAND* SIDLEY	68
20	HAMMOND JANE	WI	M	25		SSX CATSFIELD	NOT GIVEN	91
52	HAMMOND JOHN	HD	M	29	AG.LAB	SSX BEXHILL	SIDLEY GREEN	82
26	HAMMOND JOHN	HD	M	59	AG.LAB	SSX BATTLE	NOT GIVEN	92
21	HAMMOND MARY	HD	M	45	FARMER 59 AC EMP 5	SSX BATTLE	FREEZELAND* SIDLEY	68
20	HAMMOND MARY ANN	DA	U	7M		SSX BEXHILL	NOT GIVEN	91
26	HAMMOND PHILL'A	WI	M	62		SSX ST.LEONARDS	NOT GIVEN	92
20	HAMMOND RICHARD	HD	M	25	AG.LAB	SSX BEXHILL	NOT GIVEN	91
21	HAMMOND SARAH	DA	U	17		SSX BEXHILL	FREEZELAND* SIDLEY	68

21	HAMMOND SUSANNAH	DA	U	14		SSX	BEXHILL	FREEZELAND* SIDLEY	68
2	HAMMOND TILDEN	SO	U	13		SSX	CROWHURST	NOT GIVEN	128
2	HAMMOND WILLIAM	HD	M	57	AG.LAB	SSX	CROWHURST	NOT GIVEN	128
52	HAMMOND WILLIAM	SO	U	1		SSX	BEXHILL	SIDLEY GREEN	82
53	HAMMOND? EMMA	NC	U	2		SSX	BEXHILL	2 MARINE COTTAGES	29
22	HAMPTON JOSEPH	LG	U	35	RAIL LAB (AGE UNKNOWN)	UNKNOWN		RAILWAY HUT	8
65	HANCOCK CHARLES	PP	U	9	PUPIL	MDX	FINSBURY	NOT GIVEN	96
27	HANCOCK JOHN	LG	U	20	RAIL LAB	NTH	BRACKLY	RAILWAY HUT	8
48	HARDEN THOMAS	VR	U	32		HEF	TARINGTON	RAILWAY HUT	135
12	HARLAND CAROLINE	SV	U	16		SSX	BEXHILL	STEVEN'S CROUCH	121
67	HARLAND EDWARD	SV	U	19		SSX	BEXHILL	NOT GIVEN	97
54	HARLAND GEORGE	SO	U	8		SSX	BEXHILL	ALM'S HOUSE SIDLEY	82
54	HARLAND HANNAH	WI	M	36		SSX	BEXHILL	ALM'S HOUSE SIDLEY	82
54	HARLAND HENRY	SO	U	6		SSX	BEXHILL	ALM'S HOUSE SIDLEY	82
54	HARLAND JAMES	SO	U	10	AG.LAB	SSX	BEXHILL	ALM'S HOUSE SIDLEY	82
54	HARLAND JOHN	SO	U	4		SSX	BEXHILL	ALM'S HOUSE SIDLEY	82
54	HARLAND MARY ANN	DA	U	12	AG.LAB	SSX	BEXHILL	ALM'S HOUSE SIDLEY	82
54	HARLAND WILLIAM	HD	M	38	AG.LAB	SSX	BEXHILL	ALM'S HOUSE SIDLEY	82
54	HARLAND WILLIAM	SO	U	14	AG.LAB	SSX	BEXHILL	ALM'S HOUSE SIDLEY	82
66	HARMAN E J S (FEMALE)	DA	U	1M?		SSX	BEXHILL	NOT GIVEN	97
57	HARMAN HENRY	HD	M	23	AG.LAB	SSX	EWHURST	ELLINGHOURNE	239
57	HARMAN JAMES REED	GF	W	72	AG.LAB PARISH RELIEF	SSX	PETT	ELLINGHOURNE	240
66	HARMAN JOHN	HD	M	40	DRUGGIST	SSX	HASTINGS	NOT GIVEN	97
57	HARMAN LOUESA	WI	M	19		SSX	UDIMORE	ELLINGHOURNE	239
57	HARMAN MARY ANN	DA	U	6M		SSX	EWHURST	ELLINGHOURNE	239
66	HARMAN SOPHIA	WI	M	42		BRK	WOODHAY	NOT GIVEN	97
1	HARMER ELIZABETH	MO	U	76		SSX	EWHURST	CASTLE INN	215
66	HARMER GEORGE	LG	U	16	GRACER'S ASSISTANT	KEN	TONBRIDGE	EWHURST GREEN	225
23	HARMER HANNAH	DA	U	24		MDX	HAMPTON	NOT GIVEN	122
10	HARMER JOHN	GS	U	5		SSX	EWHURST	PADGHAM	216
23	HARMER JOHN	HD	M	64	GREENWICH PENSIONER	SSX	CATSFIELD	NOT GIVEN	122
1	HARMER MARY ANN	SV	U	20	SERVANT	SSX	EWHURST	CASTLE INN	215
43	HARMER MATILDA	DA	U	4		SSX	EWHURST	DAGG LANE	217
11	HARMER REUBEN	SV	U	22	AG.LAB	SSX	HEATHFIELD	WILTING FARM HOUSE	6
1	HARMER RICHARD	HD	U	50	INNKEEPER	SOM	ST.MARYS BATH	CASTLE INN	215
43	HARMER ROBERT	SO	U	8M		SSX	EWHURST	DAGG LANE	217
23	HARMER SARAH	WI	M	66	BLIND INSANE	SSX	HOOE	NOT GIVEN	122
1	HARMER WILLIAM	FA	M	82		SSX	EWHURST	CASTLE INN	215
13	HARMER? ELIZA	WI	M	35		SSX	EWHURST	DAGG LANE	217
13	HARMER? WILLIAM	HD	M	52	CORD WINDER	SSX	EWHURST	DAGG LANE	217
11	HARRIS ANN	DA	U	7		SSX	BEXHILL	NOT GIVEN	52
11	HARRIS ANN	HD	W	39	AG.LAB'S WIFE	SSX	BEXHILL	NOT GIVEN	52
37	HARRIS ANN	SV	U	17	HOUSEMAID	SSX	BEXHILL	BEXHILL STREET	27
14	HARRIS ANN	WI	M	48?		HAM	WINCHESTER	YEW TREES	173
73	HARRIS EDWARD	SO	U	17	AG.LAB	SSX	BEXHILL	NOT GIVEN	97
41	HARRIS ELIZA	DA	U	10		SSX	BEXHILL	NOT GIVEN	94
8	HARRIS ELIZA	DA	U	17		SSX	BEXHILL	BIGGS HILL SIDLEY	76
73	HARRIS ELIZA	HD	W	48	LAUNDRESS	SSX	CROWHURST	NOT GIVEN	97
41	HARRIS ELIZABETH	DA	U	8		SSX	BEXHILL	NOT GIVEN	94
73	HARRIS GEORGE	SO	U	12	SCHOLAR	SSX	BEXHILL	NOT GIVEN	97
38	HARRIS HANNAH	DA	U	12		SSX	PETT	WORK-HOUSE	156
11	HARRIS HANNAH	DA	U	14		SSX	BEXHILL	NOT GIVEN	52
8	HARRIS HANNAH	WI	M	51		SSX	WESTFIELD	BIGGS HILL SIDLEY	76
8	HARRIS JAMES	HD	M	51	FARMER 10 AC	SSX	BEXHILL	BIGGS HILL SIDLEY	76
38	HARRIS JANE	HD	W	51	LAB	KEN	NEW ROMNEY	WORK-HOUSE	156
14	HARRIS JOHN	HD	M	41	CHELSEA PENSIONER	SSX	SEDLESCOMBE	YEW TREES	173
11	HARRIS JOSHUA	SO	U	4		SSX	BEXHILL	NOT GIVEN	52
8	HARRIS MARTHA	VR	U	16		SSX	PETT	OAK COTTAGE	152
41	HARRIS MARY	HD	W	47	PAUPER	SSX	BEXHILL	NOT GIVEN	94
7	HARRIS MARY	HD	W	85	PAUPER	SSX	RIDGWICK	SCHOOL HOUSE	162
37	HARRIS MARY	SV	M	40	COOK	SSX	HEATHFIELD	BEXHILL STREET	27
28	HARRIS MARY	SV	U	15	HOUSE SERVANT	SSX	BEXHILL	WHEAT SHEAF INN	54
8	HARRIS MARY ANN	DA	U	11		SSX	BEXHILL	BIGGS HILL SIDLEY	76
41	HARRIS SARAH	DA	U	7		SSX	BEXHILL	NOT GIVEN	94
11	HARRIS SARAH	DA	U	9		SSX	BEXHILL	NOT GIVEN	52
73	HARRIS STEPHEN	SO	U	19	AG.LAB	SSX	BEXHILL	NOT GIVEN	97
11	HARRIS THOMAS	SO	U	12	AG.LAB	SSX	BEXHILL	NOT GIVEN	52
41	HARRIS WALTER	SO	U	12		SSX	BEXHILL	NOT GIVEN	94
24	HARRIS WILLIAM	LG	U	19	AG.LAB	SSX	BEXHILL	NOT GIVEN	54
8	HARRIS WILLIAM	SO	U	17	FARMER'S SO EMP AT HOME	SSX	BEXHILL	BIGGS HILL SIDLEY	76
73	HARRIS WILLIAM	SO	U	22	RAIL LAB	SSX	BEXHILL	NOT GIVEN	97
6	HARRISS SARAH	SV	U	22?	HOUSE SERVANT	SSX	NINFIELD	ROSE COTTAGE - SIDLEY	65
44	HARROD ELIZA	DA	U	13		SSX	WESTFIELD	INMANS	177
44	HARROD EMILY	DA	U	4		SSX	WESTFIELD	INMANS	178
44	HARROD ESTHER	DA	U	10		SSX	WESTFIELD	INMANS	178
44	HARROD LUCRETIA	WI	M	42		SSX	WESTFIELD	INMANS	177
44	HARROD WILLIAM	HD	M	45	AG.LAB	SSX	BREDE	INMANS	177
44	HARROD WILLIAM	SO	U	7		SSX	WESTFIELD	INMANS	178
34	HARTNIP? JABEZ	SV	U	22	FOOTMAN	KEN	CAPEL	RECTORY	205
85	HARTNUP ELIZABETH	WI	M	31		SSX	EWHURST	STAPLE CROSS	243
76	HARTNUP GEORGE	LG	U	14	BUTCHER'S BOY	KEN	SANDHURST	STAPLE CROSS	242
15	HARTNUP LOUISA	SV	U	18	HOUSE MAID	KEN	FORDLEY	CATSFIELD PLACE FARM	108
85	HARTNUP SARAH ANN	DA	U	9M		SSX	EWHURST	STAPLE CROSS	243
85	HARTNUP THOMAS	HD	M	33	BUTCHER	KEN	CAPEL	STAPLE CROSS	243
76	HARTNUP THOMAS	LG	W	59	BUTCHER JM	KEN	TONBRIDGE	STAPLE CROSS	242
76	HARTNUP WILLIAM	LG	U	25	AG.LAB	KEN	CAPEL	STAPLE CROSS	242

Ref	Surname	Forename	Rel	Cond	Age	Occupation
61	HARVEY	ANN	WI	M	66	
61	HARVEY	EDWARD	SO	U	25	AG.LAB
52	HARVEY	HENRY	SV	U	26	GROOM
32	HARVEY	HESTER ANNE	LG	M	19	
37	HARVEY	HEZEKIAH	HD	W	65	AG.LAB
61	HARVEY	JAMES	HD	M	64	AG.LAB
37	HARVEY	JAMES	SO	U	19	AG.LAB
37	HARVEY	NAOMY	DA	U	9	SCHOLAR
48	HARVEY	SAMUEL	FL	M	63?	AG.LAB
48	HARVEY	SARAH	ML	M	60	
32	HARVEY	STEPHEN	LG	M	21	SAWYER
95	HARVEY	THOMAS	LG	U	30	RAIL LAB
63	HASELDEN	HENRY	LG	U	40	RAILWAY LAB
91	HASSELL	STEPHEN	HD	U	56	SHOEMAKER
26	HAWE	REBECCA	SV	U	39	COOK
27	HAWSETT	AGNES	/	U	3	NURSE CHILD
45	HAYDEN	ANN	WI	M	33	
45	HAYDEN	ANN J	DA	U	10	SCHOLAR
45	HAYDEN	EDITH C	DA	U	4	
45	HAYDEN	HENRY	HD	M	39	COAST GUARD
45	HAYDEN	HENRY	SO	U	11	SCHOLAR
45	HAYDEN	JANE	DA	U	2	
45	HAYDEN	LOUISA L	DA	U	3M	
45	HAYDEN	MARY M	DA	U	6	
45	HAYDEN	WILLIAM	SO	U	8	SCHOLAR
29	HAYLER	EDWARD	HD	M	52	AG.LAB
29	HAYLER	EDWIN	SO	U	17	AG.LAB
33	HAYLER	ELIZA	DA	U	8	SCHOLAR
42	HAYLER	ELIZABETH	ML	W	75	
29	HAYLER	EMILY	DA	U	10	SCHOLAR
61	HAYLER	HESTER	DA	U	13?	
61	HAYLER	JANE	WI	M	43	
33	HAYLER	JOHN HENRY	SO	U	6	SCHOLAR
33	HAYLER	JOHN WILLIAM	HD	M	29	AG.LAB
61	HAYLER	LEONORA	DA	U	6	SCHOLAR
29	HAYLER	LUCY	WI	M	48	
33	HAYLER	MARY ANN	DA	U	3	
29	HAYLER	PRESSELLA	DA	U	8	SCHOLAR
33	HAYLER	SARAH	DA	U	1	
33	HAYLER	SARAH ANN	WI	M	29	
29	HAYLER	SOPHIA	DA	U	12	SCHOLAR
61	HAYLER	WILL	SO	U	10	SCHOLAR
61	HAYLER	WILLIAM	HD	M	41	AG.LAB
9	HAYLES	EDWARD	HD	M	53	AG.LAB
9	HAYLES	EDWARD	SO	U	22	AG.LAB
9	HAYLES	FREDERICK	SO	U	16	AG.LAB
9	HAYLES	GEORGE	SO	U	18	AG.LAB
9	HAYLES	HENRY	SO	U	28	SAWYER
9	HAYLES	MARY	WI	M	54	
9	HAYLES	TOM	SO	U	7	SCHOLAR
24	HAYLEY	GEORGINA M F	DA	U	3M	
24	HAYLEY	JULIA	CI	U	35	
24	HAYLEY	MARIA G	WI	M	28	
24	HAYLEY	RUSSELL	HD	M	41	RECTOR OF PARISH
70	HAYWARD	ARTHER SAMUEL	SO	U	3M	
70	HAYWARD	CHARLOTTE ANN	DA	U	3	
56	HAYWARD	JAMES	LG	W	57	AG.LAB
70	HAYWARD	JEMMA	WI	M	39	
25	HAYWARD	JOSEPH	LG	U	23	RAIL LAB
27	HAYWARD	MARIA	/	U	41?	HOUSE KEEPER
30	HAYWARD	MARY ANN	VR	U	41	DRESSMAKER
70	HAYWARD	SAMUEL	HD	M	33	MILLER
27	HAZELDEN	JOHN	SO	U	15	AG.LAB
27	HAZELDEN	JOSEPH	HD	W	64	AG.LAB
27	HAZELDEN	JOSEPH	SO	U	16	AG.LAB
27	HAZELDEN	SARAH ANN	?NC	U	22	
27	HAZELDEN	THOMAS	BR	W?	59	AG.LAB
27	HAZELDEN	THOMAS	?NP	U	26	AG.LAB
75	HEAD	ANN	WI	M	50	
75	HEAD	CHARLES	SO	U	7	
81	HEAD	CHARLOTTE	SV	U	18	NURSERY MAID
43	HEAD	CHARLOTTE	WI	M	35	
80	HEAD	EDWARD	LG	W	65	CARRIER
75	HEAD	ELIZABETH	DA	U	11	
41	HEAD	ELLEN	WI	M	27	
41	HEAD	EMMA	DA	U	3M	
41	HEAD	FANNY	DA	U	3	
78	HEAD	FRANCES	SV	U	14	
43	HEAD	HARRIOT	DA	U	8	
75	HEAD	HENRY	GS	U	2M	
41	HEAD	JOHN	HD	M	29	AG.LAB
75	HEAD	MARY	DA	U	18	
43	HEAD	ROSE	DA	U	1	
75	HEAD	SARAH	DA	U	23	
75	HEAD	STEPHEN	HD	M	45	AG.LAB
43	HEAD	STEPHEN	SO	U	4	

County	Parish	Residence	Page
SSX	CATSFIELD	AT THE STREAM	210
SSX	SEDLESCOMBE	AT THE STREAM	210
SSX	SEDLESCOMBE	GREAT SANDERS	194
SSX	EWHURST	CRIPBS COTTAGE	253
SSX	MOUNTFIELD	STRAWBERRY HILL	253
SSX	WHATLINGTON	AT THE STREAM	210
SSX	EWHURST	STRAWBERRY HILL	253
SSX	EWHURST	STRAWBERRY HILL	253
SFK	CRETON?	NO.5 GALLEY HILL	29
SFK	STONEHAM	NO.5 GALLEY HILL	29
SSX	EWHURST	CRIPPS COTTAGE	253
CAMBRIDGE TOWN		HUT	19
SSX		RAILWAY HUT	137
SSX	EWHURST	STAPLE CROSS	244
BKM	BISHAM	CATSFIELD PLACE CHURCH HSE	110
SRY	CROYDON	FORTLAND? HOUSE	123
SSX	BRIGHTON	NO.2 GALLEY HILL	28
SSX	NEWHAVEN	NO.2 GALLEY HILL	28
SSX	BEXHILL	NO.2 GALLEY HILL	29
IOW	NEWPORT	NO.2 GALLEY HILL	29
SSX	NEWHAVEN	NO.2 GALLEY HILL	28
SSX	BEXHILL	NO.2 GALLEY HILL	29
SSX	EASTBOURNE	NO.2 GALLEY HILL	29
SSX	NEWHAVEN	NO.2 GALLEY HILL	28
SSX	SEDLESCOMBE	BRICKWALL	190
SSX	BATTLE	BRICKWALL	190
SSX	SEDLESCOMBE	BREDE LANE	191
SSX	SEDLESCOMBE	POPPING HOLE LANE	206
SSX	BATTLE	BRICKWALL	190
SSX	SEDLESCOMBE	BAULKHAM GREEN	196
SSX	SEDLESCOMBE	BAULKHAM GREEN	196
SSX	WESTFIELD	BREDE LANE	191
SSX	SEDLESCOMBE	BAULKHAM GREEN	196
SSX	CATSFIELD	BRICKWALL	190
SSX	SEDLESCOMBE	BREDE LANE	191
SSX	BATTLE	BRICKWALL	190
SSX	SEDLESCOMBE	BREDE LANE	191
SSX	EWHURST	BREDE LANE	191
SSX	BATTLE	BRICKWALL	190
SSX	SEDLESCOMBE	BAULKHAM GREEN	196
SSX	SEDLESCOMBE	BAULKHAM GREEN	196
SSX	SEDLESCOMBE	BARRICKS	187
SSX	SEDLESCOMBE	BARRICKS	187
SSX	SEDLESCOMBE	BARRICKS	187
SSX	SEDLESCOMBE	BARRICKS	187
SSX	SEDLESCOMBE	BARRICKS	187
SSX	SEDLESCOMBE	BARRICKS	187
SSX	SEDLESCOMBE	BARRICKS	187
SSX	CATSFIELD	CATSFIELD RECTORY	109
SSX	BRIGHTLING	CATSFIELD RECTORY	109
HAM	SELBORN?	CATSFIELD RECTORY	109
SSX	BRIGHTLING	CATSFIELD RECTORY	109
SSX	BEXHILL	NOT GIVEN	59
SSX	BEXHILL	NOT GIVEN	59
KEN	HAWKHURST	SNAGS HALL	223
SSX	BEXHILL	NOT GIVEN	59
SSX	COOKFIELD?	QUEENS HEAD SEDLESCOMBE ST	189
SSX	SALEHURST	LONG LEES	219
SSX	WOODHURST	LITTLE COMMON	55
SSX	BEXHILL	NOT GIVEN	59
SSX	EWHURST	LONG LEES	219
SSX	SALEHURST	LONG LEES	219
SSX	EWHURST	LONG LEES	219
SSX	EWHURST	LONG LEES	219
SSX	SALEHURST	LONG LEES	219
SSX	EWHURST	LONG LEES	219
SSX	ORE	STEMPS?	15
SSX	HOLLINGTON	STEMPS?	16
SSX	HOLLINGTON	BEAUPORT HOUSE	17
SSX	BEXHILL	NOT GIVEN	56
SSX	BEXHILL	QUEENS HEAD	32
SSX	HOLLINGTON	STEMPS?	15
SSX	EASTDEAN	HOLLINGTON STREET	10
SSX	HOLLINGTON	HOLLINGTON STREET	10
SSX	HOLLINGTON	HOLLINGTON STREET	10
SSX	HOLLINGTON	STEMPS? LODGE	16
SSX	BEXHILL	NOT GIVEN	56
SSX	HOLLINGTON	STEMPS?	16
KEN	CRANBROOK	HOLLINGTON STREET	10
SSX	HOLLINGTON	STEMPS?	15
SSX	BEXHILL	NOT GIVEN	56
SSX	HOLLINGTON	STEMPS?	15
SSX	BEXHILL	NOT GIVEN	56
SSX	BEXHILL	NOT GIVEN	56

#	Name	Rel	M	Age	Occupation	Birthplace	Address	Pg
75	HEAD THOMAS	HD	M	63	WAGGONER	SSX ST.LEONARDS	STEMPS?	15
41	HEAD WILLIAM	SO	U	2		SSX HOLLINGTON	HOLLINGTON STREET	10
75	HEAD WILLIAM	SO	U	9		SSX HOLLINGTON	STEMPS?	15
64	HEARS JAMES	LG	U	21	RAILWAY LAB	CAM	RAILWAY HUT	137
64	HEATH CHARLOTTE	VR	U	18	ANNUITANT	SSX RYE	STAPLE CROSS	241
32	HEATHER DEBORAH	DA	U	19	LAUNDRESS	SSX CATSFIELD	STREAM HILL	123
32	HEATHER DEBORAH	WI	M	50	LAUNDRESS	SSX CATSFIELD	STREAM HILL	123
32	HEATHER EDWARD	HD	M	47	CARRIER	SSX CATSFIELD	STREAM HILL	123
32	HEATHER GEORGE	SO	U	11	SCHOLAR	SSX CATSFIELD	STREAM HILL	123
32	HEATHER JAMES	SO	U	13	ERRAND BOY	SSX CATSFIELD	STREAM HILL	123
32	HEATHER SARAH	DA	U	20	LAUNDRESS	SSX CATSFIELD	STREAM HILL	123
32	HEATHER THEODORHIA (SIC)	DA	U	9	SCHOLAR	SSX CATSFIELD	STREAM HILL	123
34	HEDGER HENRY	SV	U	22	SERVANT	SSX NINFIELD	COURT LODGE FARM	147
63	HEMMANY FRANCES	PP	U	9		SRY KENNINGTON	BEXHILL STREET	96
5	HENLEY ANN	DA	U	29		SSX EWHURST	COLLIERS GREEN	233
64	HENLEY ANN ELIZA	DA	U	17		SSX EWHURST	STAPLE CROSS	241
64	HENLEY ELIZA	WI	M	52		SSX RYE	STAPLE CROSS	241
64	HENLEY ELIZABETH MARY	DA	U	16		SSX EWHURST	STAPLE CROSS	241
90	HENLEY EMMA	WI	M	51		SSX EWHURST	STAPLE CROSS	244
23	HENLEY FANNY	VR	U	6		SSX ROBERTSBRIDGE	GLINE FARM SIDLEY	78
5	HENLEY HARRIET	DA	U	31		SSX EWHURST	COLLIERS GREEN	233
64	HENLEY JOSEPH	HD	M	54	CORN MERCHANT	SSX EWHURST	STAPLE CROSS	241
64	HENLEY JOSEPH	SO	U	13	SCHOLAR	SSX EWHURST	STAPLE CROSS	241
5	HENLEY MARTHA	CI	U	55		SSX EWHURST	COLLIERS GREEN	233
64	HENLEY RHODA	DA	U	8	SCHOLAR	SSX EWHURST	STAPLE CROSS	241
64	HENLEY RICHARD	SO	U	11	SCHOLAR	SSX EWHURST	STAPLE CROSS	241
90	HENLEY THOMAS	HD	M	50	CORDWAINER	SSX EWHURST	STAPLE CROSS	244
5	HENLEY THOMAS	HD	W	68	FARMER 65 AC EMP 2	SSX EWHURST	COLLIERS GREEN	233
90	HENLEY THOMAS	SO	U	16	AG.LAB	SSX EWHURST	STAPLE CROSS	244
90	HENLEY WILLIAM	SO	U	25	AG.LAB	SSX EWHURST	STAPLE CROSS	244
63	HENTLEY HENRY	LG	U	25	RAILWAY LAB	STS	RAILWAY HUT	137
16	HIBBOTT MATHEW	SL	M	26	RAILWAY TIME KEEPER	RUTLAND OAKHAM	BANKS'S HOUSE - SIDLEY	67
5	HICKMAN EMILY	DA	U	11	SCHOLAR	SSX CROWHURST	NOT GIVEN	143
5	HICKMAN HARRIETT	WI	M	46		SSX CROWHURST	NOT GIVEN	143
5	HICKMAN HARRY	SO	U	6	SCHOLAR	SSX CROWHURST	NOT GIVEN	143
5	HICKMAN WILLIAM	HD	M	46	CORDWAINER EMP 2	SSX BEXHILL	NOT GIVEN	143
5	HICKMAN WILLIAM	SO	U	9	SCHOLAR	SSX CROWHURST	NOT GIVEN	143
31	HICKMOTT HARRIOT	6D	U	4M		SSX SALEHURST	CRIPPS	253
31	HICKMOTT MARY	DA	U	19		SSX EWHURST	CRIPPS	253
31	HICKMOTT RICHARD	HD	W	55	CARRIER	KEN HORSEMONDEN	CRIPPS	253
12	HICKS MARY ANN	CL	U	12	SCHOLAR	SSX NORTHIAM	COLLIERS GREEN	233
56	HIELD ELIZABETH	WI	M	40		YKS YORK	RAILWAY STATION	30
56	HIELD JOHN	HD	M	45	CLERK S E RAILWAY	YKS YORK	RAILWAY STATION	30
41	HIGGINS ELIZABETH	WI	M	37		SSX BREDE	FORGE LANE	254
77	HIGGINS EMMA	SV	U	14	SERVANT	SSX ST.LEONARDS	STAPLE CROSS	243
41	HIGGINS FRANCES	DA	U	2		SSX BODIAM	FORGE LANE	254
32	HIGGINS HARRIET	DL	U	20		SSX EWHURST	REEVES	246
12	HIGGINS HARRIET	SV	U	14	GENERAL SERVANT	SSX EWHURST	COLLIERS GREEN	234
41	HIGGINS JAMES	HD	M	46	AG.LAB	SSX BODIAM	FORGE LANE	254
41	HIGGINS JAMES	SO	U	7	SCHOLAR	SSX EWHURST	FORGE LANE	254
41	HIGGINS MARY	DA	U	16		SSX BODIAM	FORGE LANE	254
41	HIGGINS RACHEL	DA	U	4		SSX BODIAM	FORGE LANE	254
30	HILDER ANN	HD	W	67	INN KEEPER	SSX BURWASH	CRIPPS	253
4	HILDER CAROLINE	DA	U	2		SSX SALEHURST	PADGHAM	216
25	HILDER EDWARD	HD	M	38	AG.LAB	SSX BEXHILL	CRIPPS	252
11	HILDER EDWARD	SV	U	24	FARM SERVANT	SSX WADHURST	WILTING FARM HOUSE	6
30	HILDER EDWARD B	6S	U	3		SSX SEDLESCOMBE	CRIPPS	253
30	HILDER ELIZA	DA	U	25	DRESSMAKER	SSX EWHURST	CRIPPS	253
4	HILDER ELIZABETH	DA	U	13		SSX MOUNTFIELD	PADGHAM	216
11	HILDER FRANCES	DA	U	39		SSX TICEHURST	ASHDOWNS	173
37	HILDER FRANCES SARAH	DA	U	2		SSX EWHURST	NEWHAVEN FARM	237
56	HILDER GEORGE	LG	U	21	SURVEYOR	SSX HASTINGS	VICTORIA INN	12
4	HILDER GEORGE	SO	U	1M		SSX EWHURST	PADGHAM	216
4	HILDER HARRIET	DA	U	10		SSX MOUNTFIELD	PADGHAM	216
11	HILDER HARRIETT	DA	U	41		SSX TICEHURST	ASHDOWNS	173
25	HILDER HENRY WILLIAM	SO	U	4		MDX WILSDEN	CRIPPS	252
4	HILDER JAMES	HD	M	40	AG.LAB	SSX SEDLESCOMBE	PADGHAM	216
4	HILDER JAMES	SO	U	7	SCHOLAR	SSX MOUNTFIELD	PADGHAM	216
30	HILDER JANE	DA	U	34	DRESSMAKER	KEN SANDHURST	CRIPPS	253
37	HILDER JOHN	SO	U	5		SSX EWHURST	NEWHAVEN FARM	237
4	HILDER MARY ANN	WI	M	36		SSX MOUNTFIELD	PADGHAM	216
4	HILDER ROLIN	SO	U	11		SSX SALEHURST	PADGHAM	216
11	HILDER SARAH	HD	W	72	FARMER	SSX BURWASH	ASHDOWNS	173
25	HILDER SARAH	WI	M	33		SSX MAYFIELD	CRIPPS	252
37	HILDER SARAH	WI	M	38		SSX WESTHAM	NEWHAVEN FARM	237
30	HILDER SOPHIA	DA	U	36	DRESSMAKER	KEN SANDHURST	CRIPPS	253
37	HILDER THOMAS	HD	M	39	FARM BAILIFF	SSX BURWASH	NEWHAVEN FARM	237
37	HILDER THOMAS HENRY	SO	U	9M		SSX EWHURST	NEWHAVEN FARM	237
9	HILDER WINNIFRED	HD	W	74		SSX BATTLE	SEDLESCOMBE STREET	202
16	HILL GEORGE	LG	U	39	CARPENTER	SSX HASTINGS	STEPHEN'S CROUCH	121
25	HILL THOMAS	LG	U	28	RAILWAY LAB	BDF DUNSTABLE	RANSOM'S HOUSE	145
17	HILLAY CHARLES	SV	U	26		MDX ACTON	OAKLANDS	174
46	HILLS EDWIN	SV	U	19	HOUSE SERVANT	SSX GUESTLING	MOAT	167
58	HILLS JOHN	HD	W	67	AG.LAB	KEN DIMCHURCH	NOT GIVEN	112
3	HILTON WILLIAM	SV	U	34	AG.LAB	SSX BISHOPSTOWE	BARNHORN HILL	37
81	HINKLY WILLIAM	SL	U	6	SCHOLAR	SSX WESTFIELD	BULLS EYE CORNER	182

#	Name	Rel	Age	Occupation	Co	Birthplace	Address	No
55	HIRE ESTHER	SV U	45	HOUSE SERVANT	PEM	MILFORD	SIGNAL HOUSE	44
11	HIRUNS ELIZABETH	DA U	7	SCHOLAR	BKM	CHENTWOOD?	PARK HOUSE	121
11	HIRUNS GEORGE	SO U	4		BKM	CHENTWOOD?	PARK HOUSE	121
11	HIRUNS REBACCA	WI M	36		BKM	TWYFORD	PARK HOUSE	120
11	HIRUNS THOMAS	HD M	39	FARMER 300 AC	OXF	STRATTON AUDLEY	PARK HOUSE	120
11	HIRUNS THOMAS	SO U	9	SCHOLAR	BKM	CHUTWOODS?	PARK HOUSE	120
67	HISCOCK EDMUND	HD M	38	AG.LAB	SSX	BATTLE	MOUNT PLEASANT	197
30	HISCOCK ISABELLA	GD U	8	SCHOLAR	SSX	SEDLESCOMBE	SEDLESCOMBE STREET	204
30	HISCOCK JOSHUA	SO M	32	AG.LAB	SSX	SEDLESCOMBE	SEDLESCOMBE STREET	204
30	HISCOCK LEONORA	DL M	26		SSX	SEDLESCOMBE	SEDLESCOMBE STREET	204
17	HISCOCK MARIA	SV U	32		SSX	SEDLESCOMBE	OAKLANDS	174
67	HISCOCK MARY	WI M	36		SSX	WESTFIELD	MOUNT PLEASANT	197
30	HISCOCK PHILADELPHIA	HD W	64		SSX	WHATLINGTON	SEDLESCOMBE STREET	204
30	HISCOCK SALONE	GD U	3		SSX	SEDLESCOMBE	SEDLESCOMBE STREET	204
67	HISCOCK SELINA	DA U	9		SSX	SEDLESCOMBE	MOUNT PLEASANT	197
25	HOAD ANN	SV U	23	BARMAID	SSX	LAUGHTON	QUEENS HEAD SEDLESCOMBE ST	189
55	HOAD HENRY	/ U	23	WATCH MAKER	SSX	SALEHURST	SNAGS HALL	223
23	HOAD THOMAS	VR U	25	SOLICITOR	SSX	BRIGHTLING	GLINE FARM SIDLEY	78
80	HOADLY HANNAH	SV U	16	HOUSE SERVANT	SSX	EASTDEAN	POND HOUSE (LITTLE COMMON)	47
22	HOBBS ARTHUR	SO U	2M		SSX	EWHURST	HOPHOUSE	122
22	HOBBS DEBORAH	MO W	77		NOT	GIVEN	HOPHOUSE	122
22	HOBBS EMILY	DA U	7	SCHOLAR	SSX	BATTLE	HOPHOUSE	122
22	HOBBS FANNY ELEN	DA U	5		SSX	EWHURST	HOPHOUSE	122
22	HOBBS FREDERICK	SO U	2		SSX	EWHURST	HOPHOUSE	122
22	HOBBS HARIOT	WI M	38		SSX	SHOREHAM	HOPHOUSE	122
22	HOBBS WILLIAM	HD M	40	FARMER 100 AC EMP 2	SSX	BATTLE	HOPHOUSE	122
1	HODGKINS ALFRED	SL U	14	AG.LAB	SRY	LAMBETH	CATSFIELD DOWN	106
49	HODGSKIN ANN	HD W	74	PARISH RELIEF	KEN	GOUDHURST	NOT GIVEN	111
49	HODGSKIN EDWIN	SO U	27	AG.LAB	KEN	APPLEDORE	NOT GIVEN	111
26	HOLDEN THOMAS	SV U	21	GROOM	SSX	BECKLEY	CATSFIELD PLACE CHURCH HSE	110
60	HOLESTOCK CHARLOTTE	DA U	2		SSX	SEDLESCOMBE	BAULKHAM GREEN	196
60	HOLESTOCK MARY	DA U	7	SCHOLAR	SSX	SEDLESCOMBE	BAULKHAM GREEN	196
60	HOLESTOCK SARAH	WI M	25		SSX	BREDE	BAULKHAM GREEN	196
60	HOLESTOCK THOMAS	HD M	33	AG.LAB	SSX	SEDLESCOMBE	BAULKHAM GREEN	196
60	HOLESTOCK THOMAS	SO U	1		SSX	SEDLESCOMBE	BAULKHAM GREEN	196
8	HOLLAND ANN	HD U	57	GENTLEWOMAN ANNUITANT	SSX	LEWES	BELL HILL	24
15	HOLLAND EDWARD	VR U	1		SSX	BATTLE	BLUMANS	163
8	HOLLAND ELIZA	CI U	50	GENTLEWOMAN ANNUITANT	SSX	KINGSTON	BELL HILL	24
15	HOLLAND ELIZAH	SV U	17	SERVANT	SSX	SALEHURST	BELL HILL	25
24	HOLLAND FANNY	CI U	4		SSX	SALEHURST	BEXHILL STREET	26
16	HOLLAND HANNAH E	CO U	15	SERVANT	SSX	SALEHURST	BELL HILL	25
16	HOLLAND MARY	HD U	59	GENTLEWOMAN ANNUITANT	SSX	LEWES	BELL HILL	25
24	HOLLAND MARY A	HD U	25	DRESSMAKER	SSX	BURWASH	BEXHILL STREET	26
24	HOLLAND SALLY	CI U	19	BONNETT MAKER	SSX	SALEHURST	BEXHILL STREET	26
62	HOLLANDS ANN	DA U	11		SSX	CATSFIELD	NOT GIVEN	113
28	HOLLANDS CAROLINE	DA U	4		SSX	CATSFIELD	STREAM HILL	123
62	HOLLANDS CAROLINE	DA U	5		SSX	CATSFIELD	NOT GIVEN	113
5	HOLLANDS CHARLES	SO U	5		KEN	COUDEN	SIDLEY	65
62	HOLLANDS EDWARD	HD M	36	AG.LAB	SSX	CATSFIELD	NOT GIVEN	113
28	HOLLANDS ELIZA	SA U	13	LAUNDRESS	SSX	CATSFIELD	STREAM HILL	123
62	HOLLANDS ELIZABETH	WI M	27		SSX	WATLINGTON	NOT GIVEN	113
62	HOLLANDS EMILY	DA U	8		SSX	CATSFIELD	NOT GIVEN	113
63	HOLLANDS FRANCES	PP U	8		SRY	KENNINGTON	BEXHILL STREET	96
5	HOLLANDS GEORGE	SO U	7	SCHOLAR	KEN	COUDEN	SIDLEY	65
62	HOLLANDS HANNAH	DA U	5		SSX	CATSFIELD	NOT GIVEN	113
10	HOLLANDS ISIAH	SL U	25	AG.LAB	SSX	BODIAM	PADGHAM	216
5	HOLLANDS JAMES	HD M	32	MASTER MILLER EMP 1	SSX	WESTHOATHLY	SIDLEY	65
28	HOLLANDS JAMES	SO U	7	SCHOLAR	SSX	CATSFIELD	STREAM HILL	123
5	HOLLANDS JAMES	SO U	8	SCHOLAR	KEN	COUDEN	SIDLEY	65
10	HOLLANDS JANE	GD U	5M		SSX	EWHURST	PADGHAM	216
62	HOLLANDS JOHN	SO U	2		SSX	CATSFIELD	NOT GIVEN	113
28	HOLLANDS MARIA	DA U	15	LAUNDRESS	SSX	CATSFIELD	STREAM HILL	123
28	HOLLANDS MARY	HD W	40	LAUNDRESS	SSX	CATSFIELD	STREAM HILL	123
1	HOLLANDS MARY	SV U	18	GENERAL SERVANT	SSX	EAST GRINSTEAD	CATSFIELD GREEN	119
5	HOLLANDS MARY A	WI M	27?		SSX	EWHURST	PADGHAM	216
10	HOLLANDS SARAH	DA U	18		SSX	CATSFIELD	STREAM HILL	123
28	HOLLANDS THOMAS HENRY	SO U	2M		SSX	CATSFIELD	STREAM HILL	123
28	HOLLANDS WILLIAM	SO U	9	SCHOLAR	SSX	CATSFIELD	NOT GIVEN	113
62	HOLLANDS WILLIAM	SO U	14	AG.LAB	SSX	BRIGHTLING	WATERMILL HOUSE	114
72	HOLLOWAY FREDERICK	AP U	17	MILLER'S AP	SSX	ASHBURNHAM	CATSFIELD GREEN	119
1	HOLLOWAY WILLIAM	LG U	53	COLT TRAINER?	SSX	BEXHILL	NOT GIVEN	98
74	HONEYSETT ANN	DA U	5		SSX	BEXHILL	NOT GIVEN	98
74	HONEYSETT ELIZA	DA U	8		SSX	BEXHILL	NOT GIVEN	56
39	HONEYSETT ELLEN	DA U	12	SCHOLAR	SSX	BEXHILL	NOT GIVEN	98
74	HONEYSETT HARRIET	WI M	25		SSX	BEXHILL	NOT GIVEN	98
74	HONEYSETT JOHN	SO U	2		SSX	BEXHILL	NOT GIVEN	98
74	HONEYSETT MARY	DA U	4		SSX	BEXHILL	NOT GIVEN	98
74	HONEYSETT PHILLY	DA U	11M		SSX	BEXHILL	NOT GIVEN	56
39	HONEYSETT SARAH	WI M	48		SSX	WARBLETON	NOT GIVEN	56
39	HONEYSETT THOMAS	HD M	65	AG.LAB	SSX	WESTHAM	BEXHILL STREET	26
23	HONEYSETT THOMAS	SV U	22	GROOM	SSX	WESTHAM	NOT GIVEN	98
74	HONEYSETT WILLIAM	HD M	26	RAIL LAB	SSX	BEXHILL	NOT GIVEN	58
59	HONNEYSETT GEORGE	SO U	1		SSX	BEXHILL	NOT GIVEN	58
59	HONNEYSETT JAMES	HD M	24	RAIL LAB	SSX	BEXHILL	NOT GIVEN	58
59	HONNEYSETT MARY	WI M	22		SSX	WESTFIELD	RED COTTAGE	181
68	HOOK CHARLOTTE	DA U	14					

48

	Name	Rel	St	Age	Occupation	Co	Parish	Address	No
68	HOOK EDWARD	HD	W	57	AG.LAB	SSX	SEDLESCOMBE	RED COTTAGE	181
68	HOOK EDWARD	SO	U	30	AG.LAB	SSX	WESTFIELD	RED COTTAGE	181
68	HOOK GEORGE	SO	U	25	AG.LAB	SSX	WESTFIELD	RED COTTAGE	181
64	HOOK HARRIETT	WI	M	45		SSX	SEDLESCOMBE	DURHAM FORD	210
64	HOOK HENRY	SO	U	21	AG.LAB	SSX	SEDLESCOMBE	DURHAM FORD	210
68	HOOK LEWIS	SO	U	16		SSX	WESTFIELD	RED COTTAGE	181
37	HOOK MARY	WI	M	24		SSX	SALEHURST	BRICKKILN	191
47	HOOK STEPHEN	BL	U	21	AG.LAB	SSX	WESTFIELD	MARTINS COTTAGE	178
37	HOOK THOMAS	HD	M	24	AG.LAB	SSX	SEDLESCOMBE	BRICKKILN	191
64	HOOK THOMAS	HD	M	50	AG.LAB	SSX	WAHTLINGTON	DURHAM FORD	210
25	HOOK THOMAS	SV	W	62	GROOM	KEN	TENTERDEN	QUEENS HEAD SEDLESCOMBE ST	189
9	HOPE ELLEN	DA	U	18		SSX	WARTLING	CROUCHER'S FARM	143
11	HOPE HENRY	HD	M	20	FARM LAB	SSX	BEXHILL	ADAMS FARM	143
11	HOPE HENRY	SO	U	1		SSX	CROWHURST	ADAMS FARM	143
9	HOPE JOANNA	WI	M	50		SSX	BEXHILL	CROUCHER'S FARM	143
9	HOPE JOHN	HD	M	51	BAILIF OF 40 AC EMP 2	SSX	WARTLING	CROUCHER'S FARM	143
9	HOPE KEZIA	DA	U	10		SSX	CROWHURST	CROUCHER'S FARM	143
11	HOPE SARAH	WI	M	24		SSX	CATSFIELD	ADAMS FARM	143
27	HOPPER CHARLOTTE	DA	U	15		SSX	CROWHURST	GREEN STREET	132
27	HOPPER EDWARD	GS	U	2		SSX	BATTLE	GREEN STREET	132
27	HOPPER ELIN	DA	U	6?		SSX	CROWHURST	GREEN STREET	132
25	HOPPER ELIZA	WI	M	37		SSX	BEXHILL	RANSOM'S HOUSE	145
27	HOPPER ELIZA	WI	M	40		SSX	CROWHURST	GREEN STREET	132
27	HOPPER HENRY	SO	U	18	AG.LAB	SSX	CROWHURST	GREEN STREET	132
27	HOPPER JAMES	SO	U	9	SCHOLAR	SSX	CROWHURST	GREEN STREET	132
25	HOPPER STEPHEN	HD	M	37	FARM LAB	SSX	CROWHURST	RANSOM'S HOUSE	145
27	HOPPER THOMAS	SO	U	12	SCHOLAR	SSX	CROWHURST	GREEN STREET	132
27	HOPPER WILLIAM	HD	M	46	AG.LAB	SSX	LEWES	GREEN STREET	132
25	HOPPER WILLIAM	SO	U	16		SSX	CROWHURST	RANSOM'S HOUSE	145
27	HOPPER WILLIAM	SO	U	24	AG.LAB	SSX	CROWHURST	GREEN STREET	132
81	HORSCROFT EMMA	SV	U	17		SSX	ALFRISTON	BULLS EYE CORNER	182
55	HOTTON HANNAH	VR	M	35		KEN	DOVER	BARRACKS	179
55	HOTTON JOSEPH	VR	M	37	RAIL LAB	NTH	LAMBURY	BARRACKS	179
55	HOTTON WILLIAM	VR	U	2		KEN	ROTHERHITHE	BARRACKS	179
32	HOVE CHARLES	LG	U	24	RAILWAY LAB	LEI	GILMORTON	RAILWAY HUT	146
37	HOWE CHARLOTTE	DA	U	6		SSX	BEXHILL	49 MARTELLO TOWER	42
37	HOWE FRANCES	DA	U	4		SSX	BEXHILL	49 MARTELLO TOWER	42
37	HOWE RHODA	DA	U	9		KEN	RECULVER?*	49 MARTELLO TOWER	42
37	HOWE SARAH	WI	M	42		WAR	BIRMINGHAM	49 MARTELLO TOWER	42
37	HOWE WILLIAM	HD	M	42	COM BOATMAN COAST GUARD	DOR	SYMMONDSBURY	49 MARTELLO TOWER	42
37	HOWE WILLIAM	SO	U	12	SCHOLAR	DOR	BOTHANHAMPTON	49 MARTELLO TOWER	42
9	HOYCARD? EDWARD	SV	U	21	BUTLER	YKS		PARK GATE	120
68	HUGGINGS THOMAS	LG	U	50	AG.LAB	KEN	HAWKHURST	COSSUMS	15
40	HUGHES HENRY	LG	U	26	RAILWAY LAB	ESS	FEENING?	RAILWAY HUT	134
1	HUGHES JAMES	LG	U	20	RAIL LAB		CHELMSFORD	RAILWAY HUT	4
30	HULL LOUISA	DA	U	40	SERVANT	SSX	BATTLE	BEXHILL STREET	27
48	HUMPHREY ELIZABETH	WI	M	29		KEN	WINSBURY	HOLLINGTON STREET	11
48	HUMPHREY GEORGE	HD	M	30	RAIL LAB	SRY	CHEAM	HOLLINGTON STREET	11
48	HUMPHREY SARAH	DA	U	1M		SSX	HOLLINGTON	HOLLINGTON STREET	11
17	HUMPHREY WILLIAM	LG	U	29	RAIL LAB	SSX	ROTHERFIELD	RAILWAY HUT	7
9	HUNT ELIZABETH	SV	W	30	COOK	YKS		PARK GATE	120
48	HUNT SUSANA	VR	M	57		SAL	NEW PARK	RAILWAY HUT	135
21	HUNT THOMAS	VR	U	8	SCHOLAR	SSX	BEXHILL	FREEZELAND* SIDLEY	68
7	HUTCHISON ADELAIDE	DA	U	2M		SSX	CROWHURST	NOT GIVEN	143
1	HUTCHISON CAROLINE	GD	U	7		SSX	CROWHURST	CROWHURST VILLAGE	142
1	HUTCHISON ELLEN	SV	U	17	GENERAL SERVANT	SSX	CROWHURST	CROWHURST VILLAGE	142
8	HUTCHISON FANNY	WI	M	41		SSX	CROWHURST	NOT GIVEN	143
7	HUTCHISON HARRIETT	WI	M	32		SSX	CROWHURST	NOT GIVEN	143
28	HUTCHISON HARRIOT	DA	U	13	HOUSEKEEPER	SSX	CROWHURST	GREEN STREET	132
1	HUTCHISON HENRY	GS	U	5		SSX	CROWHURST	CROWHURST VILLAGE	142
1	HUTCHISON HENRY	SO	W	39	CARPENTER JM	SSX	CROWHURST	CROWHURST VILLAGE	142
8	HUTCHISON JAMES	HD	M	48	CARPENTER JM	SSX	CROWHURST	NOT GIVEN	143
1	HUTCHISON JESSE	GS	U	3		SSX	CROWHURST	CROWHURST VILLAGE	142
7	HUTCHISON LEVENIA	DA	U	7		SSX	CROWHURST	NOT GIVEN	143
1	HUTCHISON SARAH	DA	U	11		SSX	CROWHURST	NOT GIVEN	143
8	HUTCHISON SARAH	DA	U	15		SSX	CROWHURST	NOT GIVEN	143
7	HUTCHISON THOMAS	HD	M	42	WHEELWRIGHT JM	SSX	HODE	CROWHURST VILLAGE	142
1	HUTCHISON THOMAS	HD	W	79	WHEELWRIGHT/CARPENTER EMP3	SSX	CROWHURST	NOT GIVEN	143
7	HUTCHISON THOMAS JAMES	SO	U	5		SSX	HODE	GREEN STREET	132
28	HUTCHISON WILLIAM	HD	W	82	FARM LAB	SSX	CROWHURST	GREEN STREET	132
28	HUTCHISON WILLIAM	SO	U	16	FARM LAB	SSX	SEDLESCOMBE	BAULKHAM GREEN	196
59	HYLAND ALFRED	SO	U	10	SCHOLAR	SSX	EWHURST	HOBBY HOBBS	249
1	HYLAND ALFRED	SO	U	37	BREWER	SSX	SEDLESCOMBE	SEDLESCOMBE STREET	201
3	HYLAND ALICE	WI	M	27		SSX	BREDE	CRIPPS	253
34	HYLAND AMELIA	WI	M	26		SSX	HOLLINGTON	(WILTING?)	5
6	HYLAND ANN	DA	U	1		SSX	EWHURST	HOBBY HOBBS	249
1	HYLAND CATHERINE	DA	U	34		SSX	EWHURST	SEDLESCOMBE STREET	195
57	HYLAND CATHERINE	NC	U	5		SSX	EWHURST	HOBBY HOBBS	249
1	HYLAND CHARLES	SO	U	32		SSX	WESTFIELD	APPLE TREE	182
77	HYLAND ELIZABETH	HD	W	75	HOUSEKEEPER	SSX	MOUNTFIELD	SPILSTED FARM	210
60	HYLAND ELIZABETH	WI	M	37		SSX	EWHURST	DYKES FARM	217
15	HYLAND EMILY CAROLINE	DA	U	14	SCHOLAR	SSX	WESTFIELD	BAULKHAM GREEN	196
59	HYLAND EMILY CAROLINE?	DA	U	12	SCHOLAR	SSX	SEDLESCOMBE	RECTORY	205
34	HYLAND FANNY	SV	U	20	HOUSEMAID	SSX	SEDLESCOMBE	BAULKHAM GREEN	196
59	HYLAND FRANCES	DA	U	1		SSX	SEDLESCOMBE	SEDLESCOMBE STREET	201
3	HYLAND FRANCES	DA	U	1					

#	Name	Rel	MS	Age	Occupation	County	Parish	Address	No
1	HYLAND FRANCES SOPHIA	DA	U	24		SSX	EWHURST	HOBBY HOBBS	249
3	HYLAND GEORGE	SO	U	6M		SSX	SEDLESCOMBE	SEDLESCOMBE STREET	201
60	HYLAND GEORGE	SO	U	17	AG.LAB	SSX	MOUNTFIELD	SPILSTED FARM	210
37	HYLAND HARRIETT	DA	U	13		SSX	EWHURST	FOOTLAND	205
6	HYLAND JAMES	HD	M	24	AG.LAB	SSX	BATTLE	(WILTING?)	5
60	HYLAND JAMES	SO	U	8		SSX	SEDLESCOMBE	SPILSTED FARM	210
55	HYLAND JAMES	SV	U	21	AG.LAB	SSX	WHATLINGTON	HANCOX FARM	209
77	HYLAND JANE	DA	U	54		SSX	WESTFIELD	APPLE TREE	182
59	HYLAND JANE	WI	M	32		SSX	BREDE	BAULKHAM GREEN	196
69	HYLAND JANE	WI	M	50		SSX	SEDLESCOMBE	STAPLE CROSS	241
37	HYLAND JESSE	HD	M	53	AG.LAB	SSX	EWHURST	FOOTLAND	205
59	HYLAND JOHN	HD	M	42	GAME KEEPER	SSX	BREDE	BAULKHAM GREEN	196
69	HYLAND JOHN	HD	M	59	INN KEEPER	SSX	SEDLESCOMBE	STAPLE CROSS	241
69	HYLAND JOHN	SO	U	24		SSX	SEDLESCOMBE	STAPLE CROSS	241
37	HYLAND MARIA	DA	U	22		SSX	EWHURST	FOOTLAND	205
37	HYLAND MARIA	WI	M	45		SSX	SEDLESCOMBE	FOOTLAND	205
80	HYLAND MARTHA	GS	U	6		SSX	SEDLESCOMBE	MOUN SION	182
6	HYLAND MARTHA	WI	M	24		SSX	WESTFIELD	(WILTING?)	5
60	HYLAND MARY	DA	U	5M		SSX	SEDLESCOMBE	SPILSTED FARM	210
15	HYLAND MARY	WI	M	48		SSX	EWHURST	DYKES FARM	217
15	HYLAND MARY ANN	DA	U	10	SCHOLAR	SSX	EWHURST	DYKES FARM	217
37	HYLAND MARY ANN	DA	U	16		SSX	EWHURST	FOOTLAND	205
60	HYLAND OBED	SO	U	14	AG.LAB	SSX	MOUNTFIELD	SPILSTED FARM	210
60	HYLAND SARAH	DA	U	10		SSX	MOUNTFIELD	SPILSTED FARM	210
59	HYLAND SOPHIA	DA	U	3		SSX	SEDLESCOMBE	BAULKHAM GREEN	196
1	HYLAND SOPHIA	HD	W	67	FARMER 60AC EMP 3 MEN	KEN	BENENDEN	HOBBY HOBBS	249
46	HYLAND THOMAS	GS	U	7	SCHOLAR	SSX	BATTLE	SWALES GREEN	193
34	HYLAND THOMAS	HD	M	36	FARMERS LAB	SSX	BODIAM	CRIPPS	253
60	HYLAND THOMAS	SO	U	2		SSX	SEDLESCOMBE	SPILSTED FARM	210
15	HYLAND THOMAS	SO	U	7	SCHOLAR	SSX	EWHURST	DYKES FARM	217
3	HYLAND WILLIAM	HD	M	29	AG.LAB	SSX	MOUNTFIELD	SEDLESCOMBE STREET	201
60	HYLAND WILLIAM	HD	M	44	AG.LAB	SSX	SEDLESCOMBE	SPILSTED FARM	210
60	HYLAND WILLIAM	SO	U	5		SSX	SEDLESCOMBE	SPILSTED FARM	210
59	HYLAND WILLIAM	SO	U	8	SCHOLAR	SSX	SEDLESCOMBE	BAULKHAM GREEN	196
15	HYLAND WILLIAM HENRY	SO	U	12	SERVANT	SSX	EWHURST	DYKES FARM	217
15	HYLAND WILLIAM HENRY?	HD	M	45	FARMER'S SON	SSX	EWHURST	DYKES FARM	217
38	HYSON CAROLINE	DA	U	1		SSX	BEXHILL	HILDERS COTTAGE	42
38	HYSON ELIZABETH	DA	U	2		SSX	BEXHILL	HILDERS COTTAGE	42
38	HYSON JAMES	SO	U	8	SCHOLAR	IRL		HILDERS COTTAGE	42
38	HYSON MARGARET	DA	U	10	SCHOLAR	IRL		HILDERS COTTAGE	42
38	HYSON MARGARET	WI	M	31		IRL		HILDERS COTTAGE	42
38	HYSON MARIA J	DA	U	12	SCHOLAR	IRL		HILDERS COTTAGE	42
38	HYSON MARY J	DA	U	4		SSX	PEVENSEY	HILDERS COTTAGE	42
38	HYSON PETER	SO	U	6		SSX	HASTINGS	HILDERS COTTAGE	42
38	HYSON THOMAS	HD	M	49	COAST GUARD	HAM	GOSPORT	HILDERS COTTAGE	42
12	INMAN ELIZA	DA	U	11M		SSX	SEDLESCOMBE	BARRICKS	188
12	INMAN ELIZA	WI	M	28		SSX	SEDLESCOMBE	BARRICKS	188
12	INMAN JOHN	HD	M	40	CARRIER	SSX	SEDLESCOMBE	BARRICKS	188
12	INMAN JOHN	SO	U	5	SCHOLAR	SSX	SEDLESCOMBE	BARRICKS	188
12	INMAN MARY	DA	U	10	SCHOLAR	SSX	SEDLESCOMBE	BARRICKS	188
12	INMAN THOMAS	SO	U	3		SSX	SEDLESCOMBE	BARRICKS	187
33	JACKSON BETSEY	WI	M	51		DEV	DEVONPORT	50 MARTELLO TOWER	41
6	JACKSON JOSEPH	SV	U	18	FARM LAB	SSX	WEST HOATHLY	ROSE COTTAGE - SIDLEY	65
33	JACKSON WILLIAM	HD	M	54	COAST GUARD	IRL	FETHARD WEXFORD‡	50 MARTELLO TOWER	41
71	JARMAN ELIZA	DA	U	14		SSX	EWHURST	EWHURST GREEN	225
71	JARMAN FRANCES	DA	U	2		SSX	EWHURST	EWHURST GREEN	225
2	JARMAN HARRIET	WI	M	24		SSX	WESTFIELD	SEDLESCOMBE STREET	201
71	JARMAN HARRIETT	WI	M	33		SSX	EWHURST	EWHURST GREEN	225
2	JARMAN JAMES	HD	M	23	WHEELWRIGHT EMP 2	SSX	BREDE	SEDLESCOMBE STREET	201
71	JARMAN MARY	DA	U	9	SCHOLAR	SSX	EWHURST	EWHURST GREEN	225
2	JARMAN MARY ANN	DA	U	1		SSX	SEDLESCOMBE	SEDLESCOMBE STREET	201
71	JARMAN RICHARD	SO	U	10	SCHOLAR	SSX	EWHURST	EWHURST GREEN	225
71	JARMAN SERENA	DA	U	12	SCHOLAR	SSX	EWHURST	EWHURST GREEN	225
2	JARMAN THOMAS	BR	U	13		SSX	BREDE	SEDLESCOMBE STREET	201
71	JARMAN TILDEN	HD	M	39	AG.LAB	SSX	EWHURST	EWHURST GREEN	225
71	JARMAN TILDEN	SO	U	6		SSX	EWHURST	EWHURST GREEN	225
30	JARVIS MARTHA	CI	M	27		SSX	CHILTINGTON	RAILWAY GATE HSE IN LIBERTY	41
70	JEFFERSON ELIZABETH	VR	M	87	ANNUITANT	KEN	TONBRIDGE	NOT GIVEN	97
22	JEFFERSON HENRY	GS	U	15	SCHOLAR	SSX	BEXHILL	BELL HILL	26
64	JEFFERSON JOHN	HD	M	50	SCHOOLMASTER	KEN	TONBRIDGE	NOT GIVEN	96
64	JEFFERSON MARY ANN	WI	M	43	SCHOOLMISTRESS	SSX	BEXHILL	NOT GIVEN	96
37	JEFFERY ANN	ML	M	74		SSX	WESTFIELD	OWLS CASTLE	177
59	JEFFERY CHARLOTTE	WI	M	48		SSX	BATTLE	PIXES HOUSE	240
81	JEFFERY ELIZABETH	SV	U	25	COOK	SSX	HOLLINGTON	BEAUPORT HOUSE	17
85	JEFFERY GEORGE	HD	M	66	GROCER	SSX	BATTLE	SHOP HOUSE	18
59	JEFFERY GEORGE	SO	U	4		SSX	EWHURST	PIXES HOUSE	240
12	JEFFERY HANNAH	WI	M	32		KEN	HAWKHURST	WATTS HOLE	250
41	JEFFERY HENRY	LG	U	23	AG.LAB	KEN	HAWKHURST	MARCHANTS	238
12	JEFFERY HENRY	SO	U	13	AG.LAB	SSX	EWHURST	WATTS HOLE	250
12	JEFFERY JANE	DA	U	5		SSX	EWHURST	WATTS HOLE	251
85	JEFFERY JANE	DA	U	24		SSX	HOLLINGTON	SHOP HOUSE	18
41	JEFFERY JANE	WI	M	23		SSX	BECKLEY	MARCHANTS	238
22	JEFFERY JANETTS?	SV	U	21	SERVANT	SSX	BATTLE	GATE FARM	235
12	JEFFERY JOHN	HD	M	37	AG.LAB	KEN	HAWKHURST	WATTS HOLE	250
37	JEFFERY JOHN	SL	U	15		SSX	WESTFIELD	OWLS CASTLE	177
85	JEFFERY JOHN	SO	U	22	CORD WAINER	SSX	WESTFIELD	SHOP HOUSE	18

Ref	Surname	Given Name	Rel	M	Age	Occupation	County	Place	House	No.
59	JEFFERY	MARIA	DA	U	7		SSX	EWHURST	PIXES HOUSE	240
85	JEFFERY	MARIA	WI	M	60		SSX	EASTBOURNE	SHOP HOUSE	18
21	JEFFERY	MARY	SV	U	17	GENERAL SERVANT	SSX	SEDLESCOMBE	BOYCES FARM	235
41	JEFFERY	MARY ANN	DA	U	6M		SSX	EWHURST	MARCHANTS	238
59	JEFFERY	MARY ANN	GD	U	10M		SSX	BATTLE	PIXES HOUSE	240
12	JEFFERY	NELSON	SO	U	7	SCHOLAR	SSX	EWHURST	WATTS HOLE	250
41	JEFFERY	WILLIAM	HD	M	20	AG.LAB	KEN	HAWKHURST	MARCHANTS	238
59	JEFFERY	WILLIAM	HD	M	49	AG.LAB	SSX	BATTLE	PIXES HOUSE	240
41	JEFFERY	WILLIAM	LG	W	57	AG.LAB		UNKNOWN	MARCHANTS	238
12	JEFFERY	WILLIAM	SO	U	11	AG.LAB	SSX	EWHURST	WATTS HOLE	250
59	JEFFERY	WILLIAM	SO	U	13	AG.LAB	SSX	SEDLESCOMBE	PIXES HOUSE	240
59	JEMPSON	ALFRED	SO	U	4		SSX	SEDLESCOMBE	SPILSTED FARM	209
21	JEMPSON	ANN	HD	U	77		SSX	MOUNTFIELD	SEDLESCOMBE STREET	189
59	JEMPSON	ANNE	WI	M	32?		SSX	BEXHILL	SPILSTED FARM	209
36	JEMPSON	CHARLES	HD	M	29	GATE KEEPER	SSX	MOUNTFIELD	TURNPIKE GATE	205
59	JEMPSON	CHARLES	SO	U	8	SCHOLAR	SSX	SEDLESCOMBE	SPILSTED FARM	209
36	JEMPSON	HANNAH	WI	M	28		SSX	SALEHURST	TURNPIKE GATE	205
59	JEMPSON	HARRIOTT	DA	U	6	SCHOLAR	SSX	SEDLESCOMBE	SPILSTED FARM	209
36	JEMPSON	HENRY	SO	U	3		SSX	EWHURST	TURNPIKE GATE	205
36	JEMPSON	JANE	/	U	1	NURSE CHILD	SSX	ORE	TURNPIKE GATE	205
21	JEMPSON	JANE	CI	U	61		SSX	MOUNTFIELD	SEDLESCOMBE STREET	189
52	JEMPSON	JANE ELIZABETH	SV	U	16	NURSE	SSX	SEDLESCOMBE	GREAT SANDERS	194
53	JEMPSON	JOHN	GS	U	3		SSX	BATTLE	BEECH	208
59	JEMPSON	JOHN	HD	M	34	AG.LAB	SSX	MOUNTFIELD	SPILSTED FARM	209
59	JEMPSON	JOHN	SO	U	4		SSX	SEDLESCOMBE	SPILSTED FARM	209
36	JEMPSON	MERCY	DA	U	6	SCHOLAR	SSX	EWHURST	TURNPIKE GATE	205
53	JEMPSON	MERCY	HD	W	63		KEN	HARTLIP	BEECH	208
53	JEMPSON	RICHARD	GS	U	5		SSX	SEDLESCOMBE	BEECH	208
59	JEMPSON	RICHARD	SO	U	2		SSX	SEDLESCOMBE	SPILSTED FARM	209
25	JENNER	ANNE	DA	U	5		SSX	HASTINGS	NOT GIVEN	109
25	JENNER	ANNE	WI	M	30		SSX	HASTINGS	NOT GIVEN	109
25	JENNER	CAROLINE	DA	U	6	SCHOLAR	SSX	HASTINGS	NOT GIVEN	109
24	JENNER	CATHERINE	WI	M	38	TOLL GATE KEEPER	KEN	DEAL	CRIPPS	252
25	JENNER	ELLEN	DA	U	8	SCHOLAR	SSX	HASTINGS	NOT GIVEN	109
29	JENNER	ELLEN	WD	U	13	SCHOLAR	SSX	BATTLE	CRIPPS	252
25	JENNER	GEORGE	HD	M	34	GARDENER	SSX	WALDRON	NOT GIVEN	109
25	JENNER	GEORGE	SO	U	3		SSX	HASTINGS	NOT GIVEN	109
25	JENNER	JANE	DA	U	8M		SSX	HASTINGS	NOT GIVEN	109
24	JENNER	WILLIAM	HD	M	39	FARM LAB	KEN	HAWKHURST	CRIPPS	252
20	JENNER?	ELLEN	DA	U	8	SCHOLAR	SSX	EWHURST	ODIAM FARM	218
20	JENNER?	GEORGE	SO	U	14	AG.LAB	SSX	EWHURST	ODIAM FARM	218
20	JENNER?	HENRY	HD	M	49	FARM BAILIFF	SSX	FRAMFIELD	ODIAM FARM	218
20	JENNER?	JAMES	SO	U	2		SSX	EWHURST	ODIAM FARM	218
20	JENNER?	SARAH	WI	M	39		SSX	WARBLETON	ODIAM FARM	218
20	JENNER?	WILLIAM	SO	U	11	AG.LAB	SSX	EWHURST	ODIAM FARM	218
21	JERMAN?	MARY	WI	M	48		SSX	NORTHIAM	ODIAM FARM	218
21	JERMAN?	WILLIAM	HD	M	50	AG.LAB	SSX	EWHURST	ODIAM FARM	218
22	JOHNSON	ELIZABETH	VR	U	8		SSX	NORTHIAM	GATE FARM	235
70	JOHNSON	GEORGE	SO	U	11M		MDX	HADLEY	CASTLEMANS	211
14	JOHNSON	HENRY	LG	U	24	RAILWAY LAB	KEN		NOT GIVEN	130
18	JOHNSON	HENRY	LG	U	40	AG.LAB		NORTHAMPTON BULWICK	CATTS GREEN	251
70	JOHNSON	JAMES	SO	U	11M		MDX	HADLEY	CASTLEMANS	211
70	JOHNSON	JEMIMA	WI	M	27		KEN	TUNBRIDGE WELLS	CASTLEMANS	211
45	JOHNSON	ROBERT	LG	U	33	RAILWAY LAB	YKS	GOULE	RAILWAY HUT	134
70	JOHNSON	SAMUEL	HD	M	27	RAIL LAB	KEN	TUNBRIDGE WELLS	CASTLEMANS	211
2	JOHNSON	THOMAS	LG	U	45	RAIL LAB		LINCOLN	RAILWAY HUT	4
36	JOHNSTONE	AGNES C	HD	U	19	GROCER	SSX	BATTLE	NOT GIVEN	110
36	JOHNSTONE	BENJAMIN	BR	U	13	ERRAND BOY	SSX	BATTLE	NOT GIVEN	110
31	JONES	ALFRED	HD	M	34	FARM LAB	SSX	CROWHURST	FORWARD LANE	146
14	JONES	CHARLES	HD	M	27	FARM LAB	SSX	CROWHURST	RIAL? OAK	144
7	JONES	CHARLOTTE	DA	U	14		SSX	HASTINGS	IN THE LIBERTY	38
5	JONES	CHARLOTTE	HD	W	47?		SSX	BEXHILL	FORWARD LANE	129
42	JONES	EDWARD	GS	U	7M		SSX	SEDLESCOMBE	CHITTLE BURCH	192
42	JONES	EDWARD	SO	M	28	CARPENTER JM	SSX	SEDLESCOMBE	CHITTLE BURCH	192
31	JONES	EMILY	DA	U	2		SSX	CROWHURST	FORWARD LANE	146
23	JONES	EMMA	DA	U	8	SCHOLAR	SSX	CROWHURST	RANSOM'S HOUSE	145
7	JONES	FRANCES	DA	U	8	SCHOLAR	SSX	BEXHILL	IN THE LIBERTY	38
7	JONES	GEORGE	SO	U	11M		SSX	BEXHILL	IN THE LIBERTY	38
42	JONES	HANNAH	DL	M	19		SSX	EWHURST	CHITTLE BURCH	192
31	JONES	HARRIETT	WI	M	34		SSX	BATTLE	FORWARD LANE	146
42	JONES	HENRY	HD	W	61	MASTER CARPENTER	SSX	HAILSHAM	CHITTLE BURCH	192
17	JONES	HENRY	LG	U	28	RAIL LAB		BIRMINGHAM	RAILWAY HUT	7
7	JONES	JAMES	SO	U	15		SSX	HASTINGS	IN THE LIBERTY	38
31	JONES	JANE	DA	U	7	SCHOLAR	SSX	CROWHURST	FORWARD LANE	146
14	JONES	JANE	WI	M	21		SSX	WESTFIELD	RIAL? OAK	144
28	JONES	JANE	WI	M	33		SSX	HOLLINGTON	FORWARD LANE	146
7	JONES	JANE	WI	M	39		SSX	BEXHILL	IN THE LIBERTY	38
7	JONES	JOHN	HD	M	44	AG.LAB	SSX	WARBLETON	IN THE LIBERTY	38
48	JONES	JOHN	LG	U	37		DEV		RAILWAY HUT	135
14	JONES	JOHN	SO	U	5		SSX	WESTFIELD	RIAL? OAK	144
23	JONES	JOHN	SO	U	15		SSX	ORE	RANSOM'S HOUSE	145
23	JONES	MARTHA	WI	M	49		SSX	ORE	RANSOM'S HOUSE	145
31	JONES	MARY	DA	U	9	SCHOLAR	SSX	CROWHURST	FORWARD LANE	146
23	JONES	MARY	DA	U	11	SCHOLAR	SSX	ORE	RANSOM'S HOUSE	145
36	JONES	NAOMI	SV	U	17	HOUSE SERVANT	SSX	FAIRLIGHT	NOT GIVEN	110
23	JONES	SAMUEL	HD	M	40	FARM LAB	SSX	CROWHURST	RANSOM'S HOUSE	145

No.	Surname	Forename	Rel	Cond	Age	Occupation	Birthplace	Residence	Page
31	JONES	SARAH	DA	U	5		SSX CROWHURST	FORWARD LANE	146
7	JONES	SARAH	DA	U	11		SSX BEXHILL	IN THE LIBERTY	38
7	JONES	STEPHEN	SO	U	5		SSX BEXHILL	IN THE LIBERTY	38
28	JONES	THOMAS	HD	M	39	FARM LAB	SSX CROWHURST	FORWARD LANE	146
14	JONES	WILLIAM	SO	U	3		SSX CROWHURST	RIAL? OAK	144
31	JONES	WILLIAM	SO	U	11	SCHOLAR	SSX CROWHURST	FORWARD LANE	146
50	JUDE	ELIZABETH	SV	M	56	HOUSE SERVANT	SSX BEXHILL	LITTLE COMMON	57
63	KEEVAN?	BETSY	/	W	75	FRIEND	KEN GILLINGHAM	BEXHILL STREET	96
51	KEMP	GEORGE	HD	M	31	AG.LAB	SSX BRIGHTLING	PAGES LODGE	43
47	KEMP	JAMES	SL	U	13	AG.LAB	SSX BEXHILL	COLLINGTON LANE	43
47	KEMP	JOHN	LG	U	28	AG.LAB	SSX MOUNTFIELD	HOLLINGTON STREET	11
51	KEMP	LUCY	WI	U	25		SSX HEATHFIELD	PAGES LODGE	43
2	KEMP	MARIA	SV	U	17	HOUSE SERVANT	SSX MOUNTFIELD	NEW BARN FARM	106
6	KEMP	MARY	VR	U	32		SSX FAIRLIGHT	WHEEL	162
54	KEMP	MERCY	HD	W	86	PAUPER	SSX BATTLE	BEECH	208
55	KEMP	MERCY	SV	U	12	NURSE MAID	SSX WHATLINGTON	HANCOX FARM	209
54	KEMP	RICHARD	SO	U	46	AG.LAB/DEAF & DUMB	SSX SEDLESCOMBE	BEECH	208
24	KEMP	SOLOMON	LG	U	26	AG.LAB	SSX MOUNTFIELD	LORDINE FARM	235
54	KEMP	WILLIAM	SO	U	48	AG.LAB	SSX SEDLESCOMBE	BEECH	208
46	KENEDY	ANN	VR	U	20?	DRESSMAKER	IRELAND	NO.3 GALLEY HILL	29
16	KENNARD	CHARLES	HD	M	52	POWDER MAKER	SSX CATSFIELD	GATE HOUSE	174
16	KENNARD	HANNAH	WI	M	52		SSX CATSFIELD	GATE HOUSE	174
16	KENNARD	MARY	DA	U	17		SSX WESTFIELD	GATE HOUSE	174
21	KENNARD	MARY	VR	U	36		SSX BEXHILL	SANDERS	174
16	KENNARD	RUBEN	SO	U	9		SSX WESTFIELD	GATE HOUSE	174
80	KENNARD	SPENCER	SV	U	25	BAKER JM	SSX WESTFIELD	MOUN SION	182
16	KENNARD	STEPHEN	SO	U	15		SSX WESTFIELD	GATE HOUSE	174
16	KENNARD	THOMAS	SO	U	12	DEAF & DUMB	SSX WESTFIELD	GATE HOUSE	174
16	KENNARD	WILLIAM	SO	U	24		SSX SEDLESCOMBE	GATE HOUSE	174
39	KENNEDY	ANN	WI	M	71		IRL ARMAGH	48 MARTELLO TOWER	42
39	KENNEDY	JOHN	HD	M	74	CHELSEA PENS. TOWER KEEPER	IRL ARMAGH	48 MARTELLO TOWER	42
19	KENWARD	ALFRED	SV	U	15		SSX WESTFIELD	ROSE VILLA	153
8	KENWARD	ANN	DA	U	11M		SSX CATSFIELD	NOT GIVEN	107
23	KENWARD	ANN	WI	M	55		SSX CATSFIELD	NOT GIVEN	122
8	KENWARD	CELIA	WI	M	38		SSX CATSFIELD	NOT GIVEN	107
28	KENWARD	CHARLES	SO	U	6M		SSX CATSFIELD	NOT GIVEN	110
24	KENWARD	CHARLOTTE	DA	U	6		NOT GIVEN (?WESTFIELD)	CHARITY HOUSE	154
24	KENWARD	CHARLOTTE	WI	M	49		SSX WESTFIELD	CHARITY HOUSE	154
53	KENWARD	EDMUND	HD	M	61	AG.LAB	SSX NORTHIAM	GREAT SANDERS	194
4	KENWARD	EDWIN	SV	U	21	AG.LAB	NOT GIVEN (?WESTFIELD)	PADDLESTONS	152
24	KENWARD	ELIZA	DA	U	3		NOT GIVEN (?WESTFIELD)	CHARITY HOUSE	154
31	KENWARD	ELIZA	WI	M	29		SSX CATSFIELD	STREAM HILL	123
24	KENWARD	ELIZABETH	DA	U	14		NOT GIVEN (?WESTFIELD)	CHARITY HOUSE	154
31	KENWARD	GEORGE	HD	M	39	AG.LAB	SSX CATSFIELD	STREAM HILL	123
8	KENWARD	GEORGE	SO	U	8		SSX CATSFIELD	NOT GIVEN	107
4	KENWARD	GEORGE	SV	U	17	AG.LAB	NOT GIVEN (?WESTFIELD)	PADDLESTONS	152
8	KENWARD	HARRIETT	DA	U	4		SSX CATSFIELD	NOT GIVEN	107
8	KENWARD	HENRY	SO	U	6		SSX CATSFIELD	NOT GIVEN	107
3	KENWARD	HENRY	SV	U	16		SSX WESTFIELD	COCK MARTINS	161
28	KENWARD	JAMES	HD	M	28	AG.LAB	SSX CATSFIELD	NOT GIVEN	110
23	KENWARD	JAMES	HD	M	63	AG.LAB	SSX CATSFIELD	NOT GIVEN	122
8	KENWARD	JANE	DA	U	15		SSX CATSFIELD	NOT GIVEN	107
8	KENWARD	JOHN	HD	M	35	AG.LAB	SSX CATSFIELD	NOT GIVEN	107
53	KENWARD	MARTHA	MO	W	80		KEN ROLVENDEN	GREAT SANDERS	194
28	KENWARD	MARY	WI	M	26		SSX NINFIELD	NOT GIVEN	110
24	KENWARD	RICHARD	SO	U	11		NOT GIVEN (?WESTFIELD)	CHARITY HOUSE	154
8	KENWARD	ROBERT	SO	U	11	AG.LAB	SSX CATSFIELD	NOT GIVEN	107
24	KENWARD	SAMUEL	HD	M	49	AG.LAB	SSX WESTFIELD	CHARITY HOUSE	154
24	KENWARD	SAMUEL	SO	U	22	BOOT MAKER	NOT GIVEN (?WESTFIELD)	CHARITY HOUSE	154
53	KENWARD	SARAH	WI	M	55		SSX EMHURST	GREAT SANDERS	194
8	KENWARD	WICKHAM	SO	U	2		SSX CATSFIELD	NOT GIVEN	107
24	KENWARD	WILLIAM	SO	U	24		NOT GIVEN (?WESTFIELD)	CHARITY HOUSE	154
54	KERMER	AMOS	LG	U	27	RAILWAY LAB	SSX DENGLETON?	RAILWAY HUT	135
44	KERNS	ALAXANDER	LG	U	47	RAILWAY LAB	IRL	RAILWAY HUT	134
82	KEY	SARAH	HD	W	55	PAUPER SOLDIER'S WIFE	SSX BEXHILL	NOT GIVEN (LITTLE COMMON)	47
58	KINCHETT	HENRY	HD	U	21	SCHOOLMASTER	SSX PETWORTH	SEDLESCOMBE STREET	195
19	KING	ANN	DA	U	8		SSX CROWHURST	CROWHURST VILLAGE	131
18	KING	ANN	WI	M	80		SSX EMHURST	COLLIERS GREEN	234
19	KING	CHARLES	LG	U	29	RAILWAY LAB	KEN TUNBRIDGE	CROWHURST VILLAGE	131
57	KING	EDGAR	SO	U	6	SCHOLAR	SSX EMHURST	SNAGS HALL	223
57	KING	EDWIN	SO	U	3		SSX EMHURST	SNAGS HALL	223
87	KING	ELIZABETH	LG	M	32?		BKM BIDDLESDEN	HAYWARDS	18
14	KING	GEORGE	LG	U	54	AG.LAB	SSX HAILSHAM	MAYFIELDS HOUSE	6
19	KING	HENRY	HD	M	32	AG.LAB	SSX CATSFIELD	CROWHURST VILLAGE	131
57	KING	HENRY	HD	M	34	AG.LAB	SSX EMHURST	SNAGS HALL	223
57	KING	JAMES	SO	U	12	AG.LAB	SSX EMHURST	SNAGS HALL	223
41	KING	JANE HANNA	WI	M	21		DOR BICKHAM	RAILWAY HUT	134
41	KING	JOBE ROBERTS	SO	U	1		DOR UPWAY	RAILWAY HUT	134
87	KING	JOHN	LG	M	37	RAILWAY LAB	NTH MAPPENHAM?*	HAYWARDS	18
57	KING	JOHN	SO	U	8	SCHOLAR	SSX EMHURST	SNAGS HALL	223
41	KING	JOHN ROBERTS	SO	U	3W		SSX CROWHURST	RAILWAY HUT	134
57	KING	MARIA	DA	U	6M		SSX EMHURST	SNAGS HALL	223
57	KING	MARY	DA	U	10	SCHOLAR	SSX EMHURST	SNAGS HALL	223
57	KING	MARY MARIA	WI	M	37		SSX EMHURST	SNAGS HALL	223
19	KING	PHILADELPHIA	WI	M	39		KEN NORTH FLIGHT	CROWHURST VILLAGE	131
19	KING	SARAH	DA	U	5?		SSX CROWHURST	CROWHURST VILLAGE	131

	Name			Age	Occupation	County	Parish	Address	
18	KING THOMAS	HD M	74		AG.LAB	SSX BURWASH		COLLIERS GREEN	234
41	KING WILLIAM	HD M	31		RAILWAY LAB	WEST CHELLER SHERBRIDG?		RAILWAY HUT	134
12	KINYON MATILDA	CI U	25		HOUSE SERVANT	SSX CROWHURST		BINES FARM	144
52	KIRBY? JOHN (BLOTTED)	HD M	25		RAIL LAB	KEN GODMERSHAW		HOLLINGTON STREET	12
52	KIRBY? SARAH (BLOTTED)	WI M	20			SSX HOLLINGTON		HOLLINGTON STREET	12
55	KNIGHT BENJAMIN W	HD U	31		FLORIST/MARKET GARDENER	SSX BATTLE		HOLLINGTON STREET	12
27	KNIGHT ELIZABETH	DA U	15			SRY FRIMLEY		RAILWAY HUT	8
95	KNIGHT JAMES	LG U	30		RAIL LAB	SSX TWINEHAM		HUT	19
27	KNIGHT JAMES	SO U	5			SRY BAGSHOT		RAILWAY HUT	8
27	KNIGHT JOHN	HD M	33		RAIL LAB	HAM BINSTEAD		RAILWAY HUT	8
8	KNIGHT JOHN	DA U	7		SCHOLAR	SSX RINGMER		STAR INN (IN THE LIBERTY)	38
8	KNIGHT LUCY	WI M	43			KEN EASTREA		STAR INN (IN THE LIBERTY)	38
8	KNIGHT LYDIA	WI M	34			HAM ALTON		RAILWAY HUT	8
27	KNIGHT MARY ANN	VR M	48			SSX BATTLE		COLLIERS GREEN	233
10	KNIGHT PHILADELPHIA	HD M	59		INN KEEPER	SSX RINGMER		STAR INN (IN THE LIBERTY)	38
8	KNIGHT REUBEN	GD U	13			SSX HOOE		PARISH FARM	130
15	LAMB ANN	WI M	24			SSX CHICHESTER		BEAUPORT HOUSE	16
80	LAMB ANNA	SO U	5			SSX HOLLINGTON		BEAUPORT HOUSE	16
80	LAMB ARCHIBALD	HD M	34		GENTLEMAN	SSX HOLLINGTON		BEAUPORT HOUSE	16
80	LAMB CHARLES SIR	DA U	6			SSX HOLLINGTON		BEAUPORT HOUSE	16
80	LAMB CLARA	DA U	2			SSX HOLLINGTON		BEAUPORT HOUSE	16
80	LAMB FLORA	HD M	34		AG.LAB	SSX WESTFIELD		OAK COTTAGE	152
8	LAMB GEORGE	SO U	17		AG.LAB	SSX BEXHILL		BRAGS LANE	32
73	LAMB GEORGE	HD M	59		AG.LAB	SSX PEVENSEY		BRAGS LANE	32
73	LAMB JOHN	HD M	71		AG.LAB	SSX BERWICK		SANDERS	174
21	LAMB JOHN	HD M	41		AG.LAB	SSX WESTFIELD		DOWN	176
32	LAMB LEWIS	DA U	1			SSX WESTFIELD		DOWN	176
32	LAMB MARY	DA U	8			SSX LITTLEHAMPTON		BEAUPORT HOUSE	16
80	LAMB MARY	DA U	5			SSX WESTFIELD		OAK COTTAGE	152
8	LAMB PHILA	WI M	31			SSX SEDLESCOMBE		OAK COTTAGE	152
8	LAMB PHILA	WI M	66			SSX WESTFIELD		SANDERS	174
21	LAMB PHILADELPHIA	DA U	4			SSX WESTFIELD		DOWN	176
32	LAMB SARAH	WI M	39			SSX WESTFIELD		DOWN	176
32	LAMB SARAH	WI M	58			SSX CHIDDINGLY		BRAGS LANE	32
73	LAMB SARAH	SO U	2			SSX WESTFIELD		OAK COTTAGE	152
8	LAMB THOMAS	SO U	14		AG.LAB	SSX BEXHILL		BRAGS LANE	32
73	LAMB WALTER	HD U	67		FUNDHOLDER	SSX RYE		OCKHAM	221
43	LAMB WILLIAM PHILLIP	HD W	84			SSX ST.LEONARDS		HOLLINGTON STREET	10
39	LAMBERT FANNY	SO U	50		AG.LAB	SSX HOLLINGTON		HOLLINGTON STREET	10
39	LAMBERT THOMAS	SV U	21		BRICK MAKER'S LAB	SSX HELLINGLY		SIDLEY	77
19	LAMBERT WILLIAM	PP U	7		PUPIL	CALCUTTA		NOT GIVEN	96
65	LANE A T (MALE)	SV U	21		WAGGONER	SSX CROWHURST		FARM HOUSE	133
32	LANGHAM HENRY	SV U	18		SERVANT OF ALL WORK	SSX BEXHILL		STONE HOUSE FARM	133
31	LANGHAM SOPHIA	DA U	4M			SSX SEDLESCOMBE		HERST	191
36	LANSDELL CAROLINE	NC U	24		VISITOR	SSX BEXHILL		INGREHAMS FARM - SIDLEY	75
1	LANSDELL CHARLOTTE	WI M	21			SSX SEDLESCOMBE		HERST	191
36	LANSDELL ELLEN	HD M	27		FARMER 200 AC EMP 11MEN	SSX NINFIELD		HERST	191
36	LANSDELL THOMAS STEPHEN	WI M	59?			SSX WESTDEAN		BELL HILL	25
15	LARKIN ANNA M	HD M	66		FARMER 320 AC EMP 12	SSX EWHURST		COURT LODGE FARM	147
34	LARKIN BENJAMIN	WI M	64			SSX SEDLESCOMBE		COURT LODGE FARM	147
34	LARKIN JANE	DA U	31			SSX CATSFIELD		COURT LODGE FARM	147
34	LARKIN MARTHA	HD M	63		HOUSE PROPRIETOR	SSX CROWHURST		BELL HILL	25
15	LARKIN THOMAS	SO U	30			SSX CATSFIELD		COURT LODGE FARM	147
34	LARKIN THOMAS	WI M	30			SSX BEXHILL		BELL HILL	24
3	LAURENCE ELIZABETH	NC U	9			SSX HELLINGLY		BELL HILL	24
3	LAURENCE ELLEN	DL U	11		SCHOLAR	KEN HAWKHURST		EWHURST GREEN	228
85	LAURENCE HARRIET	HD M	30		AG.LAB	SSX WARTLING		BELL HILL	24
3	LAURENCE THOMAS	SO U	1			SSX BEXHILL		BELL HILL	24
3	LAURENCE WILLIAM	SV U	26			SSX SALEHURST		ROCKS	175
24	LAVENDER HENRY	SV U	20		FARMER'S SERVANT	SSX BREDE		BREDE HIGH	251
14	LAVENDER THOMAS	LG W	45		RAILWAY LAB	MDX EDMONTON		RAILWAY HUT	136
55	LAWRENCE JOHN	/ W	66		PAUPER HOUSEKEEPER	SSX GUESTLING		NOT GIVEN	107
11	LAWS MARIA	WI M	36			KEN ELTON		BARN (SCHED.B)	137
*66	LAYDE CANCELETRY?	HD M	33		PEDLER	KEN WESTRON		BARN (SCHED.B)	137
*66	LAYDE WILLIAM	LG U	24		RAIL LAB	BKM NEWPORT PAGNELL		PIGLANDS	7
18	LAYTON THOMAS	LG U	47		RAILWAY LAB	WIL WHITE PARISH		RAILWAY HUT	134
45	LEE JAMES	HD M	51		HAWKER TRINKETS	SSX HASTINGS		TENT HOUSE (LITTLE COMMON)	46
66	LEE JOHN	SO U	18		HAWKER	SSX DENTON		TENT HOUSE (LITTLE COMMON)	46
66	LEE MARK	WI M	45		HAWKER	NBL NEWCASTLE ON TYNE		TENT HOUSE (LITTLE COMMON)	46
66	LEE MARY	LG U	28		RAIL LAB	YORKSHIRE		PUMP HOUSE	13
61	LEE ROBERT	HD M	23		RAIL LAB'S WIFE	SSX BUXTED		NOT GIVEN	91
17	LEEVES SARAH	SO U	3			SSX LEWES		NOT GIVEN	91
17	LEEVES WILLIAM	SO U	8			SSX BEXHILL		NOT GIVEN	52
10	LENNARD ALBERT	SO U	16		AG.LAB	SSX BEXHILL		NOT GIVEN	59
68	LENNARD ALFRED	WI M	55			SSX HOOE		NOT GIVEN	59
68	LENNARD ANN	DA U	16			SSX SHOREHAM		NOT GIVEN	52
10	LENNARD ANNA MARIA	SO U	1			SSX BEXHILL		WAT CLARKES	59
65	LENNARD CHARLES	DA U	10			SSX BEXHILL		WAT CLARKES	59
65	LENNARD ELIZA	DA U	13			SSX BEXHILL		(LITTLE COMMON)	55
32	LENNARD ELIZA	WI M	34			SSX BEXHILL		WAT CLARKES	59
65	LENNARD ELIZA	DA U	7			SSX BEXHILL		WAT CLARKES	59
65	LENNARD EMILY	DA U	4			SSX BEXHILL		NOT GIVEN	52
10	LENNARD FRANCES	SO U	5			SSX BEXHILL		NOT GIVEN	59
67	LENNARD GEORGE	SO U	18		AG.LAB	SSX BEXHILL		(LITTLE COMMON)	55
32	LENNARD GEORGE	SO U	3			SSX BEXHILL		NOT GIVEN	59
67	LENNARD HARRY	HD M	45		HOUSE SERVANT	SSX BEXHILL		NOT GIVEN	52
10	LENNARD HENRY								

10	LENNARD HENRY	SO	U	7		SSX	BEXHILL	NOT GIVEN	52
65	LENNARD HORACE	SO	U	2		SSX	BEXHILL	WAT CLARKES	59
10	LENNARD JANE	DA	U	10		SSX	BEXHILL	NOT GIVEN	52
32	LENNARD JANE	WI	M	58		SSX	BEXHILL	(LITTLE COMMON)	55
32	LENNARD JOHN	HD	M	67	AG.LAB	SSX	BEXHILL	(LITTLE COMMON)	55
68	LENNARD JOHN	SO	U	27	AG.LAB	SSX	BEXHILL	NOT GIVEN	59
10	LENNARD KETURAH	DA	U	6		SSX	BEXHILL	NOT GIVEN	52
67	LENNARD MARY	WI	M	23		SSX	BEXHILL	NOT GIVEN	59
67	LENNARD MARY ANN	DA	U	6		SSX	BEXHILL	NOT GIVEN	59
65	LENNARD MARY ANN	DA	U	9		SSX	BEXHILL	WAT CLARKES	59
10	LENNARD MARY ANN	DA	U	17		SSX	SHOREHAM	NOT GIVEN	52
32	LENNARD MATILDA	DA	U	11		SSX	BEXHILL	(LITTLE COMMON)	55
10	LENNARD SARAH ANN	DA	U	12		SSX	BEXHILL	NOT GIVEN	52
10	LENNARD SARAH ANN	WI	M	44		SSX	HENFIELD	NOT GIVEN	52
10	LENNARD SUSAN	DA	U	15		SSX	SHOREHAM	NOT GIVEN	52
67	LENNARD THOMAS	HD	M	30	MILLER'S LAB	SSX	BEXHILL	NOT GIVEN	59
10	LENNARD THOMAS	SO	U	4		SSX	BEXHILL	NOT GIVEN	52
65	LENNARD THOMAS	SO	U	12	AG.LAB	SSX	BEXHILL	WAT CLARKES	59
65	LENNARD WILLIAM	HD	M	28	AG.LAB	SSX	BEXHILL	WAT CLARKES	59
68	LENNARD WILLIAM	HD	M	59	AG.LAB	SSX	BEXHILL	NOT GIVEN	59
65	LENNARD WILLIAM	SO	U	4		SSX	BEXHILL	WAT CLARKES	59
95	LEONARD GEORGE	SV	U	20	HOUSE SERVANT	SSX	BEXHILL	VICARAGE	100
23	LEONARD HANNAH	SV	U	20	NURSEMAID	SSX	BEXHILL	BEXHILL STREET	26
27	LEONARD JAMES	LG	U	28	RAILWAY LAB	SSX	HOLLINGTON	FORWARD LANE	146
54	LEVETT THOMAS	SV	U	27	BAILIFF	SSX	WILMINGTON	CASTLEMANS	195
17	LEWIS CHARLES	LG	U	26	RAIL LAB	WIL	PUNTON	RAILWAY HUT	7
35	LEWRY CATHARINE	SV	U	15	HOUSE SERVANT	SSX	MARESFIELD	CROWHAM	176
35	LEWRY LUCY	WI	M	56		SSX	MARESFIELD	CROWHAM	176
35	LEWRY THOMAS	HD	M	58	FARMER 371 AC EMP 18LAB	SSX	FLETCHING	CROWHAM	176
58	LIGHT CHARLES	SV	U	23	VALET	SRY	KENNINGTON	HOLLINGTON LODGE	13
65	LINDRIGE G E? (MALE)	PP	U	6	PUPIL	SSX	HASTINGS	NOT GIVEN	96
22	LINGHAM ALFRED	HD	/	30	FARMER 70 AC EMP 4	SSX	BEXHILL	NOT GIVEN	54
22	LINGHAM BENJAMIN	BR	/	23	AG.LAB	SSX	BEXHILL	NOT GIVEN	54
13	LINGHAM ELIZABETH	HD	W	73	PAUPER AG.LAB	SSX	BATTLE	SIDLEY	76
27	LINGHAM ELLEN	SD	U	13		SSX	BEXHILL	SIDLEY	69
60	LINGHAM EMILYER	DA	U	10		SSX	BEXHILL	NOT GIVEN	58
60	LINGHAM EMILYER	WI	M	53		SSX	FIRLE	NOT GIVEN	58
27	LINGHAM GEORGE	SS	U	11		SSX	BEXHILL	SIDLEY	69
22	LINGHAM HANNAH	MO	W	57	HOUSEKEEPER	SSX	BEXHILL	NOT GIVEN	54
27	LINGHAM HENRY	SS	U	7		SSX	BEXHILL	SIDLEY	69
22	LINGHAM JOHN	BR	/	28	AG.LAB	SSX	BEXHILL	NOT GIVEN	54
60	LINGHAM JOSEPH	HD	M	52	AG.LAB	SSX	CROWHURST	NOT GIVEN	58
57	LINGHAM LESTER	SV	U	18		SSX	CROWHURST	HOLLINGTON STREET	12
27	LINGHAM UNICE	SD	U	9		SSX	BEXHILL	SIDLEY	69
60	LINGHAM WILLIAM	SO	U	16		SSX	CROWHURST	NOT GIVEN	58
50	LOCK JAMES	HD	W	65	AG.LAB	SSX	CATSFIELD	COLLINGTON LANE	43
31	LOCK JAMES	NP	U	26	SMITH	SSX	BEXHILL	BEXHILL STREET	27
5	LOCK JAMES	VR	U	30	AG.LAB	MDX	SHOREDITCH	SOUTHINGS	152
50	LOCK JANE	DA	U	29	LAUNDRESS	SSX	BEXHILL	COLLINGTON LANE	43
63	LONG SARAH C	PP	U	9		MDX		BEXHILL STREET	96
2	LONGLEY ELIZABETH	SV	U	14	GENERAL SERVANT	SSX	BEXHILL	LOWER BARNHOEN	37
64	LONGLEY EMILY	DA	U	4	SCHOLAR	SSX	BEXHILL	NOT GIVEN (LITTLE COMMON)	45
64	LONGLEY HENRY C	SO	U	1M		SSX	BEXHILL	NOT GIVEN (LITTLE COMMON)	45
64	LONGLEY JAMES	SO	U	6	SCHOLAR	SSX	BEXHILL	NOT GIVEN (LITTLE COMMON)	45
64	LONGLEY LOUISA	DA	U	2		SSX	BEXHILL	NOT GIVEN (LITTLE COMMON)	45
64	LONGLEY MARGARET	DA	U	11		SSX	BEXHILL	NOT GIVEN (LITTLE COMMON)	45
64	LONGLEY MARY	DA	U	17	DRESSMAKER	SSX	BEXHILL	NOT GIVEN (LITTLE COMMON)	45
64	LONGLEY MARY	WI	M	41		SSX	HOOE	NOT GIVEN (LITTLE COMMON)	45
64	LONGLEY THOMAS	HD	M	42	FARMER 23 AC EMP 2	SSX	WARTLING	NOT GIVEN (LITTLE COMMON)	45
64	LONGLEY TOM	SO	U	9	SCHOLAR	SSX	BEXHILL	NOT GIVEN (LITTLE COMMON)	45
52	LOVEGROVE JANE	HD	M	22	RAILWAY LAB'S WIFE	HAM		RAILWAY HUT	135
65	LOVETT J S (MALE)	PP	U	4	PUPIL	SSX	RYE	NOT GIVEN	96
53	LUCK CAROLINE	/	U	13	SERVANT	SSX	BATTLE	SNAGS HALL	222
51	LUCK MARY ANN	WI	M	37		SSX	WHATLINGTON	SPARKS FARM	239
51	LUCK SAMUEL	HD	M	44	FARMER 116 AC 4 LAB	SSX	NORTHIAM	SPARKS FARM	239
51	LUCK SARAH SUSAN	VR	U	42		SSX	NORTHIAM	SPARKS FARM	239
63	LUKES JOHN	LG	U	24	RAILWAY LAB	WIL?		RAILWAY HUT	137
52	LUXFORD CHARITY	WI	M	42		KEN	MARDEN	SNAGS HALL	222
52	LUXFORD RUTH	DA	U	9	SCHOLAR	SSX	EWHURST	SNAGS HALL	222
52	LUXFORD SARAH JANE	DA	U	1		SSX	EWHURST	SNAGS HALL	222
52	LUXFORD STEPHEN	HD	M	42	AG.LAB	SSX	EWHURST	SNAGS HALL	222
52	LUXFORD STEPHEN	SO	U	21	AG.LAB	SSX	EWHURST	SNAGS HALL	222
52	LUXFORD THOMAS	SO	U	6	SCHOLAR	SSX	EWHURST	SNAGS HALL	222
58	LUXFORD WILLIAM	LG	U	19	AG.LAB	SSX	EWHURST	SNAGS HALL	224
60	MABBOTT PHOEBE	HD	M	37	GROCER	SSX	CUCKFIELD	RAILWAY HUT	136
60	MABBOTT THOMAS	SO	U	1		SSX	ROUGHEY?	RAILWAY HUT	136
54	MACE JOHN	LG	U	29	RAILWAY LAB	NTH	IDERBON??	RAILWAY HUT	135
55	MACLEOD MARGARET S	GO	U	26	GOVERNESS	SCOTLAND		SIGNAL HOUSE	44
62	MALLING GEORGE	LG	U	31	RAIL LAB	YORKSHIRE		PUMP HOUSE	13
16	MALLYON ELIZABETH	DA	U	11	SCHOLAR	SSX	SEDLESCOMBE	SEDLESCOMBE STREET	203
16	MALLYON HENRIETTA	WI	M	50		SSX	GOUDHURST	SEDLESCOMBE STREET	203
16	MALLYON JOHN	SO	U	16		SSX	SEDLESCOMBE	SEDLESCOMBE STREET	203
16	MALLYON MARY ANN	DA	U	20	DRESSMAKER	SSX	MOUNTFIELD	SEDLESCOMBE STREET	203
16	MALLYON RICHARD	SO	U	14		SSX	DALLINGTON	SEDLESCOMBE STREET	203
16	MALLYON THOMAS	HD	M	48	BUTCHER	KEN	GOUDHURST	SEDLESCOMBE STREET	203
16	MALLYON WILLIAM	SO	U	8	SCHOLAR	SSX	SEDLESCOMBE	SEDLESCOMBE STREET	203

13	MALTMAN? ELIZABETH	VR	W	77	PARISH RELIEF	SSX DALLINGTON	STEVEN'S CROUCH		121
40	MANNERING ALFRED	SO	U	3		KEN BIDDENDEN	HOLLINGTON STREET		10
40	MANNERING GEORGE	SO	U	6		KEN BIDDENDEN	HOLLINGTON STREET		10
40	MANNERING HENRY	HD	M	39	AG.LAB	KEN HALDEN	HOLLINGTON STREET		10
38	MANNERING HENRY	SV	U	14		KEN BIDDENDEN	BUCKLANDS		10
40	MANNERING MARIA	DA	U	9		KEN BIDDENDEN	HOLLINGTON STREET		10
40	MANNERING SARAH	WI	M	45		SMARDEN	HOLLINGTON STREET		10
40	MANNERING SARAH JANE	DA	U	12		KEN BIDDENDEN	HOLLINGTON STREET		10
40	MANNERING WILLIAM	SO	U	15		KEN BIDDENDEN	HOLLINGTON STREET		10
69	MANNINGTON JOSEPH	LG	U	20	GRINDER & BAKER	SSX MARESFIELD	NOT GIVEN		59
66	MANSER CELIA	WI	M	24		KEN HADLOW	BEACH FARM		14
66	MANSER GEORGE	HD	M	30	FARM BAILIFF	KEN HADLOW	BEACH FARM		14
66	MANSER GEORGE	SO	U	3		SSX HOLLINGTON	BEACH FARM		14
66	MANSER JESSE	SO	U	1		SSX HOLLINGTON	BEACH FARM		14
66	MANSER MARY	DA	U	7M		SSX HOLLINGTON	BEACH FARM		14
20	MANTLE DAVID	SO	U	14	AG.LAB	SSX CATSFIELD	NOT GIVEN		109
20	MANTLE JOHN	SO	U	10	AG.LAB	SSX CATSFIELD	NOT GIVEN		109
20	MANTLE PHILLY	WI	M	36		SSX CROWHURST	NOT GIVEN		109
20	MANTLE RICHARD	HD	M	40	AG.LAB	SSX CATSFIELD	NOT GIVEN		109
20	MANTLE RICHARD	SO	U	4		SSX CATSFIELD	NOT GIVEN		109
20	MANTLE SARAH	DA	U	15		SSX CATSFIELD	NOT GIVEN		109
46	MAPLESDEN HANNAH	WI	M	70		SSX HOLLINGTON	MOAT		167
46	MAPLESDEN RICHARD	HD	M	73	FARMER	SSX HOLLINGTON	MOAT		167
49	MARCHANT ANN	DA	U	10		SSX ORE	HOLLINGTON STREET		11
49	MARCHANT ANN	WI	M	32		SSX ORE	HOLLINGTON STREET		11
49	MARCHANT CAROLINE	DA	U	1		SSX HOLLINGTON	HOLLINGTON STREET		11
79	MARCHANT ELIAS	SO	U	7		SSX WESTFIELD	DOWN		182
79	MARCHANT HANNAH	WI	M	28		SSX NINFIELD	DOWN		182
35	MARCHANT HARRIETT	DA	U	6		NOT GIVEN (?WESTFIELD)	LEMS		156
79	MARCHANT JAMES	HD	M	28	AG.LAB	SSX WESTFIELD	DOWN		182
49	MARCHANT JAMES	HD	M	37	BRICK BURNER	SSX ORE	HOLLINGTON STREET		11
15	MARCHANT JAMES	LG	/	23	BLACKSMITH	NOT GIVEN	MAYFIELDS HOUSE		7
49	MARCHANT JOHN	SO	U	7	SCHOLAR	SSX ORE	HOLLINGTON STREET		11
79	MARCHANT MARK	SO	U	4M		SSX WESTFIELD	DOWN		182
20	MARCHANT MARY	DA	U	12		SSX WESTFIELD	LOW COTTAGE		153
49	MARCHANT SARAH	DA	U	4		SSX ST.LEONARDS	HOLLINGTON STREET		11
20	MARCHANT SARAH	DA	U	17		SSX WESTFIELD	LOW COTTAGE		153
35	MARCHANT SARAH	WI	M	34		SSX WESTFIELD	LEMS		156
35	MARCHANT UN-NAMED INFANT BOY	SO	U	1M		NOT GIVEN (?WESTFIELD)	LEMS		156
35	MARCHANT WILLIAM	HD	M	34	AG.LAB	SSX WESTFIELD	LEMS		156
21	MARCHANT WILLIAM	LG	U	20	AG.LAB	SSX BATTLE	NOT GIVEN		109
35	MARCHANT WILLIAM	SO	U	11		NOT GIVEN (?WESTFIELD)	LEMS		156
35	MARCHANT WINIFRED	DA	U	9		NOT GIVEN (?WESTFIELD)	LEMS		156
63	MARKETT DEBORAH	WI	M	39		DEV DEVONPORT	COAST GUARD STATION		30
63	MARKETT JOHN	HD	M	53	LIEUT RN C GUARD SERVICE	IRELAND	COAST GUARD STATION		30
63	MARKETT SARAH	DA	U	11		SSX WILLINGDON	COAST GUARD STATION		30
63	MARKETT SOPHIA	DA	U	10		SSX WILLINGDON	COAST GUARD STATION		30
41	MARTIN ALBERT	SO	U	7		SSX EWHURST	OCKHAM		221
19	MARTIN ALBERT	SO	U	7	SCHOLAR	SSX BATTLE	SIDLEY		77
65	MARTIN ANN	DA	U	9	SCHOLAR	SSX EWHURST	STAPLE CROSS		241
62	MARTIN ANN	WI	M	32		SSX SEDLESCOMBE	BAULKHAM GREEN		196
48	MARTIN ANNA	GD	U	3		SSX SALEHURST	SWALES GREEN		193
26	MARTIN CALEB	SO	U	3		SSX EWHURST	FORGE FARM		219
29	MARTIN DAMORIS	WI	M	25		SSX NORTHIAM	ADAMS LANE		236
62	MARTIN EDWARD	SO	U	9M		SSX SEDLESCOMBE	BAULKHAM GREEN		196
41	MARTIN EDWIN	HD	M	34	AG.LAB	SSX EWHURST	OCKHAM		221
29	MARTIN EDWIN	SO	U	3		SSX NORTHIAM	ADAMS LANE		236
10	MARTIN FRANCIS HENRY	SO	U	17		SSX BREDE	SEDLESCOMBE STREET		202
65	MARTIN FREDERICK	HD	W	39	AG.LAB	SSX EWHURST	STAPLE CROSS		241
29	MARTIN FREDERICK	SO	U	5		SSX NORTHIAM	ADAMS LANE		236
29	MARTIN GEORGE	SO	U	2M		SSX NORTHIAM	ADAMS LANE		236
41	MARTIN GEORGE	SO	U	9		SSX BODIAM	OCKHAM		221
33	MARTIN GEORGE	SO	U	11	SCHOLAR	SSX SEDLESCOMBE	NEAR THE CHURCH		205
41	MARTIN GODFREY	SO	U	11		SSX BODIAM	OCKHAM		221
33	MARTIN HANNAH	WI	M	42		SSX BATTLE	NEAR THE CHURCH		205
72	MARTIN HARRIET	GD	U	13		SSX MOUNTFIELD	STAPLE CROSS		242
41	MARTIN HENRIETTA	WI	M	42		SSX EWHURST	OCKHAM		221
33	MARTIN HENRY	HD	M	49	COACHMAN	BRK SHRIVENHAM	NEAR THE CHURCH		205
26	MARTIN HENRY	HD	W	41	AG.LAB	SSX WHATLINGTON	FORGE FARM		219
10	MARTIN HENRY	SO	U	7		SSX EWHURST	SEDLESCOMBE STREET		202
26	MARTIN HENRY	SO	U	12	SCHOLAR	SSX EWHURST	FORGE FARM		219
65	MARTIN HENRY	SO	U	13	AG.LAB	SSX EWHURST	STAPLE CROSS		241
10	MARTIN JABEZ	SO	U	10		SSX BREDE	SEDLESCOMBE STREET		202
29	MARTIN JAMES	LG	U	15	AG.LAB	SSX EWHURST	ADAMS LANE		236
10	MARTIN JAMES	SO	U	14		SSX BREDE	SEDLESCOMBE STREET		202
19	MARTIN JAMES	SO	U	15		SSX BATTLE	SIDLEY		77
19	MARTIN JOHN	HD	M	38	BRICK & TILE MAKER	SSX BATTLE	SIDLEY		77
10	MARTIN JOHN	HD	M	50	AG.LAB	SSX WILMINGTON	SEDLESCOMBE STREET		202
19	MARTIN JOSEPH	SO	U	4		SSX BATTLE	SIDLEY		77
69	MARTIN MARK	LG	U	21	AG.LAB	KEN HADLOW	YEW TREE		15
41	MARTIN MARY	DA	U	13		SSX EWHURST	OCKHAM		221
19	MARTIN SARAH	DA	U	12	SCHOLAR	SSX BATTLE	SIDLEY		77
87	MARTIN SARAH	SV	U	16	SERVANT	SSX WHATLINGTON	STAPLE CROSS		244
28	MARTIN SARAH	WI	M	26		KEN ASHFORD	RAILWAY HUT		8
19	MARTIN SARAH	WI	M	34		KEN CHATHAM	SIDLEY		77
29	MARTIN SELENA	DA	U	2		SSX NORTHIAM	ADAMS LANE		236

No.	Name	Rel	M	Age	Occupation	Birth County	Birth Place	Address	Pg
48	MARTIN SIDNEY	HD	M	44	FARMER 38AC EMP 2	SSX	BATTLE	WESTBROOK	178
48	MARTIN STELLA	WI	M	43		SSX	WESTFIELD	WESTBROOK	178
10	MARTIN SUSANNAH	DA	U	3		SSX	SEDLESCOMBE	SEDLESCOMBE STREET	202
10	MARTIN SUSANNAH	WI	M	45		SSX	BREDE	SEDLESCOMBE STREET	202
38	MARTIN THOMAS	LG	U	22	AG.LAB	SSX	EWHURST	MARCHANTS	237
29	MARTIN WILLIAM	HD	M	26	AG.LAB	SSX	EWHURST	ADAMS LANE	236
28	MARTIN WILLIAM	HD	M	31	RAIL LAB	WAR	KINGSTON	RAILWAY HUT	8
62	MARTIN WILLIAM	HD	M	44	CHELSEA PENSIONER	SSX	WILMINGTON	BAULKHAM GREEN	196
41	MARTIN WILLIAM	SO	U	9M		SSX	EWHURST	OCKHAM	221
1	MASTERS EMILY	VR	U	12		SSX	NORTHIAM	KNIGHTS	151
63	MASTERS JULIA	AS	U	23	GOVERNESS	ST GEORGES	- ? (SIC)	BEXHILL STREET	96
34	MATHIS ALLENDER	DA	U	1	(14M)	SSX	HAILSHAM	NOT GIVEN	124
34	MATHIS CROLINE (SIC)	DA	U	14	SCHOLAR	SSX	HAILSHAM	NOT GIVEN	124
34	MATHIS HANNAH	WI	M	36		SSX	HAILSHAM	NOT GIVEN	124
37	MATHIS JANE	SV	U	14	NURSE MAID	SSX	BATTLE	BEXHILL STREET	27
34	MATHIS JOHN	HD	M	40	BASKET MAKER	KEN	HADLOW	NOT GIVEN	124
34	MATHIS MARIA	DA	U	12	SCHOLAR	SSX	HAILSHAM	NOT GIVEN	124
34	MATHIS MARY	DA	U	16		SSX	HAILSHAM	NOT GIVEN	124
22	MATT HENRY	HD	M	84	POSTMASTER	DOR	BERE REGIS	BELL HILL	26
22	MATT MARY	WI	M	78?		SSX	EWHURST	BELL HILL	26
7	MAWLE ANN	CI	U	18		SSX	WESTFIELD	PLATNIX	173
7	MAWLE ELIZABETH	CI	U	25		SSX	WESTFIELD	PLATNIX	173
7	MAWLE JOHN	HD	U	27	FARMER	SSX	BREDE	PLATNIX	173
68	MAY CHARLES	SO	U	9	SCHOLAR	SSX	BEXHILL	46 MARTELLO TOWER	31
68	MAY ELIZABETH	DA	U	5		SSX	BEXHILL	46 MARTELLO TOWER	31
34	MAY ELLEN	DA	U	21		SSX	CATSFIELD	NOT GIVEN	110
34	MAY HANNAH	HD	W	69	PAUPER	SSX	BEXHILL	NOT GIVEN	110
34	MAY HARRIET	GD	U	10	SCHOLAR	KEN	GREENWICH	NOT GIVEN	110
34	MAY HENRY	SO	U	35	AG.LAB	SSX	CATSFIELD	NOT GIVEN	110
30	MAY JAMES	HD	M	33	AG.LAB	SSX	BRIGHTLING	NOT GIVEN	110
68	MAY JAMES	SO	U	12	SCHOLAR	SSX	BEXHILL	46 MARTELLO TOWER	31
30	MAY RHODA	WI	M	37		SSX	BATTLE	NOT GIVEN	110
68	MAY RICHARD	HD	M	44	COAST GUARD	COR	FALMOUTH	46 MARTELLO TOWER	31
68	MAY SARAH	DA	U	17		COR	FALMOUTH	46 MARTELLO TOWER	31
68	MAY SARAH	WI	M	40?		COR	ST.COLUMB	46 MARTELLO TOWER	31
42	MAYNARD HANNAH	WI	M	41		SRY	NARHAM?	RAILWAY HUT	134
42	MAYNARD JOHN	HD	M	45	RAILWAY LAB	KEN	TUNBRIDGE	RAILWAY HUT	134
42	MAYNARD WILLIAM HENRY	NP	U	9		SRY	NARHAM?	RAILWAY HUT	134
54	MAYO JOHN	LG	U	43	RAILWAY LAB	DOR	POOLE	RAILWAY HUT	135
50	MCCARTHY DENIS	VR	M	43	MARINER	IRELAND		GALLEY HILL	29
67	MCCARTHY PRISCILLA	HD	M	42	PROPRIETOR OF HOUSES	KEN	ASH	1 BELLENDER COTTAGE	46
77	MCLAUCHTON CHARLOTTE	LG	U	76	FUNDHOLDER	SCOTLAND		STEMPS? LODGE	16
64	MCLEISH ANN	DA	U	8?		SSX	HOLLINGTON	NEW COTTAGE	14
64	MCLEISH ARCHIBALD WILLIAM	SO	U	10			SSX HASTINGS	NEW COTTAGE	14
64	MCLEISH DAVID	HD	M	49	SERVANT	MDX	ST.G HAN SQUARE	NEW COTTAGE	14
64	MCLEISH MARY	DA	U	5		SSX	HOLLINGTON	NEW COTTAGE	14
64	MCLEISH MARY ANN	WI	M	34		SSX	BREDE	NEW COTTAGE	14
26	MCNAUGHTON ELIZABETH	SV	U	28	HOUSE MAID	SCOTLAND (+CROSSED OUT)		CATSFIELD PLACE CHURCH HSE	110
73	MCVEAN JOHN	LG	U	37	GARDENER	CUL	LONG TOWN	STEMPS?	15
80	MENDHAM EDWARD	VR	U	32	GENTLEMAN	MDX	LONDON	BELL HOTEL	99
8	MEPHAM ANN	DA	U	17		SSX	NORTHIAM	STOCKLANDS	250
8	MEPHAM CAROLINE	WI	M	36		SSX	NORTHIAM	STOCKLANDS	250
8	MEPHAM EDMUND	SO	U	8	SCHOLAR	SSX	EWHURST	STOCKLANDS	250
8	MEPHAM JAMES	SO	U	3		SSX	EWHURST	STOCKLANDS	250
8	MEPHAM JOHN	SO	U	6		SSX	EWHURST	STOCKLANDS	250
8	MEPHAM MARY	DA	U	11	SCHOLAR	SSX	EWHURST	STOCKLANDS	250
8	MEPHAM NELSON	HD	M	41	AG.LAB	SSX	EWHURST	STOCKLANDS	250
80	MEPHAM SARAH	/	W	34	HOUSE KEEPER	SSX	BECKLEY	EWHURST GREEN	227
47	MEPPEM AMOS	SO	U	1		SSX	EWHURST	NOT GIVEN	238
58	MEPPEM EDWIN	SO	U	23	AG.LAB	SSX	EWHURST	ELLINGHALL	240
47	MEPPEM MARTHA	WI	M	28		SSX	BECKLEY	NOT GIVEN	238
58	MEPPEM PHILADELPHIA	WI	M	53		SSX	BRIGHTLING	ELLINGBALL	240
58	MEPPEM SAMUEL	HD	M	65	WOODREEVE	SSX	EWHURST	ELLINGHALL	240
47	MEPPEM WILLIAM	HD	M	33	AG.LAB	SSX	EWHURST	NOT GIVEN	238
88	MERCER ANN	DA	U	5		SSX	TICEHURST	NOT GIVEN	99
88	MERCER CHARLES	HD	M	35	BRICKMAKER	KEN	STAPLEHURST	NOT GIVEN	99
88	MERCER ELIZABETH	DA	U	1M		SSX	BEXHILL	NOT GIVEN	99
88	MERCER EMMA	DA	U	2		SSX	WINCHELSEA	NOT GIVEN	99
88	MERCER SARAH	WI	M	25		SSX	NORTHIAM	NOT GIVEN	99
25	MERCER THOMAS	LG	U	21	AG.LAB	SSX	HURSTMONCEUX	SAMPSONS SIDLEY	69
85	MERCHANT ANN	SV	U	22		SSX	WESTFIELD	SHOP HOUSE	18
112	MERCHANT JANE	ML	W	75	PAUPER LAUNDRESS	SSX	HERSTMONCEUX	NOT GIVEN	102
37	MERCHANT JERIMIAH	SV	U	50	AG.LAB	SSX	GUESTLING	BEXHILL STREET	27
75	MEWETT MARY	WI	M	76		SSX	CATSFIELD	NOT GIVEN	32
75	MEWETT ROBERT	HD	M	81	COOPER	SSX	BEXHILL	NOT GIVEN	32
21	MICHEL JOHN	BR	U	51	CHELSEA PENSIONER	SSX	HERSTMONCEUX	MARLPITS	122
21	MICHEL THOMAS	HD	U	65	AG.LAB	SSX	HERSTMONCEUX	MARLPITS	122
21	MICHEL WILLIAM	BR	U	44	AG.LAB	SSX	HERSTMONCEUX	MARLPITS	122
66	MIDDLEDITCH EMILY	DA	U	7	SCHOLAR	SSX	HASTINGS	COAST GUARD STATION	31
66	MIDDLEDITCH HARRIETT	DA	U	5	SCHOLAR	SSX	HASTINGS	COAST GUARD STATION	31
66	MIDDLEDITCH MARY A	DA	U	12	SCHOLAR	SSX	HASTINGS	COAST GUARD STATION	31
66	MIDDLEDITCH MARY A	WI	M	45		KEN	UPERON?*	COAST GUARD STATION	31
66	MIDDLEDITCH RICHARD	SO	U	3M		SSX	BEXHILL	COAST GUARD STATION	31
66	MIDDLEDITCH THOMAS	HD	M	43	COAST GUARD	KEN	CHATHAM	COAST GUARD STATION	31
66	MIDDLEDITCH WILLIAM	SO	U	9	SCHOLAR	SSX	HASTINGS	COAST GUARD STATION	31
96	MIDDLETON GEORGE	HD	W	62	RAIL LAB	YKS		HUT	19

	Name			Age	Occupation	County	Parish	Address	Page
13	MIDDLETON MARY	LG	U	29		SSX	PETWORTH	MAYFIELDS RAILWAY HUT	6
3	MILES ELIZABETH	WI	M	73		SSX	WESTFIELD?	NOT GIVEN	106
3	MILES HENRY	HD	M	69	LAB	SSX	CATSFIELD	NOT GIVEN	106
11	MILES WILLIAM	VR	U	5	COAST GUARD'S SON	SSX	RYE	IN THE LIBERTY	38
64	MILFORD GEORGE	LG	W	39	RAILWAY LAB	WIL	*(SIC) WITHIHAM	RAILWAY HUT	137
13	MILFORD WILLIAM	LG	U	22	RAIL LAB	BRK	FINEHAMPSTEAD	MAYFIELDS RAILWAY HUT	6
45	MILHAM ANN	WI	M	35?		SSX	NORTHIAM	NOT GIVEN	238
30	MILHAM CAROLINE	DA	U	3M	TWIN	SSX	EWHURST	RENS	219
30	MILHAM CHARLOTTE	WI	M	26		SSX	BREDE	RENS	219
30	MILHAM CLARA	DA	U	3M	TWIN	SSX	EWHURST	RENS	219
53	MILHAM DAVID	HD	M	45	AG.LAB	SSX	EWHURST	STOCKWOOD FARM	239
20	MILHAM DAVID	SO	U	3		KEN	SANDHURST	CATTS GREEN	252
53	MILHAM ELIZABETH	WI	M	45		SSX	SEDLESCOMBE	STOCKWOOD FARM	239
45	MILHAM FRANK	SO	U	10		SSX	NORTHIAM	NOT GIVEN	238
30	MILHAM GEORGE	HD	M	30	FARMER 65 ACRS EMP 1	SSX	BREDE	RENS	219
45	MILHAM GEORGE	SO	U	4		SSX	EWHURST	NOT GIVEN	238
63	MILHAM JANE	HD	U	58	HOUSE KEEPER	SSX	BREDE	RECTORY HOUSE	224
20	MILHAM JANE	WI	M	24		KEN	SANDHURST	CATTS GREEN	252
30	MILHAM LEWIS	SO	U	5		SSX	BREDE	RENS	219
45	MILHAM THOMAS	SO	U	7M		SSX	EWHURST	NOT GIVEN	238
20	MILHAM THOMAS	SO	U	5		KEN	SANDHURST	CATTS GREEN	252
20	MILHAM WILLIAM	HD	M	23	AG.LAB	SSX	EWHURST	CATTS GREEN	251
45	MILHAM WILLIAM	HD	M	32	AG.LAB	SSX	EWHURST	NOT GIVEN	238
30	MILHAM WILLIAM	SO	U	2		SSX	BREDE	RENS	219
45	MILHAM WILLIAM	SO	U	7		SSX	NORTHIAM	NOT GIVEN	238
33	MILLER AMELIA	DA	U	3		SSX	BATTLE	MOORS FARM	147
11	MILLER ANN	DA	U	7	SCHOLAR	SSX	BEXHILL	SIDLEY	76
33	MILLER CHARLES	SO	U	9		SSX	WARTLING	MOORS FARM	147
76	MILLER EDWIN	VR	U	29	MARINER	SSX	BEXHILL	BELL HILL	32
56	MILLER ELIZA	WI	M	28		KEN	WHISTABLE	RAILWAY HUT	136
76	MILLER EMILY	DA	U	13		SSX	BEXHILL	NOT GIVEN (LITTLE COMMON)	47
56	MILLER GEORGE	HD	M	34	RAILWAY LAB	NTH		RAILWAY HUT	136
8	MILLER GEORGE	SO	U	20	RAIL LAB	KEN	ASHFORD	RAILWAY HUT	5
83	MILLER HANNAH	NC	U	20	HOUSE SERVANT	SSX	BEXHILL	NOT GIVEN (LITTLE COMMON)	47
38	MILLER HANNAH	SV	U	26	HOUSE SERVANT	SSX	HERSTMONCEUX	SHOP HOUSES	124
62	MILLER HARRIETT	DA	U	5		SSX	HOLLINGTON	PUMP HOUSE	13
11	MILLER HENRY	HD	M	45	SHEPHERD	SSX	BATTLE	SIDLEY	76
62	MILLER JAMES	HD	M	46	AG.LAB	SSX	MAYFIELD	PUMP HOUSE	13
11	MILLER JAMES	SO	U	13		SSX	BEXHILL	SIDLEY	76
62	MILLER JAMES	SO	U	21	AG.LAB	SSX	CROWHURST	PUMP HOUSE	13
33	MILLER JEMIMA	DA	U	11		SSX	WARTLING	MOORS FARM	146
33	MILLER JEMIMA	WI	M	46		SSX	HEATHFIELD	MOORS FARM	146
8	MILLER JOHN	6S	U	4?		KEN	CANTERBURY	RAILWAY HUT	5
33	MILLER JOHN	HD	M	51	FARMER 61 AC EMP 2	SSX	HEATHFIELD	MOORS FARM	146
95	MILLER JOHN	LG	U	30	RAIL LAB	SSX	KEYMER	HUT	19
8	MILLER JOHN	SO	U	7		KEN	ASHFORD	RAILWAY HUT	5
62	MILLER JOHN	SO	U	9		SSX	HOLLINGTON	PUMP HOUSE	13
33	MILLER JONATHAN	SO	U	13		SSX	WARTLING	MOORS FARM	146
77	MILLER LUCY	WI	M	39		SSX	RINGMER	NOT GIVEN (LITTLE COMMON)	47
66	MILLER MARIA	SV	U	19	HOUSE MAID	SSX	CROWHURST	BEACH FARM	14
3	MILLER MARY	SV	U	25	HOUSE SERVANT	SSX	BEXHILL	BARNHORN HILL	37
76	MILLER MARY	WI	M	47		SSX	BEXHILL	NOT GIVEN (LITTLE COMMON)	47
11	MILLER MARY ANN	WI	M	38		SSX	BEXHILL	SIDLEY	76
11	MILLER PHILLIP	SO	U	5	SCHOLAR	SSX	BEXHILL	SIDLEY	76
62	MILLER PHOEBE	WI	M	47		SSX	BATTLE	PUMP HOUSE	13
63	MILLER RICHARD	HD	M	65	AG.LAB	SSX	BEXHILL	PINNIERS (LITTLE COMMON)	45
11	MILLER SAMUEL	SO	U	3		SSX	BEXHILL	SIDLEY	76
33	MILLER SARAH	DA	U	15		SSX	WARTLING	MOORS FARM	146
11	MILLER THOMAS	FA	W	71	AG.LAB	SSX	BEXHILL	SIDLEY	76
77	MILLER THOMAS	HD	M	41	AG.LAB	SSX	BEXHILL	NOT GIVEN (LITTLE COMMON)	47
11	MILLER THOMAS	SO	U	9		SSX	BEXHILL	SIDLEY	76
76	MILLER WILLIAM	HD	M	50	AG.LAB	SSX	HASTINGS	NOT GIVEN (LITTLE COMMON)	47
62	MILLER WILLIAM	SO	U	17		SSX	CROWHURST	PUMP HOUSE	13
33	MILLER WILLIAM	SO	U	17		SSX	WARTLING	MOORS FARM	146
8	MILLER WILLIAM	SO	U	18	RAIL LAB	KEN	ASHFORD	RAILWAY HUT	5
74	MILLS CHARLOTTE	WI	M	25		KEN	HAWKHURST	EWHURST GREEN	226
74	MILLS EDWARD	SO	U	5M		SSX	EWHURST	EWHURST GREEN	226
42	MILLS EDWIN	SO	U	5		SSX	EWHURST	FORGE LANE	254
74	MILLS ELIZA	DA	U	2		SSX	EWHURST	EWHURST GREEN	226
42	MILLS ELIZABETH	WI	M	37		SSX	BECKLEY	FORGE LANE	254
74	MILLS FANNY	DA	U	3		SSX	EWHURST	EWHURST GREEN	226
32	MILLS GEORGE	SO	U	3M		SSX	NORTHIAM	MADDAMS	220
10	MILLS GEORGE WILLIAM	SO	U	6		SSX	EWHURST	COLLIERS GREEN	233
7	MILLS HANNAH	WI	M	59		SSX	NORTHIAM	PADGHAM	216
32	MILLS HARRIET	WI	M	28		SSX	NORTHIAM	MADDAMS	220
10	MILLS HARRIET	WI	M	34		SSX	BATTLE	COLLIERS GREEN	233
10	MILLS HENRY	HD	M	30	AG.LAB	SSX	EWHURST	COLLIERS GREEN	233
32	MILLS JAMES	HD	M	24	AG.LAB	SSX	EWHURST	MADDAMS	220
42	MILLS JOHN	HD	M	36	AG.LAB	SSX	EWHURST	FORGE LANE	254
7	MILLS JOHN	HD	M	59	AG.LAB	SSX	WHATLINGTON	PADGHAM	216
51	MILLS MARY JANE	NC	U	11	SCHOLAR	SSX	WHATLINGTON	SPARKS FARM	239
42	MILLS NORMAN	SO	U	2		SSX	EWHURST	FORGE LANE	254
7	MILLS SAMUEL	6S	U	16	AG.LAB	SSX	EWHURST	PADGHAM	216
37	MILLS THOMAS	LG	U	28	RAILWAY LAB	SSX	MOUNTFIELD	RAILWAY HUT	133
74	MILLS WILLIAM	HD	M	28	AG.LAB	SSX	EWHURST	EWHURST GREEN	226
82	MILSTED ELIZA	DA	U	1M		SSX	EWHURST	STAPLE CROSS	243

No.	Name	Code	Age	Occupation	County Parish	Location	Ref
82	MILSTED HARRIET	DA U	6	SCHOLAR	KEN SANDHURST	STAPLE CROSS	243
82	MILSTED HARRIET	WI M	33		KEN SANDHURST	STAPLE CROSS	243
82	MILSTED JAMES	SO U	3		SSI EWHURST	STAPLE CROSS	243
82	MILSTED MARY ANN	DA U	8	SCHOLAR	SSI TENTERDEN	STAPLE CROSS	243
82	MILSTED WILLIAM	HD M	34	SADDLER	KEN TENTERDEN	STAPLE CROSS	243
82	MILSTED WILLIAM	SO U	9	SCHOLAR	SSI SANDHURST	STAPLE CROSS	243
19	MITCHEL ANN	DA U	17		SSI NINFIELD	BURNT BARNS	122
19	MITCHEL ELIZABETH	WI M	44		SSI NINFIELD	BURNT BARNS	122
19	MITCHEL HENERY	SO U	13	AG.LAB	SSI NINFIELD	BURNT BARNS	122
19	MITCHEL RICHARD	HD M	55	AG.LAB	SSI NINFIELD	BURNT BARNS	122
19	MITCHEL THOMAS	SO U	15	AG.LAB	SSI NINFIELD	BURNT BARNS	122
23	MITCHELL ELLEN	DA U	16		SSI BEXHILL	MOUNT PLEASANT - SIDLEY	68
11	MITCHELL JAMES	SV W	60	AG.LAB	SRY GUILDFORD	WILTING FARM HOUSE	6
23	MITCHELL JANE	DA U	24		SSI BATTLE	MOUNT PLEASANT - SIDLEY	68
23	MITCHELL JOHN	HD M	68	PROPRIETOR OF HOUSES	KEN STAPLECHURCH	MOUNT PLEASANT - SIDLEY	68
23	MITCHELL MARY	WI M	57		SSI BEXHILL	MOUNT PLEASANT - SIDLEY	68
66	MITTEN ANN	GD U	5		SSI BEXHILL	NOT GIVEN	59
66	MITTEN ARON	GS U	3		SSI BEXHILL	NOT GIVEN	59
71	MITTEN DELIA	DA U	6	SCHOLAR	SSI BEXHILL	NOT GIVEN (LITTLE COMMON)	46
35	MITTEN ELIZA	GD U	10		SSI BEXHILL	NOT GIVEN	55
66	MITTEN ESTHER	GD U	9		SSI BEXHILL	NOT GIVEN	59
71	MITTEN GEORGE	SO U	9	SCHOLAR	SSI BEXHILL	NOT GIVEN (LITTLE COMMON)	46
71	MITTEN HANNAH	HD M	39	PAUPER AG.LAB'S WIFE	SSI BEXHILL	NOT GIVEN (LITTLE COMMON)	46
35	MITTEN HARRIOT	GD U	4		SSI BEXHILL	NOT GIVEN	55
64	MITTEN JAMES	SV U	20	AG.LAB	SSI BEXHILL	NOT GIVEN (LITTLE COMMON)	45
71	MITTEN JANE	DA U	11	SCHOLAR	SSI BEXHILL	NOT GIVEN (LITTLE COMMON)	46
66	MITTEN JOHN	GS U	11	SCHOLAR	SSI BEXHILL	NOT GIVEN	59
71	MITTEN JOHN	SO U	5		SSI BEXHILL	NOT GIVEN (LITTLE COMMON)	46
66	MITTEN JOSEPH	GS U	13	SCHOLAR	SSI BEXHILL	NOT GIVEN	59
38	MITTEN JOSEPH	HD W	67	RETIRED FARMER	SSI BEXHILL	NOT GIVEN	93
66	MITTEN JOSEPH JNR	SO U	36	AG.LAB	SSI BEXHILL	NOT GIVEN	59
66	MITTEN JOSEPH SNR	HD W	69	FARMER 7 AC	SSI BEXHILL	NOT GIVEN	59
35	MITTEN MARY	DL M	33		SSI BEXHILL	NOT GIVEN	55
35	MITTEN MARY	GD U	14		SSI BEXHILL	NOT GIVEN	55
57	MITTEN MARY	L6 U	81	PARISH ANNUITANT	MDX	WHITE HILL COTTAGE	58
12	MITTEN MARY ANN	SV U	17	HOUSE SERVANT	SSI BEXHILL	WHYDOWN	52
66	MITTEN ORPHA	GD U	7		SSI BEXHILL	NOT GIVEN	59
35	MITTEN RICHARD	SO M	35	AG.LAB	SSI BEXHILL	NOT GIVEN	55
71	MITTEN RICHARD	SO U	15	AG.LAB	SSI BEXHILL	NOT GIVEN (LITTLE COMMON)	46
66	MITTEN SOPHIA	DL M	36		SSI BEXHILL	NOT GIVEN	59
35	MITTEN THOMAS	GS U	6		SSI BEXHILL	NOT GIVEN	55
35	MITTEN WILLIAM	HD W	76	FARMER 7 ACRES	SSI BREDE	NOT GIVEN	55
71	MITTEN WILLIAM	SO U	13	AG.LAB	SSI BEXHILL	NOT GIVEN (LITTLE COMMON)	46
117	MOCKFORD HANNAH	HD W	86	ANNUITANT	SSI BEXHILL	NOT GIVEN	102
17	MOON CALEB	SO U	12		SSI WESTFIELD	BUCKHURST	163
64	MOON CHARLOTTE	DA U	7		SSI WESTFIELD	ONION HILL	180
13	MOON CHARLOTTE	NC U	20		SSI MOUNTFIELD	YEW TREES	173
45	MOON ELIZA A	DA U	8		SSI WESTFIELD	BOWERS COTTAGE	178
17	MOON ELIZABETH	DA U	3	SCHOLAR	SSI WESTFIELD	BUCKHURST	164
45	MOON ELIZABETH J	DA U	6		SSI WESTFIELD	BOWERS COTTAGE	178
34	MOON GEORGE S	HD M	45	CARPENTER	KENT MARDEN	BEXHILL STREET	27
64	MOON HANNAH	DA U	10	SCHOLAR	SSI WESTFIELD	ONION HILL	180
17	MOON HANNAH	DA U	20		SSI WESTFIELD	BUCKHURST	163
1	MOON HARRIETT	SV U	22	HOUSE SERVANT	SSI WESTFIELD	VICARAGE HOUSE	161
64	MOON JAMES	HD M	42	AG.LAB	SSI WESTFIELD	ONION HILL	180
86	MOON JAMES	SV U	16		SSI WESTFIELD	HARROW INN	18
17	MOON JOHN	SO U	10	SCHOLAR	SSI WESTFIELD	BUCKHURST	163
17	MOON LEWES	SO U	18		SSI WESTFIELD	BUCKHURST	163
45	MOON LEWIS	HD M	35	AG.LAB	SSI WESTFIELD	BOWERS COTTAGE	178
64	MOON MARK	SO U	4		SSI WESTFIELD	ONION HILL	180
64	MOON MARTHA	DA U	1		SSI WESTFIELD	ONION HILL	180
45	MOON MARTHA	DA U	4		SSI WESTFIELD	BOWERS COTTAGE	178
20	MOON MARY	SV U	13		SSI WESTFIELD	REDLEYS	174
64	MOON MARY	WI M	33		SSI WESTFIELD	ONION HILL	180
17	MOON MARY	WI M	43		SSI MOUNTFIELD	BUCKHURST	163
45	MOON RICHARD	FA W	74	AG.LAB	SSI WESTFIELD	BOWERS COTTAGE	178
17	MOON RICHARD	HD M	45	AG.LAB	SSI WESTFIELD	BUCKHURST	163
45	MOON RICHARD T	SO U	8		SSI WESTFIELD	BOWERS COTTAGE	178
45	MOON SARAH	WI M	36		SSI WESTFIELD	BOWERS COTTAGE	178
45	MOON SOPHEE H	DA U	1		SSI WESTFIELD	BOWERS COTTAGE	178
71	MOOR HENRY	SV U	16	AG.LAB	SSI BEXHILL	WOODS FARM SIDLEY	85
16	MOORE EMMA	DA U	15		MDX PADDINGTON	RAILWAY HUT	7
16	MOORE MARIA	DA U	13		MDX HISTON	RAILWAY HUT	7
16	MOORE ROBERT	SO U	10		MDX PADDINGTON	RAILWAY HUT	7
13	MOORE WILLIAM	SV U	20	FARM LAB	SSI EASTBOURNE	MILL HOUSE - SIDLEY	66
32	MORGAN DANIEL	SO U	29	SEAMAN	CARDIGAN NEWQUAY	51 MARTELLO TOWER	41
32	MORGAN ELIZABETH	DA U	18		SSI RYE	51 MARTELLO TOWER	41
82	MORGAN ELIZABETH	WI M	33		LAN MANCHESTER	GATE HOUSE	17
32	MORGAN LOIS	DA U	11		SSI BEXHILL	51 MARTELLO TOWER	41
82	MORGAN MARTHA	DA U	7		LAN MANCHESTER	GATE HOUSE	17
32	MORGAN MARY	WI M	56		GLAMORGAN PENMARINE	51 MARTELLO TOWER	41
82	MORGAN UN-NAMED INFANT GIRL	DA U	2D		SSI HOLLINGTON	GATE HOUSE	17
82	MORGAN WILLIAM	HD M	41	RAILWAY LAB	WALES MONGOMERYSHIRE	GATE HOUSE	17
32	MORGAN WILLIAM	HD M	57	COAST GUARD	GLAMORGAN PENRICE	51 MATELLO TOWER	41
82	MORGAN WILLIAM	SO U	2		STS WALSALL	GATE HOUSE	17

House	Surname	Name	Rel	MS	Age	Occupation	County	Birthplace	Address	Pg
16	MORLEY	ANN	GD	U	5	SCHOLAR	SSX	BEXHILL	BANKS'S HOUSE - SIDLEY	67
16	MORLEY	CHARLES	SO	U	14	AG.LAB	SSX	BEXHILL	BANKS'S HOUSE - SIDLEY	67
16	MORLEY	EDWARD	SO	U	14		SSX	BEXHILL	BANKS'S HOUSE - SIDLEY	67
16	MORLEY	JOHN	GS	U	11		SSX	BEXHILL	BANKS'S HOUSE - SIDLEY	67
16	MORLEY	MARY	DA	U	32		SSX	BEXHILL	BANKS'S HOUSE - SIDLEY	67
16	MORLEY	MARY	GD	U	7	SCHOLAR	SSX	GARDNER STREET	BANKS'S HOUSE - SIDLEY	67
16	MORLEY	RICHARD	SO	U	28	AG.LAB	SSX	BEXHILL	BANKS'S HOUSE - SIDLEY	67
16	MORLEY	STEPHEN	SO	U	19	AG.LAB	SSX	BEXHILL	BANKS'S HOUSE - SIDLEY	67
16	MORLEY	THOMAS	HD	W	65	FARMER 6 ACRES	SSX	OFFHAM	BANKS'S HOUSE - SIDLEY	67
61	MORPHEE	CHARLOTTE	SV	U	19		SSX	BREDE	NOT GIVEN	95
60	MORRIS	ANN	DA	U	2		SSX	HOLLINGTON	HOLLINGTON STREET	13
22	MORRIS	ANN	DA	U	7	SCHOLAR	SSX	WESTFIELD	HARTS GREEN	164
39	MORRIS	CAROLINE	HD	W	40	SHOEBINDER	SSX	BEXHILL	BEXHILL STREET	28
60	MORRIS	CHARLOTTE	DA	U	5?		SSX	BATTLE	HOLLINGTON STREET	13
60	MORRIS	DELIA	WI	M	33		SSX	NINFIELD	HOLLINGTON STREET	13
9	MORRIS	EDWARD	SV	U	16		SSX	BATTLE	WIDOWS	173
22	MORRIS	ELIZA	WI	M	27		SSX	WESTFIELD	HARTS GREEN	164
39	MORRIS	ELIZABETH	DA	U	5		SSX	BEXHILL	BEXHILL STREET	28
39	MORRIS	ELIZABETH	DA	U	17	SERVANT	SSX	BEXHILL	BEXHILL STREET	28
89	MORRIS	ELIZABETH	GD	U	7		SSX	WARTLING	NOT GIVEN	99
3	MORRIS	ELLEN	DA	U	14	SCHOLAR	SSX	CROWHURST	NOT GIVEN	142
22	MORRIS	EMILY	DA	U	5	SCHOLAR	SSX	WESTFIELD	HARTS GREEN	164
22	MORRIS	GEORGE	HD	M	33	AG.LAB	SSX	CROWHURST	HARTS GREEN	164
60	MORRIS	HANNAH	DA	U	5?		SSX	BATTLE	HOLLINGTON STREET	13
39	MORRIS	HARRIOTT	DA	U	14		SSX	BEXHILL	BEXHILL STREET	28
3	MORRIS	JAMES	HD	M	43	CORDWAINER	SSX	CROWHURST	NOT GIVEN	142
60	MORRIS	JAMES	SO	U	10		SSX	BATTLE	HOLLINGTON STREET	13
54	MORRIS	JAMES	SV	U	12	FARM LAB	SSX	BATTLE	CASTLEMANS	195
60	MORRIS	JOHN	SO	U	12		SSX	BATTLE	HOLLINGTON STREET	13
5	MORRIS	MARY	HD	W	64	PAUPER	SSX	WARBLETON	BELL HILL	24
60	MORRIS	PETER	HD	M	38	WAGGONER	SSX	BATTLE	HOLLINGTON STREET	13
3	MORRIS	SARAH	DA	U	15		SSX	CROWHURST	NOT GIVEN	142
3	MORRIS	SARAH	WI	M	50		SSX	BEXHILL	NOT GIVEN	142
28	MORRIS	WILLIAM	LG	U	21	FARM LAB	SSX	HOLLINGTON	FORWARD LANE	146
15	MORRIS	WILLIAM	NP	U	9	SCHOLAR	SSX	BEXHILL	RIST WOOD SIDLEY	77
22	MORRISSON	ELIZA	WI	M	23		KEN	QUEENBOROUGH	IN THE LIBERTY	40
22	MORRISSON	JAMES	HD	M	23	COAST GUARD SERVICE	HAM	ELVERSTOKE	IN THE LIBERTY	40
63	MORTEN	WILLIAM	LG	U	29	RAILWAY LAB	HAM		RAILWAY HUT	137
26	MOSLEY	CHARLOTTE	DA	U	3		NTH	BRACKLY	RAILWAY HUT	8
26	MOSLEY	HANNAH	WI	M	29		SSX	WORTH	RAILWAY HUT	8
26	MOSLEY	HENRY	HD	M	33	RAIL LAB	NTH	BRACKLY	RAILWAY HUT	8
26	MOSLEY	JOHN	SO	U	5		SRY	CROYDON	RAILWAY HUT	8
18	MOTT	CHARLES	SO	U	20	AG.LAB	KEN	HAWKHURST	NOT GIVEN	53
18	MOTT	EDWIN	SO	U	22	AG.LAB	SSX	ROTHERFIELD	NOT GIVEN	53
18	MOTT	HANNAH	DA	U	14	HOUSE SERVANT	KEN	HAWKHURST	NOT GIVEN	53
18	MOTT	HESTER	DA	U	16	HOUSE SERVANT	KEN	HAWKHURST	NOT GIVEN	53
18	MOTT	JAMES	SO	U	12	AG.LAB	KEN	HAWKHURST	NOT GIVEN	53
18	MOTT	JESSE	SO	U	3		SSX	BEXHILL	NOT GIVEN	53
18	MOTT	JOSEPH	SO	U	18	AG.LAB	KEN	HAWKHURST	NOT GIVEN	53
18	MOTT	MARY	WI	M	51		KEN	MAIDSTONE	NOT GIVEN	53
18	MOTT	MARY ANN	DA	U	25	HOUSE SERVANT	SSX	BEXHILL	NOT GIVEN	53
18	MOTT	WILLIAM	HD	M	48	AG.LAB	SSX	BEXHILL	NOT GIVEN	53
30	MOULS	FREDERICK	LG	U	34	RAILWAY LAB	ESS		FORWARD LANE	146
3	MUGGERIDGE	EMMA	/	U	1	NURSE CHILD	SSX	BATTLE	CATSFIELD GREEN	120
15	MUGGRIDGE	HANNAH	DA	U	28		SSX	FAIRLIGHT	DEER PARK	121
15	MUGGRIDGE	JANE	WI	M	67		SSX	CHIDDINGLY	DEER PARK	121
15	MUGGRIDGE	STEPHEN	HD	M	70	PARK KEEPER	SSX	HEATHFIELD	DEER PARK	121
15	MUGGRIDGE	STEPHEN	SO	U	26	KEEPER	SSX	CATSFIELD	DEER PARK	121
44	MULHALL	THOMAS	LG	U	34	RAILWAY LAB	IRL		RAILWAY HUT	134
48	MUNN	GEORGE	GS	U	5		SSX	BEXHILL	SIDLEY GREEN	81
62	MUNN	GEORGE	HD	M	38	AG.LAB	SSX	HOOE	SIDLEY GREEN	83
42	MUNN	GEORGE	SO	U	7		SSX	BEXHILL	NOT GIVEN	42
42	MUNN	HANNAH	DA	U	9	SCHOLAR	SSX	BEXHILL	NOT GIVEN	42
68	MUNN	JAMES	SO	U	3		SSX	BEXHILL	2 BELLENDER COTTAGE	46
42	MUNN	JOHN	HD	M	34	AG.LAB	SSX	BEXHILL	NOT GIVEN	42
42	MUNN	JOHN	SO	U	3		SSX	BEXHILL	NOT GIVEN	42
62	MUNN	LUCY	WI	M	24		SSX	LEWES	SIDLEY GREEN	83
9	MUNN	MARY	WI	M	26		SSX	PEVENSEY	SIDLEY	66
42	MUNN	MARY	WI	M	36		SSX	BEXHILL	NOT GIVEN	42
68	MUNN	MARY A	WI	M	24		SSX	BEXHILL	2 BELLENDER COTTAGE	46
1	MUNN	NAOMI	DA	U	21		SSX	BEXHILL	SIDLEY CORNER	64
9	MUNN	PETER	HD	M	27	AG.LAB	SSX	BEXHILL	SIDLEY	66
62	MUNN	SARAH	DA	U	2		SSX	BEXHILL	SIDLEY GREEN	83
68	MUNN	SPENCER	HD	M	31	AG.LAB	SSX	BEXHILL	2 BELLENDER COTTAGE	46
1	MUNN	THOMAS	HD	W	63	PAUPER AG.LAB	SSX	BEXHILL	SIDLEY CORNER	64
62	MUNN	UN-NAMED INFANT	SO	U	3D		SSX	BEXHILL	SIDLEY GREEN	83
9	MUNN	WILLIAM P	SO	U	2		SSX	BEXHILL	SIDLEY	66
19	MYNN	CHARLOTTE F	WI	M	46		SSX	FUNTINGTON	NOT GIVEN	53
19	MYNN	JOHN	HD	M	54	FARMER 73 AC EMP 4	SSX	HAILSHAM	NOT GIVEN	53
38	NABS	SUSANNAH	DL	U	15		SSX	GUESTLING	OWLS CASTLE	177
22	NASH	ANN J	ML	U	53		KEN	DOVER	IN THE LIBERTY	40
42	NASH	ANNA	AU	M	73	ANNUITANT	SSX	SEDLESCOMBE	STONE HOUSE	167
22	NASH	SMITH	FL	M	60	SUPERANNUATED FROM C.G.S.	KEN	DOVER	IN THE LIBERTY	40
5	NEELY	WILLIAM	HD	W	60	PENSIONER ARTILERY	IRL		SIDLEY	90
81	NELSON	AGNESS	SV	U	24	HOUSE MAID	SCOTLAND	MAYBOLE*	BEAUPORT HOUSE	17
81	NELSON	THOMAS	HD	U	34	BUTLER	SCT	MAYBOLE*	BEAUPORT HOUSE	17

59

No.	Name	Status	Age	Occupation	Birthplace	Location	No.
38	NEVE ANN	DA U	21	MILLINER & DRESSMAKER	SSX BEXHILL	ROSEPLATT COTTAGE SIDLEY	80
72	NEVE CHARLES	SO U	22	FARMERS SON EMP AT HOME	SSX BATTLE	GLOVERS FARM SIDLEY	85
72	NEVE CHARLOTTE A	DA U	18	FARMER'S DA EMP AT HOME	SSX BEXHILL	GLOVERS FARM SIDLEY	85
31	NEVE CORDELIA	SV U	17	HOUSE SERVANT	SSX BEXHILL	BUCKHOLT SIDLEY	79
38	NEVE DAVID	SO U	10	SCHOLAR	SSX BEXHILL	ROSEPLATT COTTAGE SIDLEY	80
32	NEVE ELIZA	WI M	37		SSX SEDLESCOMBE	STONE HOUSE	9
41	NEVE ELIZABETH	SV U	15	HOUSE SERVANT	SSX BEXHILL	PRESTON FARM SIDLEY	81
72	NEVE GEORGE	HD M	48	FARMER 124 AC EMP 5	SSX CROWHURST	GLOVERS FARM SIDLEY	85
38	NEVE GEORGE	SO U	8	SCHOLAR	SSX BEXHILL	ROSEPLATT COTTAGE SIDLEY	80
32	NEVE JOHN	HD M	45	FARM BAILIFF	SSX CROWHURST	STONE HOUSE	9
38	NEVE MARY	DA U	13		SSX BEXHILL	ROSEPLATT COTTAGE SIDLEY	80
32	NEVE SARAH	DA U	2		SSX HOLLINGTON	STONE HOUSE	9
38	NEVE STEPHEN	HD M	46	FARMER 20 ACRES	SSX BUXTED	ROSEPLATT COTTAGE SIDLEY	80
38	NEVE STEPHEN	SO U	24	CARPENTER & JOINER	SSX BEXHILL	ROSEPLATT COTTAGE SIDLEY	80
38	NEVE SUSANNA	WI M	51		SSX CATSFIELD	ROSEPLATT COTTAGE SIDLEY	80
38	NEVE WILLIAM	SO U	19	FARMERS SO EMP AT HOME	SSX BEXHILL	ROSEPLATT COTTAGE SIDLEY	80
104	NEVES JAMES	HD M	26	PLATE LAYER	SSX BEXHILL	NOT GIVEN	101
104	NEVES MARY	WI M	26		SSX BEXHILL	NOT GIVEN	101
104	NEVES STEPHEN	FA W	55	AG.LAB	SSX BEXHILL	NOT GIVEN	101
61	NEW WILLIAM	LG U	33	RAIL LAB	PORTSMOUTH	PUMP HOUSE	13
61	NEWBLE HARRY?	SO U	10M		SSX EWHURST	SNAGS HALL	224
61	NEWBLE HENRY	HD M	43	SHOEMAKER	SSX NORTHIAM	SNAGS HALL	224
61	NEWBLE SARAH	DA U	3		SSX EWHURST	SNAGS HALL	224
61	NEWBLE SARAH	WI M	34		KEN CRANBROOK	SNAGS HALL	224
54	NEWICK SARAH	DA W	58	PAUPER	SSX UDIMORE	BEECH	208
63	NENINGTON MARY	PP U	13		SSX BURWASH	BEXHILL STREET	96
80	NEWMAN MARY ANN	CL U	39	ANNUITANT	SSX TREYFORD	STAPLE CROSS	243
16	NEWNHAM RICHARD	/ M	51	MILLER JM	SSX FRAMPFIELD	NOT GIVEN	91
29	NICHOLLS THOMAS	LG U	24	RAIL LAB	NOT GIVEN	BAGGERS HOLE	9
13	NICKOLL ANNE	WI M	50		BKM AYLESBURY	OFFICERS COTTAGE IN LIBERTY	39
13	NICKOLL ANNE E	DA U	16		KEN HARBLEDOWN	OFFICERS COTTAGE IN LIBERTY	39
13	NICKOLL JAMES H	HD M	56	LIEUT R N	KEN BARHAM	OFFICERS COTTAGE IN LIBERTY	39
48	NOAKES ALFRED	SO U	9		SSX SEDLESCOMBE	POPPING HOLE LANE	207
48	NOAKES ANN	DA U	7		SSX SEDLESCOMBE	POPPING HOLE LANE	207
56	NOAKES CHARLOTTE	DA U	2		SSX RYE	NOT GIVEN	112
56	NOAKES CHARLOTTE	WI M	27		SSX ICKLESHAM	NOT GIVEN	112
2	NOAKES DAVID	SO U	8	SCHOLAR	SSX WESTFIELD	PLACE	161
48	NOAKES ELIZA	WI M	34		SSX EWHURST	POPPING HOLE LANE	207
56	NOAKES ELIZABETH	DA U	1M		SSX PEASMARSH	NOT GIVEN	112
48	NOAKES ELIZABETH	DA U	5		SSX BEXHILL	SIDLEY GREEN	81
48	NOAKES ELIZABETH	DA U	11		SSX SEDLESCOMBE	POPPING HOLE LANE	207
14	NOAKES ELIZABETH	WI M	52		SSX PENHURST	TAN YARD	153
2	NOAKES ELLEN	DA U	11		SSX WESTFIELD	PLACE	161
22	NOAKES ELLEN	NC U	17		NOT GIVEN (?WESTFIELD)	BAKERS	154
14	NOAKES FRANCES	DA U	24		SRY BERMONDSEY	TAN YARD	153
48	NOAKES FRANCES J	DA U	2		SSX BEXHILL	SIDLEY GREEN	81
48	NOAKES GEORGE	HD M	38	AG.LAB	SSX SEDLESCOMBE	POPPING HOLE LANE	207
48	NOAKES GEORGE	SO U	2		SSX SEDLESCOMBE	POPPING HOLE LANE	207
48	NOAKES GEORGE	SO U	13		SSX HOOE	SIDLEY GREEN	81
2	NOAKES HENRY	HD M	43	FARMER	SSX ASHBURNHAM	PLACE	161
2	NOAKES HORACE	SO U	5		SSX WESTFIELD	PLACE	161
56	NOAKES JAMES	HD M	24	POLICE CONSTABLE	SSX PEASMARSH	NOT GIVEN	112
48	NOAKES JAMES	HD M	48	BUTCHER	SSX BEXHILL	SIDLEY GREEN	81
48	NOAKES JAMES	SO U	15		SSX LEWES	SIDLEY GREEN	81
6	NOAKES JAMES	SO U	34		NOT GIVEN (?WESTFIELD)	DOWN OAKS	152
2	NOAKES JANE	WI M	44		SSX CATSFIELD	PLACE	161
48	NOAKES JOHN	SO U	15	AG.LAB	SSX SEDLESCOMBE	POPPING HOLE LANE	207
6	NOAKES JOHN	SO U	32		NOT GIVEN (?WESTFIELD)	DOWN OAKS	152
14	NOAKES JOHN P	HD M	49	MASTER FELLMONGER	SSX ASHBURNHAM	TAN YARD	153
2	NOAKES JOSEPH	SO U	21		SSX PENHURST	PLACE	161
6	NOAKES JOSEPH	SO U	27		NOT GIVEN (?WESTFIELD)	DOWN OAKS	152
48	NOAKES LUCY	WI M	48		SSX STANMORE	SIDLEY GREEN	81
2	NOAKES MARGARET	DA U	16		SSX PENHURST	PLACE	161
6	NOAKES MARIA	DA U	40		SSX WESTFIELD	DOWN OAKS	152
6	NOAKES MARIA	WI M	67		SSX ORE	DOWN OAKS	152
6	NOAKES MARY	DA U	24		NOT GIVEN (?WESTFIELD)	DOWN OAKS	152
13	NOAKES MARY	GD U	22	SERVANT	SSX CATSFIELD	STEVEN'S CROUCH	121
6	NOAKES ROBERT	HD M	70	FARMER	SSX WESTFIELD	DOWN OAKS	152
48	NOAKES ROBERT	SO U	11		SSX HOOE	SIDLEY GREEN	81
48	NOAKES SAMUEL	SO U	7	SCHOLAR	SSX HOOE	SIDLEY GREEN	81
6	NOAKES SARAH	DA U	30		NOT GIVEN (?WESTFIELD)	DOWN OAKS	152
48	NOAKES THOMAS	SO U	5		SSX SEDLESCOMBE	POPPING HOLE LANE	207
6	NOAKES THOMAS	SO U	37		SSX WESTFIELD	DOWN OAKS	152
28	NOAKS ANN	WI M	60		SSX ASHBURNHAM	BRICKWALL	190
46	NOAKS ELIZABETH	WI M	56		YKS SHEFFIELD	SWALES GREEN	193
46	NOAKS GEORGE	HD M	65	AG.LAB	SSX SEDLESCOMBE	SWALES GREEN	193
28	NOAKS HENRY	HD M	60	CARPENTER JM	SSX BREDE	BRICKWALL	190
28	NOAKS THOMAS	SO U	18	AG.LAB	SSX SEDLESCOMBE	BRICKWALL	190
24	NOKES MARY ELIZABETH	GD U	4		SSX HERSTMONCEUX	SAMPSON'S FARM	131
10	NORMAN SAMUEL	LG U	23	RAIL LAB	DEV AXMINSTER	RAILWAY HUT	5
29	NORTH DANIEL	LG U	20	RAILWAY LAB	HAM YUKELY?	GREEN STREET	132
24	NYE HENRY	HD M	33	EXCAVATOR	SRY KINGSTON	RANSOM'S HOUSE	145
24	NYE MARTHA	WI M	32		HRT HATFIELD	RANSOM'S HOUSE	145
5	OCKENDEN ANN	HK U	69	HOUSE KEEPER	SSX BEXHILL	NEW INN SIDLEY	76
75	OCKENDEN ANNE	DA U	11		SSX BEXHILL	NOT GIVEN	98
17	OCKENDEN CHARLOTTE	DA U	18	DRESSMAKER	SSX BEXHILL	BELL HILL	25

	Name	Rel	St	Age	Occupation	Co	Parish	Location	Fol
17	OCKENDEN CHARLOTTE	WI	M	40		SSX	BEXHILL	BELL HILL	25
5	OCKENDEN EDMUND	VR	M	49	STONEMASON	SSX	BEXHILL	NEW INN SIDLEY	76
57	OCKENDEN ELLEN	DA	U	10		SSX	CATSFIELD	NOT GIVEN	112
17	OCKENDEN HENRY	SO	U	16	CARPENTER	SSX	BEXHILL	BELL HILL	25
75	OCKENDEN JAMES	HD	M	42	GROCER & DRAPER	SSX	BEXHILL	NOT GIVEN	98
17	OCKENDEN JAMES	SO	U	12		SSX	BEXHILL	BELL HILL	25
17	OCKENDEN JANE	DA	U	13		SSX	BEXHILL	BELL HILL	25
75	OCKENDEN JOSHUA	SO	U	1		SSX	BEXHILL	NOT GIVEN	98
75	OCKENDEN MATILDA	WI	M	38		SSX	BEXHILL	NOT GIVEN	98
75	OCKENDEN OLIVER	SO	U	9		SSX	BEXHILL	NOT GIVEN	98
57	OCKENDEN RICHARD	SO	U	14		SSX	CATSFIELD	NOT GIVEN	112
57	OCKENDEN ROBERT	SO	U	12		SSX	CATSFIELD	NOT GIVEN	112
17	OCKENDEN SAMUEL	HD	M	44	CARPENTER	SSX	BEXHILL	BELL HILL	25
17	OCKENDEN SAMUEL	SO	U	9		SSX	BEXHILL	BELL HILL	25
57	OCKENDEN THOMAS	HD	W	46	CORDWAINER	SSX	WARTLING	NOT GIVEN	112
57	OCKENDEN THOMAS	SO	U	18	AG.LAB	SSX	BATTLE	NOT GIVEN	112
16	OCKWELL ANN	HD	W	75	CHARWOMAN	SSX		PARKERS	153
9	OFFIN ALFRED	SO	U	20	BRICKLAYER	SSX	WESTFIELD	SCHOOL HOUSE	162
43	OFFIN ELIZA	DA	U	1		SSX	WESTFIELD	BROOKS	177
43	OFFIN ESTHER	WI	M	33		SSX	WESTFIELD	BROOKS	177
9	OFFIN HANNAH	WI	M	47		SSX	HERSTMONCEUX	SCHOOL HOUSE	162
49	OFFIN JAMES	BL	U	26	AG.LAB	SSX	WESTFIELD	BADCOX	178
9	OFFIN JAMES	HD	M	49	BRICKLAYER	SSX	WESTFIELD	SCHOOL HOUSE	162
43	OFFIN JAMES	SO	U	4		SSX	WESTFIELD	BROOKS	177
43	OFFIN JOHN	SO	U	7		SSX	WESTFIELD	BROOKS	177
9	OFFIN JOHN	SO	U	12		SSX	WESTFIELD	SCHOOL HOUSE	162
9	OFFIN MARY A	DA	U	14		SSX	WESTFIELD	SCHOOL HOUSE	162
43	OFFIN WILLIAM	HD	M	48	AG.LAB	SSX	WESTFIELD	BROOKS	177
10	OLIVER ANN	DA	U	14		SSX	BEXHILL	SIDLEY	90
35	OLIVER ELLEN	DA	U	9		SSX	HOLLINGTON	MILWARDS	10
75	OLIVER EMILY	NC	U	13		SSX	HOLLINGTON	NOT GIVEN	98
35	OLIVER EMMA	DA	U	4		SSX	HOLLINGTON	MILWARDS	10
10	OLIVER HARRIET	DA	U	11		SSX	BEXHILL	SIDLEY	90
10	OLIVER HARRIET	WI	M	43		SSX	HERSTMONCEUX	SIDLEY	90
35	OLIVER JAMES	HD	M	39	FARMER 90 AC EMP 4 MEN	SSX	BEXHILL	MILWARDS	9
35	OLIVER JAMES ALBERT	SO	U	7		SSX	HOLLINGTON	MILWARDS	10
35	OLIVER JANE	WI	M	36		SSX	SEDLESCOMBE	MILWARDS	9
35	OLIVER JESSE	DA	U	9M		SSX	HOLLINGTON	MILWARDS	10
10	OLIVER JESSE	SO	U	18		SSX	BEXHILL	SIDLEY	90
23	OLIVER JOHN	HD	M	50	OUT PENSIONER CHELSEA	SSX	NORTHIAM	CRIPPS	252
10	OLIVER JOHN	SO	U	15		SSX	BEXHILL	SIDLEY	90
10	OLIVER JOSEPH	HD	M	43	GROCER & DRAPER	SSX	BEXHILL	SIDLEY	90
35	OLIVER MAHALA	DA	U	11		SSX	HOLLINGTON	MILWARDS	10
23	OLIVER MARY ANN	DA	U	1		SSX	EWHURST	CRIPPS	252
23	OLIVER MARY ANN	WI	M	32		SSX	SALEHURST	CRIPPS	252
35	OLIVER RUTH	DA	U	2		SSX	HOLLINGTON	MILWARDS	10
10	OLIVER RUTH	DA	U	6		SSX	BEXHILL	SIDLEY	90
10	OLIVER SARAH	DA	U	17		SSX	BEXHILL	SIDLEY	90
35	OLIVER SARAH ANN	DA	U	14		SSX	HOLLINGTON	MILWARDS	9
47	ORAN HENRY	HD	M	40	COAST GUARD	HAM	PORTSMOUTH	NO.4 GALLEY HILL	29
47	ORAN HENRY P	SO	U	4		SSX	BEXHILL	NO.4 GALLEY HILL	29
47	ORAN MARY A	WI	M	40		HAM	PORTSMOUTH	NO.4 GALLEY HILL	29
47	ORAN MARY J	DA	U	6	SCHOLAR	SSX	ST.LEONARDS	NO.4 GALLEY HILL	29
51	OSBORN CAROLINE	DA	U	12		SSX	SEDLESCOMBE	SWALES GREEN	208
51	OSBORN EDWIN	SO	U	19	CARRIER	SSX	SEDLESCOMBE	SWALES GREEN	208
51	OSBORN ELIJAH	SO	U	9		SSX	SEDLESCOMBE	SWALES GREEN	208
51	OSBORN JAMES	SO	U	7		SSX	SEDLESCOMBE	SWALES GREEN	208
33	OSBORN JOHN	SV	U	63	WHEELWRIGHT	SSX	BEXHILL	BEXHILL STREET	27
51	OSBORN MARY	DA	U	16		SSX	SEDLESCOMBE	SWALES GREEN	208
51	OSBORN MARY	WI	M	42		SSX	SALEHURST	SWALES GREEN	208
51	OSBORN THOMAS	SO	U	21	CARRIER	MDX	CHELSEA	SWALES GREEN	208
51	OSBORN WILLIAM	HD	M	41	CARRIER	SSX	SEDLESCOMBE	SWALES GREEN	208
51	OSBORN WILLIAM	SO	U	14		SSX	SEDLESCOMBE	SWALES GREEN	208
7	OSBORNE ANN	HK	U	24		SSX	EWHURST	COLLIERS GREEN	233
7	OSBORNE ANN ELIZABETH	/	U	3	HK'S DAUGHTER	KEN	HIGH HALDEN	COLLIERS GREEN	233
86	OSBORNE ANTHONY	LG	U	28	AG.LAB	SSX	EWHURST	STAPLE CROSS	243
86	OSBORNE ANTHONY	LG	W	60	AG.LAB	SSX	EWHURST	STAPLE CROSS	243
95	OSBORNE ELEANOR	HD	M	57		SSX	EWHURST	STAPLE CROSS	244
86	OSBORNE JAMES	WS	U	2		SSX	EWHURST	STAPLE CROSS	243
86	OSBORNE JOHN	WS	U	4		SSX	BATTLE	STAPLE CROSS	243
15	OVERY MARY	SV	U	50	HOUSEKEEPER	SSX	CROWHURST	CATSFIELD PLACE FARM	108
3	OVERY RICHARD C	AP	U	19	MILLER AP	SSX	GUESTLING	BEACON MILL	249
69	OVERY ROBERT	VR	M	57	ANNUITANT	SSX	SALEHURST	STAPLE CROSS	241
78	PACKHAM HENRY	HD	W	71	TOLL COLLECTOR	SSX	NORTHIAM	GATE HOUSE	243
87	PADGHAM AMANDA	SV	U	19	HOUSE MAID	KEN	SANDHURST	SOGGS FARM	228
9	PADGHAM DAVID	SO	U	17	WESLEYAN DAY SCHOOLTEACHER	SSX	EWHURST	ALLENHALL LANE	250
9	PADGHAM HENRIETTA	WI	M	49		SSX	EWHURST	ALLENHALL LANE	250
15	PADGHAM PHILADELPHIA	WI	M	21		SSX	UDIMORE	BREDE HIGH	251
15	PADGHAM THOMAS	HD	M	25	FARMER'S SERVANT	SSX	EWHURST	BREDE HIGH	251
9	PADGHAM THOMAS	HD	M	58	AG.LAB	SSX	BECKLEY	ALLENHALL LANE	250
15	PADGHAM THOMAS	SO	U	1		SSX	EWHURST	BREDE HIGH	251
12	PAGE EDWIN	HD	M	28	LOADER	SSX	BEXHILL	SIDLEY	66
44	PAGE FANNY	GD	U	4		SSX	SEDLESCOMBE	POPPING HOLE LANE	207
12	PAGE FRANCES	WI	M	27		SSX	NINFIELD	SIDLEY	66
12	PAGE HEPHZABAH	DA	U	2		SSX	BEXHILL	SIDLEY	66
6	PAGE ISAAC	HD	U	50	LAB	ESS		SIDLEY GREEN	76

	Name	Rel	St	Age	Occupation	Birthplace	Residence	No.
9	PAGE JESSE	HD	U	25	AG.LAB	SSX BEXHILL	SIDLEY	90
44	PAGE MARY	GD	U	6		KEN GRAVESEND	POPPING HOLE LANE	207
12	PAGE SUSANNAH	DA	U	1		SSX BEXHILL	SIDLEY	66
29	PAIN? EMILY	WI	M	16		SSX CATSFIELD	BEXHILL STREET	26
29	PAIN? SAMUEL	HD	M	26	BAKER	SSX BEXHILL	BEXHILL STREET	26
61	PAINE WILLIAM	LG	U	24	AG.LAB	SSX PENHURST	PUMP HOUSE	13
26	PANKHURST CHARLES	SO	U	21		NOT GIVEN (?WESTFIELD)	WHEELERS	154
26	PANKHURST CHARLOTTE	DA	U	17		NOT GIVEN (?WESTFIELD)	WHEELERS	154
26	PANKHURST HARRIETT	DA	U	13		NOT GIVEN (?WESTFIELD)	WHEELERS	154
25	PANKHURST JAMES	HD	M	53	AG.LAB	SSX SEDLESCOMBE	SEDLESCOMBE STREET	204
26	PANKHURST JOSEPH	SO	U	20		NOT GIVEN (?WESTFIELD)	WHEELERS	154
25	PANKHURST MARIA	WI	M	60		SSX SEDLESCOMBE	SEDLESCOMBE STREET	204
64	PANKHURST PHILLY	LG	U	27		SSX MOUNTFIELD	NEW COTTAGE	14
26	PANKHURST SARAH	WI	M	62		SSX WESTFIELD	WHEELERS	154
26	PANKHURST WILLIAM	HD	M	64	CARPENTER	SSX WESTFIELD	WHEELERS	154
51	PANTING HARRIOT	WI	M	38		WINSER (SIC)	RAILWAY HUT	135
51	PANTING JOSEPH	HD	M	46	BRICKMAKER	BRK	RAILWAY HUT	135
65	PAPPEN LYDIA	WI	M	39		COR GERRINS (SIC)	COAST GUARD STATION	30
65	PAPPEN MARY J	DA	U	1		SSX BEXHILL	COAST GUARD STATION	30
65	PAPPEN WILLIAM	HD	M	35	COAST GUARD	GUERNSEY	COAST GUARD STATION	30
11	PARIS JAMES	HD	M	60	FISH MERCHANT	SSX WESTFIELD	UPPER FISHPOND	153
11	PARIS JANE	DA	U	34		SSX (?WESTFIELD)	UPPER FISHPOND	153
61	PARK HANNAH	SV	U	22	COOK	SSX BURWASH	HURCHINGTON	58
53	PARKER ALICE	DA	U	4		SSX BEXHILL	NOT GIVEN	95
89	PARKER ANN	SV	U	26	HOUSE SERVANT	SSX BEXHILL	NOT GIVEN	99
51	PARKER EDWARD	SO	U	17	CARPENTER	SSX BEXHILL	NOT GIVEN	94
60	PARKER EMILY	DA	U	1		SSX CATSFIELD	NOT GIVEN	113
53	PARKER EMMA	DA	U	7		SSX BEXHILL	NOT GIVEN	95
53	PARKER FREDERICK WILLIAM	SO	U	7M		SSX BEXHILL	NOT GIVEN	95
78	PARKER HENRY	HD	M	24	CARPENTER	SSX BEXHILL	BELL HILL	32
60	PARKER JAMES	SO	U	3		SSX CATSFIELD	NOT GIVEN	113
51	PARKER JOHN	HD	M	63	CARPENTER	SSX BEXHILL	NOT GIVEN	94
63	PARKER JOHN	LG	U	17	RAILWAY LAB	STS	RAILWAY HUT	137
51	PARKER LOUISA	GD	U	8	SCHOLAR	SSX BEXHILL	NOT GIVEN	94
53	PARKER MARY ANN	DA	U	10		SSX BEXHILL	NOT GIVEN	95
53	PARKER MARY ANN	WI	M	35		SSX NINFIELD	NOT GIVEN	95
78	PARKER MARY E	WI	M	26		SSX BEXHILL	BELL HILL	32
51	PARKER PHILL'A	WI	M	63		SSX BEXHILL	NOT GIVEN	94
78	PARKER ROWLAND	SO	U	1		SSX BEXHILL	BELL HILL	32
60	PARKER SOPHIA	WI	M	22		SSX CATSFIELD	NOT GIVEN	113
60	PARKER THOMAS	HD	M	28	CARPENTER	SSX NINFIELD	NOT GIVEN	113
53	PARKER WILLIAM	HD	M	36	CARPENTER	SSX BEXHILL	NOT GIVEN	95
45	PARKS ANNE	DA	U	13		SSX SEDLESCOMBE	SWALES GREEN	193
45	PARKS CATHERINE	WI	M	45		SSX SALEHURST	SWALES GREEN	193
17	PARKS CHARLOTTE	DA	U	7		SSX BEXHILL	NOT GIVEN	53
45	PARKS DARKHURST?	DA	U	1		SSX SEDLESCOMBE	SWALES GREEN	193
17	PARKS DAVID	SO	U	9		SSX BEXHILL	NOT GIVEN	53
45	PARKS EMILY	DA	U	11		SSX SEDLESCOMBE	SWALES GREEN	193
17	PARKS HARRIOT	WI	M	31		SSX BEXHILL	NOT GIVEN	53
95	PARKS HEZEKIAH	LG	U	47	AG.LAB	SSX EWHURST	STAPLE CROSS	244
42	PARKS JESSE	LG	W	57	PEDLAR	SSX EWHURST	FORGE LANE	254
45	PARKS MARGARET	DA	U	7		SSX SEDLESCOMBE	SWALES GREEN	193
45	PARKS MARY	DA	U	20		SSX SEDLESCOMBE	SWALES GREEN	193
65	PARKS MARY	DA	U	24		SSX EWHURST	EWHURST GREEN	224
65	PARKS MARY	WI	M	52		SSX EWHURST	EWHURST GREEN	224
17	PARKS PHILIP	SO	U	4		SSX BEXHILL	NOT GIVEN	53
65	PARKS SABINA	DA	U	24		SSX EWHURST	EWHURST GREEN	224
17	PARKS SAMPSON	SO	U	5		SSX BEXHILL	NOT GIVEN	53
23	PARKS SARAH	SV	U	20	HOUSE SERVANT	SSX WARBLETON	GLINE FARM SIDLEY	78
65	PARKS STEPHEN	HD	M	55	WHEELWRIGHT	SSX EWHURST	EWHURST GREEN	224
17	PARKS STEPHEN	SO	U	2		SSX BEXHILL	NOT GIVEN	53
17	PARKS THOMAS	HD	M	34	AG.LAB	SSX BEXHILL	NOT GIVEN	53
17	PARKS THOMAS	SO	U	3M		SSX BEXHILL	NOT GIVEN	53
45	PARKS WILLIAM	HD	M	43	HAWKER CARRYING BASKET+	SSX SEDLESCOMBE	SWALES GREEN	193
9	PARRER EDWARD	SO	U	14		SSX HASTINGS	RAILWAY HUT	129
9	PARRER ELIZ	HD	M	40		SSX HASTINGS	RAILWAY HUT	129
20	PARRIS REUBEN	LG	U	20	RAILWAY LAB	SSX JEVINGTON	CROWHURST VILLAGE	131
10	PARSONS AGNES	DA	U	13		SSX SEDLESCOMBE	HARTS GREEN	173
30	PARSONS CHARLOTTE	SV	U	20		NOT GIVEN (?WESTFIELD)	LANKHURST COT	155
30	PARSONS ELIZA	VR	U	6		SSX BATTLE	LANKHURST COT	155
30	PARSONS ELIZA	WI	M	32		SSX WESTFIELD	LANKHURST COT	155
30	PARSONS GEORGE	HD	M	40	AG.LAB	SSX WESTFIELD	LANKHURST COT	155
10	PARSONS HANNAH	DA	U	11		SSX SEDLESCOMBE	HARTS GREEN	173
10	PARSONS HANNAH	WI	M	41		SSX EWHURST	HARTS GREEN	173
10	PARSONS HELLEN	DA	U	2		SSX WESTFIELD	HARTS GREEN	173
10	PARSONS JAMES	SO	U	7		SSX WESTFIELD	HARTS GREEN	173
10	PARSONS JANE	DA	U	4		SSX WESTFIELD	HARTS GREEN	173
30	PARSONS LEWES	VR	U	3M		SSX BREDE	LANKHURST COT	155
10	PARSONS ROBERT	SO	U	5		SSX WESTFIELD	HARTS GREEN	173
10	PARSONS SARAH	DA	U	2M		SSX WETSFIELD	HARTS GREEN	173
10	PARSONS SUSAN	DA	U	9		SSX WESTFIELD	HARTS GREEN	173
10	PARSONS THOMAS	HD	M	41	AG.LAB	SSX BREDE	HARTS GREEN	173
41	PATTISON FANNY	DA	U	5		SSX BREDE	MILL COTTAGE	177
41	PATTISON HENRY	HD	W	35	AG.LAB	SSX WESTFIELD	MILL COTTAGE	177
41	PATTISON HENRY	SO	U	8		SSX WESTFIELD	MILL COTTAGE	177

	Name	Rel/St	Age	Occupation	County	Parish	Address	No.
41	PATTISON JOHN	SO U	4		SSX	WESTFIELD	MILL COTTAGE	177
41	PATTISON MARTHA	DA U	2		SSX	WESTFIELD	MILL COTTAGE	177
44	PEACHAM ALBERT	SO U	18		SSX	BATTLE	HOLLINGTON STREET	11
44	PEACHAM ANN	DA U	19		SSX	BATTLE	HOLLINGTON STREET	11
44	PEACHAM ANN	WI M	49		SSX	BATTLE	HOLLINGTON STREET	11
33	PEACHAM HARRIETT	WI M	25		SSX	ORE	PARSONAGE	9
44	PEACHAM JAMES	SO U	16		SSX	BATTLE	HOLLINGTON STREET	11
33	PEACHAM JOHN	HD M	26	AG.LAB	SSX	BATTLE	PARSONAGE	9
44	PEACHAM JOHN	HD M	48	AG.LAB	HAM	GOSPORT	HOLLINGTON STREET	11
33	PEACHAM JOHN	SO U	3		SSX	HOLLINGTON	PARSONAGE	9
44	PEACHAM NORMAN	SO U	14		SSX	BATTLE	HOLLINGTON STREET	11
33	PEACHAM WILLIAM	SO U	1		SSX	HOLLINGTON	PARSONAGE	9
32	PEACOCK ELLEN	DA U	11	SCHOLAR AT HOME	CAMBERWELL		BEXHILL STREET	27
32	PEACOCK JEMIMA	HD W	43?	GENTLEWOMAN ANNUITANT	MDX		BEXHILL STREET	27
81	PEARSON ALFRED	SO U	6	SCHOLAR	SSX	EWHURST	EWHURST GREEN	227
18	PEARSON CHARLOTTE	DA U	9	SCHOLAR	SSX	EWHURST	ODIAM FARM	218
81	PEARSON CHARLOTTE	DA U	22		SSX	EWHURST	EWHURST GREEN	227
18	PEARSON ELIZA	DA U	18	SERVANT	SSX	EWHURST	ODIAM FARM	218
81	PEARSON ELLEN	DA U	12	SCHOLAR	SSX	EWHURST	EWHURST GREEN	227
7	PEARSON EMILY P	DA U	1		SSX	EWHURST	STOCKLANDS	250
18	PEARSON GEORGE	SO U	6		SSX	EWHURST	ODIAM FARM	218
18	PEARSON HARRIET	DA U	11	SCHOLAR	SSX	EWHURST	ODIAM FARM	218
7	PEARSON HENRY	HD M	37	AG.LAB	SSX	EWHURST	STOCKLANDS	250
18	PEARSON HENRY	SO U	4		SSX	EWHURST	ODIAM FARM	218
7	PEARSON JANE	DA U	9	SCHOLAR	SSX	EWHURST	STOCKLANDS	250
7	PEARSON JANE	WI M	37		SSX	SEDLESCOMBE	STOCKLANDS	250
32	PEARSON JANE	WI M	60		SSX	BECKLEY	REEVES	236
81	PEARSON JEMIMA	WI M	48		SSX	EWHURST	EWHURST GREEN	227
40	PEARSON MARY	WI M	22		SSX	EWHURST	FORGE LANE	254
18	PEARSON MIRIAM	DA U	16	DUMB	SSX	EWHURST	ODIAM FARM	218
18	PEARSON SARAH	WI M	40		SSX	EWHURST	ODIAM FARM	218
32	PEARSON THOMAS	HD M	43	AG.LAB	SSX	EWHURST	REEVES	236
81	PEARSON THOMAS	HD M	51	AG.LAB	SSX	EWHURST	EWHURST GREEN	227
32	PEARSON THOMAS	LG W	76	AG.LAB	SSX	EWHURST	REEVES	237
18	PEARSON THOMAS	SO U	13	AG.LAB	SSX	EWHURST	ODIAM FARM	218
81	PEARSON THOMAS	SO U	16	AG.LAB	SSX	EWHURST	EWHURST GREEN	227
40	PEARSON WILLIAM	HD M	25	AG.LAB	SSX	EWHURST	FORGE LANE	254
18	PEARSON WILLIAM	HD M	48	AG.LAB	SSX	EWHURST	ODIAM FARM	218
40	PEARSON WILLIAM	SO U	1		SSX	EWHURST	FORGE LANE	254
18	PEARSON WILLIAM	SO U	15	AG.LAB	SSX	EWHURST	ODIAM FARM	218
65	PEDDIE ANN	DA U	4		SSX	HOLLINGTON	GATE COTTAGE	14
65	PEDDIE ELIZABETH	DA U	8		SSX	HOLLINGTON	GATE COTTAGE	14
65	PEDDIE GEORGE	HD M	46	(SERVANT)	SCOTLAND		GATE COTTAGE	14
65	PEDDIE GEORGE	SO U	2		SSX	HOLLINGTON	GATE COTTAGE	14
65	PEDDIE SARAH	DA U	4?		SSX	HOLLINGTON	GATE COTTAGE	14
65	PEDDIE SARAH	WI M	32		SSX	HOLLINGTON	GATE COTTAGE	14
30	PEDDLESDEN ELIZABETH	WI M	32	RAILWAY GATE KEEPER	SSX	CHILTINGTON	RAILWAY GATE HSE IN LIBERTY	41
30	PEDDLESDEN JOHN	HD M	29	RAIL LAB	SSX	BERWICK	RAILWAY GATE HSE IN LIBERTY	41
116	PELLING DEARING	HD M	63	RETIRED CORDWAINER	SSX	WEST TARRING	NOT GIVEN	102
116	PELLING EDMUND	SO U	30	CORDWAINER	SSX	BEXHILL	NOT GIVEN	102
51	PELLING ELIZA	WI M	29		SSX	WARBLETON	HOLLINGTON STREET	12
116	PELLING JOHN	BR U	53	CORDWAINER	SSX	WEST TARRING	NOT GIVEN	102
51	PELLING JOHN	HD M	29	POTTER	SSX	HELLINGLY	HOLLINGTON STREET	12
51	PELLING JOHN	SO U	8		SSX	HURSTMONCEUX	HOLLINGTON STREET	12
51	PELLING MARY ANN	DA U	4		SSX	HOLLINGTON	HOLLINGTON STREET	12
51	PELLING PERCIVAL	SO U	6		SSX	ST.LEONARDS	HOLLINGTON STREET	12
51	PELLING TREYTON	SO U	3		SSX	HOLLINGTON	HOLLINGTON STREET	12
81	PEMPLE MARY	SV U	24	HOUSE MAID	WIL	TEA	BEAUPORT HOUSE	17
63	PENFOLD FANNY	PP U	12		SSX	UNKNOWN	BEXHILL STREET	96
63	PENNINGTON ANN	PP U	9		SRY	KENNINGTON	BEXHILL STREET	96
63	PENNINGTON EMILY	DA U	25	GOVERNESS	SSX	ASHBURNHAM	BEXHILL STREET	96
63	PENNINGTON HRRIETTA	DA U	39	GOVERNESS	SSX	ASHBURNHAM	BEXHILL STREET	96
65	PENNINGTON LOUISA	HD U	37	GOVERNESS	SSX	ASHBURNHAM	NOT GIVEN	96
63	PENNINGTON MARY	NC U	16	PUPIL	MDX	DALSTON	BEXHILL STREET	96
63	PENNINGTON WAL'	GS U	5		MDX	HACKNEY	BEXHILL STREET	96
63	PENNINGTON WILLIAM	HD W	74	ANNUITANT	SFK	BARKIN	BEXHILL STREET	96
2	PENTON CHARLES	LG U	30	RAIL LAB	HAM	HORLEY	RAILWAY HUT	4
68	PEPPER HANNAH	CI U	40		SSX	BATTLE	NOT GIVEN	97
68	PEPPER MARIAH	CI U	38		SSX	BATTLE	NOT GIVEN	97
3	PEPPERCORNE HARRIET	WI M	71		MDX	ISLINGTON	NOT GIVEN	51
3	PEPPERCORNE WILLIAM	HD M	69	RETIRED STOCK BROKER	MDX	STRATFORD+	NOT GIVEN	51
63	PERRY ELIZA J	PP U	9		DEV	BARBICAN	BEXHILL STREET	96
54	PETERS GEORGE	HD M	37	AG.LAB	SSX	BEXHILL	LODGE	179
54	PETERS HARRIETT	WI M	20?		SSX	BEXHILL	LODGE	179
54	PETERS JAMES	SO U	2		SSX	WESTFIELD	LODGE	179
69	PETERS MARY	SV W	65		SSX	WESTFIELD	MOUNT PLEASANT	181
30	PETITT GEORGE	LG U	25		SSX	NINFIELD	IRON LATCH	9
6	PETTETT CHARLES	HD M	42	AG.LAB	SSX	CATSFIELD	NOT GIVEN	107
6	PETTETT CHARLES	SO U	8		SSX	CATSFIELD	NOT GIVEN	107
6	PETTETT ELIZABETH	DA U	12	SCHOLAR	SSX	CATSFIELD	NOT GIVEN	107
6	PETTETT FRANCES	WI M	41		SSX	CATSFIELD	NOT GIVEN	107
6	PETTETT HARRIETT	DA U	1		SSX	CATSFIELD	NOT GIVEN	107
52	PETTETT HENRY	SO U	13	AG.LAB	SSX	BEXHILL	NOT GIVEN	112
52	PETTETT JAMES	HD M	36	AG.LAB	SSX	NINFIELD	NOT GIVEN	112
6	PETTETT JAMES	SO U	6		SSX	CATSFIELD	NOT GIVEN	107
6	PETTETT MARY	DA U	11	SCHOLAR	SSX	CATSFIELD	NOT GIVEN	107

63

	Name			Age	Occupation	Birthplace	Address	No.
52	PETTETT MARY	WI	M	40		SSX BEXHILL	NOT GIVEN	112
52	PETTETT WILLIAM	SO	U	6	SCHOLAR	SSX CATSFIELD	NOT GIVEN	112
5	PETTETT WILLIAM	SV	U	18	FARM LAB	SSX CATSFIELD	NOT GIVEN	107
2	PETTITT HENRY	SV	U	18		SSX ASHBURNHAM	PLACE	107
41	PHILCOX ESTHER	WI	M	43		NOT GIVEN (?BREDE)	WALNUT TREE	161
41	PHILCOX JAMES	HD	M	49	GARDENER	SSX BREDE	WALNUT TREE	156
21	PHILCOX WILLIAM	NP	U	19	AG.LAB	SSX BATTLE	MARLPITS	122
55	PHILIPPS ELIZABETH	DA	U	23		PEM MILFORD	SIGNAL HOUSE	44
55	PHILIPPS ELLEN M	DA	U	16		SCOTLAND	SIGNAL HOUSE	44
55	PHILIPPS GEORGE	HD	M	54	CHIEF OFFICER COAST GUARD	PEM JEFFRESTON	SIGNAL HOUSE	44
55	PHILIPPS JANE P	DA	U	8	SCHOLAR	SCOTLAND	SIGNAL HOUSE	44
55	PHILIPPS JOHN L	SO	U	20	MARINER	SCOTLAND	SIGNAL HOUSE	44
55	PHILIPPS MARTHA	DA	U	5	SCHOLAR	SCOTLAND	SIGNAL HOUSE	44
55	PHILIPPS MARTHA	WI	M	46		PEM MILFORD	SIGNAL HOUSE	44
55	PHILIPPS MARY A	DA	U	13	SCHOLAR	SCOTLAND	SIGNAL HOUSE	44
55	PHILIPPS RICHARD	SO	U	22		PEM MILFORD	SIGNAL HOUSE	44
67	PHILIPS LOUISA	VR	U	5	SCHOLAR	SSX EASTBOURNE	1 BELLENDER COTTAGE	46
43	PHILLIPS ANN	HD	M	32	LAUNDRESS	SSX BEXHILL	NOT GIVEN	94
43	PHILLIPS BENJAMIN	SO	U	3M		SSX BEXHILL	NOT GIVEN	94
43	PHILLIPS HENRY	SO	U	2		SSX BEXHILL	NOT GIVEN	94
43	PHILLIPS JANE	DA	U	5		SSX ST.LEONARDS	NOT GIVEN	94
43	PHILLIPS THOMAS	SO	U	3		SSX ST.LEONARDS	NOT GIVEN	94
7	PICKELS JOHN	HD	M	30	RAILWAY LAB	YKS SOWERBY?*	DUKE FARM	129
7	PICKELS MAREY	WI	M	25		SFK ELMSWELL*	DUKE FARM	129
5	PICKNELL WILLIAM	SV	U	27	CARTER	SSX BOLNEY	SOUTHINGS	152
29	PIDDLESDEN ANN	VR	U	6	SCHOLAR	SSX BRIGHTON	IN THE LIBERTY	41
29	PIDDLESDEN HERBERT	VR	U	8	SCHOLAR	SSX PATCHAM	IN THE LIBERTY	41
23	PIDDLESTON ELIZA	VR	U	40		SSX WESTFIELD	CHARITY HOUSE	154
23	PIDDLESTON HENRY	/	U	9		SSX ORE	CHARITY HOUSE	154
46	PIDELSDEN JOHN	SV	U	16	HOUSE SERVANT	SSX ORE	MOAT	167
87	PILBEAM ELIZA	WI	M	30		SSX BURWASH	HAYWARDS	18
87	PILBEAM LEVI	HD	M	33	BLACKSMITH	SSX BURWASH	HAYWARDS	18
15	PILBEN CARCTOLIE (SIC)	WI	M	64		SSX MAYFIELD	PARISH FARM	130
15	PILBEN WILLIAM	HD	M	67	FARMER	SSX HOOE	PARISH FARM	130
26	PILKINGTON ANDREW	HD	M	74	LT GENERAL ARMY RCB	SAL BRIDGNORTH	CATSFIELD PLACE CHURCH HSE	110
26	PILKINGTON LOUISA E	DA	U	26		KEN HAYES	CATSFIELD PLACE CHURCH HSE	110
26	PILKINGTON MARIA E	WI	M	65		LONDON	CATSFIELD PLACE CHURCH HSE	110
87	PIOLL ELLENOR ELIZABETH	SV	U	20	COOK	KEN BRENZETT	SOGGS FARM	228
7	PIPER ALFRED	SO	U	7	SCHOLAR	SSX EWHURST	COLLIERS GREEN	233
2	PIPER AMOS	GS	U	7	SCHOLAR	SSX WESTFIELD	WATTLE HILL	249
5	PIPER ELIZA	WI	M	42		SSX FOREST ROW	TAN HOUSE SEDLESCOMBE ST	187
5	PIPER HERBERT	SO	U	10	SCHOLAR	KEN CRANBROOK	TAN HOUSE SEDLESCOMBE ST	187
62	PIPER JESSEY (MALE)	/	U	17	SERVANT	SSX NORTHIAM	EWHURST GREEN	224
81	PIPER JOHN	HD	W	65	AG.LAB	SSX WADHURST	STAPLE CROSS	243
2	PIPER PHILADELPHIA	WI	M	51		SSX WESTFIELD	WATTLE HILL	249
7	PIPER ROSANNA	DA	U	11		SSX EWHURST	COLLIERS GREEN	233
50	PIPER THOMAS	LG	U	23	SAWYER?	SSX EWHURST	SNAGS HALL	222
5	PIPER WILLIAM	HD	M	44	FELMONGER EMP 3	KEN COWDEN	TAN HOUSE SEDLESCOMBE ST	187
2	PIPER WILLIAM	HD	M	57	FARMER 154 AC EMP 4 MEN	SSX BREDE	WATTLE HILL	249
7	PIPER WILLIAM	HD	W	33	SAWYER	SSX EWHURST	COLLIERS GREEN	233
56	PLAYFORD ALBERT	SO	U	6	SCHOLAR	SSX EWHURST	SNAGS HALL	223
43	PLAYFORD ANN	WI	M	37		SSX WESTFIELD	POPPING HOLE LANE	206
43	PLAYFORD GEORGE	BR	U	41	AG.LAB	SSX WARTLING	POPPING HOLE LANE	206
56	PLAYFORD GEORGE	SO	U	1		SSX EWHURST	SNAGS HALL	223
56	PLAYFORD HARRIET	DA	U	14		SSX EWHURST	SNAGS HALL	223
56	PLAYFORD HARRIET	WI	M	36		SSX EWHURST	SNAGS HALL	223
43	PLAYFORD HENRY	SO	U	11		SSX SEDLESCOMBE	POPPING HOLE LANE	206
43	PLAYFORD JABEZ	SO	U	5		SSX SEDLESCOMBE	POPPING HOLE LANE	206
56	PLAYFORD JAMES	HD	M	36	AG.LAB	SSX NORTHIAM	SNAGS HALL	223
43	PLAYFORD JAMES	HD	M	36	AG.LAB	SSX SEDLESCOMBE	POPPING HOLE LANE	206
29	PLAYFORD JAMES	HD	M	37	GARDENER	SSX BECKLEY	CRIPPS	252
43	PLAYFORD JANE	DA	U	8		SSX SEDLESCOMBE	POPPING HOLE LANE	206
29	PLAYFORD JANE	WI	M	34		SSX BATTLE	CRIPPS	252
56	PLAYFORD JOHN	SO	U	12		SSX SEDLESCOMBE	SNAGS HALL	223
56	PLAYFORD MARY ANN	DA	U	4		SSX EWHURST	SNAGS HALL	223
40	PLAYFORD MARY JANE	WI	M	26		SSX NORTHIAM	NEAR FOOTLAND	206
43	PLAYFORD ROBERT	SO	U	13		SSX SEDLESCOMBE	POPPING HOLE LANE	206
29	PLAYFORD SILVESTER	SO	U	2		SSX BATTLE	CRIPPS	252
40	PLAYFORD SPENCER	HD	M	32	AG.LAB	SSX SEDLESCOMBE	NEAR FOOTLAND	206
40	PLAYFORD SPENCER	SO	U	1		SSX SEDLESCOMBE	NEAR FOOTLAND	206
43	PLAYFORD WILLIAM	SO	U	3		SSX SEDLESCOMBE	POPPING HOLE LANE	206
56	PLAYFORD WILLIAM	SO	U	6	SCHOLAR	SSX EWHURST	SNAGS HALL	223
28	PLUMB JOHN	HD	M	25	INNKEEPER EMP 1	MDI CLERKENWELL	WHEAT SHEAF INN	54
28	PLUMB MARY	WI	M	27		WIL SALISBURY	WHEAT SHEAF INN	54
80	PLUMLEY GEORGE R	SO	U	9	SCHOLAR	SSX CATSFIELD	QUEENS HEAD	32
80	PLUMLEY JANE E	WI	M	38		SSX BEXHILL	QUEENS HEAD	32
80	PLUMLEY JANE V	DA	U	1		SSX BEXHILL	QUEENS HEAD	32
80	PLUMLEY URIAH	HD	M	48	INN KEEPER	SSX PEVENSEY	QUEENS HEAD	32
80	PLUMLEY URIAH E	SO	U	11	SCHOLAR	SSX CATSFIELD	QUEENS HEAD	32
38	POCOCK ANN	DA	U	8	SCHOLAR	SSX CATSFIELD	NOT GIVEN	111
11	POCOCK ANN	WI	M	40		SSX HOOE	WILTING FARM HOUSE	6
67	POCOCK C T (MALE)	SO	U	1		SSX BEXHILL	NOT GIVEN	97
51	POCOCK ELIZABETH	DA	U	7	SCHOLAR	SSX EWHURST	SNAGS HALL	222
38	POCOCK FRANCES	DA	U	9	SCHOLAR	SSX CATSFIELD	NOT GIVEN	111
67	POCOCK FREDERICK	SO	U	3		SSX BEXHILL	NOT GIVEN	97

	Name	Rel	MS	Age	Occupation	County	Birthplace	Address	No
38	POCOCK HARRIE C	SO	U	6	SCHOLAR	SSX	CATSFIELD	NOT GIVEN	111
67	POCOCK JAMES	HD	M	35	BUTCHER (4 MEN)	SSX	HOOE	NOT GIVEN	97
67	POCOCK JANE	WI	M	32		SSX	BEXHILL	NOT GIVEN	97
38	POCOCK JANE	WI	M	38		SSX	HOLLINGTON	NOT GIVEN	111
62	POCOCK JOHN	HD	W	73	MARKET GARDENER	SSX	HOOE	NOT GIVEN	58
51	POCOCK JOHN BAKER	HD	M	33	AG.LAB	SSX	BATTLE	SNAGS HALL	222
51	POCOCK MARIA	WI	M	33		SSX	EWHURST	SNAGS HALL	222
51	POCOCK MARTHA	DA	U	9	SCHOLAR	SSX	EWHURST	SNAGS HALL	222
41	POCOCK MARY	VR	U	7	SCHOLAR	SSX	HELLINGLY	NOT GIVEN	111
38	POCOCK MARY J	DA	U	3		SSX	CATSFIELD	NOT GIVEN	111
2	POCOCK SAMUEL	SV	U	30	SERVANT	SSX	HOOE	PLOUGH INN	142
38	POCOCK THOMAS	SO	U	1		SSX	CATSFIELD	NOT GIVEN	111
100	POCOCK WILLIAM	GS	U	4	SCHOLAR	SSX	BEXHILL	NOT GIVEN	101
11	POCOCK WILLIAM	HD	M	65	FARMER 457 AC EMP 22 LAB	SSX	HOOE	WILTING FARM HOUSE	6
38	POCOCK WILLIAM H	HD	M	52	GARDENER	SSX	UCKFIELD	NOT GIVEN	111
51	POCOCK WILLIAM HENRY	SO	U	5	SCHOLAR	SSX	EWHURST	SNAGS HALL	222
46	POLHILL ANN	WI	M	22		SSX	EWHURST	POPPING HOLE LANE	207
32	POLHILL ANNE	DA	U	11	SCHOLAR	SSX	SEDLESCOMBE	BREDE LANE	191
32	POLHILL ANNE	WI	M	32		SSX	HASTINGS	BREDE LANE	191
1	POLHILL EDGAR	SO	U	9	SCHOLAR	SSX	EWHURST	STOCKWOOD FARM	232
53	POLHILL EDMOND	SO	U	23	AG.LAB	SSX	EWHURST	SNAGS HALL	222
1	POLHILL EDMUND	SO	U	17	AG.LAB	SSX	EWHURST	STOCKWOOD FARM	232
1	POLHILL EDWARD	SO	U	19	AG.LAB	SSX	EWHURST	STOCKWOOD FARM	232
46	POLHILL EDWIN	SO	U	5		SSX	EWHURST	POPPING HOLE LANE	207
32	POLHILL ELIZABETH	DA	U	6	SCHOLAR	SSX	SEDLESCOMBE	BREDE LANE	191
32	POLHILL GEORGE	SO	U	17	AG.LAB	SSX	SEDLESCOMBE	BREDE LANE	191
32	POLHILL HARRIET	DA	U	14		SSX	SEDLESCOMBE	BREDE LANE	191
1	POLHILL HARRIET	WI	M	46		SSX	MOUNTFIELD	STOCKWOOD FARM	232
32	POLHILL HENRY	SO	U	9	SCHOLAR	SSX	SEDLESCOMBE	BREDE LANE	191
46	POLHILL JAMES	HD	M	32	AG.LAB	SSX	SALEHURST	POPPING HOLE LANE	207
53	POLHILL JANE	WI	M	65		KEN	HAWKHURST	SNAGS HALL	222
31	POLHILL JANE	WI	M	67		SSX	SEDLESCOMBE	SEDLESCOMBE PLACE	204
1	POLHILL PHEBE	DA	U	11		SSX	EWHURST	STOCKWOOD FARM	232
31	POLHILL SAMUEL	HD	M	70	PAUPER AG.LAB	SSX	WESTFIELD	SEDLESCOMBE STREET	204
1	POLHILL SAMUEL	SO	U	7	SCHOLAR	SSX	EWHURST	STOCKWOOD FARM	232
32	POLHILL SPENCER	HD	M	45	AG.LAB	SSX	WESTFIELD	BREDE LANE	191
1	POLHILL THOMAS	HD	M	40	AG.LAB	SSX	SALEHURST	STOCKWOOD FARM	232
53	POLHILL THOMAS	HD	M	59	GAME KEEPER	SSX	WHATLINGTON	SNAGS HALL	222
36	POMPHREY MARIA	HD	U	65	GENTLEWOMAN ANNUITANT	SSX	HASTINGS	BEXHILL STREET	27
16	PONT ANN	WI	M	28		SSX	CATSFIELD	STEPHEN'S CROUCH	121
16	PONT ELIZABETH	DA	U	2		SSX	CATSFIELD	STEPHEN'S CROUCH	121
9	PONT JAMES	SV	U	20		SSX	CROWHURST	WIDOWS	173
16	PONT MARIANN	DA	U	4		SSX	CATSFIELD	STEPHEN'S CROUCH	121
68	PONT MARY	CI	M	52		SSX	BATTLE	NOT GIVEN	97
16	PONT MATHEW	HD	M	32	BLACKSMITH	SSX	DALLINGTON	STEPHEN'S CROUCH	121
16	PONT MATHEW	SO	U	6M		SSX	HASTINGS	STEPHEN'S CROUCH	121
32	POPKIN E F	DA	U	19	GENTLEWOMAN	MDX	LONDON	BEXHILL STREET	27
32	POPKIN ELIZABETH	DA	U	21	GENTLEWOMAN	MDX	LONDON	BEXHILL STREET	27
32	POPKIN J M	DA	U	16	GENTLEWOMAN		CAMBERWELL	BEXHILL STREET	27
32	POPKIN JEMIMA	DA	U	23	GENTLEWOMAN	MDX	LONDON	BEXHILL STREET	27
32	POPKIN N M	DA	U	17	GENTLEWOMAN	MDX	LONDON	BEXHILL STREET	27
5	PORT WILLIAM	SV	U	23	LEATHER DRESSER	SAL		TAN HOUSE SEDLESCOMBE ST	187
34	PRATT EDWARD B	SO	U	31	LATE IN THE ARMY	SSX	SEDLESCOMBE	RECTORY	205
34	PRATT HARRIETT CATHERINE	DA	U	41		SSX	SEDLESCOMBE	RECTORY	205
34	PRATT JOHN	HD	W	77	RECTOR OF SEDLESCOMBE	KEN	ORPINGTON	RECTORY	205
34	PRATT JOHN JOSEPH	SO	U	40	CLERGYMAN	SSX	SEDLESCOMBE	RECTORY	205
34	PRATT RICHARD FREDERICK	SO	U	33	OCCUPIER 103 AC EMP 8	SSX	SEDLESCOMBE	RECTORY	205
34	PRATT SOPHIA ELIZABETH	DA	U	43		SSX	SEDLESCOMBE	RECTORY	205
87	PRIOR ALFRED	HD	U	41	CORDWAINER	SSX	BEXHILL	NOT GIVEN	99
76	PRIOR CHARLES	SO	U	24	AG.LAB	SSX	BEXHILL	BELL HILL	32
80	PRIOR CHARLES	SV	U	31	HOSTLER	SSX	BEXHILL	BELL HOTEL	99
81	PRIOR DELIA S	DA	U	29		SSX	BEXHILL	CHURCH STREET	99
84	PRIOR EDWARD	HD	W	90	PAUPER CORDWAINER	SSX	BEXHILL	CHURCH STREET	99
84	PRIOR ELIZA	DA	U	33		SSX	BEXHILL	CHURCH STREET	99
76	PRIOR ELIZABETH	WI	M	50		SSX	BEXHILL	BELL HILL	32
76	PRIOR ELLEN	DA	U	19		SSX	BEXHILL	BELL HILL	32
76	PRIOR GEORGE	SO	U	13	AG.LAB	SSX	BEXHILL	BELL HILL	32
81	PRIOR JANE	HD	W	61	PAUPER MARINER'S WIDOW	SSX	NINFIELD	CHURCH STREET	99
70	PRIOR MAHALA	NC	U	21		SSX	BEXHILL	POTMANS	114
76	PRIOR NEWMAN	SO	U	8	SCHOLAR	SSX	BEXHILL	BELL HILL	32
83	PRIOR PHILADELPHIA	DL	U	18		SSX	BEXHILL	CHURCH STREET	99
76	PRIOR RICHARD	HD	M	52	AG.LAB	SSX	BEXHILL	BELL HILL	32
55	PURFIELD ANN	DA	U	8	SCHOLAR	SSX	SALEHURST	4 MARINE COTTAGES	30
55	PURFIELD FREDERICK	SO	U	14		SSX	BATTLE	4 MARINE COTTAGES	30
55	PURFIELD HENRY	GS	U	5	SCHOLAR	SSX	LEWES	4 MARINE COTTAGES	30
55	PURFIELD MARIA	WI	M	43		SSX	BATTLE	4 MARINE COTTAGES	30
55	PURFIELD SAMUEL	HD	M	50	AG.LAB	SSX	BATTLE	4 MARINE COTTAGES	30
69	PUTLAND CALEB	SO	U	15	ASSISTANT ENGINEER	SSX	ST.MAGDALEN	EWHURST GREEN	225
69	PUTLAND ESTHER	DA	U	6		SSX	SALEHURST	EWHURST GREEN	225
69	PUTLAND ESTHER	WI	M	36		SSX	CLAPHAM	EWHURST GREEN	225
69	PUTLAND HENRY	SO	U	10	SCHOLAR	SSX	ST.MAGDALEN	EWHURST GREEN	225
13	PUTLAND MARY	DA	U	12	SCHOLAR	SSX	CROWHURST	NOT GIVEN	108
13	PUTLAND MARY	WI	M	39		SSX	CATSFIELD	NOT GIVEN	108
69	PUTLAND NELSON	SO	U	12	SCHOLAR	SSX	ST.MAGDALEN	EWHURST GREEN	225
69	PUTLAND SAMUEL	HD	M	39	CIVIL ENGINEER & SURVEYOR	SSX	NORTHIAM	EWHURST GREEN	225
69	PUTLAND SAMUEL	SO	U	8	SCHOLAR	SSX	EWHURST	EWHURST GREEN	225

13	PUTLAND SARAH	DA	U	3		SSX	CATSFIELD	NOT GIVEN	108
69	PUTLAND STEPHEN	SO	U	1		SSX	WESTFIELD	EWHURST GREEN	225
15	PUTLAND THOMAS	SV	U	15	ERRAND BOY	SSX	CROWHURST	CATSFIELD PLACE FARM	108
13	PUTLAND WILLIAM	HD	M	45	AG.LAB	SSX	CROWHURST	NOT GIVEN	108
40	PUTLAND* JOHN	HD	M	36	AG.LAB	SSX	CROWHURST	SHOP HOUSES	124
40	PUTLAND* MARY	WI	M	31		SSX	DALLINGTON	SHOP HOUSES	124
45	PUXTED MARY	WI	M	55		SSX	BATTLE	SHOREHAM	221
45	PUXTED WILLIAM	HD	M	41	FARMER 72 AC EMP 3	SSX	EWHURST	SHOREHAM	221
45	PUXTED WILLIAM	SL	U	33	AG.LAB	SSX	BATTLE	SHOREHAM	221
16	QUAIFE ALDRED	SO	U	11		SSX	CATSFIELD	NOT GIVEN	108
16	QUAIFE AMOS	SO	U	5	SCHOLAR	SSX	CATSFIELD	NOT GIVEN	108
17	QUAIFE ANN	WI	M	27		SSX	CATSFIELD	NOT GIVEN	108
39	QUAIFE ANNE	DA	U	5		SSX	CATSFIELD	SHOP HOUSES	124
16	QUAIFE ANSLEY?	DA	U	6	SCHOLAR	SSX	CATSFIELD	NOT GIVEN	108
19	QUAIFE DELIA	DA	U	13		SSX	CROWHURST	NASHES	145
19	QUAIFE DIANA	WI	M	44?		SSX	CATSFIELD	NASHES	144
39	QUAIFE EDWARD	HD	M	31	AG.LAB	SSX	CATSFIELD	SHOP HOUSES	124
31	QUAIFE ELIZABETH	DA	U	2		SSX	SEDLESCOMBE	BREDE LANE	190
39	QUAIFE ELIZABETH	DA	U	7	SCHOLAR	SSX	CATSFIELD	SHOP HOUSES	124
1	QUAIFE FRANCES	VR	U	24		SSX	CATSFIELD	STOCKWOOD FARM	232
17	QUAIFE FREDERICK	HD	M	27	AG.LAB	SSX	CATSFIELD	NOT GIVEN	108
17	QUAIFE FREDERICK	SO	U	4		SSX	CATSFIELD	NOT GIVEN	108
19	QUAIFE GEORGE	HD	M	49	FARM LAB	SSX	CATSFIELD	NASHES	144
16	QUAIFE HARRIET	WI	M	47		SSX	CATSFIELD	NOT GIVEN	108
17	QUAIFE HENRY	SO	U	1		SSX	CATSFIELD	NOT GIVEN	108
15	QUAIFE HORACE	SV	U	14	(AG.LAB)	SSX	CATSFIELD	CATSFIELD PLACE FARM	108
71	QUAIFE JAMES	SO	U	9	CARTERS BOY	SSX	BEXHILL	WATERMILL COTTAGE	114
19	QUAIFE JAMES	SO	U	12		SSX	CROWHURST	NASHES	145
70	QUAIFE JOHN	LG	U	22	AG.LAB	SSX	CATSFIELD	SIDLEY	84
71	QUAIFE MARY A	WI	M	36		SSX	BEXHILL	WATERMILL COTTAGE	114
39	QUAIFE MARY ANN	DA	U	3		SSX	FRAMFIELD	SHOP HOUSES	124
18	QUAIFE MARY ANN	DA	U	17		SSX	BEXHILL	NOT GIVEN	108
39	QUAIFE MARY ANN	WI	M	30		SSX	BREDE	SHOP HOUSES	124
71	QUAIFE MARY J	DA	U	7		SSX	CATSFIELD	WATERMILL COTTAGE	114
71	QUAIFE ROBERT	HD	M	43	AG.LAB	SSX	CATSFIELD	WATERMILL COTTAGE	114
16	QUAIFE SAMUEL	HD	M	46	AG.LAB	SSX	CATSFIELD	NOT GIVEN	108
3	QUAIFE SAMUEL	LG	W	72	HOUSE SERVANT	SSX	CATSFIELD	CATSFIELD GREEN	120
19	QUAIFE SARAH	DA	U	9	SCHOLAR	SSX	CROWHURST	NASHES	145
16	QUAIFE SARAH	DA	U	18		SSX	CATSFIELD	NOT GIVEN	108
71	QUAIFE SARAH A	DA	U	11	SCHOLAR	SSX	CATSFIELD	WATERMILL COTTAGE	114
18	QUAIFE SOPHIA	WI	M	49		SSX	CATSFIELD	NOT GIVEN	108
18	QUAIFE WALTER	HD	M	51	AG.LAB	SSX	CATSFIELD	NOT GIVEN	108
17	QUAIFE WALTER	SO	U	3		SSX	CATSFIELD	NOT GIVEN	108
31	QUIAFE MARIA	DA	U	6	SCHOLAR	SSX	SEDLESCOMBE	BREDE LANE	190
31	QUIAFE MARY	WI	M	43		SSX	NINFIELD	BREDE LANE	190
31	QUIAFE MARY ELIZA	DA	U	4		SSX	WESTFIELD	BREDE LANE	190
31	QUIAFE ROBERT	HD	M	45	AG.LAB	SSX	CATSFIELD	BREDE LANE	190
16	RAGLESS OLIVER	LG	U	28	CARPENTER	SSX	ANGMERING	STEPHEN'S CROUCH	121
34	RAINGER ELIZABETH	WI	M	38		LND		DAIRY HOUSE	133
34	RAINGER HARRIOT	DA	U	7		SSX	LEWES	DAIRY HOUSE	133
34	RAINGER HENRY	HD	M	34	RAILWAY LAB	LND		DAIRY HOUSE	133
34	RAINGER JOHN	SO	U	10		SSX	LEWES	DAIRY HOUSE	133
22	RANSOM ALFRED	SO	U	12		SSX	CROWHURST	RANSOM'S HOUSE	145
3	RANSOM ANN	DA	U	8M		SSX	BEXHILL	SIDLEY CORNER	65
11	RANSOM ANN	DA	U	1		SSX	CROWHURST	MADKITS?	129
104	RANSOM ANN M	NC	U	4		SSX	BEXHILL	NOT GIVEN	101
10	RANSOM BARBARY	SV	U	17	HOUSE SERVANT	SSX	CROWHURST	ADAMS FARM	143
45	RANSOM CAROLINE	WI	M	37		SSX	PEASMARSH	SIDLEY GREEN	81
36	RANSOM CHARLOTTE	DA	U	14		SSX	BEXHILL	COCKRELLS SIDLEY	80
20	RANSOM CHARLOTTE	WI	M	63		SRY	HORLEY	TWO HOUSES SIDLEY	77
60	RANSOM CHARLOTTE	WI	M	79		SSX	BEXHILL	LANES END	30
34	RANSOM EDMUND	SV	U	20	SERVANT	SSX	CROWHURST	COURT LODGE FARM	147
33	RANSOM EDWARD	HD	M	43	AG.LAB	SSX	BEXHILL	WATER MILL SIDLEY	80
36	RANSOM EDWARD	SO	U	27	FARM LAB	SSX	CROWHURST	NOT GIVEN	133
13	RANSOM EDWIN	SO	U	25		SSX	CROWHURST	RIAL? OAK	144
17	RANSOM EDWIN	SV	U	17	FARM SERVANT	SSX	CROWHURST	HILL FARM	144
113	RANSOM ELIZA	WI	M	36		SSX	BEXHILL	NOT GIVEN	102
7	RANSOM ELIZABETH	DA	U	4		SSX	HOLLINGTON	WILTING	5
33	RANSOM ELIZABETH	HD	M	91	HOUSE KEEPER	SSX	WATLINGTON	CRIPPS	253
22	RANSOM ELIZABETH	WI	M	22		SSX	BEXHILL	TWO HOUSES SIDLEY	78
7	RANSOM ELIZABETH	WI	M	34		SSX	NINFIELD	WILTING	5
33	RANSOM ELIZABETH	WI	M	35		SSX	BEXHILL	WATER MILL SIDLEY	80
22	RANSOM ELIZABETH	WI	M	48		SSX	CROWHURST	RANSOM'S HOUSE	145
21	RANSOM ELIZABETH	WI	M	52		SSX	WARTLING	NOT GIVEN	109
12	RANSOM ELIZABETH	WI	M	63		SSX	BEXHILL	RIST WOOD SIDLEY	76
33	RANSOM ELIZABETH F	DA	U	8		SSX	CATSFIELD	WATER MILL SIDLEY	80
55	RANSOM FANNY	LG	U	30	DRESSMAKER	SSX	CROWHURST	NOT GIVEN	112
22	RANSOM FREDERIC B	SO	U	1		SSX	BEXHILL	TWO HOUSES SIDLEY	78
113	RANSOM FREDERICK	SO	U	3		SSX	BEXHILL	NOT GIVEN	102
10	RANSOM FREDERICK	SV	U	23	FARM LAB	SSX	CROWHURST	ADAMS FARM	143
21	RANSOM GEORGE	HD	M	60	AG.LAB	SSX	BEXHILL	NOT GIVEN	109
3	RANSOM GEORGE	SO	U	3		SSX	BEXHILL	SIDLEY CORNER	65
33	RANSOM GEORGE	SO	U	4		SSX	BEXHILL	WATER MILL SIDLEY	80
36	RANSOM HANNAH	WI	M	57		SSX	BEXHILL	COCKRELLS SIDLEY	80
13	RANSOM HANNAH	WI	M	57		SSX	BEXHILL	RIAL? OAK	144
7	RANSOM HARRIETT	DA	U	7M		SSX	HOLLINGTON	WILTING	5

66

34	RANSOM HARRIETT	SV	U	21	SERVANT	SSX	CROWHURST	COURT LODGE FARM	147
33	RANSOM HENRY	SO	U	10M		SSX	BEXHILL	WATER MILL SIDLEY	80
57	RANSOM HENRY	SO	U	7	SCHOLAR	SSX	BEXHILL	KEWHURST	44
22	RANSOM JAMES	HD	M	23	AG.LAB	SSX	BEXHILL	TWO HOUSES SIDLEY	78
13	RANSOM JAMES	HD	M	59	FARM LAB	SSX	CROWHURST	RIAL? OAK	144
8	RANSOM JAMES	LG	U	40	FARM LAB	SSX	CROWHURST	NOT GIVEN	143
33	RANSOM JAMES	SO	U	6		SSX	CATSFIELD	WATER MILL SIDLEY	80
13	RANSOM JAMES	SO	U	21		SSX	CROWHURST	RIAL? OAK	144
37	RANSOM JAMES	SV	U	23	AG.LAB	SSX	BEXHILL	BEXHILL STREET	27
12	RANSOM JESSE	SO	U	16	AG.LAB	SSX	BEXHILL	RIST WOOD SIDLEY	76
37	RANSOM JESSE	SV	U	19	AG.LAB	SSX	BEXHILL	BEXHILL STREET	27
45	RANSOM JOHN	HD	M	39	AG.LAB	SSX	BEXHILL	SIDLEY GREEN	81
12	RANSOM JOHN	HD	M	64	AG.LAB	SSX	BEXHILL	RIST WOOD SIDLEY	76
20	RANSOM JOHN	HD	M	69	AG.LAB	SSX	BEXHILL	TWO HOUSES SIDLEY	77
11	RANSOM JOHN	SV	U	20	AG.LAB	SSX	CROWHURST	WILTING FARM HOUSE	6
3	RANSOM MAHALA	WI	M	29		SSX	BEXHILL	SIDLEY CORNER	65
11	RANSOM MAREY	WI	M	36		SSX	CATSFIELD	MADKITS?	129
57	RANSOM MARIA	WI	M	31		SSX	CROWHURST	KEWHURST	44
11	RANSOM MARY	DA	U	8		SSX	CROWHURST	MADKITS?	129
36	RANSOM MARY	DA	U	24		SSX	CROWHURST	NOT GIVEN	133
36	RANSOM MARY	WI	M	60		SSX	MOUNTFIELD	NOT GIVEN	133
12	RANSOM MARY	WI	M	60		SSX	TICEHURST	NOT GIVEN	90
36	RANSOM SAMUEL	SO	U	16	AG.LAB	SSX	BEXHILL	COCKRELLS SIDLEY	80
11	RANSOM SARAH	DA	U	3		SSX	CROWHURST	MADKITS?	129
13	RANSOM SARAH	DA	U	16		SSX	CROWHURST	RIAL? OAK	144
22	RANSOM SOPHIA	DA	U	25		SSX	CROWHURST	RANSOM'S HOUSE	145
113	RANSOM SPENCER	HD	M	35	AG.LAB	SSX	BEXHILL	NOT GIVEN	102
7	RANSOM STEPHEN	HD	M	33	AG.LAB	SSX	BEXHILL	WILTING	5
113	RANSOM STEPHEN	SO	U	9		SSX	BEXHILL	NOT GIVEN	102
11	RANSOM THOMAS	HD	M	36	AG.LAB	SSX	CROWHURST	MADKITS?	129
36	RANSOM THOMAS	HD	M	63	FARM LAB	SSX	CROWHURST	NOT GIVEN	133
60	RANSOM THOMAS	HD	M	77	PAUPER	SSX	BEXHILL	LANES END	30
22	RANSOM THOMAS	SO	U	4		SSX	BEXHILL	TWO HOUSES SIDLEY	78
11	RANSOM THOMAS	SO	U	6		SSX	CROWHURST	MADKITS?	129
33	RANSOM THOMAS	SO	U	11	AG.LAB	SSX	CATSFIELD	WATER MILL SIDLEY	80
21	RANSOM THOMAS	SO	U	16	AG.LAB	SSX	CATSFIELD	NOT GIVEN	109
3	RANSOM WILLIAM	HD	M	29	AG.LAB	SSX	BEXHILL	SIDLEY CORNER	65
57	RANSOM WILLIAM	HD	M	31	AG.LAB	SSX	BEXHILL	KEWHURST	44
22	RANSOM WILLIAM	HD	M	57	FARM LAB	SSX	CROWHURST	RANSOM'S HOUSE	145
36	RANSOM WILLIAM	HD	M	58	AG.LAB	SSX	BEXHILL	COCKRELLS SIDLEY	80
12	RANSOM WILLIAM	HD	M	70	CORDWAINER	SSX	BEXHILL	NOT GIVEN	90
57	RANSOM WILLIAM	SO	U	5	SCHOLAR	SSX	BEXHILL	KEWHURST	44
22	RANSOM WILLIAM	SO	U	10		SSX	CROWHURST	RANSOM'S HOUSE	145
31	RANSOM WILLIAM	SV	U	17	WAGGONER	SSX	CATSFIELD	STONE HOUSE FARM	133
38	RANSON JOSEPH	HD	M	40	AG.LAB	SSX	BEXHILL	BEXHILL STREET	28
38	RANSON JOSEPH	SO	U	1		SSX	BEXHILL	BEXHILL STREET	28
38	RANSON MARY	DA	U	8		SSX	BEXHILL	BEXHILL STREET	28
38	RANSON SOPHIA	DA	U	12		SSX	BEXHILL	BEXHILL STREET	28
38	RANSON SOPHIA	WI	M	34		SSX	BEXHILL	BEXHILL STREET	28
38	RANSON WILLIAM	SO	U	5	SCHOLAR	SSX	BEXHILL	BEXHILL STREET	28
51	RAY DAVID	SO	U	24	AG.LAB	SSX	WESTFIELD	RANSOMS	178
46	RAY ELLEN	CO	U	11	SCHOLAR	HAM	SOUTHAMPTON	NO.3 GALLEY HILL	29
55	RAY ESTHER	WI	M	30		SSX	NORTHIAM	BARRACKS	179
55	RAY HENRY	SO	U	3		SSX	WESTFIELD	BARRACKS	179
55	RAY JESSE	HD	M	32	AG.LAB	SSX	WESTFIELD	BARRACKS	179
51	RAY RICHARD	HD	M	56	AG.LAB	SSX	WESTFIELD	RANSOMS	178
59	RAY RICHARD T	HD	U	29	CORDWAINER	SSX	WESTFIELD	BAKEHOUSE	180
51	RAY ROBERT	SO	U	16		SSX	WESTFIELD	RANSOMS	178
51	RAY SAMUEL	SO	U	22		SSX	WESTFIELD	RANSOMS	178
51	RAY SARAH	WI	M	56		SSX	JEVINGTON	RANSOMS	178
55	RAY WILLIAM	SO	U	8		SSX	WESTFIELD	BARRACKS	179
12	RAYINGER? JOSEPH	LG	U	30		LIN		MDKITS?	130
48	RAYMER JOHN	LG	U	33		SSX		RAILWAY HUT	135
70	REED ANSLEY	DA	U	17		SSX	EWHURST	STAPLE CROSS	241
12	REED DAVID	LG	U	17	BRICKLAYER'S LAB	SSX	SEDLESCOMBE	SEDLESCOMBE STREET	202
37	REED EDWARD	HD	M	39	RAILWAY CONTRACTOR	SSX	ALFRISTON	RAILWAY HUT	133
41	REED GEORGE	SO	U	8	SCHOLAR	SSX	SEDLESCOMBE	HAILSFORD	192
38	REED HARRIET JANE	DA	U	6	SCHOLAR	SSX	SEDLESCOMBE	BRICKKILN	192
41	REED MARK	SO	U	2		SSX	SEDLESCOMBE	HAILSFORD	192
70	REED MARY	HD	W	54		SSX	EWHURST	STAPLE CROSS	241
38	REED MARY ANN	DA	U	11	SCHOLAR	SSX	SEDLESCOMBE	BRICKKILN	192
41	REED MERIA	WI	M	40		SSX	EWHURST	HAILSFORD	192
41	REED PHILLIP	SO	U	12	SCHOLAR	SSX	SEDLESCOMBE	HAILSFORD	192
38	REED SAMUEL	HD	M	35	AG.LAB	SSX	EWHURST	BRICKKILN	192
37	REED SAMUEL EDWARD	SO	U	19	RAILWAY LAB	SSX	ALFRISTON	RAILWAY HUT	133
38	REED SARAH	WI	M	34		KEN	HALKHURST (SIC)	BRICKKILN	192
37	REED SARAH	WI	M	41		SSX	ALFRISTON	RAILWAY HUT	133
37	REED SARAH JANE	DA	U	16		SSX	ALFRISTON	RAILWAY HUT	133
38	REED THOMAS	LG	W	76	PARISH RELIEF/PAUPER LAB	SSX	SEDLESCOMBE	BRICKKILN	192
41	REED WILLIAM	HD	M	43	AG.LAB	SSX	SEDLESCOMBE	HAILSFORD	192
37	REED WILLIAM	SO	U	8	SCHOLAR	ESS	KELVEDON	RAILWAY HUT	133
41	REED WILLIAM	SO	U	14	SCHOLAR	SSX	SEDLESCOMBE	HAILSFORD	192
15	REEVES ALFRED	SO	U	11		SSX	HOLLINGTON	MAYFIELDS HOUSE	7
15	REEVES ANN	WI	M	51		SSX	ST.LEONARDS	MAYFIELDS HOUSE	6
79	REEVES CHARLES	BR	U	22	GROCER & DRAPER	SSX	BEXHILL	NOT GIVEN	98
15	REEVES CHARLOTTE	DA	U	26		SSX	HOLLINGTON	MAYFIELDS HOUSE	6

No.	Name	Rel	St	Age	Occupation	County	Birthplace	Address	No.
78	REEVES ELLEN	DA	U	12		SSX	BEXHILL	NOT GIVEN	98
15	REEVES GEORGE	SO	U	16	AG.LAB	SSX	HOLLINGTON	MAYFIELDS HOUSE	7
15	REEVES HANNAH	DA	U	10		SSX	HOLLINGTON	MAYFIELDS HOUSE	7
78	REEVES HENRY	HD	M	56	FARMER 279AC EMP 16	SSX	BEXHILL	NOT GIVEN	98
79	REEVES HENRY	HD	U	31	GROCER & DRAPER	SSX	BEXHILL	NOT GIVEN	98
78	REEVES JANE	DA	U	8		SSX	BEXHILL	NOT GIVEN	98
15	REEVES JOHN	SO	U	18	AG.LAB	SSX	HOLLINGTON	MAYFIELDS HOUSE	7
78	REEVES LUCY	DA	U	17		SSX	BEXHILL	NOT GIVEN	98
78	REEVES LUCY	WI	M	52		SSX	BEXHILL	NOT GIVEN	98
15	REEVES MARY ANN	DA	U	14		SSX	HOLLINGTON	MAYFIELDS HOUSE	7
15	REEVES SARAH ANN	GD	U	1		SSX	HASTINGS	MAYFIELDS HOUSE	7
24	REEVES THOMAS	HD	W	73	FARMER 94 AC EMP 3	SSX	CROWHURST	SAMPSON'S FARM	131
15	REEVES WILLIAM	HD	M	55	AG.LAB	SSX	ST.MARY IN THE CASTLE	MAYFIELDS HOUSE	6
42	RELFE JOHN	HD	M	49	AG.LAB	SSX	EWHURST	OCKHAM	221
42	RELFE SARAH	WI	M	44		SSX	SEDLESCOMBE	OCKHAM	221
22	REYNOLDS JAMES	LG	U	NK30	RAIL LAB	UNKNOWN		RAILWAY HUT	8
31	RICH ALICE	DA	U	33	DRESS MAKER	SSX	EAST HOATHLY	LUNSFORDS LANE SIDLEY	70
31	RICH FRANCIS	HD	M	58	CARPENTER	SSX	EAST HOATHLY	LUNSFORDS LANE SIDLEY	70
31	RICH FREDERICK	SO	U	21	CARPENTER	SSX	EAST HOATHLY	LUNSFORDS LANE SIDLEY	70
31	RICH HARRIET	WI	M	51?		SSX	EAST HOATHLY	LUNSFORDS LANE SIDLEY	70
98	RICH HENRY	HD	M	32	SADLER	SSX	BEXHILL	NOT GIVEN	100
98	RICH HENRY T	SO	U	2		SSX	BEXHILL	NOT GIVEN	100
31	RICH JOHN	SO	U	27	CARPENTER	SSX	EAST HOATHLY	LUNSFORDS LANE SIDLEY	70
100	RICH MARY	WI	M	66		SSX	WINCHELSEA	NOT GIVEN	101
98	RICH MARY A	DA	U	8M		SSX	BEXHILL	NOT GIVEN	100
98	RICH SARAH	WI	M	27		SSX	WESTHAM	NOT GIVEN	100
100	RICH WILLIAM	HD	M	66	RETIRED SADLER	SSX	BEXHILL	NOT GIVEN	101
13	RICHARDS WILLIAM	LG	U	21	RAIL LAB	HAM	YATELY	MAYFIELDS RAILWAY HUT	6
22	RICHARDSON CHARLOTTE	WI	M	55		SSX	SEDLESCOMBE	EDGINGTON	252
22	RICHARDSON ELIZA	DA	U	24		SSX	EWHURST	EDGINGTON	252
22	RICHARDSON ELIZABETH	DA	U	9	SCHOLAR	SSX	EWHURST	EDGINGTON	252
79	RICHARDSON EMMA	WI	M	27		SSX	EWHURST	STAPLE CROSS	243
79	RICHARDSON HENRY	HD	M	30	MILLER	SSX	EWHURST	STAPLE CROSS	243
22	RICHARDSON HESTOR	DA	U	14		SSX	EWHURST	EDGINGTON	252
15	RICHARDSON LOUISA	GS	U	4	VISITOR	KEN	TUNBRIDGE WELLS	HIGH HOUSE	144
22	RICHARDSON THOMAS	HD	M	64	FARMER 84 AC EMP 8	SSX	EWHURST	EDGINGTON	252
22	RICHARDSON WILLIAM	SO	U	22		SSX	EWHURST	EDGINGTON	252
11	RICKES JOHN	LG	U	28		WIL	SWINDON	MADKITS?	129
63	RICKMAN CATHRINE	PP	U	6		SSX	HELLINGLY	BEXHILL STREET	96
33	RIDDLE CAROLINE	DA	U	3		SSX	CATSFIELD	POWDER MILL LANE	110
17	RIDDLE DAVID	LG	U	35	RAIL LAB	SSX	ARUNDLE	RAILWAY HUT	7
33	RIDDLE ELIZABETH	WI	M	31		SSX	HOOE	POWDER MILL LANE	110
33	RIDDLE GEORGE	HD	M	36	AG.LAB	UNKNOWN		POWDER MILL LANE	110
33	RIDDLE GEORGE	SO	U	8	SCHOLAR	SSX	CATSFIELD	POWDER MILL LANE	110
33	RIDDLE MARY A	DA	U	1		SSX	CATSFIELD	POWDER MILL LANE	110
76	RIDDLE MARY ANN	LG	W	62		SSX	BATTLE	STEMPS?	16
77	RINTOUL GRACE	DA	U	8	SCHOLAR	SSX	HOLLINGTON	STEMPS? LODGE	16
77	RINTOUL ISABELLA	WI	M	39		SCOTLAND		STEMPS? LODGE	16
77	RINTOUL JOHN	HD	M	51	LAND STEWARD	SCOTLAND		STEMPS? LODGE	16
77	RINTOUL MARY	DA	U	10	SCHOLAR	SSX	HOLLINGTON	STEMPS? LODGE	16
63	RINTOUL MARY	PP	U	9		SSX	HOLLINGTON	BEXHILL STREET	96
77	RINTOUL WILLIAM	SO	U	5		SSX	HOLLINGTON	STEMPS? LODGE	16
47	ROBERTS ANN	DA	U	2		SSX	BEXHILL	LITTLE COMMON	57
20	ROBERTS CHARLES	SO	U	11M		SSX	GUESTLING	RAILWAY HUT	7
47	ROBERTS EDWARD	HD	M	30	AG.LAB	SSX	BEXHILL	LITTLE COMMON	57
70	ROBERTS EDWARD	HD	M	61	AG.LAB	SSX	BEXHILL	COWDEN GATE (LITTLE COMMON)	46
20	ROBERTS HANNAH	DA	U	2		STS	WOLVERHAMPTON	RAILWAY HUT	7
47	ROBERTS HARRIOT	WI	M	26		SSX	HOOE	LITTLE COMMON	57
47	ROBERTS HENRY	SO	U	7		SSX	BEXHILL	LITTLE COMMON	57
6	ROBERTS JAMES	HD	M	37	FARMER 4 AC	SSX	BEXHILL	PEAR TREES	52
34	ROBERTS JOHN	HD	U	56	AG.LAB	SSX	BEXHILL	COWDEN HOUSE	41
70	ROBERTS MARTHA	WI	M	55		SSX	BEXHILL	COWDEN GATE (LITTLE COMMON)	46
6	ROBERTS MARY	WI	M	40		KEN	STAPLEHURST	PEAR TREES	52
70	ROBERTS MOSES J	SO	U	15	AG.LAB	SSX	BEXHILL	COWDEN GATE (LITTLE COMMON)	46
20	ROBERTS ROBERT	HD	M	36	RAIL LAB	SSX	BEEDING	RAILWAY HUT	7
34	ROBERTS RUTH	SV	U	21	GENERAL SERVANT	SSX	BEXHILL	COWDEN HOUSE	41
20	ROBERTS SARAH	WI	M	26		SRY	CROYDON	RAILWAY HUT	7
47	ROBERTS WALTER	SO	U	7M		SSX	BEXHILL	LITTLE COMMON	57
47	ROBERTS WILLIAM	SO	U	4		SSX	BEXHILL	LITTLE COMMON	57
70	ROBERTS WILLIAM H	SO	U	16	AG.LAB	SSX	BEXHILL	COWDEN GATE (LITTLE COMMON)	46
40	ROBESON JOHN	SO	U	7		ESS	HANAM	RAILWAY HUT	134
40	ROBESON SARAH	DA	U	9		KEN	EDENBRIDGE	RAILWAY HUT	134
34	ROBINSON BENJAMIN	GS	U	9		SSX	HASTINGS	COURT LODGE FARM	147
34	ROBINSON ELLIS	WI	M	37		SSX	UDIMORE	LODGE	176
34	ROBINSON GEORGE	HD	M	40	AG.LAB	KEN	TENTERDEN	LODGE	176
34	ROBINSON GEORGE	SO	U	12		SSX	WESTFIELD	LODGE	176
40	ROBINSON HENRY	LG	U	25		NOT GIVEN (?WESTFIELD)		WORK-HOUSE?	156
34	ROBINSON JANE	DA	U	32		SSX	CATSFIELD	COURT LODGE FARM	147
34	ROBINSON JOHN	SO	U	7		SSX	WESTFIELD	LODGE	176
34	ROBINSON JOSEPH	SO	U	3		SSX	WESTFIELD	LODGE	176
34	ROBINSON LUCY	GD	U	6		MDX	RENSELLIYUN?	COURT LODGE FARM	147
58	ROBINSON LUCY	VR	W	65	HOUSEKEEPER	SSX	WITHYAM	NOT GIVEN	112
69	ROGERS EMMA	DA	U	11M		SSX	BEXHILL	2 BELLENDER COTTAGE	46
69	ROGERS JOHN	HD	M	37	COAST GUARD BOATMAN	COR	ANTONY	2 BELLENDER COTTAGE	46
69	ROGERS JOHN	SO	U	3		SSX	BEXHILL	2 BELLENDER COTTAGE	46
69	ROGERS MARGARET	DA	U	6	SCHOLAR	SSX	BEXHILL	2 BELLENDER COTTAGE	46

	Name	Rel	St	Age	Occupation	Co	Birthplace	Address	No
69	ROGERS MARGARET	WI	M	28		NOR	SHERINGHAM	2 BELLENDER COTTAGE	46
23	ROLFE ANN	DA	U	10		SSX	EWHURST	ODIAM FARM	219
23	ROLFE HESTER	DA	U	25	SERVANT	SSX	SEDLESCOMBE	ODIAM FARM	218
23	ROLFE JANE	GD	U	9		SSX	BATTLE	ODIAM FARM	219
23	ROLFE LUCY	DA	U	13		SSX	EWHURST	ODIAM FARM	218
23	ROLFE MARY	DA	U	18	SERVANT	SSX	EWHURST	ODIAM FARM	218
23	ROLFE MARY	HD	W	52		SSX	MOUNTFIELD	ODIAM FARM	218
23	ROLFE WILLIAM	SO	U	22	AG.LAB	SSX	EWHURST	ODIAM FARM	218
1	ROLLS GEORGE	LG	W	29	RAILWAY LAB	SSX		KNIGHTS	151
1	ROLLS HENRY	LG	U	19	RAILWAY LAB	SSX		KNIGHTS	151
62	ROOTES MARY ANN	/	U	28	SERVANT	SSX	NORTHIAM	EWHURST GREEN	224
51	ROOTS JOHN	SV	U	41	FARM SERVANT	SSX	EWHURST	SPARKS FARM	239
17	ROSE WILLIAM	LG	U	38	RAIL LAB	HAM	LOCKLEY	RAILWAY HUT	7
61	ROUTH HANNAH	WI	M	70		DEV	MAMHEAD*	HURCHINGTON	58
61	ROUTH HANNAH GAIN?	DA	U	37		ESS	EPPING	HURCHINGTON	58
61	ROUTH JOHN	HD	M	84	LANDED/HOUSE PROPRIETOR	YKS	GAYLE	HURCHINGTON	58
61	ROUTH JOHN OSWALD	SO	U	35	VICAR OF HOOE SUSSEX	MDX	HOMERTON	HURCHINGTON	58
*67	ROWLE EMILY	VR	U	19		DURHAM	CACKFIELD	TENT (SCHED.B)	138
2	RUSCOE THOMAS	LG	U	46	RAIL LAB	WALES		RAILWAY HUT	4
13	RUSH ELLEN	DA	U	25		SSX	CROWHURST	PARSONAGE	130
13	RUSH H J REV'D	HD	M	62	CURATE OF CROWHURST	LND		PARSONAGE	130
13	RUSH HENRY JOHN	SO	U	29		SSX	CROWHURST	PARSONAGE	130
13	RUSH JULIA	DA	U	20		SSX	CROWHURST	PARSONAGE	130
13	RUSH MARY ANN	DA	U	30		KEN	SELING	PARSONAGE	130
13	RUSH MARY ANN	WI	M	58		KEN	SELING	PARSONAGE	130
13	RUSH WILLIAM	SO	U	26		SSX	CROWHURST	PARSONAGE	130
35	RUSSELL ALBERT	SO	U	8	SCHOLAR	SSX	CATSFIELD	WATER MILL SIDLEY	80
33	RUSSELL BURTON	SO	U	13	AG.LAB	SSX	BEXHILL	NOT GIVEN	93
45	RUSSELL CAROLINE	WI	M	21		SSX	BEXHILL	NOT GIVEN	43
33	RUSSELL EDWARD	SO	U	15	AG.LAB	SSX	BEXHILL	NOT GIVEN	93
35	RUSSELL ELIZA	DA	U	11	SCHOLAR	SSX	CATSFIELD	WATER MILL SIDLEY	80
35	RUSSELL EMILY	DA	U	5	SCHOLAR	SSX	CATSFIELD	WATER MILL SIDLEY	80
14	RUSSELL EMILY	DA	U	9	SCHOLAR	SSX	SEDLESCOMBE	SEDLESCOMBE STREET	188
33	RUSSELL GEORGE	SO	U	18	AG.LAB	SSX	BEXHILL	NOT GIVEN	93
35	RUSSELL HANNAH	DA	U	25		SSX	CATSFIELD	WATER MILL SIDLEY	80
11	RUSSELL HANNAH	WI	M	33		IRL	CORK WHITEGATE	IN THE LIBERTY	38
27	RUSSELL HENRY B	SO	U	3		SSX	SEDLESCOMBE	LITTLE WORSHAM SIDLEY	79
6	RUSSELL HENRY WILLIAM	SO	U	4		SSX	SEDLESCOMBE	SEDLESCOMBE STREET	202
33	RUSSELL JACOB	HD	W	46	STREET DRIVER	SSX	BEXHILL	NOT GIVEN	93
27	RUSSELL JAMES	HD	M	53	FARMER 300 AC EMP 14	SSX	BEXHILL	LITTLE WORSHAM SIDLEY	78
27	RUSSELL JAMES	SO	U	10	SCHOLAR AT HOME	SSX	BEXHILL	LITTLE WORSHAM SIDLEY	78
45	RUSSELL JANE	DA	U	5		SSX	BATTLE	NOT GIVEN	43
27	RUSSELL JOSIAH	SO	U	6	SCHOLAR AT HOME	SSX	BEXHILL	LITTLE WORSHAM SIDLEY	78
27	RUSSELL MARGARET	DA	U	8	SCHOLAR AT HOME	SSX	BEXHILL	LITTLE WORSHAM SIDLEY	78
35	RUSSELL MARY	WI	M	48		SSX	CATSFIELD	WATER MILL SIDLEY	80
33	RUSSELL MARY ANN	DA	U	7	SCHOLAR	SSX	BEXHILL	NOT GIVEN	93
11	RUSSELL MICHAEL	HD	M	35	COAST GUARD	IRL	CORK WHITEGATE	IN THE LIBERTY	38
6	RUSSELL PHOEBE	WI	M	23		SSX	WESTFIELD	SEDLESCPMBE STREET	202
33	RUSSELL RICHARD	SO	U	21	AG.LAB	SSX	BEXHILL	NOT GIVEN	93
6	RUSSELL ROWLAND	SO	U	1		SSX	SEDLESCOMBE	SEDLESCOMBE STREET	202
35	RUSSELL SAMUEL	HD	M	57	TAILOR	SSX	CATSFIELD	WATER MILL SIDLEY	80
27	RUSSELL SARAH	WI	M	43?		SSX	ASHBURNHAM	LITTLE WORSHAM SIDLEY	78
33	RUSSELL SARAH ANN	DA	U	7	SCHOLAR	SSX	BEXHILL	NOT GIVEN	93
27	RUSSELL SARAH JANE	DA	U	14	SCHOLAR AT HOME	SSX	BEXHILL	LITTLE WORSHAM SIDLEY	78
14	RUSSELL SUSANNAH	WI	M	47		SSX	BREDE	SEDLESCOMBE STREET	188
35	RUSSELL THOMAS	BR	W	66	SHOEMAKER	SSX	CATSFIELD	WATER MILL SIDLEY	80
6	RUSSELL THOMAS	HD	M	28	CARPENTER	SSX	SEDLESCOMBE	SEDLESCOMBE STREET	202
45	RUSSELL THOMAS	HD	M	31	AG.LAB	SSX	HOOE	NOT GIVEN	43
27	RUSSELL THOMAS	SO	U	12	SCHOLAR AT HOME	SSX	BEXHILL	LITTLE WORSHAM SIDLEY	78
14	RUSSELL WILLIAM	HD	M	85	SHOEMAKER	SSX	CATSFIELD	SEDLESCOMBE STREET	188
30	RUSSELL WILLIAM	LG	U	28	RAILWAY CARPENTER	SRY		FORWARD LANE	146
45	RUSSELL WILLIAM	SO	U	3		WAR	SOLIHULL	NOT GIVEN	43
27	RUSSELL WILLIAM P	SO	U	1		SSX	BEXHILL	LITTLE WORSHAM SIDLEY	79
74	RUSSLE HARRIOTT	HD	M	21		SSX	BEXHILL	BRAGS LANE	32
74	RUSSLE JOHN	SO	U	1M		SSX	BEXHILL	BRAGS LANE	32
64	RYDER WILLIAM	HD	U	26	AG.LAB	UNKNOWN		NOT GIVEN	113
13	SAGENT ANN	SV	U	23		SSX	BATTLE	PARSONAGE	130
*67	SAMSON FRANCES	DA	U	4		SSX	CROWHURST	TENT (SCHED.B)	138
*67	SAMSON HENRY	SO	U	7		KEN	TENTERDEN	TENT (SCHED.B)	138
*67	SAMSON JAMES	SO	U	3M		KEN	HAWKHURST	TENT (SCHED.B)	138
*67	SAMSON MARY	HD	M	43	TRAVELLER'S WIFE	SUMBEREY?		TENT (SCHED.B)	137
*67	SAMSON SARAH	DA	U	9	(WHOLE ENTRY CROSSED OUT)	SANDHURST		TENT (SCHED.B)	137
*67	SAMSON WILLIAM	SO	U	11		BACKLEY		TENT (SCHED.B)	137
75	SANDS HANNAH	DA	U	1		SSX	EWHURST	EWHURST GREEN	226
75	SANDS JAMES	SO	U	9	SCHOLAR	SSX	EWHURST	EWHURST GREEN	226
75	SANDS MARTHA	DA	U	4		SSX	EWHURST	EWHURST GREEN	226
75	SANDS MARTHA	WI	M	34		SSX	NORTHIAM	EWHURST GREEN	226
75	SANDS MARY ANNE	DA	U	7	SCHOLAR	SSX	EWHURST	EWHURST GREEN	226
75	SANDS SAMUEL	HD	M	38	AG.LAB	SSX	EWHURST	EWHURST GREEN	226
75	SANDS THOMAS	SO	U	13	AG.LAB	SSX	EWHURST	EWHURST GREEN	226
75	SANDS WILLIAM	SO	U	11	SCHOLAR	SSX	EWHURST	EWHURST GREEN	226
65	SAPARES? CAROLINE	WI	M	32		MDX	CHELSEA	NATIONAL SCHOOL	137
65	SAPARES? LYDIA	DA	U	6		SSX	CROWHURST	NATIONAL SCHOOL	137
65	SAPARES? RICHARD	HD	M	33	SCHOOL MASTER	SSX	WESTERGATE	NATIONAL SCHOOL	137
47	SARGEANT ELIZABETH	DA	U	7		SSX	BEXHILL	COLLINGTON LANE	43
96	SARGEANT HARRIET	DA	M	40		SSX	BEXHILL	NOT GIVEN	100

69

#	Name	Rel	St	Age	Occupation	County	Place	Address	No
1	SARGEANT JAMES	HD	M	73	AG.LAB	SSX	HURSTMONCEUX	GUNTERS	51
39	SARGEANT JOHN	HD	W	47	AG.LAB	SSX	HOLLINGTON	NOT GIVEN	93
47	SARGEANT JOHN	SO	U	6		SSX	BEXHILL	COLLINGTON LANE	43
39	SARGEANT JOHN	SO	U	21	SEAMAN	SSX	BEXHILL	NOT GIVEN	93
47	SARGEANT JOSEPH	HD	M	40	CARRIER	SSX	BEXHILL	COLLINGTON LANE	43
47	SARGEANT JOSEPH	SO	U	9		SSX	BEXHILL	COLLINGTON LANE	43
47	SARGEANT MARY	DA	U	6M		SSX	BEXHILL	COLLINGTON LANE	43
47	SARGEANT MARY	WI	M	33		SSX	BEXHILL	COLLINGTON LANE	43
47	SARGEANT SARAH ANN	DA	U	4		SSX	BEXHILL	COLLINGTON LANE	43
96	SARGEANT WILLIAM	SL	M	37	BRICKLAYER	SSX	HOOE	NOT GIVEN	100
73	SARGENT ALBERT	LG	U	3		SSX	WESTFIELD	PEAR TREE	189
73	SARGENT CAROLINE	LG	U	29		SSX	BATTLE	PEAR TREE	181
1	SARGENT DINAH	WI	M	66		SSX	BEXHILL	GUNTERS	51
70	SARGENT GEORGE	HD	M	56	FARMER 105 AC EMP 2	SSX	NINFIELD	POTMANS	114
1	SARGENT JAMES	SO	U	42	AG.LAB	SSX	BEXHILL	GUNTERS	51
1	SARGENT JOHN	GS	U	25	SHOPMAN TO GROCER	SSX	BEXHILL	GUNTERS	51
73	SARGENT MARTHA	LG	U	2M		SSX	WESTFIELD	PEAR TREE	181
70	SARGENT MARY	WI	M	54		SSX	NINFIELD	POTMANS	114
1	SARGENT THOMAS	HD	W	63	POWDER MAKER	SSX	BATTLE	POWDERMILLS	201
1	SARGENT THOMAS	SO	U	22	AG.LAB	SSX	BATTLE	POWDERMILLS	201
46	SAVAGE CHARLES	SO	U	21	AG.LAB	SSX	BEXHILL	NOT GIVEN	43
46	SAVAGE GEORGE	SO	U	26	AG.LAB	SSX	BEXHILL	NOT GIVEN	43
49	SAVAGE JOHN	HD	M	24	AG.LAB	SSX	BEXHILL	COLLINGTON COTTAGE	43
46	SAVAGE JOHN	LG	W	82	PAUPER AG.LAB	SSX	BEXHILL	NOT GIVEN	43
46	SAVAGE MARY	WI	M	55		SSX	BEXHILL	NOT GIVEN	43
49	SAVAGE MARY A	WI	M	18		SSX	BEXHILL	COLLINGTON COTTAGE	43
46	SAVAGE THOMAS	LG	U	59	GARDENER	SSX	BEXHILL	NOT GIVEN	43
46	SAVAGE WILLIAM	HD	M	51	AG.LAB	SSX	BEXHILL	NOT GIVEN	43
46	SAVAGE WILLIAM	SO	U	23	AG.LAB	SSX	BEXHILL	NOT GIVEN	43
43	SAWYERS MARIAH	WI	M	43		KEN	LYDD	RAILWAY HUT	134
43	SAWYERS MORRIS	HD	M	46	RAILWAY LAB	SSX	ROCKHAM	RAILWAY HUT	134
11	SAXBY ANN	DA	U	7		SSX	CATSFIELD	ADAMS FARM	143
26	SAXBY ANN	DA	U	8	SCHOLAR	SSX	CROWHURST	GREEN STREET	132
17	SAXBY EDWARD	HD	M	57	AG.LAB	SSX	CATSFIELD	BANDY'S FOLLY - SIDLEY	67
50	SAXBY ELIZA	DA	U	6M		SSX	CATSFIELD	NOT GIVEN	112
17	SAXBY ELIZABETH	DA	U	24		SSX	BEXHILL	BANDY'S FOLLY - SIDLEY	67
17	SAXBY ELIZABETH	WI	M	57		SSX	HOOE	BANDYS FOLLY - SIDLEY	67
40	SAXBY ELIZABETH	WI	M	74		SSX	PEASMARSH	NOT GIVEN	111
26	SAXBY FANEY	DA	U	13		SSX	CATSFIELD	GREEN STREET	132
12	SAXBY FRANCES	DA	U	6		SSX	CROWHURST	MADKITS?	130
12	SAXBY FRANCES	WI	M	28		SSX	CATSFIELD	MADKITS?	130
79	SAXBY GEORGE	HD	M	30	AG.LAB	SSX	BEXHILL	NOT GIVEN	32
17	SAXBY HENRY	SO	U	15	AG.LAB	SSX	BEXHILL	BANDY'S FOLLY - SIDLEY	67
41	SAXBY HENRY	SO	U	19	CARPENTER	SSX	CATSFIELD	NOT GIVEN	111
26	SAXBY HENRY	SO	U	20		SSX	CATSFIELD	GREEN STREET	132
41	SAXBY HORACE	SO	U	17	CARPENTER	SSX	CATSFIELD	NOT GIVEN	111
12	SAXBY JAMES	SO	U	10M		SSX	CROWHURST	MADKITS?	130
17	SAXBY JAMES	SO	U	35	AG.LAB	SSX	NINFIELD	BANDY'S FOLLY - SIDLEY	67
26	SAXBY JANE	DA	U	16		SSX	CATSFIELD	GREEN STREET	132
41	SAXBY JANE	WI	M	37		SSX	CATSFIELD	NOT GIVEN	111
41	SAXBY JOHN	HD	M	41	CARPENTER	SSX	CATSFIELD	NOT GIVEN	111
26	SAXBY JOHN	SO	U	11	SCHOLAR	SSX	CATSFIELD	GREEN STREET	132
79	SAXBY MARIA	WI	M	27		SSX	BEXHILL	NOT GIVEN	32
26	SAXBY NAOMI	DA	U	14		SSX	CATSFIELD	GREEN STREET	132
34	SAXBY ROBERT	HD	M	26	AG.LAB	SSX	BEXHILL	WATER MILL SIDLEY	80
50	SAXBY ROBERT	HD	M	30	CARPENTER	SSX	CATSFIELD	NOT GIVEN	111
26	SAXBY SAMUEL	HD	M	50	WOODREIVE	SSX	CATSFIELD	GREEN STREET	132
40	SAXBY SAMUEL	HD	M	73	PARISH RELIEF - CARPENTER	SSX	CATSFIELD	NOT GIVEN	111
12	SAXBY SAMUEL	SO	U	2		SSX	CROWHURST	MADKITS?	130
17	SAXBY SAMUEL	SO	U	17	AG.LAB	SSX	BEXHILL	BANDY'S FOLLY - SIDLEY	67
26	SAXBY SAMUEL	SO	U	18		SSX	CATSFIELD	GREEN STREET	132
12	SAXBY SARAH	DA	U	4		SSX	CROWHURST	MADKITS?	130
34	SAXBY SARAH	WI	M	26		SSX	UDIMORE	WATER MILL SIDLEY	80
50	SAXBY SARAH	WI	M	29		SSX	CATSFIELD	NOT GIVEN	111
26	SAXBY SARAH	WI	M	43		SSX	HOOE	GREEN STREET	132
12	SAXBY STEPHEN	HD	M	28	GAMEKEEPER	SSX	CATSFIELD	MADKITS?	130
12	SAXBY STEPHEN	SO	U	5		SSX	CROWHURST	MADKITS?	130
50	SAXBY THOMAS	SO	U	4		SSX	CATSFIELD	NOT GIVEN	112
50	SAXBY WILLIAM	SO	U	9		SSX	CATSFIELD	NOT GIVEN	112
34	SAYERS ELIZABETH	GD	U	3		KEN	TUNBRIDGE WELLS	NOT GIVEN	55
34	SAYERS JAMES	GS	U	6M		SSX	ST.LEONARDS	NOT GIVEN	55
34	SAYERS LUCY	DA	M	22	RAIL LAB'S WIFE	SSX	BEXHILL	NOT GIVEN	55
69	SCOTCHER ANN	DA	U	2		SSX	BEXHILL	NOT GIVEN	59
69	SCOTCHER EMMA	DA	U	9M		SSX	BEXHILL	NOT GIVEN	59
69	SCOTCHER MARY RHODA	WI	M	28		KEN	HYTHE	NOT GIVEN	59
69	SCOTCHER WILLIAM	HD	M	34	GRINDER FLOUR MILL	SSX	ASHBURNHAM	NOT GIVEN	59
32	SCOTT AMELIA	SV	U	32	COOK	KEN	ROCHESTER	BEXHILL STREET	27
64	SCOTT FANNY	/	U	7	SCHOLAR	SSX	BATTLE	NOT GIVEN	96
64	SCOTT JANE	/	U	8	SCHOLAR	SSX	BATTLE	NOT GIVEN	96
64	SCOTT M A (FEMALE)	/	U	10	SCHOLAR	SSX	BEXHILL	NOT GIVEN	96
60	SCOTT WILLIAM	LG	U	30	RAILWAY LAB	SSX	SELSEY	RAILWAY HUT	136
63	SCRASE EMMA J	PP	U	11		SSX	EAST DEAN	BEXHILL STREET	96
63	SCRASE FANNY	PP	U	10		SSX	EAST DEAN	BEXHILL STREET	96
6	SEARLE MARY	WI	M	26		OXF	CAVERSHAM	NOT GIVEN	143
6	SEARLE WILLIAM	HD	M	30	RAILWAY SUB CONTRACTOR	SRY	ASH	NOT GIVEN	143
5	SELDEN ANN	DA	U	2		SSX	WESTFIELD	SPRAYS	172

Ref	Surname	Name	Code	St	Age	Occupation	County	Parish	Address	Page
88	SELDEN	ANN	DL	M	25		SSX	BATTLE	HAYWARDS	18
37	SELDEN	ANN	WI	M	35		SSX	WESTFIELD	OWLS CASTLE	177
27	SELDEN	ELIZABETH	WI	M	74		SSX	SEDLESCOMBE	SEDLESCOMBE STREET	204
37	SELDEN	GEORGE	SO	U	6		SSX	WESTFIELD	OWLS CASTLE	177
37	SELDEN	HENRY	HD	M	32	AG.LAB	SSX	WESTFIELD	OWLS CASTLE	177
47	SELDEN	HENRY	HD	M	63	AG.LAB	SSX	ORE	WHYBORNES	167
37	SELDEN	HENRY	SO	U	1		SSX	WESTFIELD	OWLS CASTLE	177
20	SELDEN	HENRY	SO	U	8		SSX	WESTFIELD	LOW COTTAGE	153
18	SELDEN	ISAAC	SV	U	16		SSX	WESTFIELD	WOODHOUSE	174
28	SELDEN	JAMES	HD	M	27	AG.LAB	SSX	WESTFIELD	KENT STREET	165
47	SELDEN	JOHN	SO	U	25		SSX	WESTFIELD	WHYBORNES	167
20	SELDEN	MARY	HD	M	37	LAUNDRESS	KEN	BETHERDEN	LOW COTTAGE	153
88	SELDEN	MARY A	6D	U	5W		SSX	WESTFIELD	HAYWARDS	18
37	SELDEN	MARYANN	DA	U	3		SSX	WESTFIELD	OWLS CASTLE	177
28	SELDEN	MATILDA	WI	M	26		SSX	PETT	KENT STREET	165
88	SELDEN	PHILADELPHIA	6D	U	2		SSX	WESTFIELD	HAYWARDS	18
47	SELDEN	PHILADELPHIA	WI	M	61		SSX	SEDLESCOMBE	WHYBORNES	167
88	SELDEN	SARAH	HD	W	70		SSX	WESTFIELD	HAYWARDS	18
5	SELDEN	SARAH	WI	M	23		SSX	PETT	SPRAYS	172
5	SELDEN	STEPHEN	HD	M	30	AG.LAB	SSX	PETT	SPRAYS	172
88	SELDEN	THOMAS	SO	M	27	AG.LAB	SSX	WESTFIELD	HAYWARDS	18
27	SELDEN	WILLIAM	HD	M	75	AG.LAB	SSX	WESTFIELD	SEDLESCOMBE STREET	204
3	SELDEN	WILLIAM	SV	U	40	AG.LAB	SSX	WESTFIELD	DOLEHAM	152
17	SELLENS	ALFRED	SO	U	21		SSX	CROWHURST	HILL FARM	144
18	SELLENS	CARLINE	WI	M	22		SSX	CROWHURST	CROWHURST VILLAGE	131
41	SELLENS	CHARLOTTE	WI	M	33		SSX	SEDLESCOMBE	SWALES GREEN	206
17	SELLENS	EDMUND	SO	U	24		SSX	CROWHURST	HILL FARM	144
17	SELLENS	ELIZA	DA	U	17		SSX	CROWHURST	HILL FARM	144
3	SELLENS	ELIZABETH	WI	M	30		SSX	WESTFIELD	SEDLESCOMBE STREET	186
30	SELLENS	ELLEN	DA	U	5		SSX	BEXHILL	LUNSFORDS CROSS HSE SIDLEY	70
18	SELLENS	FREDERICK	SO	U	13		SSX	WESTFIELD	WOODHOUSE	174
18	SELLENS	GEORGE	HD	M	27	CORDWAINER	SSX	SEDLESCOMBE	CROWHURST VILLAGE	131
3	SELLENS	GEORGE	SO	U	3		SSX	SEDLESCOMBE	SEDLESCOMBE STREET	186
30	SELLENS	JAMES	SO	U	1		SSX	BEXHILL	LUNSFORDS CROSS HSE SIDLEY	70
18	SELLENS	JAMES	SO	U	17		SSX	WESTFIELD	WOODHOUSE	174
3	SELLENS	JANE	DA	U	1		SSX	SEDLESCOMBE	SEDLESCOMBE STREET	186
18	SELLENS	JANE	DA	U	11		SSX	WESTFIELD	WOODHOUSE	174
41	SELLENS	JANE	DA	U	11	SCHOLAR	SSX	SEDLESCOMBE	SWALES GREEN	206
17	SELLENS	JOHN	HD	M	63	FARMER 270 AC EMP 2	SSX	SEDLESCOMBE	HILL FARM	144
17	SELLENS	JOHN	SO	U	31		SSX	CROWHURST	CROWHURST VILLAGE	131
18	SELLENS	LOUISA	DA	U	2?		SSX	EWHURST	HILL FARM	144
49	SELLENS	MARTHA	SV	U	14	GEN SERVANT	SSX	CROWHURST	HILL FARM	144
17	SELLENS	MARY	WI	M	60		SSX	WESTFIELD	SWALES GREEN	207
17	SELLENS	MARY ANN	DA	U	19		SSX	CROWHURST	HILL FARM	144
41	SELLENS	MARYANN	DA	U	8	SCHOLAR	SSX	CROWHURST	HILL FARM	144
18	SELLENS	PHILADELPHIA	DA	U	21		SSX	SEDLESCOMBE	SWALES GREEN	206
18	SELLENS	PHILADELPHIA	WI	M	50		SSX	WESTFIELD	WOODHOUSE	174
67	SELLENS	ROBERT	LG	U	65	RETIRED FARMER	SSX	WHATLINGTON	WOODHOUSE	174
41	SELLENS	SARAH	DA	U	7		SSX	SEDLESCOMBE	MOUNT PLEASANT	197
52	SELLENS	SARAH	SV	U	19	HOUSE SERVANT	SSX	SEDLESCOMBE	SWALES GREEN	206
30	SELLENS	SARAH	WI	M	24		SSX	WHATLINGTON	GREAT SANDERS	194
73	SELLENS	STEPHEN	HD	M	37	AG.LAB	SSX	NINFIELD	LUNSFORDS CROSS HSE SIDLEY	70
18	SELLENS	SUSAN	DA	U	7		SSX	WESTFIELD	PEAR TREE	181
73	SELLENS	SUSAN	WI	M	33		SSX	WESTFIELD	WOODHOUSE	174
3	SELLENS	THOMAS	HD	M	32	AG.LAB	SSX	BATTLE	PEAR TREE	181
30	SELLENS	THOMAS	HD	M	37	FARMER 100 AC EMP 1	SSX	SEDLESCOMBE	SEDLESCOMBE STREET	186
18	SELLENS	THOMAS	HD	M	55	FARMER 72 AC 1 LAB	SSX	CROWHURST	LUNSFORDS CROSS HSE SIDLEY	70
3	SELLENS	THOMAS	SO	U	5	SCHOLAR	SSX	WESTFIELD	WOODHOUSE	174
18	SELLENS	THOMAS	SO	U	23	MILLER	SSX	SEDLESCOMBE	SEDLESCOMBE STREET	186
41	SELLENS	WALTER	HD	M	34	AG.LAB	SSX	SEDLESCOMBE	WOODHOUSE	174
41	SELLENS	WALTER	SO	U	3		SSX	SEDLESCOMBE	SWALES GREEN	206
13	SELLENS	WILLIAM	SO	U	26	GROCER'S SHOPMAN	SSX	SEDLESCOMBE	SWALES GREEN	206
23	SELLMAN	GEORGE	SV	U	23	GROOM & GARDENER	SSX	CROWHURST	SEDLESCOMBE STREET	188
25	SELLMAN	JAMES	SO	U	17	AG.LAB	SSX	EWHURST	LORDINE	235
25	SELLMAN	LEONORA FRANCES	WI	M	41		SSX	EWHURST	LORDINE FARM	235
25	SELLMAN	MARY	DA	U	13	SCHOLAR	SSX	EWHURST	LORDINE FARM	235
73	SELLMAN	MARY ANN	SV	U	14	SERVANT	SSX	EWHURST	LORDINE FARM	235
25	SELLMAN	MOSES	SO	U	20	AG.LAB	SSX	EWHURST	STAPLE CROSS	242
72	SELLMAN	STEPHEN	6S	U	5W		SSX	EWHURST	LORDINE FARM	235
25	SELLMAN	STEPHEN	HD	M	50	AG.LAB	SSX	EWHURST	EWHURST GREEN	226
24	SELLMAN	WILLIAM	LG	U	27	AG.LAB	SSX	EWHURST	LORDINE FARM	235
39	SELMAN	JAMES	SO	U	7	SCHOLAR	SSX	EWHURST	LORDINE FARM	235
39	SELMAN	JOHN	SO	U	10	SCHOLAR	SSX	EWHURST	FORGE LANE	254
39	SELMAN	MATILDA	WI	M	39		SSX	EWHURST	FORGE LANE	254
18	SELMAN	OBEDIAH	LG	U	22	AG.LAB	SSX	EWHURST	FORGE LANE	254
39	SELMAN	THOMAS	HD	M	39	AG.LAB	SSX	EWHURST	CATTS GREEN	251
39	SELMAN	WILLIAM	SO	U	18	AG.LAB	SSX	EWHURST	FORGE LANE	254
76	SELMAN?	STEPHEN	LG	U	29	AG.LAB	SSX	EWHURST	FORGE LANE	254
43	SELMES	ANN	DA	U	45		SSX	EWHURST	STAPLE CROSS	242
5	SELMES	ANN	WI	M	45		SSX	WESTFIELD	IRELAND	167
48	SELMES	CHARLOTTE	WI	M	47		HAM	ELING	WHEEL	162
39	SELMES	CORDELIA	DA	U	18		SSX	HASTINGS	HOLLY COTTAGE	167
39	SELMES	EDWIN	SO	U	13		SSX	WESTFIELD	PIG HILL	166
43	SELMES	EDWIN	SO	U	39		SSX	WESTFIELD	PIG HILL	166
43	SELMES	ELIZA	DA	U	41		SSX	WESTFIELD	IRELAND	167
36	SELMES	ELIZA	SV	U	13	HOUSE SERVANT	SSX	WHATLINGTON	HERST	191

	Name			Age	Occupation	County	Place	Address	No.
5	SELMES ELIZA F	DA	U	8	SCHOLAR	SSX	WESTFIELD	WHEEL	162
5	SELMES ELIZABETH A	DA	U	19		SSX	WESTFIELD	WHEEL	162
5	SELMES HARRIETT	DA	U	17		SSX	WESTFIELD	WHEEL	162
43	SELMES HARRIETT	DA	U	36		SSX	WESTFIELD	IRELAND	167
43	SELMES JAMES	HD	W	76	FARMER	SSX	WESTFIELD	IRELAND	167
5	SELMES JAMES F	SO	U	13	SCHOLAR	SSX	WESTFIELD	WHEEL	162
5	SELMES JMES	HD	M	43	GROCER	SSX	WESTFIELD	WHEEL	162
5	SELMES LOUISA	DA	U	15		SSX	WESTFIELD	WHEEL	162
39	SELMES PHILADELPHIA M	DA	U	1		SSX	WESTFIELD	PIG HILL	166
39	SELMES SARAH	WI	M	56		SSX	BATTLE	PIG HILL	166
9	SELMES SPENCER	SV	U	27		SSX	BREDE	WIDOWS	173
48	SELMES STEPHEN	HD	M	51	PROPRIETOR OF HOUSES	SSX	WESTFIELD	HOLLY COTTAGE	167
39	SELMES THOMAS	HD	M	59	AG.LAB	SSX	BECKLEY	PIG HILL	166
5	SELMES TILDEN R	SO	U	11	SCHOLAR	SSX	WESTFIELD	WHEEL	162
39	SELMES WILLIAM	SO	U	29		SSX	WESTFIELD	PIG HILL	166
62	SHANFIELD? MARY	/	M	35	HOUSEKEEPER	SSX	BEXHILL	NOT GIVEN	58
58	SHARP ANN	HD	W	79	PAUPER	SSX	CATSFIELD	NOT GIVEN	95
32	SHARP ANN	WI	M	27		LEI	LUTTERWORTH	RAILWAY HUT	146
21	SHARP CAROLINE	WI	M	29		SSX	CATSFIELD	WATER MILL HOUSE	145
77	SHARP ELIZABETH	WI	M	53		SSX	HOOE	BEXHILL DOWN	32
20	SHARP ELIZABETH	WI	M	72		SSX	HOLLINGTON	WATER MILL HOUSE	145
37	SHARP HANNAH	SV	U	30	HOUSEMAID	SSX	BEXHILL	BEXHILL STREET	27
21	SHARP JAMES	SO	U	1		SSX	CROWHURST	WATER MILL HOUSE	145
32	SHARP JOHN	HD	M	26	RAILWAY LAB	LEI	LUTTERWORTH	RAILWAY HUT	146
23	SHARP LUCY	SV	U	24*	NURSEMAID AGE ?14	SSX	BEXHILL	BEXHILL STREET	26
32	SHARP MARY ANN	DA	U	11M		LEI	LUTTERWORTH	RAILWAY HUT	146
77	SHARP RICHARD	HD	M	55	AG.LAB	SSX	BEXHILL	BEXHILL DOWN	32
77	SHARP RICHARD	SO	U	28	AG.LAB	SSX	BEXHILL	BEXHILL DOWN	32
32	SHARP SAMUEL	SO	U	4		LEI	LUTTERWORTH	RAILWAY HUT	146
21	SHARP THOMAS	SO	U	6		SSX	CROWHURST	WATER MILL HOUSE	145
21	SHARP THOMAS JNR	HD	M	35	FARM LAB	SSX	CROWHURST	WATER MILL HOUSE	145
20	SHARP THOMAS SNR	HD	M	69	FARMER 15 1/2 AC EMP 2	SSX	BEXHILL	WATER MILL HOUSE	145
21	SHARP WILLIAM	SO	U	3		SSX	CROWHURST	WATER MILL HOUSE	145
30	SHARPE ANN	DA	U	9		SSX	BEXHILL	ACTONS SIDLEY	79
30	SHARPE EDWARD	SO	U	7		SSX	BEXHILL	ACTONS SIDLEY	79
30	SHARPE JOSEPH	HD	M	43	AG.LAB	SSX	BEXHILL	ACTONS SIDLEY	79
30	SHARPE JOSEPH	SO	U	1		SSX	BEXHILL	ACTONS SIDLEY	79
30	SHARPE LUCY	WI	M	42		KEN	TENTERDEN	ACTONS SIDLEY	79
34	SHARPLES ELLICE	WI	M	25		LEI		LEMS	156
34	SHARPLES GEORGE	HD	M	28	RAIL LAB	LEI		LEMS	156
34	SHARPLES WILLIAM	SO	U	11M		NOT GIVEN (?LEI)		LEMS	156
14	SHAW ANN	HD	M	49	LODGING HOUSE KEEPER	KEN	MARGATE	BELL HILL	25
14	SHEARWOOD HENRY	LG	U	33	RAILWAY LAB	SRY		NOT GIVEN	130
14	SHEARWOOD JAMES	LG	U	24	RAILWAY LAB	SRY		NOT GIVEN	130
7	SHEATHER ALBERT	SO	U	1		SSX	CATSFIELD	NOT GIVEN	107
68	SHEATHER ANN	DA	U	20	DRESSMAKER	SSX	CATSFIELD	SIDLEY GREEN	84
15	SHEATHER CAROLINE	SV	U	12	NURSE	SSX	CATSFIELD	CATSFIELD PLACE FARM	108
7	SHEATHER CHARLOTTE	WI	M	26		SSX	SEDLESCOMBE	NOT GIVEN	107
7	SHEATHER ELIZA	DA	U	4		SSX	CATSFIELD	NOT GIVEN	107
9	SHEATHER ELLEN	GD	U	8		SSX	CATSFIELD	NOT GIVEN	107
68	SHEATHER EMILY	DA	U	18		SSX	CATSFIELD	SIDLEY GREEN	84
9	SHEATHER EMILY	GD	U	4		SSX	CATSFIELD	NOT GIVEN	107
9	SHEATHER FRANCES	DA	U	32		SSX	CATSFIELD	NOT GIVEN	107
7	SHEATHER FRANCES	HD	M	30	AG.LAB	SSX	CATSFIELD	NOT GIVEN	107
7	SHEATHER FRANK	SO	U	3		SSX	CATSFIELD	NOT GIVEN	107
68	SHEATHER HENRY	HD	M	41	POLICEMAN	SSX	CATSFIELD	SIDLEY GREEN	84
9	SHEATHER HENRY	HD	M	72	AG.LAB	SSX	NINFIELD	NOT GIVEN	107
68	SHEATHER HENRY	SO	U	16	BLACKSMITH'S AP	SSX	CATSFIELD	SIDLEY GREEN	84
27	SHEATHER JANE	SV	U	19	HOUSE SERVANT	SSX	NINFIELD	LITTLE WORSHAM SIDLEY	79
9	SHEATHER JANE	WI	M	71		SSX	CATSFIELD	NOT GIVEN	107
68	SHEATHER SARAH	WI	M	50		SSX	BATTLE	SIDLEY GREEN	84
59	SHEATHER THOMAS	SV	U	16	AG.LAB	SSX	CATSFIELD	NOT GIVEN	113
1	SHEATHER WILLIAM	SO	U	25	GENERAL SERVANT	SSX	CATSFIELD	CATSFIELD GREEN	119
9	SHEATHER/SHA-HATHER* ELIZ'TH	SV	U	12	HOUSEMAID	LONDON		PARK LANE	120
19	SHELTON ANN	VR	W	44		NOT GIVEN		SEDLESCOMBE STREET	188
26	SHEPPARD CHARLES	SO	U	5	SCHOLAR	KEN	MINSTER THANET	53 MARTELLO TOWER IN LIBERTY	40
26	SHEPPARD EDWARD T	SO	U	3		KEN	MINSTER THANET	53 MARTELLO TOWER IN LIBERTY	40
26	SHEPPARD FREDERICK J	SO	U	1		SSX	BEXHILL	53 MARTELLO TOWER IN LIBERTY	40
26	SHEPPARD GEORGE	SO	U	11	SCHOLAR	KEN	BIRCHINGTON	53 MARTELLO TOWER IN LIBERTY	40
26	SHEPPARD MARY	WI	M	31		KEN	WALMER	53 MARTELLO TOWER IN LIBERTY	40
26	SHEPPARD RICHARD	SO	U	9	SCHOLAR	KEN	BIRCHINGTON	53 MARTELLO TOWER IN LIBERTY	40
26	SHEPPARD SUSANNAH E	DA	U	7	SCHOLAR	KEN	BIRCHINGTON	53 MARTELLO TOWER IN LIBERTY	40
26	SHEPPARD WILLIAM	HD	M	42	COAST GUARD COM.BOATMAN	HAM	PORTSMOUTH	53 MARTELLO TOWER IN LIBERTY	40
3	SHERING RICHARD	LG	U	23	BRICKMAKER	HORSHAM		FORWARD LANE	128
44	SHERLEY WILLIAM	LG	W	40	RAILWAY LAB	SSX	BOLNEY	RAILWAY HUT	134
25	SHINGLETON JAMES	LG	U	29	RAIL LAB	SSX	HEATHFIELD	QUEENS HEAD SEDLESCOMBE ST	189
56	SHOESMITH ALFRED	SO	U	9	SCHOLAR	SSX	BEXHILL	ALMS HOUSE SIDLEY	83
106	SHOESMITH ANN	DA	U	14		SSX	BEXHILL	NOT GIVEN	101
32	SHOESMITH ANN	SV	U	17	HOUSEMAID	SSX	BEXHILL	BEXHILL STREET	27
106	SHOESMITH ANN	WI	M	52		SSX	BEXHILL	NOT GIVEN	101
25	SHOESMITH C (FEMALE)	CL	U	13		SSX	BEXHILL	NOT GIVEN	92
1	SHOESMITH CAROLINE	DA	U	1		SSX	BEXHILL	HOLYERS HILL	89
26	SHOESMITH CAROLINE	SV	U	21	HOUSE MAID	SSX	BEXHILL	BEXHILL STREET	26
56	SHOESMITH CHARLES	SO	U	15		SSX	BEXHILL	ALMS HOUSE SIDLEY	83
1	SHOESMITH CHARLOTTE	DA	U	2		SSX	BEXHILL	HOLYERS HILL	89
1	SHOESMITH CHARLOTTE	WI	M	30?		SSX	CROWHURST	HOLYERS HILL	89

19	SHOESMITH DAVID	SO U	12	AG.LAB	SSX BEXHILL	NOT GIVEN	91
1	SHOESMITH ELIZABETH	DA U	4	SCHOLAR	SSX BEXHILL	HOLYERS HILL	89
105	SHOESMITH EMILY	SV U	18		SSX BEXHILL	ROSE COTTAGE	101
25	SHOESMITH EMMA	DA U	8M		SSX BEXHILL	NOT GIVEN	92
60	SHOESMITH GEORGE	HD M	25	GARDENER	SSX BEXHILL	NOT GIVEN	95
4	SHOESMITH GEORGE	HD M	60	AG.LAB	SSX BEXHILL	GUNSES?	51
60	SHOESMITH GEORGE	SO U	1		SSX BEXHILL	NOT GIVEN	95
56	SHOESMITH GEORGE	SO U	6		SSX BEXHILL	ALMS HOUSE SIDLEY	83
19	SHOESMITH GEORGE	SO U	12	AG.LAB	SSX BEXHILL	NOT GIVEN	91
38	SHOESMITH HARRIET	WI M	41		SSX BEXHILL	SIDLEY	71
60	SHOESMITH HARRIETT	WI M	25		SSX BEXHILL	NOT GIVEN	95
25	SHOESMITH JAMES	SO U	2		SSX BEXHILL	NOT GIVEN	92
106	SHOESMITH JOHN	HD M	48	GARDENER	SSX BEXHILL	NOT GIVEN	101
1	SHOESMITH JOSEPH	HD M	43	AG.LAB	SSX BEXHILL	HOLYERS HILL	89
56	SHOESMITH JUDITH	WI M	48		SSX BEXHILL	ALMS HOUSE SIDLEY	83
106	SHOESMITH LOUIS	SO U	10		SSX BEXHILL	NOT GIVEN	101
25	SHOESMITH M (FEMALE)	CL U	28	SERVANT	SSX BEXHILL	NOT GIVEN	92
19	SHOESMITH MARIA	WI M	50		SSX FAIRLIGHT	NOT GIVEN	91
107	SHOESMITH MARY	WI M	61		SSX WHATLINGTON	NOT GIVEN	101
5	SHOESMITH SARAH	DA M	34		SSX EWHURST	MILISES	250
1	SHOESMITH SARAH	DA U	7	SCHOLAR	SSX BEXHILL	HOLYERS HILL	89
4	SHOESMITH SARAH	WI M	55		SSX BEXHILL	GUNSES?	51
19	SHOESMITH STEPHEN	HD M	61	AG.LAB	SSX BEXHILL	NOT GIVEN	91
19	SHOESMITH STEPHEN	SO U	8	SCHOLAR	SSX BEXHILL	NOT GIVEN	91
56	SHOESMITH THOMAS	HD M	50	AG.LAB	SSX BEXHILL	ALMS HOUSE SIDLEY	83
107	SHOESMITH THOMAS	HD M	65	PAUPER	SSX BEXHILL	NOT GIVEN	101
56	SHOESMITH THOMAS	SO U	4		SSX BEXHILL	ALMS HOUSE SIDLEY	83
38	SHOESMITH WILLIAM	HD M	43	PENSIONER ARMY	SSX BEXHILL	SIDLEY	71
1	SHOESMITH WILLIAM	SO U	5	SCHOLAR	SSX BEXHILL	HOLYERS HILL	89
56	SHOESMITH WILLIAM	SO U	6		SSX BEXHILL	ALMS HOUSE SIDLEY	83
19	SHOESMITH WILLIAM	SO U	6	SCHOLAR	SSX BEXHILL	NOT GIVEN	91
60	SHOOSMITH ANN	GM W	90	PAUPER AG.LAB'S WIFE	SSX HOLLINGTON	BIRCHINGTON	45
72	SHOOSMITH HARRIETT	WI M	57		SSX CATSFIELD	NOT GIVEN (LITTLE COMMON)	46
3	SHOOSMITH WALTER	SV U	25	AG.LAB	SSX BEXHILL	BARNHORN HILL	37
72	SHOOSMITH WILLIAM	HD M	52	AG.LAB	SSX BEXHILL	NOT GIVEN (LITTLE COMMON)	46
50	SIBSON ANN	WI M	55?		CUM BOWNESS	GALLEY HILL	29
50	SIBSON JOSEPH	HD M	56	COAST GUARD	CUM KIRKBRIDE*	GALLEY HILL	29
50	SIBSON JOSEPH	SO U	29	GREENWICH PENSIONER	CUM BOLNESS (SIC)	GALLEY HILL	29
50	SIBSON MARY J	DA U	18		SSX BEXHILL	GALLEY HILL	29
17	SIDDERS HENRY	LG M	54	BLACKSMITH	KEN MARGATE	BELL VILLA	153
59	SILHICK KETURAH	DA U	11		SOM DODINGTON	NOT GIVEN	113
59	SILHICK MARY	WI M	37		DEV HONITON	NOT GIVEN	112
59	SILHICK THOMAS	HD M	46	AGENT & FARMER 367 AC EMP9	SOM DODINGTON	NOT GIVEN	112
59	SILHICK TOMAZINE -?	DA U	6	SCHOLAR	SOM DODINGTON	NOT GIVEN	113
42	SIMES ANNA	CI U	40	VISITOR	SSX PEASMARSH	STONE HOUSE	167
15	SIMES ASHTON	SO U	1		SSX CATSFIELD	CATSFIELD PLACE FARM	108
55	SIMES AUGUSTA	DA U	4		SSX SEDLESCOMBE	HANCOX FARM	209
55	SIMES CAROLINE	WI M	36		SSX HASTINGS	HANCOX FARM	209
55	SIMES CAROLINE M	DA U	2		SSX SEDLESCOMBE	HANCOX FARM	209
38	SIMES CHARLOTTE	CI M	40		SSX HOLLINGTON	NOT GIVEN	111
6	SIMES CLARA	DA U	8		SSX SALEHURST	STOCKLANDS	250
42	SIMES ELIZABETH	DA U	4		SSX WESTFIELD	STONE HOUSE	167
15	SIMES ELIZABETH A	DA U	4		SSX CATSFIELD	CATSFIELD PLACE FARM	108
15	SIMES ERNEST?	SO U	2		SSX CATSFIELD	CATSFIELD PLACE FARM	108
42	SIMES FRANCES	DA U	9		SSX ST.CLEMENT	STONE HOUSE	167
55	SIMES FREDERICK	SO U	1		SSX SEDLESCOMBE	HANCOX FARM	209
65	SIMES G J (MALE)	PP U	5	PUPIL	SSX CATSFIELD	NOT GIVEN	96
52	SIMES HANNAH	VR U	35	FARMER'S DAUGHTER	SSX WHATLINGTON	GREAT SANDERS	194
42	SIMES HANNAH	WI M	43		YKS MARR	STONE HOUSE	167
42	SIMES HENRY	HD M	42	GAME KEEPER	SSX PEASMARSH	STONE HOUSE	167
6	SIMES HENRY	HD M	47	RETIRED FARMER	SSX WHATLINGTON	STOCKLANDS	250
42	SIMES HENRY	SO U	6		SSX WESTFIELD	STONE HOUSE	167
52	SIMES HORACE	VR U	30	FARMER	SSX WHATLINGTON	GREAT SANDERS	194
63	SIMES JANE	SV U	19		SSX BATTLE	BEXHILL STREET	96
6	SIMES JANE CATHERINE	WI M	38		DOR CHARMINSTER	STOCKLANDS	250
55	SIMES JOHN	HD M	48	FARMER 304 AC EMP 16	SSX WHATLINGTON	HANCOX FARM	209
15	SIMES JOSHUA	HD M	42	FARMER 400 AC EMP 12	SSX WHATLINGTON	CATSFIELD PLACE FARM	108
15	SIMES MARY ANN	WI M	28		SSX FRANT	CTASFIELD PLACE FARM	108
62	SIMMONDS EDWARD	HD M	46	AG.LAB	KEN TENTERDEN	LANES END	30
16	SIMMONDS GEORGE	SO U	5	DUMB	SSX EWHURST	GREAT WORSHAM SIDLEY	77
16	SIMMONDS SARAH	WI M	40		SSX BEXHILL	GREAT WORSHAM SIDLEY	77
16	SIMMONDS WILLIAM	HD M	38	AG.LAB	KEN TENTERDEN	GREAT WORSHAM SIDLEY	77
16	SIMMONDS WILLIAM	SO U	12		SSX BEXHILL	GREAT WORSHAM SIDLEY	77
64	SIMONS CHARLES	LG U	23	RAILWAY LAB	IRL	RAILWAY HUT	137
95	SIMPSON A B (MALE)	SO U	23	B A CAMBRIDGE	MDX EALING	VICARAGE	100
95	SIMPSON ADELAID	DA U	20		ST.GEO HANOVER SQUARE	VICARAGE	100
95	SIMPSON ELLA M	DA U	17		MDX EALING	VICARAGE	100
95	SIMPSON H G (MALE)	SO U	27	LIENT R N	MDX EALING	VICARAGE	100
95	SIMPSON HENRY W	HD W	58	VICAR OF BEXHILL	LND ST.D CONNISIERN?*	VICARAGE	100
66	SINDEN ALBERT	HD M	23	BLACKSMITH MASTER EMP 1MAN	SSX BEXHILL	MOUNT PLEASANT	197
71	SINDEN CORDELIA	WI M	47		SSX BEXHILL	WOODS FARM SIDLEY	84
75	SINDEN EDMUND	AP U	19	GROCER & DRAPER AP	SSX BEXHILL	NOT GIVEN	98
32	SINDEN EDWARD	HD M	64	AG.LAB	SSX CATSFIELD	NOT GIVEN	110
31	SINDEN EMILY	DA U	3		SSX CATSFIELD	NOT GIVEN	110
48	SINDEN HANNAH	HD U	50	CHARWOMAN	SSX BEXHILL	NOT GIVEN	94
14	SINDEN HENRY	SO U	4		SSX BEXHILL	SIDLEY	67

	Name			Occupation	Birthplace	Address	
71	SINDEN HENRY	SO U	6	SCHOLAR	SSX BEXHILL	WOODS FARM SIDLEY	85
11	SINDEN JAMES	HD W	79	AG.LAB	SSX CATSFIELD	NOT GIVEN	107
71	SINDEN JAMES	SO U	4		SSX BEXHILL	WOODS FARM SIDLEY	85
14	SINDEN JAMES	SO U	6?	SCHOLAR	SSX BEXHILL	SIDLEY	67
14	SINDEN JANE	WI M	33		SSX BEXHILL	SIDLEY	67
3	SINDEN JESSE	HD M	42	AG.LAB	SSX CATSFIELD	CATSFIELD GREEN	120
71	SINDEN JOHN	HD M	51	BLACKSMITH/FARMER 38 AC	SSX BEXHILL	WOODS FARM SIDLEY	84
13	SINDEN JOSEPH	HD M	71	BLACKSMITH	SSX CATSFIELD	STEVEN'S CROUCH	121
3	SINDEN MARGARET	DA U	18		SSX CATSFIELD	CATSFIELD GREEN	120
108	SINDEN MARIA	HD W	66	ANNUITANT	SSX WARBLETON	NOT GIVEN	101
3	SINDEN MARTHA	WI M	43		SSX WESTFIELD	CATSFIELD GREEN	120
32	SINDEN MARY	WI M	67		SSX CATSFIELD	NOT GIVEN	110
13	SINDEN MARY	WI M	67		SSX DALLINGTON	STEVEN'S CROUCH	121
14	SINDEN MARY A	DA U	9	SCHOLAR	SSX BEXHILL	SIDLEY	67
66	SINDEN PHILLY	WI M	18		SSX BREDE	MOUNT PLEASANT	197
14	SINDEN SAMUEL	SO U	11		SSX HERSTMONCEUX	SIDLEY	67
14	SINDEN SARAH	DA U	13		SSX BEXHILL	SIDLEY	67
48	SINDEN SARAH ANN	DA U	18	SERVANT	SSX BEXHILL	NOT GIVEN	94
26	SINDEN SARAH E	SV U	26	LADIES MAID	SSX BEXHILL	BEXHILL STREET	26
13	SINDEN SOLOMON	/ U	15	GROCER'S SHOPBOY AP	SSX BEXHILL	SEDLESCOMBE STREET	188
71	SINDEN STEPHEN	SO U	8	SCHOLAR	SSX BEXHILL	WOODS FARM SIDLEY	84
31	SINDEN SUSANNAH	WI M	38		SSX CROWHURST	NOT GIVEN	110
9	SINDEN THOMAS	L6 U	41		SSX SEDLESCOMBE	SEDLESCOMBE STREET	202
14	SINDEN THOMAS	SO U	6W		SSX BEXHILL	SIDLEY	67
31	SINDEN WILLIAM	HD M	32	AG.LAB	SSX CATSFIELD	NOT GIVEN	110
14	SINDEN WILLIAM	HD M	51	PAUPER AG.LAB	KEN BETHERSDEN	SIDLEY	67
31	SINDEN WILLIAM	HD U	57	FARMER 28 ACRES EMP 3 LAB	SSX BEXHILL	BEXHILL STREET	27
31	SINDEN WILLIAM	SO U	1		SSX CATSFIELD	NOT GIVEN	110
71	SINDEN WILLIAM	SO U	14		SSX BEXHILL	WOODS FARM SIDLEY	84
14	SINDEN WILLIAM	SO U	15		SSX BEXHILL	SIDLEY	67
8	SINGER JOHN	HD M	29	RAIL LAB	BKM IVER	RAILWAY HUT	5
8	SINGER MARIA	WI M	44		KEN INKSEL	RAILWAY HUT	5
42	SINHOCK?* GEORGE	VR W	66	AG.LAB	SSX BATTLE	NOT GIVEN	111
15	SINNOCK JAMES W	SO U	17	CORDWAINER	SSX WESTFIELD	GATE HOUSE	174
15	SINNOCK MARY	WI M	53		SSX HAMSY	GATE HOUSE	174
15	SINNOCK SAMUEL	HD M	57	CORDWAINER	SSX HAILSHAM	GATE HOUSE	173
15	SINNOCK THOMAS	SO U	14		SSX WESTFIELD	GATE HOUSE	174
31	SIVIOR EMMA	WI M	30		KEN GOUDHURST	ADAMS LANE	236
31	SIVIOR JOHN	HD M	37	AG.LAB	SSX EWHURST	ADAMS LANE	236
31	SIVIOR SUSAN	DA U	9		SSX SHADOXHURST	ADAMS LANE	236
32	SKINER JOHN	SV U	50		KEN BETHERSDEN	FARM HOUSE	133
73	SKINNER ALFRED	SO U	2		SSX HOLLINGTON	STEMPS?	15
73	SKINNER ELIZA	DA U	16		SSX HOLLINGTON	STEMPS?	15
73	SKINNER ELIZABETH	DA U	13		SSX HOLLINGTON	STEMPS?	15
73	SKINNER ELIZABETH	WI M	41		SSX EWHURST	STEMPS?	15
81	SKINNER SARAH A	SV U	18	LAUNDRY MAID	SSX HOLLINGTON	BEAUPORT HOUSE	17
78	SKINNER SOPHIA	HD U	18	DAIRY WOMAN -FARM	SSX BATTLE	STEMPS? LODGE	16
73	SKINNER WILLIAM	HD M	51	GARDENER	SSX CROWHURST	STEMPS?	15
73	SKINNER WILLIAM	SO U	9		SSX HOLLINGTON	STEMPS?	15
77	SMALL JANE	NC U	20	ASSISTANT (DRAPER/GROCER)	KEN GREAT CHART	STAPLE CROSS	243
52	SMITH (FARMER) ABSENT			FARMER		GREAT SANDERS	194
74	SMITH ABRAHAM	SO U	17	AG.LAB	SSX HOLLINGTON	STEMPS?	15
54	SMITH ALBERT	HD M	26	FARMER 227 AC EMP 6	SSX BREDE	CASTLEMANS	195
19	SMITH ALBERT	SO U	4		SSX BEXHILL	COBS MILL HOUSE - SIDLEY	68
20	SMITH ALBERT	SO U	4		SSX BEXHILL	SIDLEY	69
52	SMITH ALFRED	SO U	6		SSX SEDLESCOMBE	GREAT SANDERS	194
49	SMITH ALLEN	SO U	25	GROCER & DRAPER	SSX EWHURST	SNAGS HALL	222
54	SMITH AMELIA	WI M	32		KEN SMARDEN	CASTLEMANS	195
51	SMITH ANN	DA U	4		SSX SEDLESCOMBE	COMPASSES	194
30	SMITH ANN	DA U	5		SSX NORTHIAM	ADAMS LANE	236
45	SMITH ANN	WI M	28		SSX CROWHURST	HOLLINGTON STREET	11
51	SMITH ANN	WI M	34		SSX FLETCHING	COMPASSES	194
62	SMITH ANN	?DA M	22		SSX EWHURST	STAPLE CROSS	240
67	SMITH ARTHUR	SV U	22		SSX BEXHILL	NOT GIVEN	97
53	SMITH BENJAMIN	HD M	67	AG.LAB	SSX CROWHURST	HOLLINGTON STREET	12
52	SMITH BERTRAM	SO U	4		SSX SEDLESCOMBE	GREAT SANDERS	194
54	SMITH CAROLINE	CI U	24		SSX BREDE	CASTLEMANS	195
19	SMITH CAROLINE	WI M	30	SCHOOLMISTRESS	FRANCE BRITISH SUBJECT	COBS MILL HOUSE - SIDLEY	68
60	SMITH CHARLES	L6 U	21	RAILWAY LAB	YKS BRAMTON	RAILWAY HUT	136
63	SMITH CHARLES	L6 U	45	RAILWAY LAB	BRK READING	RAILWAY HUT	137
44	SMITH CHARLOTTE	DA U	3?		SSX BEXHILL	NOT GIVEN	43
59	SMITH CHARLOTTE	DA U	14		SSX BEXHILL	NOT GIVEN	95
88	SMITH CHARLOTTE	DL U	15		SSX EWHURST	MILL PLATT	228
44	SMITH CHARLOTTE	WI M	38		SSX EWHURST	NOT GIVEN	43
52	SMITH CLARA	DA U	8		SSX SEDLESCOMBE	GREAT SANDERS	194
48	SMITH ELEANOR	DA U	21		SSX EWHURST	NOT GIVEN	239
52	SMITH ELIZA	WI M	38	FARMER'S WIFE	SSX WHATLINGTON	GREAT SANDERS	194
62	SMITH ELIZABETH	/ U	1M		SSX BEXHILL	LANES END	30
16	SMITH ELIZABETH	DA U	4		SSX EWHURST	COLLIERS GREEN	234
30	SMITH ELIZABETH	DA U	4		SSX NORTHIAM	ADAMS LANE	236
54	SMITH ELIZABETH	VR U	50	ANNUITANT	HERTFORD	CASTLEMANS	195
28	SMITH ELIZABETH	WI M	38?		SSX CROWHURST	SIDLEY	69
16	SMITH ELLIOT	SO U	1		SSX EWHURST	COLLIERS GREEN	234
59	SMITH EMMA	DA U	11		SSX BEXHILL	NOT GIVEN	95
81	SMITH ESTHER	CO U	26	HOUSE KEEPER	SSX WESTFIELD	BULLS EYE CORNER	182
45	SMITH FRANCES	DA U	5		SSX HOLLINGTON	HOLLINGTON STREET	11

ID	Name	Code	Status	Age	Occupation	County	Place	Location	No.
45	SMITH GEORGE	LG	U	21	RAILWAY LAB	NOR	DISS	RAILWAY HUT	134
1	SMITH GEORGE	LG	U	24	RAIL LAB	STS	COLCHESTER	CATSFIELD GREEN	119
58	SMITH GEORGE	LG	U	25	AG.LAB	SSX	EWHURST	ELLINGHALL	240
51	SMITH GEORGE	SO	U	2M		SSX	SEDLESCOMBE	COMPASSES	194
28	SMITH GEORGE	SO	U	10		SSX	BEXHILL	SIDLEY	69
74	SMITH HANNAH	DA	U	9		SSX	HOLLINGTON	STEMPS?	15
53	SMITH HANNAH	DA	U	17		SSX	HOLLINGTON	HOLLINGTON STREET	12
26	SMITH HANNAH	SV	U	19?	COOK	SSX	HASTINGS	BEXHILL STREET	26
59	SMITH HARRIET	WI	M	30		SSX	BEXHILL	NOT GIVEN	95
10	SMITH HARRIET	WI	M	42	AG.LAB'S WIFE	SSX	EWHURST	PADGHAM	216
8	SMITH HARRIET	WI	M	50		SSX	BEXHILL	SIDLEY	90
51	SMITH HARRIETT	DA	U	8		SSX	SEDLESCOMBE	COMPASSES	194
46	SMITH HARRIOTT	WI	M	38		HAM	FAREHAM	NO.3 GALLEY HILL	29
45	SMITH HENRY	SO	U	8		SSX	HOLLINGTON	HOLLINGTON STREET	11
62	SMITH IAN	LG	U	28	RAILWAY LAB	NOR	LYNN*	RAILWAY HUT	136
49	SMITH JABEZ	SO	U	15	PUPIL TEACHER	SSX	EWHURST	SNAGS HALL	222
62	SMITH JACK	LG	U	28	RAILWAY LAB	KEN	SMARDEN	RAILWAY HUT	136
55	SMITH JAMES	HD	M	32	AG.LAB	SSX	SEDLESCOMBE	ELLINGHOURNE	239
11	SMITH JAMES	HD	M	49	SAWYER	SSX	EWHURST	COLLIERS GREEN	233
8	SMITH JAMES	HD	M	50	AG.LAB	SSX	BEXHILL	SIDLEY	90
86	SMITH JAMES	LG	W	25	AG.LAB	KEN	SANDHURST	HARROW INN	18
28	SMITH JAMES	SO	U	1		SSX	BEXHILL	SIDLEY	69
55	SMITH JAMES	SO	U	9	AG.LAB	SSX	EWHURST	ELLINGHOURNE	239
51	SMITH JAMES	SO	U	14	AG.LAB	SSX	EWHURST	COMPASSES	194
11	SMITH JAMES	SO	U	23	WHEELWRIGHT AP	SSX	EWHURST	COLLIERS GREEN	233
30	SMITH JANE	DA	U	2		SSX	NORTHIAM	ADAMS LANE	236
44	SMITH JESSE	SO	U	19	AG.LAB	SSX	BEXHILL	NOT GIVEN	43
45	SMITH JOHN	HD	M	40	AG.LAB	SSX	HOLLINGTON	HOLLINGTON STREET	11
3	SMITH JOHN	LG	U	22	BRICKMAKER'S LAB	SSX	BRIGHTON	FORWARD LANE	128
10	SMITH JOHN	LG	U	22	RAILWAY LAB	UNKNOWN		FORWARD LANE	129
48	SMITH JOHN	SO	U	7		SSX	EWHURST	NOT GIVEN	239
55	SMITH JOHN	SO	U	7	SCHOLAR	SSX	EWHURST	ELLINGHOURNE	239
16	SMITH JOSEPH	HD	M	26	AG.LAB	SSX	EWHURST	COLLIERS GREEN	234
96	SMITH JOSEPH	HD	W	71	RETIRED BRICKLAYER	SSX	BEXHILL	NOT GIVEN	100
53	SMITH JOSEPH	SO	U	9	SCHOLAR	SSX	HOLLINGTON	HOLLINGTON STREET	12
52	SMITH KATE	DA	U	2		SSX	SEDLESCOMBE	GREAT SANDERS	194
74	SMITH LOUIZA	DA	U	4		SSX	HOLLINGTON	STEMPS?	15
62	SMITH LUCY A	SV	U	19	HOUSE SERVANT	SSX	BEXHILL	LANES END	30
48	SMITH MAHALA	DA	U	5		SSX	EWHURST	NOT GIVEN	239
86	SMITH MARTHA	LG	U	6		KEN	SANDHURST	HARROW INN	18
48	SMITH MARY	DA	U	20		SSX	SEDLESCOMBE	SWALES GREEN	193
88	SMITH MARY	DL	U	20		SSX	EWHURST	MILL PLATT	228
62	SMITH MARY	GD	U	1		SSX	BATTLE	STAPLE CROSS	241
109	SMITH MARY	HD	W	72	PAUPER	SSX	BEXHILL	NOT GIVEN	101
30	SMITH MARY	WI	M	26		SSX	EWHURST	ADAMS LANE	236
74	SMITH MARY	WI	M	49		SSX	CROWHURST	STEMPS?	15
45	SMITH MARY A	DA	U	7		SSX	HOLLINGTON	HOLLINGTON STREET	11
26	SMITH MARY ANN	/	U	4	NURSE CHILD	SSX	WINCHELSEA	RANSOM'S COTTAGE	145
16	SMITH MARY ANN	DA	U	3		SSX	EWHURST	COLLIERS GREEN	234
55	SMITH MARY ANN	DA	U	4		SSX	EWHURST	ELLINGHOURNE	239
44	SMITH MARY ANN	DA	U	8?	SCHOLAR	SSX	BEXHILL	NOT GIVEN	43
93	SMITH MARY ANN	SV	U	14?	SERVANT	SSX	EWHURST	STAPLE CROSS	244
11	SMITH MARY ANN	WI	M	45		SSX	NORTHIAM	COLLIERS GREEN	233
53	SMITH RACHEL	DA	U	23		SSX	HOLLINGTON	HOLLINGTON STREET	12
72	SMITH RICHARD	AP	U	18	MILLER'S AP	SSX	ASHBURNHAM	WATERMILL HOUSE	114
51	SMITH RICHARD	HD	M	37	AG.LAB	SSX	SEDLESCOMBE	COMPASSES	194
46	SMITH RICHARD	HD	M	41	COAST GUARD	SSX	TARRANT (SIC)	NO.3 GALLEY HILL	29
28	SMITH RICHARD	HD	M	43	AG.LAB	SSX	BEXHILL	SIDLEY	69
48	SMITH RICHARD	HD	W	61	AG.LAB	SSX	MOUNTFIELD	SWALES GREEN	193
28	SMITH RICHARD	SO	U	7	SCHOLAR	SSX	BEXHILL	SIDLEY	69
48	SMITH SABAN	SO	U	11		SSX	EWHURST	NOT GIVEN	239
25	SMITH SAMUEL	LG	U	39	RAILWAY LAB	ESS	COLCHESTER	RANSOM'S HOUSE	145
62	SMITH SAMUEL	SL	M	28		SSX	SEDLESCOMBE	STAPLE CROSS	240
19	SMITH SAMUEL	SO	U	1		SSX	BEXHILL	COBS MILL HOUSE - SIDLEY	68
49	SMITH SAMUEL L	SO	U	8	SCHOLAR	SSX	EWHURST	SNAGS HALL	222
74	SMITH SARAH	DA	U	12		SSX	HOLLINGTON	STEMPS?	15
16	SMITH SARAH	WI	M	25		SSX	EWHURST	COLLIERS GREEN	234
55	SMITH SARAH	WI	M	30		SSX	EWHURST	ELLINGHOURNE	239
19	SMITH SARAH A	DA	U	9	SCHOLAR	SSX	BEXHILL	COBS MILL HOUSE - SIDLEY	68
70	SMITH SARAH A	VR	U	16		SSX	BEXHILL	NOT GIVEN	97
49	SMITH SARAH RABACCA	WI	M	52		SSX	EWHURST	SNAGS HALL	222
48	SMITH SERENA	DA	U	12		SSX	ST.LEONARDS	NOT GIVEN	239
30	SMITH SOPHIA	DA	U	1M		SSX		ADAMS LANE	236
53	SMITH SOPHIA	WI	M	47		SSX	HOLLINGTON	HOLLINGTON STREET	12
48	SMITH SPENCER	SO	U	23	AG.LAB	SSX	SEDLESCOMBE	SWALES GREEN	193
59	SMITH STEPHEN	HD	M	41	AG.LAB	SSX	BEXHILL	NOT GIVEN	95
28	SMITH STEPHEN	SO	U	12		SSX	BEXHILL	SIDLEY	69
48	SMITH THOMAS	HD	M	38	SAWYER	SSX	EWHURST	NOT GIVEN	238
63	SMITH THOMAS	LG	U	19	RAILWAY LAB	SSX		RAILWAY HUT	137
51	SMITH THOMAS	SO	U	6		SSX	SEDLESCOMBE	COMPASSES	194
53	SMITH THOMAS	SO	U	12		SSX	HOLLINGTON	HOLLINGTON STREET	12
30	SMITH TILDEN	HD	M	29	AG.LAB	SSX	SEDLESCOMBE	ADAMS LANE	236
51	SMITH TILDEN	SO	U	2		SSX	SEDLESCOMBE	COMPASSES	194
116	SMITH TOM?	SV	U	23	CORDWAINER	SSX	HERSTMONCEUX	NOT GIVEN	102
62	SMITH WILLIAM	GS	U	4		SSX	EWHURST	STAPLE CROSS	241
19	SMITH WILLIAM	HD	M	39	LOADER	SSX	BEXHILL	COBS MILL HOUSE - SIDLEY	68

ID	Name	Rel	M	Age	Occupation	County	Parish	Place	No.
44	SMITH WILLIAM	HD	M	51	AG.LAB	SSX	BEXHILL	NOT GIVEN	43
74	SMITH WILLIAM	HD	M	51	AG.LAB	SSX	HOLLINGTON	STEMPS?	15
49	SMITH WILLIAM	HD	M	52	ROPE MANUFACTURER	SSX	BATTLE	SNAGS HALL	222
1	SMITH WILLIAM	LG	U	22	RAIL LAB	STS	COLCHESTER	CATSFIELD GREEN	119
13	SMITH WILLIAM	LG	U	27	RAIL LAB	HRT		MAYFIELDS RAILWAY HUT	6
45	SMITH WILLIAM	SO	U	2		SSX	HOLLINGTON	HOLLINGTON STREET	11
51	SMITH WILLIAM	SO	U	10	AG.LAB	SSX	SEDLESCOMBE	COMPASSES	194
55	SMITH WILLIAM	SO	U	11	AG.LAB	SSX	EWHURST	ELLINGHOURNE	239
74	SMITH WILLIAM	SO	U	18	AG.LAB	SSX	HOLLINGTON	STEMPS?	15
49	SMITH WILLIAM	SO	U	29	ROPE MAKER	SSX	EWHURST	SNAGS HALL	222
2	SMITH WILLIAM	SV	U	15	FARM SERVANT	SSX	BEXHILL	WAKEHAMS	89
19	SMITH WILLIAM D	SO	U	7	SCHOLAR	SSX	BEXHILL	COBS MILL HOUSE - SIDLEY	68
4	SNASHALL EMILY	DA	U	18		SSX	BATTLE	BELL HILL	24
4	SNASHALL MARY	WI	M	60		SSX	BATTLE	BELL HILL	24
4	SNASHALL THOMAS	HD	M	68	AG.LAB	SSX	BALCOMB	BELL HILL	24
95	SNELL SARAH	SV	U	32	HOUSE SERVANT	KEN	TUNBRIDGE WELLS	VICARAGE	100
4	SPEARS ALICE	WI	M	60?		SSX	PENHURST	SEDLESCOMBE STREET	201
63	SPEARS CHARLOTTE	WI	M	51		SSX	BATTLE	DURHAM FORD	210
11	SPEARS DRUSILLA	SV	U	20	HOUSE MAID	SSX	BATTLE	WILTING FARM HOUSE	6
63	SPEARS ELIZA	DA	U	14		SSX	SEDLESCOMBE	DURHAM FORD	210
4	SPEARS GEORGE	HD	M	65	FARMER	SSX	SEDLESCOMBE	SEDLESCOMBE STREET	201
78	SPEARS HANNAH	SV	U	25	HOUSE SERVANT	SSX	BATTLE	NOT GIVEN	98
1	SPEARS HARRIETT	SV	U	32	HOUSE SERVANT	SSX	SEDLESCOMBE	VICARAGE HOUSE	161
4	SPEARS HENRY	*	U	3	SON OF ANN THOMPSON	SSX	BATTLE	CATSFIELD GREEN	120
43	SPEARS MARY	WI	M	26		SSX	WESTFIELD	SWALES GREEN	192
11	SPEARS ROBERT	LG	U	24	AG.LAB	SSX	BATTLE	YEW TREE	163
43	SPEARS SAMUEL	HD	M	24	AG.LAB	SSX	SEDLESCOMBE	SWALES GREEN	192
63	SPEARS SAMUEL	HD	M	53	AG.LAB	SSX	SEDLESCOMBE	DURHAM FORD	210
12	SPICE CAROLINE	DA	U	12		SSX	AMBERLEY	RAILWAY HUT	6
12	SPICE EMMA	DA	U	2		SSX	ST.LEONARDS	RAILWAY HUT	6
12	SPICE FREDERIC	SO	U	3		ESS	MOUNT BURES	RAILWAY HUT	6
12	SPICE JANE	WI	M	34		SSX	AMBERLEY	RAILWAY HUT	6
12	SPICE MARIA	DA	U	6	SCHOLAR	SSX	ST.LEONARDS	RAILWAY HUT	6
81	SPICE MARIA	SV	U	16	STILLROOM MAID	SSX	BEXHILL	BEAUPORT HOUSE	17
12	SPICE WILLIAM	HD	M	37	RAIL LAB	SSX	SEDLESCOMBE	RAILWAY HUT	6
47	SPILSTEAD EMMA	WI	M	30		SSX	SALEHURST	SWALES GREEN	193
47	SPILSTEAD HARRIET	DA	U	20		SSX	SALEHURST	SWALES GREEN	193
47	SPILSTEAD THOMAS	HD	M	46	AG.LAB	SSX	SEDLESCOMBE	SWALES GREEN	193
20	SPILSTED AGNESS	GD	U	5		SSX	EWHURST	COLLIERS GREEN	234
20	SPILSTED HARRIET	DA	U	31	DRESSMAKER	SSX	EWHURST	COLLIERS GREEN	234
20	SPILSTED HENRY	SO	U	22	WHEELWRIGHT	SSX	EWHURST	COLLIERS GREEN	234
14	SPILSTED JOSHUA	SV	U	19	FARMER'S SERVANT	SSX	SEDLESCOMBE	BREDE HIGH	251
20	SPILSTED WILLIAM	HD	M	61	AG.LAB	SSX	WHATLINGTON	COLLIERS GREEN	234
20	SPILSTED WILLIAM	SO	U	34	AG.LAB	SSX	EWHURST	COLLIERS GREEN	234
55	SPILSTED WILLIAM	SV	U	16	AG.LAB	SSX	WHATLINGTON	HANCOX FARM	209
5	SPITTELS WILLIAM	SV	U	26	LEATHER DRESSER	KEN	COWDEN	TAN HOUSE SEDLESCOMBE ST	187
21	SPLISTED MAREY	VR	U	42		SSX	SEDLESCOMBE	NOT GIVEN	131
2	SPRAY DELEY	WI	M	45		SSX	CROWHURST	PLOUGH INN	142
32	SPRAY DELIA	SV	U	15	HOUSE MAID	SSX	CROWHURST	STONE HOUSE	9
33	SPRAY EDMUND	HD	M	24	AG.LAB	SSX	NINFIELD	LUNSFORDS LANE SIDLEY	70
33	SPRAY ELIZABETH	WI	M	25		SSX	BEXHILL	LUNSFORDS LANE SIDLEY	70
2	SPRAY EMILY	DA	U	12		SSX	CROWHURST	PLOUGH INN	142
2	SPRAY FANNY	DA	U	25		SSX	CROWHURST	PLOUGH INN	142
1	SPRAY HARRIETT	WI	M	29		SSX	CATSFIELD	MILLERS COTTAGE	37
2	SPRAY JAMES	SO	U	10		SSX	CROWHURST	PLOUGH INN	142
37	SPRAY JAMES	SV	U	44	AG.LAB	SSX	BEXHILL	BEXHILL STREET	28
33	SPRAY JANE	DA	U	1		SSX	BEXHILL	LUNSFORDS LANE SIDLEY	70
72	SPRAY JANE	SV	U	30	HOUSE SERVANT	SSX	NINFIELD	NOT GIVEN	97
39	SPRAY MARY	VR	U	22	HOUSE SERVANT	SSX	BEXHILL	NOT GIVEN	56
33	SPRAY MARY A	DA	U	2		SSX	BEXHILL	LUNSFORDS LANE SIDLEY	70
2	SPRAY SARAH	DA	U	7		SSX	CROWHURST	PLOUGH INN	142
2	SPRAY SETH	SO	U	24		SSX	CROWHURST	PLOUGH INN	142
1	SPRAY WALTER	HD	M	29	AG.LAB	SSX	NINFIELD	MILLERS COTTAGE	37
2	SPRAY WILLIAM	HD	M	62	BLACKSMITH & INNKEEPER	SSX	NINFIELD	PLOUGH INN	142
1	SPRAY WILLIAM	SO	U	5		SSX	BEXHILL	MILLERS COTTAGE	37
2	SPRAY WILLIAM	SO	U	22		SSX	CROWHURST	PLOUGH INN	142
6	SPRAY?* ELIZABETH	WI	M	62		SSX	FAIRLIGHT	DUKE FARM	129
6	SPRAY?* WILLIAM (V.UNCLEAR)	HD	M	68	FARMER 37 AC EMP 1	SSX	BATTLE	DUKE FARM	129
29	STACE CHARLES	SO	U	13	AG.LAB	SSX	EWHURST	RENS	219
39	STACE GEORGE	SV	U	19	AG.SERVANT	SSX	EWHURST	PRAWLES FARM	221
29	STACE HARRIET	WI	M	45		SSX	NORTHIAM	RENS	219
29	STACE SAMUEL	HD	M	49	AG.LAB	STS	EWHURST	RENS	219
89	STACE WALTER	LG	U	30	AG.LAB	SSX	EWHURST	HOLLOW WALLS	244
29	STACE WALTER	SO	U	21	AG.LAB	SSX	EWHURST	RENS	219
27	STAMP EUGENE	SO	U	8M		SSX	CATSFIELD	NOT GIVEN	110
27	STAMP JAMES	HD	M	23	SCHOOLMASTER	SSX	CHICHESTER	NOT GIVEN	110
27	STAMP SARAH S	WI	M	23		DEV	EXETER	NOT GIVEN	110
25	STANDEN ANN	WI	M	51		SSX	CASTLE	FORGE	175
25	STANDEN CHARLES	SO	U	12	DUMB	SSX	WESTFIELD	FORGE	175
23	STANDEN CHARLOTTE	DA	U	6		SSX	WESTFIELD	OLD HOUSE	175
33	STANDEN CHARLOTTE	WI	M	28		SSX	SEDLESCOMBE	DOWN	176
23	STANDEN EMILY	DA	U	3		SSX	WESTFIELD	OLD HOUSE	175
72	STANDEN GEORGE	HD	M	21	AG.LAB	SSX	WESTFIELD	DOWN	181
25	STANDEN GEORGE	HD	M	53	AG.LAB	SSX	HOLLINGTON	FORGE	175
33	STANDEN GEORGE	SO	U	7	AG.LAB (SIC)	SSX	WESTFIELD	DOWN	176
23	STANDEN HANNAH	DA	U	1		SSX	WESTFIELD	OLD HOUSE	175

#	Surname	Given Name			Age	Occupation	County	Parish	Location	No.
72	STANDEN	HANNAH	WI	M	21		SSX	ICKLESHAM	DOWN	181
23	STANDEN	HANNAH	WI	M	22		SSX	WESTFIELD	OLD HOUSE	175
23	STANDEN	JAMES	HD	M	32	AG.LAB	SSX	WESTFIELD	OLD HOUSE	175
46	STANDEN	JAMES	HD	M	55	AG.LAB	SSX	HOLLINGTON	HOLLINGTON STREET	11
75	STANDEN	JAMES	LG	U	50	AG.LAB	MDX		STEMPS?	16
33	STANDEN	JANE	DA	U	3		SSX	WESTFIELD	DOWN	176
46	STANDEN	JANE	WI	M	50		SSX	HAILSHAM	HOLLINGTON STREET	11
33	STANDEN	JOHN	HD	M	28	AG.LAB	SSX	WESTFIELD	DOWN	176
33	STANDEN	LIPORIA	DA	U	8M		SSX	WESTFIELD	DOWN	176
35	STANDEN	MARIA	SV	U	18	HOUSE SERVANT	SSX	WESTFIELD	CROWHAM	176
89	STANDEN	MARY	WI	M	48		SSX	ST.MARY MAGDALEN	EVERSFIELDS	18
14	STANDEN	SAMUEL	SV	U	16		SSX	WESTFIELD	TAN YARD	153
46	STANDEN	SELVINA	DA	U	15		SSX	HOLLINGTON	HOLLINGTON STREET	11
25	STANDEN	STEPHEN	SO	U	10		SSX	WESTFIELD	FORGE	175
89	STANDEN	THOMAS	HD	M	55	FARMER 55 AC EMP 2 MEN	SSX	ST.MARY IN THE CASTLE	EVERSFIELDS	18
33	STANDEN	WILLIAM	SO	U	5		SSX	SEDLESCOMBE	DOWN	176
9	STANLEY	ELIZABETH	HD	W	67	GROCER	SSX	BEXHILL	BELL HILL	24
9	STANLEY	MARY ANN	GD	U	14	SCHOLAR	SSX	BEXHILL	BELL HILL	24
64	STAPLEY	ALFRED	SO	U	22	AG.LAB	SSX	SEDLESCOMBE	BAULKHAM GREEN	196
64	STAPLEY	ANGELINA	DA	U	18		SSX	SEDLESCOMBE	BAULKHAM GREEN	196
64	STAPLEY	CALIB	SO	U	20	AG.LAB	SSX	SEDLESCOMBE	BAULKHAM GREEN	196
64	STAPLEY	CHARLES	GS	U	9		SSX	BATTLE	BAULKHAM GREEN	196
4	STAPLEY	CHARLES	HD	M	31	AG.LAB	SSX	SEDLESCOMBE	SEDLESCOMBE STREET	186
64	STAPLEY	CHARLES	HD	M	62	AG.LAB	SSX	SEDLESCOMBE	BAULKHAM GREEN	196
18	STAPLEY	CHARLES	HD	U	27	VETINARY SURGEON	SSX	ALBOURNE	BELL HILL	25
64	STAPLEY	CHARLOTTE	DA	U	34		SSX	SEDLESCOMBE	BAULKHAM GREEN	196
63	STAPLEY	ELIZABETH	DA	U	1		SSX	SEDLESCOMBE	BAULKHAM GREEN	196
32	STAPLEY	ELIZABETH	HD	W	57		SSX	BATTLE	SEDLESCOMBE STREET	205
9	STAPLEY	ELIZABETH	WI	M	52		SSX	BUXTED	WIDOWS	173
4	STAPLEY	FANNY	WI	M	28		SSX	BATTLE	SEDLESCOMBE STREET	186
32	STAPLEY	GEORGE	SO	U	28	AG.LAB	SSX	BATTLE	SEDLESCOMBE STREET	205
18	STAPLEY	HENRY	VR	U	21	DRAPER	SSX	ALBOURNE	BELL HILL	25
55	STAPLEY	JAMES	SO	U	5		SSX	SEDLESCOMBE	SEDLESCOMBE STREET	195
64	STAPLEY	JOHN	GS	U	7		SSX	SEDLESCOMBE	BAULKHAM GREEN	196
55	STAPLEY	JOHN	HD	M	35	AG.LAB	SSX	SEDLESCOMBE	SEDLESCOMBE STREET	195
64	STAPLEY	JULIA	GD	U	6		SSX	SEDLESCOMBE	BAULKHAM GREEN	196
55	STAPLEY	MARY	DA	U	8		SSX	SEDLESCOMBE	SEDLESCOMBE STREET	195
55	STAPLEY	MARY	WI	M	29		SSX	BATTLE	SEDLESCOMBE STREET	195
32	STAPLEY	PHILADELPHIA	DA	U	30	DRESSMAKER	SSX	SEDLESCOMBE	SEDLESCOMBE STREET	205
36	STAPLEY	PHILADELPHIA	LG	/?	40		SSX	MOUNTFIELD	MADDAMS	220
64	STAPLEY	REBECKA	WI	M	52		SSX	WHATLINGTON	BAULKHAM GREEN	196
32	STAPLEY	ROBERT	SO	U	30	AG.LAB	SSX	SEDLESCOMBE	SEDLESCOMBE STREET	205
63	STAPLEY	SABINA	WI	M	22		SSX	BATTLE	BAULKHAM GREEN	196
64	STAPLEY	SPENCER	SO	U	27	AG.LAB	SSX	SEDLESCOMBE	BAULKHAM GREEN	196
63	STAPLEY	THOMAS	HD	M	25	AG.LAB	SSX	SEDLESCOMBE	BAULKHAM GREEN	196
9	STAPLEY	THOMAS	HD	M	46	FARMER 124 AC EMP 2	SSX	BUXTED	WIDOWS	173
4	STAPLEY	UN-NAMED INFANT GIRL	DA	U	14D		SSX	SEDLESCOMBE	SEDLESCOMBE STREET	186
11	STEVENS	BENJAMIN	SO	U	7	SCHOLAR	SSX	BATTLE	MILL COTTAGE - SIDLEY	66
57	STEVENS	CHARLOTTE	WI	M	33		SSX	PETT	RAILWAY COTTAGE	30
10	STEVENS	JAMES	HD	M	60	SHEPHERD	BKM	CHAYDORN?*	PARK COTTAGE	120
11	STEVENS	JAMES	SO	U	15		SSX	BATTLE	MILL COTTAGE - SIDLEY	66
11	STEVENS	JOHN	SO	U	2		SSX	BEXHILL	MILL COTTAGE - SIDLEY	66
11	STEVENS	LOUISA	WI	M	40?		SSX	WILLINGDON	MILL COTTAGE - SIDLEY	66
54	STEVENS	MARY ANN	CI	U	30		KEN	SMARDEN	CASTLEMANS	195
11	STEVENS	RACHEL	DA	U	9	SCHOLAR	SSX	BATTLE	MILL COTTAGE - SIDLEY	66
57	STEVENS	SALLEY	DA	U	1		SSX	BEXHILL	RAILWAY COTTAGE	30
11	STEVENS	SAMUEL	SO	U	5	SCHOLAR	SSX	BATTLE	MILL COTTAGE - SIDLEY	66
10	STEVENS	SARAH	WI	M	48		BKM	UNKNOWN	PARK COTTAGE	120
57	STEVENS	WILLIAM	HD	M	26	RAILWAY LAB	SSX	BEXHILL	RAILWAY COTTAGE	30
11	STEVENS	WILLIAM	HD	M	61	MILLER	SSX	BEXHILL	MILL COTTAGE - SIDLEY	66
10	STEVENS	WILLIAM	LG	U	22	RAILWAY LAB	SSX	PORTSLADE	FORWARD LANE	129
11	STEVENS	WILLIAM	SO	U	11		SSX	BATTLE	MILL COTTAGE - SIDLEY	66
28	STEY	ALICE	DA	U	1		SSX	BEXHILL	52 MARTELLO TOWER IN LIBERTY	40
28	STEY	CHARLES	SO	U	4		SSX	BEXHILL	52 MARTELLO TOWER IN LIBERTY	40
28	STEY	ELIZABETH	WI	M	26		SSX	PETT	52 MARTELLO TOWER IN LIBERTY	40
28	STEY	HENRY	HD	M	30	COAST GUARD SERVICE	SSX	BRIGHTON	52 MARTELLO TOWER IN LIBERTY	40
28	STEY	JAMES	SO	U	2		SSX	BEXHILL	52 MARTELLO TOWER IN LIBERTY	40
27	STILES	AMY R	DA	U	8	SCHOLAR	ESS	HARWICH	52 MARTELLO TOWER IN LIBERTY	40
27	STILES	JAMES	HD	M	40	COAST GUARD SERVICE	SSX	BEXHILL	52 MARTELLO TOWER IN LIBERTY	40
27	STILES	JOHN J	SO	U	4M		SRY	LAMBETH	52 MARTELLO TOWER IN LIBERTY	40
27	STILES	LOUISIA	DA	U	10		DEV	EXETER	RAILWAY HUT	5
27	STILES	MARY A	WI	M	38		SSX	BEXHILL	(BARNHORN HILL?)	38
10	STILES	WILLIAM	LG	M	24	RAIL LAB	SSX	BEXHILL	NOT GIVEN	93
4	STONE	ALFRED	LG	U	16	AG.LAB	SSX	WESTFIELD	YEW TREE	162
34	STONE	ARTHUR	SO	U	7	SCHOLAR	SSX	WESTFIELD	YEW TREE	163
10	STONE	EDMUND	SO	U	21		BKM	NEWPORT PAGNELL	PIGLANDS	7
10	STONE	ELIZA	DA	U	5	SCHOLAR	SSX	BEXHILL	NOT GIVEN	93
18	STONE	ELIZABETH	WI	M	37		SSX	WESTFIELD	YEW TREE	163
34	STONE	ELLEN	DA	U	5	SCHOLAR	SSX	BEXHILL	NOT GIVEN	93
10	STONE	EMILY	DA	U	9	SCHOLAR	SSX	BEXHILL	NOT GIVEN	94
34	STONE	HANNAH	DA	U	10	SCHOLAR	KEN	ROMNEY	STAPLE CROSS	241
46	STONE	HANNAH	SV	U	11		SSX	WESTFIELD	YEW TREE	162
64	STONE	HARRIET	SV	U	20	SERVANT	SSX	BEXHILL	NOT GIVEN	93
10	STONE	JOHN	HD	M	55	AG.LAB	SSX	WESTFIELD	YEW TREE	162
10	STONE	JOHN	SO	U	14	AG.LAB				
10	STONE	JOHN	SO	U	16					

	Name		Age	Occupation	County	Place	
34	STONE MARY	DA U	12	SCHOLAR	SSX BEXHILL	NOT GIVEN	93
10	STONE MARY	WI M	48		SSX GUESTLING	YEW TREE	162
34	STONE MARY ANN	HD W	37	PAUPER	GERMANY	NOT GIVEN	93
34	STONE SARAH	DA U	5M		SSX BEXHILL	NOT GIVEN	93
18	STONE THOMAS	HD M	37	RAILROAD CONTRACTOR	BDF BACTON	PIGLANDS	7
10	STONE WILLIAM	SO U	12	SCHOLAR	SSX WESTFIELD	YEW TREE	162
19	STONHAM MATILDA	DA U	26		SSX IDEN	ROSE VILLA	153
28	STREETER AMOS F	SO U	5		SSX BATTLE	BREDE BRIDGE	175
28	STREETER CALIB H	SO U	3		SSX WESTFIELD	BREDE BRIDGE	175
29	STREETER CHARLES	SO U	14	AG.LAB	SSX HOLLINGTON	BAGGERS HOLE	9
29	STREETER EMILY	DA U	22		SSX HOLLINGTON	BAGGERS HOLE	9
28	STREETER EMMA	DA U	7		SSX BATTLE	BREDE BRIDGE	176
25	STREETER EMMA	WI M	66		SSX BECKLEY	NEW ENGLAND	165
25	STREETER FREDERIC	SO U	20	AG.LAB	SSX BATTLE	NEW ENGLAND	165
28	STREETER GEORGE	HD M	37	BRICKMAKER	SSX PEASMARSH	BREDE BRIDGE	175
28	STREETER GEORGE	SO U	9		SSX BREDE	BREDE BRIDGE	175
46	STREETER HANNAH	VR U	11		SSX ST.LEONARDS	NOT GIVEN	43
30	STREETER JANE	SV U	15	HOUSE SERVANT	KEN WAREHORN	STONE HOUSE	132
25	STREETER JOHN	HD M	70	AG.LAB	SSX HOLLINGTON	NEW ENGLAND	165
28	STREETER LEWIS R	SO U	9M		SSX WESTFIELD	BREDE BRIDGE	176
28	STREETER LOUISA	DA U	12		SSX BREDE	BREDE BRIDGE	175
28	STREETER LOUISA	WI M	35		SSX BREDE	BREDE BRIDGE	175
18	STREETER MARY A	GD U	12		KEN BRENZETT	CATTS GREEN	251
29	STREETER MATILDA	DA U	17		SSX HOLLINGTON	BAGGERS HOLE	9
28	STREETER SARAH	DA U	13		SSX WESTFIELD	BREDE BRIDGE	175
29	STREETER WILLIAM	HD W	44	WAGGONER	SSX ASHBURNHAM	BAGGERS HOLE	9
28	STREETER WILLIAM	SO U	15		SSX BATTLE	BREDE BRIDGE	175
46	STRIDE ROBERT	HD W	71	RETIRED GROCER	HAM EMSWORTH	LITTLE COMMON	57
58	STRODE JAMES CRANBOURNE ESQ	HD M	33	FUNDHOLDER	SSX FRANT	HOLLINGTON LODGE	12
13	STROUD SOPHIA	WI M	26		WIL LOCKRIDGE	MAYFIELDS RAILWAY HUT	6
13	STROUD THOMAS	HD M	29	CARPENTER	WIL ALDBURN	MAYFIELDS RAILWAY HUT	6
92	STUBBERFIELD ANN	DA U	18		SSX BEXHILL	NOT GIVEN	100
44	STUBBERFIELD CHARLOTTE	DA U	23		SSX BEXHILL	NOT GIVEN	94
92	STUBBERFIELD DELIA	DA U	7		SSX BEXHILL	NOT GIVEN	100
101	STUBBERFIELD EDWARD	HD M	53	FISHMONGER	SSX HODE	NOT GIVEN	101
101	STUBBERFIELD EDWARD	SO U	11		SSX BEXHILL	NOT GIVEN	101
41	STUBBERFIELD ELIZABETH	WI M	51		SSX SALEHURST	STONE HOUSE	167
49	STUBBERFIELD EMILY	DA U	3		SSX WESTFIELD	HOADS WOOD	168
12	STUBBERFIELD EMILY	DA U	5		SSX BEXHILL	WHYDOWN	52
98	STUBBERFIELD FANNY	SV U	13	HOUSE SERVANT	SSX BEXHILL	NOT GIVEN	100
101	STUBBERFIELD FRANCES	WI M	50		SSX HORSEBRIDGE	NOT GIVEN	101
92	STUBBERFIELD GEORGE	SO U	4		SSX BEXHILL	NOT GIVEN	100
12	STUBBERFIELD GEORGE	SO U	16	AG.LAB	SSX BEXHILL	WHYDOWN	52
40	STUBBERFIELD GEORGE	SO U	19	CORDWAINER	SSX BEXHILL	NOT GIVEN	93
92	STUBBERFIELD HANNAH	WI M	43		SSX BEXHILL	NOT GIVEN	100
40	STUBBERFIELD HANNAH	WI M	52		SSX BEXHILL	NOT GIVEN	93
40	STUBBERFIELD HARRIET	DA U	17		SSX BEXHILL	NOT GIVEN	93
44	STUBBERFIELD HARRIET	HD W	68	PAUPER	SSX HAILSHAM	NOT GIVEN	94
49	STUBBERFIELD HARRIETT	WI M	32		SSX BREDE	HOADS WOOD	168
12	STUBBERFIELD HILDER?	SO U	12	AG.LAB	SSX BEXHILL	WHYDOWN	52
12	STUBBERFIELD JAMES	SO U	10	AG.LAB	SSX BEXHILL	WHYDOWN	52
92	STUBBERFIELD JAMES	SO U	16	AG.LAB	SSX BEXHILL	NOT GIVEN	100
101	STUBBERFIELD JOHN	SO U	8		SSX BEXHILL	NOT GIVEN	101
92	STUBBERFIELD JOHN	SO U	9		SSX BEXHILL	NOT GIVEN	100
12	STUBBERFIELD MARY ANN	DA U	9		SSX BEXHILL	WHYDOWN	52
40	STUBBERFIELD MARY ANN	DA U	12		SSX BEXHILL	NOT GIVEN	93
49	STUBBERFIELD NAOMI	SL U	20	DRESSMAKER	SSX BEXHILL	SIDLEY GREEN	82
100	STUBBERFIELD PHILLY	SV U	14	HOUSE SERVANT	SSX BEXHILL	NOT GIVEN	101
40	STUBBERFIELD ROBERT	HD M	52	CORDWAINER	SSX RIPE	NOT GIVEN	93
92	STUBBERFIELD SAMUEL	HD M	48	AG.LAB	SSX BEXHILL	NOT GIVEN	100
12	STUBBERFIELD SAMUEL	SO U	7		SSX BEXHILL	WHYDOWN	52
92	STUBBERFIELD SAMUEL	SO U	11		SSX BEXHILL	NOT GIVEN	100
41	STUBBERFIELD STEPHEN	HD M	76	INDEPENDANT	SSX BEXHILL	STONE HOUSE	167
40	STUBBERFIELD STEPHEN	SO U	9		SSX BEXHILL	NOT GIVEN	93
12	STUBBERFIELD STEPHEN	SO U	18	AG.LAB	SSX BEXHILL	WHYDOWN	52
49	STUBBERFIELD THOMAS	HD M	32	GAME KEEPER	SSX HASTINGS	HOADS WOOD	168
12	STUBBERFIELD WILLIAM	HD W	54	AG.LAB	SSX BEXHILL	WHYDOWN	52
12	STUBBERFIELD WILLIAM	SO U	20	AG.LAB	SSX BEXHILL	WHYDOWN	52
42	STUNT ANDREW R	SO U	5		SSX WESTFIELD	MILL COTTAGE	177
66	STUNT ANN	DA U	2		SSX WESTFIELD	ONION HILL	181
26	STUNT ANN	DA U	7		SSX WESTFIELD	FORGE	175
26	STUNT CALEB	SO U	9M		SSX WESTFIELD	FORGE	175
42	STUNT CAROLINE E	DA U	7		SSX WESTFIELD	MILL COTTAGE	177
30	STUNT DAVID	SO U	23		SSX WESTFIELD	GATE COTTAGE	176
26	STUNT ELIZA	DA U	3		SSX WESTFIELD	FORGE	175
102	STUNT ELIZABETH	HD U	70	ANNUITANT	SSX BEXHILL	NOT GIVEN	101
66	STUNT HANNAH	WI M	30		SSX WESTFIELD	ONION HILL	181
30	STUNT HANNAH	WI M	60	DEAF	SSX SEDLESCOMBE	GATE COTTAGE	176
66	STUNT HANNAH B	DA U	5		SSX WESTFIELD	ONION HILL	181
42	STUNT HARRIETT	WI M	27		SSX WESTFIELD	MILL COTTAGE	177
56	STUNT JANE	WI M	61		SSX BATTLE	BARRACKS	179
66	STUNT JANE R	DA U	8		SSX WESTFIELD	ONION HILL	181
30	STUNT JOSEPH	SO U	25		SSX WESTFIELD	GATE COTTAGE	176
26	STUNT JOSHUA	SO U	9M		SSX WESTFIELD	FORGE	175
56	STUNT LESTER	SO U	24	AG.LAB	SSX WESTFIELD	BARRACKS	179
42	STUNT MARGARET	DA U	2		SSX WESTFIELD	MILL COTTAGE	177

No.	Name	Rel	St	Age	Occupation	Birthplace	Place	Pg
28	STUNT MARY	WI	M	57		NOT GIVEN (?WESTFIELD)	PLOUGH INN	155
61	STUNT MATHEW	LG	M	25	BRICKLAYER	SSX BATTLE	BAULKHAM GREEN	196
61	STUNT PHILLY	LW	M	17		SSX SEDLESCOMBE	BAULKHAM GREEN	196
26	STUNT SABINA	WI	M	32		SSX WESTFIELD	FORGE	175
66	STUNT SALLY	DA	U	2M		SSX WESTFIELD	ONION HILL	181
42	STUNT SUMMERFIELD	HD	M	29	AG.LAB	SSX WESTFIELD	MILL COTTAGE	177
26	STUNT THOMAS	HD	M	33	AG.LAB	SSX WESTFIELD	FORGE	175
28	STUNT THOMAS	HD	M	55	VICTUALLER	SSX (?WESTFIELD)	PLOUGH INN	155
30	STUNT THOMAS	HD	M	62	AG.LAB	SSX BATTLE	GATE COTTAGE	176
70	STUNT THOMAS	HD	W	84	FARMER	SSX WESTFIELD	DOWN	181
56	STUNT WILLIAM	HD	M	61	AG.LAB	SSX BATTLE	BARRACKS	179
66	STUNT WILLIAM H	HD	M	32	AG.LAB	SSX BATTLE	ONION HILL	181
26	SWADLING CHARLOTTE	WI	M	47		SSX WESTFIELD	WHY DOWN	165
26	SWADLING ELIZA	DA	U	16		SSX SEDLESCOMBE	WHY DOWN	165
26	SWADLING FRANCES	DA	U	7		SSX WESTFIELD	WHY DOWN	165
26	SWADLING GEORGE	HD	M	41	AG.LAB	SSX SEDLESCOMBE	WHY DOWN	165
18	SWADLING GEORGE	NP	/	18	BUTCHER'S BOY LODGER	SSX SEDLESCOMBE	SEDLESCOMBE STREET	203
26	SWADLING LYDIA	DA	U	4		SSX WESTFIELD	WHY DOWN	165
26	SWADLING SARAH E	DA	U	9		SSX WESTFIELD	WHY DOWN	165
86	SWADLING THOMAS	LG	W	24	AG.LAB	SSX SEDLESCOMBE	HARROW INN	18
26	SWADLING WILLIAM	SO	U	11		SSX WESTFIELD	WHY DOWN	165
41	SWETMAN RICHARD A	SV	U	13		KEN SANDHURST	STONE HOUSE	167
17	TANNER JANE	HD	U	50	STRAW BONNET MAKER	SSX CATSFIELD	STEPHEN'S CROUCH	121
1	TARRENS THOMAS	SL	U	19	AG.LAB	SSX ST.LEONARDS	CATSFIELD DOWN	106
95	TAYLER GEORGE	HD	M	36	RAILWAY LAB	SRY BISLEY	HUT	19
95	TAYLER MARY	WI	M	24		SRY WINDLESONE (SIC)	HUT	19
95	TAYLER MARY A	DA	U	4?		SRY BISLEY	HUT	19
29	TAYLOR CHARLES	SO	U	3		SSX CROWHURST	FORWARD LANE	146
17	TAYLOR CHARLES	SV	U	14	FARM SERVANT	SSX HOLLINGTON	HILL FARM	144
34	TAYLOR CHARLOTTE	DA	U	12		SSX HASTINGS	DAIRY HOUSE	133
36	TAYLOR CHARLOTTE	HD	W	25	LAUNDRESS	SSX ORE	EMMARYS	10
23	TAYLOR CHARLOTTE	VR	U	15		KEN DEPTFORD	LORDINE	235
28	TAYLOR EDGAR	/	I	4	NURSE CHILD	SSX CROWHURST	FORWARD LANE	146
4	TAYLOR EDWARD	SO	U	12	SCHOLAR	SSX HOLLINGTON	NOT GIVEN	143
16	TAYLOR ELIZA	DA	U	6	SCHOLAR	SSX CROWHURST	HIGH COTTAGE	144
4	TAYLOR ELIZA	DA	U	17		SSX HOLLINGTON	NOT GIVEN	143
12	TAYLOR ELIZA	WI	M	28		SSX CROWHURST	BINES FARM	143
4	TAYLOR ELIZA	WI	M	46		SSX CROWHURST	NOT GIVEN	143
12	TAYLOR ELLEN	DA	U	8		SSX CROWHURST	BINES FARM	143
16	TAYLOR ELLEN	DA	U	8	SCHOLAR	SSX CROWHURST	HIGH COTTAGE	144
12	TAYLOR EMILY	DA	U	4		SSX CROWHURST	BINES FARM	144
16	TAYLOR EMILY	DA	U	10	SCHOLAR	SSX CROWHURST	HIGH COTTAGE	144
39	TAYLOR ESTHER	WI	M	28		SSX EWHURST	MARCHANTS	238
12	TAYLOR FREDRICK	SO	U	6		SSX CROWHURST	BINES FARM	144
29	TAYLOR GEORGE	HD	M	48	FARM LAB	SSX BATTLE	FORWARD LANE	146
94	TAYLOR HARRIET	DA	U	17		SSX EWHURST	STAPLE CROSS	244
94	TAYLOR HARRIET	WI	M	44		SSX SEDLESCOMBE	STAPLE CROSS	244
16	TAYLOR HENRY	SO	U	15		SSX CROWHURST	HIGH COTTAGE	144
23	TAYLOR HENRY P	VR	M	26	VICTUALLER	KEN DEPTFORD	LORDINE	235
4	TAYLOR JAMES	HD	M	43	FARM LAB	SSX BATTLE	NOT GIVEN	143
29	TAYLOR JAMES	SO	U	14		SSX CROWHURST	FORWARD LANE	146
24	TAYLOR JAMES	SV	U	18	WAGGONER	SSX CROWHURST	SAMPSON'S FARM	131
29	TAYLOR JANE	WI	M	47		SSX BATTLE	FORWARD LANE	146
68	TAYLOR JANE	WI	M	50		SSX HOOE	COSSUMS	15
39	TAYLOR JOHN	HD	M	39	AG.LAB	SSX EWHURST	MARCHANTS	237
11	TAYLOR JOHN	HD	M	66	AG.LAB	SSX EWHURST	WINTER LANDS	250
34	TAYLOR JOHN	HD	W	51	AG.LAB	SSX HASTINGS	DAIRY HOUSE	133
30	TAYLOR JOHN	SO	U	11		SSX HOLLINGTON	IRON LATCH	9
29	TAYLOR JOHN	SO	U	18		SSX CROWHURST	FORWARD LANE	146
30	TAYLOR MARIA	DA	U	7		SSX HOLLINGTON	IRON LATCH	9
58	TAYLOR MARIA	VR	U	21	HOUSE SERVANT	SSX CROWHURST	NOT GIVEN	58
34	TAYLOR MARKE	SO	U	15	AG.LAB	SSX HASTINGS	DAIRY HOUSE	133
30	TAYLOR MARY	DA	U	4		SSX HOLLINGTON	IRON LATCH	9
11	TAYLOR MARY	WI	M	63		SSX WESTFIELD	WINTER LANDS	250
68	TAYLOR MARY ANN	DA	U	18	DRESSMAKER	SSX CROWHURST	COSSUMS	15
19	TAYLOR REBECCA	SV	U	18	HOUSE SERVANT	SSX CROWHURST	NOT GIVEN	53
19	TAYLOR SAMUEL	HD	M	36	AG.LAB	SSX CASTLE - HASTINGS	COLLIERS GREEN	234
30	TAYLOR SARAH	DA	U	9		SSX HOLLINGTON	IRON LATCH	9
58	TAYLOR SARAH	SV	U	16	KITCHEN MAID	SSX CROWHURST	HOLLINGTON LODGE	13
30	TAYLOR SARAH	WI	M	35		SSX SEDLESCOMBE	IRON LATCH	9
19	TAYLOR SARAH	WI	M	36		SSX NORTHIAM	COLLIERS GREEN	234
68	TAYLOR SARAH ANN	DA	U	17		SSX HOLLINGTON	COSSUMS	15
19	TAYLOR SARAH ESTHER	DA	U	8		SSX EWHURST	COLLIERS GREEN	234
16	TAYLOR SOPHIA	WI	M	43		SSX NINFIELD	HIGH COTTAGE	144
12	TAYLOR STEPHEN	HD	M	32	FARMER 80 AC	SSX BATTLE	BINES FARM	143
68	TAYLOR STEPHEN	HD	M	50	AG.LAB	SSX BATTLE	COSSUMS	15
29	TAYLOR STEPHEN	SO	U	7	SCHOLAR	SSX CROWHURST	FORWARD LANE	146
30	TAYLOR THOMAS	HD	M	42	WAGGONER	SSX HOLLINGTON	IRON LATCH	9
85	TAYLOR THOMAS	LG	U	55	AG.LAB	SSX SALEHURST	SHOP HOUSE	18
30	TAYLOR THOMAS	SO	U	1		SSX HOLLINGTON	IRON LATCH	9
29	TAYLOR THOMAS	SO	U	11		SSX CROWHURST	FORWARD LANE	146
48	TAYLOR THOMAS	VR	U	24	RAILWAY LAB	OXF	RAILWAY HUT	135
29	TAYLOR UN-NAMED INFANT BOY	SO	U	3W		SSX CROWHURST	FORWARD LANE	146
16	TAYLOR WILLIAM	HD	M	41	FARM LAB	SSX BATTLE	HIGH COTTAGE	144
94	TAYLOR WILLIAM	HD	M	43	AG.LAB	SSX WESTFIELD	STAPLE CROSS	244
12	TAYLOR WILLIAM	SO	U	1		SSX CROWHURST	BINES FARM	144

#	Name	Status	Age	Occupation	County/Parish	Place	Ref
16	TAYLOR WILLIAM	SO U	4		SSX CROWHURST	HIGH COTTAGE	144
30	TAYLOR WILLIAM	SO U	13		SSX HOLLINGTON	IRON LATCH	9
29	TAYLOR WILLIAM	SO U	16		SSX CROWHURST	FORWARD LANE	146
94	TAYLOR WILLIAM	SO U	18	AG.LAB	SSX EWHURST	STAPLE CROSS	244
58	TAYLOR WILLIAM	SV U	24	AG.LAB	KEN TUDLEY	HOLLINGTON LODGE	13
108	TEDHAMS HENRY	NP U	24	AG.LAB	SSX ASHBURNHAM	NOT GIVEN	101
108	TEDHAMS WILLIAM	NP U	19	AG.LAB	SSX ASHBURNHAM	NOT GIVEN	101
27	TEDMAN EPHRAIM	SV U	23	AG.LAB	SSX WALBERTON	LITTLE WORSHAM SIDLEY	79
14	TERRY CAROLINE	DA U	6	SCHOLAR	SSX BEXHILL	RIST WOOD SIDLEY	77
14	TERRY CHARLOTTE	DA U	17		SSX BEXHILL	RIST WOOD SIDLEY	77
14	TERRY EDWARD	SO U	14	AG.LAB	SSX BEXHILL	RIST WOOD SIDLEY	77
14	TERRY GEORGE	BR U	40	AG.LAB	SSX BEXHILL	RIST WOOD SIDLEY	77
14	TERRY GEORGE	SO U	19	AG.LAB	SSX BEXHILL	RIST WOOD SIDLEY	77
14	TERRY JOHN	SO U	5	SCHOLAR	SSX BEXHILL	RIST WOOD SIDLEY	77
14	TERRY LUCY	DA U	11	SCHOLAR	SSX BEXHILL	RIST WOOD SIDLEY	77
14	TERRY PHILLY	DA U	9	SCHOLAR	SSX BEXHILL	RIST WOOD SIDLEY	77
14	TERRY SARAH	WI M	49		SSX MOUNTFIELD	RIST WOOD SIDLEY	77
14	TERRY WILLIAM	HD M	50	AG.LAB	SSX BEXHILL	RIST WOOD SIDLEY	77
52	TESTER CHARLES	HD M	27	GARDENER	SSX BATTLE	NOT GIVEN	94
52	TESTER ELIZABETH	WI M	30		SSX BEXHILL	NOT GIVEN	94
52	TESTER M E (FEMALE)	DA U	3M		SSX BEXHILL	NOT GIVEN	94
24	TESTER PHILLEYDELPHIA	DA W	41	HOUSEKEEPER	SSX CROWHURST	SAMPSON'S FARM	131
11	TESTER SARAH	HD U	39		SSX CATSFIELD	BELL HILL	25
53	TESTER SARAH JANE	DL U	15		SSX HASTINGS	NOT GIVEN	
11	TESTER SUSAN	DA U	7	SCHOLAR	SSX BEXHILL	BELL HILL	25
17	TEYNHAM DOWAGER LADY	HD W	60	PEERESS	IRL MAYO	OAKLANDS	174
58	THARRARD OWEN	VR U	20	AG.LAB	SSX HELLINGLY	BARRACKS	180
19	THOMAS AGNES	SV U	14	HOUSE SERVANT	NOT GIVEN	SEDLESCOMBE STREET	188
50	THOMAS ALFRED	HD M	40	BLACKSMITH	SSX BEXHILL	SIDLEY GREEN	82
83	THOMAS ALFRED	SV U	17	BLACKSMITH JM	SSX BEXHILL	NOT GIVEN (LITTLE COMMON)	47
63	THOMAS ANN	DA U	20		SSX BEXHILL	SIDLEY GREEN	83
42	THOMAS ANN	WI M	36		SSX GUESTLING	WORK-HOUSE	157
30	THOMAS BENJAMIN	SO U	10		SSX WESTFIELD	KENT STREET	165
65	THOMAS CHARLES	SO U	14		SSX WHATLINGTON	CASTLEMANS	210
1	THOMAS CHARLES	SO U	21	CABINET MAKER	SSX WESTFIELD	INGREHAMS FARM - SIDLEY	75
63	THOMAS CICLY	DA U	22		SSX BEXHILL	SIDLEY GREEN	83
42	THOMAS DELIA	DA U	11		NOT GIVEN (?WESTFIELD)	WORK-HOUSE	157
13	THOMAS DOROTHY	WI M	57		SSX BEXHILL	MILL HOUSE - SIDLEY	66
1	THOMAS EDWARD	SO U	27	EMPLOYED ON FATHER'S FARM	SSX BEXHILL	INGREHAMS FARM - SIDLEY	75
30	THOMAS EDWIN	SO U	1		SSX WESTFIELD	KENT STREET	165
32	THOMAS EDWIN	SO U	9		SSX WESTFIELD	KENT STREET	166
32	THOMAS ELIZA	WI M	50		SSX FAIRLIGHT	KENT STREET	166
114	THOMAS ELIZABETH	WI M	50		SSX BEXHILL	NOT GIVEN	102
65	THOMAS ELLEN	DA U	9M		SSX SEDLESCOMBE	CASTLEMANS	210
36	THOMAS FOOTS	SV U	68	HOUSE SERVANT	SSX CHICHESTER	HERST	191
30	THOMAS GEORGE	HD M	48	AG.LAB	SSX WESTFIELD	KENT STREET	165
1	THOMAS GEORGE	HD M	60	FARMER 180 AC EMP 6	SSX WESTFIELD	INGREHAMS FARM - SIDLEY	75
6	THOMAS GEORGE	NP U	23	AG.LAB	SSX WESTFIELD	WHEEL	162
38	THOMAS GODFREY URBAN	SO U	6	SCHOLAR	SSX MOUNTFIELD	FOOTLAND	206
32	THOMAS HANNAH	DA U	17		SSX WESTFIELD	KENT STREET	166
63	THOMAS HARRIET	DA U	24		SSX BEXHILL	SIDLEY GREEN	83
65	THOMAS HARRIETT	DA U	3		SSX SEDLESCOMBE	CASTLEMANS	210
6	THOMAS HARRIETT	WI M	34		SSX FAIRLIGHT	WHEEL	162
32	THOMAS HENRY	HD M	53	AG.LAB	SSX WESTFIELD	KENT STREET	166
30	THOMAS HENRY	SO U	8		SSX WESTFIELD	KENT STREET	165
65	THOMAS HORACE	SO U	7		SSX SEDLESCOMBE	CASTLEMANS	210
6	THOMAS JAMES	HD M	34	AG.LAB	SSX ORE	WHEEL	162
6	THOMAS JAMES	SO U	2		SSX WESTFIELD	WHEEL	162
65	THOMAS JAMES	SO U	11		SSX SEDLESCOMBE	CASTLEMANS	210
30	THOMAS JAMES	SO U	14		SSX WESTFIELD	KENT STREET	165
114	THOMAS JAMES	SO U	14	AG.LAB	SSX GUESTLING	NOT GIVEN	102
50	THOMAS JANE	WI M	45		SSX CATSFIELD	SIDLEY GREEN	82
52	THOMAS JANE EDITH	SV U	19	COOK	SSX MOUNTFIELD	GREAT SANDERS	194
25	THOMAS JESSE	SO U	3M		SSX WESTFIELD	WHEELERS COT	154
42	THOMAS JOHN	HD M	40	AG.LAB	SSX WESTFIELD	WORK-HOUSE	157
114	THOMAS JOHN	HD M	49	SURVEYOR	SSX HOLLINGTON	NOT GIVEN	102
42	THOMAS JOHN	SO U	13		NOT GIVEN (?WESTFIELD)	WORK-HOUSE	157
114	THOMAS JOHN	SO U	17	AG.LAB	SSX BEXHILL	NOT GIVEN	102
38	THOMAS JULIA ANN	DA U	1		SSX SEDLESCOMBE	FOOTLAND	206
38	THOMAS LAURA MIRIAM	DA U	1		SSX SEDLESCOMBE	FOOTLAND	206
114	THOMAS LOUISA	DA U	8	SCHOLAR	SSX BEXHILL	NOT GIVEN	102
63	THOMAS MARGARET	DA U	6	SCHOLAR	SSX BEXHILL	SIDLEY GREEN	83
1	THOMAS MARGARET	DA U	25	EMPLOYED AT HOME	SSX WESTFIELD	INGREHAMS FARM - SIDLEY	75
42	THOMAS MARIA	DA U	7		NOT GIVEN (?WESTFIELD)	WORK-HOUSE	157
6	THOMAS MARY	DA U	1		SSX WESTFIELD	WHEEL	162
25	THOMAS MARY	DA U	2		SSX WESTFIELD	WHEELERS COT	154
65	THOMAS MARY	DA U	16		SSX WHATLINGTON	CASTLEMANS	210
1	THOMAS MARY	WI M	57		SSX BEXHILL	INGREHAMS FARM - SIDLEY	75
44	THOMAS MARY	WI M	67		SSX BEXHILL	POPPING HOLE LANE	207
42	THOMAS MARY ANN	DA U	3		NOT GIVEN (?WESTFIELD)	WORK-HOUSE	157
38	THOMAS MIRIAM	WI M	32		SSX SEDLECOMBE	FOOTLAND	206
19	THOMAS PHILADELPHIA	VR U	54		SSX WESTFIELD	COTTAGE	174
42	THOMAS PHILIDELPHIA	VR W	81		NOT GIVEN (?WESTFIELD)	WORK-HOUSE	157
65	THOMAS REBECCA	WI M	35		SSX WHATLINGTON	CASTLEMANS	210
25	THOMAS RICHARD	HD M	26	AG.LAB	SSX WESTFIELD	WHEELERS COT	154
65	THOMAS RICHARD	HD M	38	SAWYER	SSX MOUNTFIELD	CASTLEMANS	210

	Name	Rel		Age	Occupation	Birth County	Birthplace	Address	No
25	THOMAS RICHARD	SO	U	4		SSX	BREDE	WHEELERS COT	154
25	THOMAS SARAH	WI	M	25		SSX	UDIMORE	WHEELERS COT	154
30	THOMAS SARAH	WI	M	44		SSX	WESTFIELD	KENT STREET	165
38	THOMAS SARAH MATILDA	DA	U	3		SSX	MOUNTFIELD	FOOTLAND	206
65	THOMAS SELINA	DA	U	9		SSX	SEDLESCOMBE	CASTLEMANS	210
38	THOMAS STEPHEN	HD	M	30	CARPENTER	SSX	MOUNTFIELD	FOOTLAND	206
63	THOMAS STEPHEN	HD	W	45	REGISTRAR	SSX	BEXHILL	SIDLEY GREEN	83
63	THOMAS STEPHEN	SO	U	18		SSX	BEXHILL	SIDLEY GREEN	83
42	THOMAS WALTER	SO	U	15		SSX	WESTFIELD	WORK-HOUSE	157
13	THOMAS WILLIAM	HD	M	63	FARMER 18 AC EMP 1	SSX	WESTFIELD	MILL HOUSE - SIDLEY	66
44	THOMAS WILLIAM	HD	M	64	AG.LAB	SSX	MOUNTFIELD	POPPING HOLE LANE	207
6	THOMAS WILLIAM	SO	U	3		SSX	WESTFIELD	WHEEL	162
42	THOMAS WILLIAM	SO	U	4		NOT GIVEN (?WESTFIELD)		WORK HOUSE	157
32	THOMAS WILLIAM	SO	U	15		SSX	WESTFIELD	KENT STREET	166
1	THOMAS WILLIAM	SO	U	29	EMPLOYED ON FATHER'S FARM	SSX	BEXHILL	INGREHAMS FARM - SIDLEY	75
61	THOMPSETT ALFRED	SO	U	17	AG.LAB	NOT GIVEN		PUMP HOUSE	13
61	THOMPSETT ANN	WI	M	49		NOT GIVEN		PUMP HOUSE	13
61	THOMPSETT BENJAMIN	SO	U	7		NOT GIVEN		PUMP HOUSE	13
67	THOMPSETT CHARLES	SO	U	1		SSX	HOLLINGTON	COSSUMS	14
67	THOMPSETT EDWARD	HD	M	24	AG.LAB	SSX	CROWHURST	COSSUMS	14
67	THOMPSETT ELLEN	DA	U	3M		SSX	HOLLINGTON	COSSUMS	14
61	THOMPSETT EMILY	DA	U	13		NOT GIVEN		PUMP HOUSE	13
67	THOMPSETT FRANCES	WI	M	24		SSX	HOLLINGTON	COSSUMS	14
61	THOMPSETT LESTER	SO	U	20	AG.LAB	NOT GIVEN		PUMP HOUSE	13
67	THOMPSETT MARY ANN	DA	U	3		SSX	HOLLINGTON	COSSUMS	14
61	THOMPSETT SARAH	DA	U	10		NOT GIVEN		PUMP HOUSE	13
61	THOMPSETT WILLIAM	HD	M	50	AG.LAB	NOT GIVEN		PUMP HOUSE	13
4	THOMPSON ANN	DL	M	24		SSX	BATTLE	CATSFIELD GREEN	120
4	THOMPSON SUSSANNAH	WI	M	55		SSX	NORTHIAM	CATSFIELD GREEN	120
31	THOMPSON THOMAS	LG	U	29	AG.LAB	SSX	CATSFIELD	STREAM HILL	123
4	THOMPSON WILLIAM	HD	M	56	AG.LAB	SSX	BATTLE	CATSFIELD GREEN	120
64	THOMSON JOHN	LG	M	30	RAILWAY LAB	IRL		RAILWAY HUT	137
35	THORN ELIZABETH	GD	U	2		SSX	CROWHURST	DAIRY HOUSE	133
35	THORN MARIA	DA	U	20		SSX	CROWHURST	DAIRY HOUSE	133
42	THORNE ANN ELIZABETH	DA	U	7M		SSX	HOLLINGTON	OLD CORNER	10
42	THORNE CHARLOTTE	WI	M	26		SSX	HASTINGS	OLD CORNER	10
39	THORNE ELLEN	GD	U	1		SSX	CATSFIELD	NOT GIVEN	111
42	THORNE ESAU WILLIAM	SO	U	5		SSX	CATSFIELD	OLD CORNER	10
39	THORNE JOSEPH	HD	M	60	HUCKSTER	DOR	STURMINSTER	NOT GIVEN	111
42	THORNE JOSEPH	SO	U	3		SSX	CATSFIELD	OLD CORNER	10
39	THORNE PHILLEY	WI	M	36		SSX	CATSFIELD	NOT GIVEN	111
42	THORNE WILLIAM	HD	M	27	AG.LAB	KEN	APPLEDORE	OLD CORNER	10
26	THORNE? BETSY	CI	U	14		SSX	CATSFIELD	CATSFIELD STREAM	123
26	THORNE? GEORGE	BR	U	24		SSX	CATSFIELD	CATSFIELD STREAM	123
54	THURSTON? ELIZABETH	NS	M	65	NURSE	SSX	BREDE	CASTLEMANS	195
28	THWAITES ELIZABETH	HD	M	21	BUTCHER'S WIFE	SSX	BATTLE	BEXHILL STREET	26
28	THWAITES GEORGE	SO	U	11M		SSX	BEXHILL	BEXHILL STREET	26
72	THWAITES SARAH	WI	M	51		SSX	BEXHILL	NOT GIVEN	97
72	THWAITES THOMAS	HD	M	54	FARMER 100AC EMP 5	KEN	STAPLEHURST	NOT GIVEN	97
72	THWAITES THOMAS	SO	U	15		SSX	BEXHILL	NOT GIVEN	97
20	TICEHURST ALFRED	SO	U	10		SSX	BEXHILL	IN THE LIBERTY	39
9	TICEHURST ALFRED	SO	U	26		SSX	BEXHILL	ROCK HSE BANK IN THE LIBERTY	38
19	TICEHURST ELIZABETH	DA	U	2		SSX	BEXHILL	IN THE LIBERTY	39
19	TICEHURST EMMA	DA	U	9	SCHOLAR	SSX	PEVENSEY	IN THE LIBERTY	39
7	TICEHURST FRANCIS	HD	W	66	PAUPER AG.LAB	SSX	WARTLING	SIDLEY	90
19	TICEHURST FRANCIS	SO	U	4	SCHOLAR	SSX	BEXHILL	IN THE LIBERTY	39
19	TICEHURST GEORGE	HD	M	40	CARPENTER JM	SSX	BEXHILL	IN THE LIBERTY	39
19	TICEHURST GEORGE	SO	U	6	SCHOLAR	SSX	BEXHILL	IN THE LIBERTY	39
20	TICEHURST HANNAH	DA	U	6?		SSX	BEXHILL	IN THE LIBERTY	40
20	TICEHURST HORACE	SO	U	7M		SSX	BEXHILL	IN THE LIBERTY	40
20	TICEHURST JAMES	HD	M	38	AG.LAB	SSX	BEXHILL	IN THE LIBERTY	39
9	TICEHURST JAMES	HD	M	74	LOOKER	SSX	NINFIELD	ROCK HSE BANK IN THE LIBERTY	38
82	TICEHURST JOSEPH	HD	U	34	GARDENER	SSX	BATTLE	CHURCH STREET	99
20	TICEHURST MARY A	WI	M	33		SSX	HOLLINGTON	IN THE LIBERTY	39
20	TICEHURST SARAH	DA	U	12		SSX	BEXHILL	IN THE LIBERTY	39
9	TICEHURST SARAH	WI	M	71		SSX	CATSFIELD	ROCK HSE BANK IN THE LIBERTY	38
19	TICEHURST TAMER	WI	M	36		SSX	PEVENSEY	IN THE LIBERTY	39
10	TITMUS JOHN	LG	U	25	RAIL LAB	MDX		RAILWAY HUT	5
3	TOLHURST JAMES	SO	U	1		SSX	WESTFIELD	COCK MARTINS	161
3	TOLHURST JAMES	SV	M	46	GENERAL SERVANT	SSX	ICKLESHAM	COCK MARTINS	162
3	TOLHURST MARY	SV	U	44		SSX	ORE	COCK MARTINS	162
3	TOLHURST MARY A	DA	U	7		SSX	GUESTLING	COCK MARTINS	161
3	TOLHURST SARAH	WI	M	38		SSX	BREDE	COCK MARTINS	161
3	TOLHURST THOMAS	HD	M	46	FARMER	SSX	ORE	COCK MARTINS	161
3	TOLHURST THOMAS	SO	U	4		SSX	GUESTLING	COCK MARTINS	161
76	TOLHURST WILLIAM	VR	U	17	AG.LAB	SSX	BATTLE	APPLE TREE	182
54	TOMPSETT CHARLES	LG	U	26	AG.LAB	SSX	CATSFIELD	PARSONAGE	9
55	TOMPSETT JABEZ	/	U	22	WHEELWRIGHT'S JM	KEN	GOUDHURST	EWHURST GREEN	224
58	TOURE LEWES?	LG	U	31	RAILWAY LAB	DEV	EXETER	RAILWAY HUT	136
40	TREE CAROLINE	SV	U	20		SSX	BREDE	MILL	177
50	TREE CHARLOTTE	SV	U	26		SSX	BODIAM	SWALES GREEN	208
49	TREMBLE ALEXANDER	HD	M	33	COAST GUARD	CUM	WHITEHAVEN	NO.5 GALLEY HILL	29
54	TREMBLE ALEXANDER	HD	M	61	COAST GUARD	CUM	WHITEHAVEN	COAST GUARD STATION	30
49	TREMBLE EDWARD T	SO	U	4		SSX	HASTINGS	NO.6 GALLEY HILL	29
54	TREMBLE EDWIN	SO	U	16	SCHOLAR AT HOME	SSI	WINCHELSEA	COAST GUARD STATION	30
54	TREMBLE ELLEN	WI	M	55		CUM	WHITEHAVEN	COAST GUARD STATION	30

	Name			Age	Occupation	County	Birthplace	Dwelling	No.
49	TREMBLE SARAH A	WI	M	23		DEV	RINGMORE	NO.6 GALLEY HILL	29
49	TREMBLE SARAH E	DA	U	2		SSX	BEXHILL	NO.6 GALLEY HILL	29
60	TREMBLE WILLIAM	/	U	1	NURSECHILD	SSX	BEXHILL	SIDLEY GREEN	83
49	TREMBLE WILLIAM	SO	U	1		SSX	BEXHILL	NO.6 GALLEY HILL	29
18	TROTTER JOHN	LG	/	33	JOINER	SCT		STEPHEN'S CROUCH	121
105	TROTTMAN NATHANIEL	HD	U	69	FUND HOLDER	MDX	HOXTON	ROSE COTTAGE	101
52	TRUSLER FREDERICK	VR	U	42	GROOM	SSX	BRIGHTON	HOPPOLE CASTLE	179
66	TUCK R HOLMES	LG	U	33	CURATE OF THE PARISH	NFK	LINSWOOD	EWHURST GREEN	225
18	TUCKEY G	LG	U	24	RAIL LAB	SSX	WEST THORNEY	PIGLANDS	7
64	TUNEY THOMAS	LG	U	21	RAILWAY LAB	IRL		RAILWAY HUT	137
22	TURNER ABRAHAM	SO	U	4		YKS	MORLEY	RAILWAY HUT	8
23	TURNER ALFRED	BR	U	22		SSX	BEXHILL	GLINE FARM SIDLEY	78
55	TURNER AMELIA (FURNER?)	SV	U	22	GENERAL SERVANT	SSX	WHATLINGTON	HANCOX FARM	209
24	TURNER ANN	WI	M	54?		SSX	BEXHILL	SIDLEY	69
28	TURNER BARBARY	SV	U	20		SSX	WESTFIELD	PLOUGH INN	155
21	TURNER BENJAMIN	SV	U	17	AG.LAB	SSX	BEXHILL	FREEZELAND? SIDLEY	68
11	TURNER CALEB	SO	U	13	AG.LAB	SSX	SEDLESCOMBE	SEDLESCOMBE STREET	202
24	TURNER CHARLOTTE	DA	U	8	SCHOLAR	SSX	BATTLE	SIDLEY	69
5	TURNER CHARLOTTE	SV	U	17	HOUSE SERVANT	SSX	WESTFIELD	NOT GIVEN	106
23	TURNER ELIZA	CI	U	30		SSX	RYE	GLINE FARM SIDLEY	78
23	TURNER ELLEN	CI	U	24		SSX	BEXHILL	GLINE FARM SIDLEY	78
11	TURNER ELLEN	DA	U	11	SCHOLAR	SSX	SEDLESCOMBE	SEDLESCOMBE STREET	202
11	TURNER EMILY	DA	U	6	SCHOLAR	SSX	SEDLESCOMBE	SEDLESCOMBE STREET	202
21	TURNER EMILY	WI	M	22?		SSX	WESTFIELD	SAW PIT COTTAGE	154
22	TURNER EMMA	DA	U	6		KEN	TUNBRIDGE WELLS	RAILWAY HUT	8
18	TURNER GEORGE	HD	M	24	BRICKMAKER	SSX	LAUGHTON	SEDLESCOMBE STREET	188
21	TURNER GEORGE	HD	M	34	AG.LAB	SSX	WESTFIELD	SAW PIT COTTAGE	154
56	TURNER GEORGE	LG	M	37	AG.LAB	SSX	WESTFIELD	BARRACKS	179
53	TURNER GEORGE	LG	U	18	BRICKLAYER'S LAB	SSX	MOUNTFIELD	BEECH	208
18	TURNER GEORGE	SO	U	3	SCHOLAR	SSX	LAUGHTON	SEDLESCOMBE STREET	188
67	TURNER HANNAH	WI	M	61		SSX	WESTFIELD	ONION HILL	181
23	TURNER HARRIET	CI	U	24		SSX	BEXHILL	GLINE FARM SIDLEY	78
24	TURNER HARRIET	DA	U	13		SSX	BEXHILL	SIDLEY	69
25	TURNER HARRIET	WI	M	35		SSX	RIPE	QUEENS HEAD SEDLESCOMBE ST	189
18	TURNER HESTER	WI	M	26		SSX	LAUGHTON	SEDLESCOMBE STREET	188
22	TURNER ISAAC	HD	M	40	RAIL LAB	NOT GIVEN		RAILWAY HUT	8
22	TURNER ISAAC	SO	U	11		SSX	BALCOMBE	RAILWAY HUT	8
86	TURNER JAMES	HD	M	47	INN KEEPER	SSX	BREDE	HARROW INN	18
23	TURNER JAMES	HD	U	45	FARMER 300 AC EMP 8	SSX	LITTLEHAMPTON	GLINE FARM SIDLEY	78
11	TURNER JAMES	SO	U	20	AG.LAB	SSX	SEDLESCOMBE	SEDLESCOMBE STREET	202
24	TURNER JAMES	SO	U	29	AG.LAB	SSX	BEXHILL	SIDLEY	69
23	TURNER JANE	CI	U	26		SSX	BEXHILL	GLINE FARM SIDLEY	78
18	TURNER JANE	DA	U	5M		SSX	SEDLESCOMBE	SEDLESCOMBE STREET	188
56	TURNER JANE	LG	M	35		SSX	BATTLE	BARRACKS	179
22	TURNER JOHN	SO	U	1M		SSX	HOLLINGTON	RAILWAY HUT	8
23	TURNER MARGARET	CI	U	34		KEN	WHITSTABLE	GLINE FARM SIDLEY	78
21	TURNER MARIA	WI	M	23	RAIL LAB (SIC)	YKS	LEEDS	RAILWAY HUT	7
86	TURNER MARIA	WI	M	45		SSX	BREDE	HARROW INN	18
55	TURNER MARTHA (FURNER?)	SV	U	24	GENERAL SERVANT	SSX	WHATLINGTON	HANCOX FARM	209
18	TURNER MARY	DA	U	2		SSX	SEDLESCOMBE	SEDLESCOMBE STREET	189
1	TURNER MARY	DL	U	10	SCHOLAR	KEN	DOVER	HOLYERS HILL	89
13	TURNER MARY	SV	U	21		SSX	BEXHILL	PARSONAGE	130
11	TURNER MARY	WI	M	50		SSX	NINFIELD	SEDLESCOMBE STREET	202
8	TURNER MARY ANN	HK	U	27		SSX	MOUNTFIELD	COLLIERS GREEN	233
22	TURNER PHILADELPHIA	WI	M	40		NOT GIVEN		RAILWAY HUT	8
53	TURNER PHILLY	WI	M	23		SSX	BEXHILL	2 MARINE COTTAGES	29
22	TURNER REBECCA	DA	U	14		HORSTED KEYNES		RAILWAY HUT	8
67	TURNER RICHARD	HD	M	62	THATCHER	SSX	WESTFIELD	ONION HILL	181
25	TURNER RICHARD	SO	U	16		SSX	LAUGHTON	QUEENS HEAD SEDLESCOMBE ST	189
11	TURNER ROBERT	SO	U	19	AG.LAB	SSX	SEDLESCOMBE	SEDLESCOMBE STREET	202
49	TURNER SAMUEL	VR	U	32	RAILWAY LAB	SSX	HASTINGS	RAILWAY HUT	135
24	TURNER SARAH	DA	U	27		SSX	BEXHILL	SIDLEY	69
21	TURNER STEPHEN	SO	U	1		HUDDERSFIELD		RAILWAY HUT	7
25	TURNER THOMAS	HD	M	49	INN KEEPER	SSX	EAST HOATHLY	QUEENS HEAD SEDLESCOMBE ST	189
24	TURNER THOMAS	HD	M	65	AG.LAB	SSX	MAYFIELD	SIDLEY	69
25	TURNER THOMAS	SO	U	11	SCHOLAR	SSX	LAUGHTON	QUEENS HEAD SEDLESCOMBE ST	189
11	TURNER TOM	SO	U	9	SCHOLAR	SSX	SEDLESCOMBE	SEDLESCOMBE STREET	202
53	TURNER WILLIAM	HD	M	33	AG.LAB	SSX	BEXHILL	2 MARINE COTTAGES	29
11	TURNER WILLIAM	HD	M	56	AG.LAB	SSX	SEDLESCOMBE	SEDLESCOMBE STREET	202
80	TURNER WILLIAM	SV	W	70	MILLER JM	SSX	HAILSHAM	MOUN SION	182
23	TURNER WILLIAM	VR	U	33	GROCER	KEN	WHITSTABLE	GLINE FARM SIDLEY	78
21	TURNER WILLIAM ROBERT	HD	M	22	RAIL LAB	SSX	HORSTED KEYNES	RAILWAY HUT	7
85	TUTT WILLIAM	GS	U	13		SSX	HOLLINGTON	SHOP HOUSE	18
19	TYHURST ELIZABETH	DA	U	19		SSX	WESTFIELD	ROSE VILLA	153
19	TYHURST JOHN	HD	M	56	FARMER	SSX	WESTFIELD	ROSE VILLA	153
19	TYHURST MATILDA	WI	M	49		SSX	BECKLEY	ROSE VILLA	153
96	TYSOME SAMUEL	LG	W	40	RAIL LAB	BKM	EMMERTON	HUT	19
47	UMSTANE FREDERICK	HD	M	28	RAILWAY LAB	UNKNOWN		RAILWAY HUT	134
47	UMSTANE JANE	WI	M	26		SSX	BATTLE	RAILWAY HUT	134
47	UMSTANE MARKE	SO	U	1		FEVERSHAM		RAILWAY HUT	134
23	UNDERWOOD SARAH	CI	U	23		SSX	BEXHILL	BEXHILL STREET	26
83	UNICOMB JAMES	HD	U	73	SHOEMAKER	SSX	EWHURST	STAPLE CROSS	243
13	UNSCOMBE HANNAH	DL	U	9	SCHOLAR	SSX	EWHURST	DAGG LANE	217
13	UNSCOMBE JAMES	SL	U	11	AG.LAB	SSX	EWHURST	DAGG LANE	217
13	UNSCOMBE MARY ANN	DL	U	7	SCHOLAR	SSX	EWHURST	DAGG LANE	217
13	UNSCOMBE WILLIAM	SL	U	14	AG.LAB/BLIND IN ONE EYE	SSX	EWHURST	DAGG LANE	217

	Name	Rel	Age	Occupation	County	Birthplace	Address	No
30	UPFIELD ANNE JANE	DA U	2		SSX	WARBLETON	STREAM HILL	123
30	UPFIELD EMILY	DA U	3		SSX	WARBLETON	STREAM HILL	123
30	UPFIELD HARIOT	WI M	39?		SSX	WARBLETON	STREAM HILL	123
30	UPFIELD JOHN	HD M	33	MILLWRIGHT	SSX	WARBLETON	STREAM HILL	123
1	UPTON ELIZA	WI M	35		SSX	NORTHIAM	KNIGHTS	151
1	UPTON JAMES	HD M	31	AG.LAB	SSX	NORTHIAM	KNIGHTS	151
1	UPTON JAMES	SO U	1M		SSX	WESTFIELD	KNIGHTS	151
95	UPTON SARAH	SV U	41	HOUSE SERVANT	SSX	BREDE	VICARAGE	100
1	UPTON WILLIAM	SO U	1		SSX	WESTFIELD	KNIGHTS	151
15	VANN ANN	HD U	21	DRESSMAKER	SSX	BATTLE	SEDLESCOMBE STREET	188
22	VEENESS ALFRED	BR U	31	AG.LAB	SSX	NINFIELD	NOT GIVEN	131
22	VEENESS GEORGE	HD W	35	UNWELL	SSX	NINFIELD	NOT GIVEN	131
4	VENESS ALFRED	GS U	4		SSX	ST.LEONARDS ON SEA	LITTLE WILTING	5
30	VENESS ELIZABETH	SV U	15		SSX	BEXHILL	LUNSFORDS CROSS HSE SIDLEY	70
4	VENESS ELIZABETH	WI M	59		SSX	BEXHILL	LITTLE WILTING	5
26	VENESS FRANCES	DA U	10		SSX	NINFIELD	SIDLEY	69
26	VENESS GEORGE	SO U	8		SSX	NINFIELD	SIDLEY	69
26	VENESS JAMES	HD M	38	AG.LAB	SSX	NINFIELD	SIDLEY	69
70	VENESS JAMES	SV U	18	AG.LAB	SSX	NINFIELD	POTMANS	114
90	VENESS JANE	HD W	85?	PAUPER	SSX	PENHURST	NOT GIVEN	100
90	VENESS MOSES	SO U	42	GARDENER	SSX	BEXHILL	NOT GIVEN	100
26	VENESS PHILLY	WI M	39		SSX	BRIGHTLING	SIDLEY	69
4	VENESS ROBERT	HD M	63	WAGGONER	SSX	BEXHILL	LITTLE WILTING	5
5	VENESS SARAH	/ W	85	FORMERLY FARMER'S WIFE	SSX	NINFIELD	KITES NEST	51
66	VENESS STEPHEN	SV U	21	WAGGONER	SSX	NINFIELD	BEACH FARM	14
11	VENESS THOMAS	SV U	24	AG.LAB	SSX	NINFIELD	WILTING FARM HOUSE	6
27	VENIS EDWARD	SV U	65	AG.LAB	SSX	PENHURST	LITTLE WORSHAM SIDLEY	79
1	VERNON BOWATER H	BR U	56	CAPTAIN - ARMY	WOR	PERDISWELL	VICARAGE HOUSE	161
1	VERNON MARK H	HD M	54	VICAR WESTFIELD	WOR	WHITE LADY ASTON	VICARAGE HOUSE	161
1	VERNON MARY M	WI M	41		HRT		VICARAGE HOUSE	161
50	VICKERY LAURENCE	HD M	52	TAILOR	SOM	LANGPORT	NOT GIVEN	94
50	VICKERY M S (FEMALE)	WI M	42		SRY	KINGSTON	NOT GIVEN	94
35	VIDLER ALICE	SV U	16	HOUSE MAID	SSX	BATTLE	MILWARDS	10
80	VIDLER ANN	SV U	19		SSX	BEXHILL	BELL HOTEL	99
29	VIDLER ANN	WI M	65		SSX	HOLLINGTON	NOT GIVEN	92
39	VIDLER CHARLES	SO U	1		SSX	SEDLESCOMBE	HAILSFORD	192
29	VIDLER E A (FEMALE)	GD U	1		SSX	BEXHILL	NOT GIVEN	92
29	VIDLER EDWARD	HD M	60	AG.LAB	SSX	HOOE	NOT GIVEN	92
39	VIDLER HESTER	WI M	25		SSX	SEDLESCOMBE	HAILSFORD	192
2	VIDLER JAMES	HD M	68	AG.LAB	SSX	HOOE	LOWER BARNHORN	37
39	VIDLER JAMES COLEMAN	HD M	25	FARMER 386 AC EMP 19	SSX	RYE	HAILSFORD	192
80	VIDLER MARY	SV U	24		SSX	BEXHILL	BELL HOTEL	99
2	VIDLER MARY	WI M	62		SSX	HOOE	LOWER BARNHORN	37
3	VIDLER PHILLY	SV U	33	HOUSE SERVANT	SSX	HOOE	BARNHORN HILL	37
34	VINSEN WILLIAM	VR U	21	BRICKLAYER	SSX	WADHURST	BEXHILL STREET	27
99	VYE MARY	WI M	57		DOR	SHIPPEN (SIC) GEORGE	NOT GIVEN	101
99	VYE THOMAS	HD M	54	COAST GUARD	DOR	WEST LULWORTH	NOT GIVEN	101
29	WAIL CHARLES	HD M	28	AG.LAB	SSX	CATSFIELD	STREAM HILL	123
29	WAIL CHARLES	SO U	1		SSX	BATTLE	STREAM HILL	123
6	WAIL DAVID	HD M	40	AG.LAB	SSX	CATSFIELD	CATSFIELD GREEN	120
14	WAIL DAVID	HD M	72	AG.LAB	SSX	CROWHURST	PORTER'S LODGE	121
6	WAIL DAVID	SO U	2		SSX	CATSFIELD	CATSFIELD GREEN	120
29	WAIL ELIZABETH	DA U	4		SSX	BATTLE	STREAM HILL	123
29	WAIL ELIZABETH	WI M	25		SSX	BATTLE	STREAM HILL	123
14	WAIL ELIZABETH	WI M	54		SSX	CHICHESTER	PORTER'S LODGE	121
6	WAIL FRANCES	WI M	41		SSX	SEDLESCOMBE	CATSFIELD GREEN	120
6	WAIL HANNAH	DA U	17		SSX	CATSFIELD	CATSFIELD GREEN	120
29	WAIL JAMES	SO U	2		SSX	BATTLE	STREAM HILL	123
6	WAIL JANE	DA U	14		SSX	CATSFIELD	CATSFIELD GREEN	120
6	WAIL MARY	DA U	10		SSX	CATSFIELD	CATSFIELD GREEN	120
11	WAIL MARY ANN	SV U	17	HOUSEMAID	SSX	CATSFIELD	PARK HOUSE	121
29	WAIL WILLIAM	SO U	6	SCHOLAR	SSX	BATTLE	STREAM HILL	123
25	WAISCOAT JESSE	LG M	39	RAIL LAB	SSX	WELDRON	QUEENS HEAD SEDLESCOMBE ST	189
1	WAITE ALDRED B	SO U	6		SSX	CATSFIELD	CATSFIELD DOWN	106
61	WAITE ELIZA	DA U	3M		SSX	CATSFIELD	NOT GIVEN	113
37	WAITE FANNY	DA U	17	HOUSE SERVANT	SSX	CATSFIELD	NOT GIVEN	110
89	WAITE GEORGE	SO U	26	BUTCHER	SSX	WARTLING	NOT GIVEN	99
37	WAITE HARRIETT	DA U	13	SCHOLAR	SSX	CATSFIELD	NOT GIVEN	111
1	WAITE JAMES	SO U	1		SSX	CATSFIELD	CATSFIELD DOWN	106
37	WAITE LUCY	WI M	54	CHARWOMAN	SSX	CATSFIELD	NOT GIVEN	110
89	WAITE MARY	HD W	67	ANNUITANT	SSX	HERSTMONCEUX	NOT GIVEN	99
1	WAITE MARY	WI M	43		SSX	CATSFIELD	CATSFIELD DOWN	106
1	WAITE MICHAEL	HD M	37	LAB	SSX	SEDLESCOMBE	CATSFIELD DOWN	106
61	WAITE ROBERT	HD M	26	AG.LAB	SSX	CATSFIELD	NOT GIVEN	113
61	WAITE SILVESTER	WI M	28		SSX	HAILSHAM	NOT GIVEN	113
6	WAITE THOMAS	LG W	55	LEATHER DRESSER	WIL	LOCKERRAGE	COACH & HORSES	187
61	WAITE THOMAS	SO U	3		SSX	CATSFIELD	NOT GIVEN	113
61	WAITE TOBERT	SO U	2		SSX	CATSFIELD	NOT GIVEN	113
37	WAITE WILLIAM	HD M	58	GUN POWDER MAKER	SSX	CATSFIELD	NOT GIVEN	110
11	WALKER EMILY	LG U	20	ASSISTANT IN FARM HOUSE	SSX	LAMBERHURST	WILTING FARM HOUSE	6
49	WALKER JOSEPH	VR U	25	RAILWAY LAB	SSX	HASTINGS	RAILWAY HUT	135
96	WALL WILLIAM	LG U	25	RAIL LAB	NTH	EARTHLINGHAM	HUT	19
24	WALLERS DAVID	SO U	4		SSX	CATSFIELD	CATSFIELD STREAM	122
24	WALLERS ELLEN	DA U	11	SCHOLAR	SSX	CATSFIELD	CATSFIELD STREAM	122
24	WALLERS ESTER	DA U	18		SSX	CATSFIELD	CATSFIELD STREAM	122
24	WALLERS GEORGE	SO U	8	SCHOLAR	SSX	CATSFIELD	CATSFIELD STREAM	122

	Name			Age	Occupation	County	Birthplace	Location	No.
24	WALLERS GODFREY	SO	U	18	AG.LAB	SSX	CATSFIELD	CATSFIELD STREAM	122
24	WALLERS HARIOT	WI	M	40		SSX	CATSFIELD	CATSFIELD STREAM	122
24	WALLERS MARY	DA	U	3		SSX	CATSFIELD	CATSFIELD STREAM	122
24	WALLERS THOMAS	HD	M	40	AG.LAB	SSX	CATSFIELD	CATSFIELD STREAM	122
24	WALLERS THOMAS	SO	U	9	SCHOLAR	SSX	CATSFIELD	CATSFIELD STREAM	122
23	WALLIS FREDERICK	HD	M	35	SURGEON LIC.APOTH.HALL	SSX	HARTFIELD	BEXHILL STREET	26
23	WALLIS FREDERICK M	SO	U	3		SSX	BEXHILL	BEXHILL STREET	26
23	WALLIS JAMES R	SO	U	2		SSX	BEXHILL	BEXHILL STREET	26
23	WALLIS MARY	WI	M	29		NTH	PITSFORD	BEXHILL STREET	26
23	WALLIS MARY C	DA	U	4		NTH	PITSFORD	BEXHILL STREET	26
23	WALLIS PETER	SO	U	1M		SSX	BEXHILL	BEXHILL STREET	26
44	WALSH JAMES	HD	M	36	EXCAVATOR	IRL		RAILWAY HUT	134
44	WALSH JOHN	SO	U	13		SCT		RAILWAY HUT	134
44	WALSH MARGRET	DA	U	2		HRT		RAILWAY HUT	134
44	WALSH MARY	DA	U	8		FRANCE		RAILWAY HUT	134
44	WALSH MARY	WI	M	34		IRL		RAILWAY HUT	134
44	WALSH MICHAL	SO	U	5		FRANCE		RAILWAY HUT	134
3	WALTER ALFRED	SO	U	5		SSX	HOLLINGTON	LITTLE WILTING	4
3	WALTER ANN	DA	U	2		SSX	HOLLINGTON	LITTLE WILTING	4
3	WALTER HARRIETT	DA	U	8	SCHOLAR	SSX	HOLLINGTON	LITTLE WILTING	4
3	WALTER JOHN	HD	M	41	AG.LAB	SSX	ROBERTSBRIDGE	LITTLE WILTING	4
3	WALTER MARY	DA	U	10	SCHOLAR	SSX	HOLLINGTON	LITTLE WILTING	4
3	WALTER MARY	WI	M	33		SSX	NINFIELD	LITTLE WILTING	4
103	WARD JANE	HD	W	71	ANNUITANT	SSX	BEXHILL	NOT GIVEN	101
26	WARREN ELIZABETH	GD	U	32	ANNUITANT	MDX	ST.MARTIN IN FIELD	BEXHILL STREET	26
8	WARREN JOHN	LG	U	30	RAIL LAB	DEV	NORTH BOVEY	RAILWAY HUT	5
14	WATERS BENJAMIN	BR	U	28	AG.LAB	SSX	CATSFIELD	NOT GIVEN	108
17	WATERS BETSY	DA	U	13		SSX	CROWHURST	CROWHURST VILLAGE	130
17	WATERS CHARLES	SO	U	11		SSX	CROWHURST	CROWHURST VILLAGE	130
14	WATERS DANIEL	BR	U	23	AG.LAB	SSX	CATSFIELD	NOT GIVEN	108
41	WATERS EDWIN	LG	U	21	RAILWAY LAB	UPWHAY		RAILWAY HUT	134
14	WATERS ELIZABETH	CI	U	39		SSX	CATSFIELD	NOT GIVEN	108
17	WATERS GUSTAVIOUS	SO	U	3		SSX	CROWHURST	CROWHURST VILLAGE	131
14	WATERS HENRY	BR	U	31	AG.LAB	SSX	CATSFIELD	NOT GIVEN	108
14	WATERS MARY	MO	W	64		SSX	SEDLESCOMBE	NOT GIVEN	108
17	WATERS MARY	WI	M	31		SSX	CROWHURST	CROWHURST VILLAGE	130
14	WATERS RICHARD	HD	U	36	FARMER 40 AC	SSX	BRIGHTLING?*	NOT GIVEN	108
17	WATERS SUSANNA	DA	U	4		SSX	CROWHURST	CROWHURST VILLAGE	131
17	WATERS THOMAS	HD	M	41	BLACKSMITH	SSX	WARBLETON	CROWHURST VILLAGE	130
33	WATERS THOMAS	VR	W	60		SSX	HOLLINGTON	MOOR FARM	155
17	WATERS TILDEN	SO	U	14		SSX	CROWHURST	CROWHURST VILLAGE	130
17	WATERS TOM HAMMOND	SO	U	2		SSX	CROWHURST	CROWHURST VILLAGE	131
4	WATSON GEORGE	SV	U	24	AG.LAB	NOT GIVEN (?WESTFIELD)		PADDLESTONS	152
12	WATSON HARRIET	WI	M	26	DEAF	SSX	NORTHIAM	COLLIERS GREEN	233
63	WATSON JAMES	HD	M	30	SHOEMAKER	SSX	EWHURST	HILL SHOP	180
11	WATSON JAMES	LG	U	26	AG.LAB	OXF	HENTH?	PARK HOUSE	121
63	WATSON MARTHA	WI	M	25	GROCER	SSX	BREDE	HILL SHOP	180
32	WATSON MARY	SV	U	41	GENERAL SERVANT	SSX	BREDE	CRIPPS COTTAGE	253
18	WATSON MATILDA	HD	U	30?	HOUSE KEEPER	SSX	EWHURST	SEDLESCOMBE STREET	203
12	WATSON RICHARD	SO	U	2		SSX	WESTFIELD	COLLIERS GREEN	233
63	WATSON ROLAND H	SO	U	2		SSX	EWHURST	HILL SHOP	180
63	WATSON SAMUEL	LG	W	76	CROSS POSTMAN	SSX	SEDLESCOMBE	BAULKHAM GREEN	196
12	WATSON WILLIAM	HD	M	27	CORDWAINER	SSX	NORTHIAM	COLLIERS GREEN	233
12	WATSON WILLIAM	SO	U	2		SSX	EWHURST	COLLIERS GREEN	233
18	WATSON WILLIAM	SO	U	6		SSX	SEDLESCOMBE	SEDLESCOMBE STREET	203
64	WAY WILLIAM	BD	/	3		MDX	OLD COMPTON ST SOHO	NEW COTTAGE	14
10	WEBB CAROLINE	DA	U	12	SCHOLAR	SSX	CATSFIELD	NOT GIVEN	107
10	WEBB CAROLINE	WI	M	31		SSX	CATSFIELD	NOT GIVEN	107
27	WEBB EMMA	WI	M	64		SSX	BEXHILL	WHY DOWN	165
10	WEBB FRANCES	DA	U	4		SSX	CATSFIELD	NOT GIVEN	107
59	WEBB GEORGE	SO	U	3		NTH	ASHTON	RAILWAY COTTAGE	30
10	WEBB JAMES	SO	U	8	SCHOLAR	SSX	CATSFIELD	NOT GIVEN	107
10	WEBB JAMES	VR	U	20	MILLER	SSX	CATSFIELD	NOT GIVEN	107
10	WEBB JOHN	SO	U	10	SCHOLAR	SSX	CATSFIELD	NOT GIVEN	107
27	WEBB MARY	DA	U	24		SSX	WESTFIELD	WHY DOWN	165
10	WEBB MARY	MO	W	77	ANNUITANT	SSX	CATSFIELD	NOT GIVEN	107
59	WEBB MARY	WI	M	32		BKM	STONY STRATFORD*	RAILWAY COTTAGE	30
77	WEBB NATHANIEL	LG	W	79	FUNDHOLDER	ESS	KELVEDON	STEMPS? LODGE	16
10	WEBB STEPHEN	HD	M	32	AG.LAB	SSX	CATSFIELD	NOT GIVEN	107
10	WEBB STEPHEN	SO	U	7M		SSX	CATSFIELD	NOT GIVEN	107
13	WEBB SUSANNAH	HD	M	44	GROCER & DRAPER EMP2	SSX	SEDLESCOMBE	SEDLESCOMBE STREET	188
59	WEBB THOMAS	HD	M	37	RAIL LAB	NTH	ASHTON	RAILWAY COTTAGE	30
27	WEBB WILLIAM	HD	M	63	AG.LAB	SSX	SEDLESCOMBE	WHY DOWN	165
10	WEBB WILLIAM	LG	U	19	RAILWAY LAB	SFK	BENTLEY	FORWARD LANE	129
59	WEBB WILLIAM	SO	U	9M		SSX	BEXHILL	RAILWAY COTTAGE	30
27	WEBB WILLIAM H	SO	U	6		SSX	WESTFIELD	WHY DOWN	165
88	WEEKES ELIZABETH	WI	M	37		SSX	HOOE	HOLLOW WALLS	244
88	WEEKES ELLEN	DA	U	16		SSX	EWHURST	HOLLOW WALLS	244
88	WEEKES SARAH	DA	U	7		SSX	EWHURST	HOLLOW WALLS	244
88	WEEKES WILLIAM	HD	M	42	AG.LAB	SSX	EWHURST	HOLLOW WALLS	244
88	WEEKES WILLIAM	SO	U	19	AG.LAB	SSX	EWHURST	HOLLOW WALLS	244
24	WEEKS ELIZABETH	CI	U	27		SSX	SALEHURST	ROCKS	175
24	WEEKS GEORGE W	HD	U	24	FARMER 150 AC EMP 5LAB	SSX	SALEHURST	ROCKS	175
2	WEEKS JAMES	LG	U	50	AG.LAB	UNKNOWN		CATSFIELD GREEN	119
24	WEEKS MARY	CI	U	29		SSX	SALEHURST	ROCKS	175
24	WEEKS THOMAS J	VR	U	20		SSX	SALEHURST	ROCKS	175

	Name			Age	Occupation	Birthplace	Address	
13	WELFARE MARY	WI	M	60		SSX CATSFIELD	PICKNELL GREEN	52
13	WELFARE STEPHEN	HD	M	53	AG.LAB	SSX BEXHILL	PICKNELL GREEN	52
36	WELLARD CHARLES	SO	U	5		SSX ST.LEONARDS	EMMARYS	10
36	WELLARD ELIZABETH	CI	U	17		SSX ORE	EMMARYS	10
63	WELLER AMELIA	DA	U	10		SSX HOLLINGTON	LAMBS COTTAGE	14
59	WELLER ANN	DA	U	1W		SSX CROWHURST	RAILWAY HUT	136
63	WELLER CAROLINE	DA	U	5		SSX HOLLINGTON	LAMBS COTTAGE	14
59	WELLER CHARLOTTE	DA	U	2		SSX HASTINGS	RAILWAY HUT	136
63	WELLER EDWARD	HD	M	50	CARPENTER	SSX HOLLINGTON	LAMBS COTTAGE	14
10	WELLER EDWARD	LG	U	20	RAIL LAB	SRY DORKING	RAILWAY HUT	5
41	WELLER ELIZA	/	/	30	DAUGHTER OF SARAH	SSX EWHURST	OCKHAM	221
63	WELLER ELIZABETH	DA	U	19	SERVANT	NOT GIVEN	LAMBS COTTAGE	14
79	WELLER ELIZABETH	HD	W	83	HOUSEKEEPER	SSX BREDE	STEMPS?	16
79	WELLER ELIZABETH	WI	M	43		SSX BATTLE	LAMBS COTTAGE	14
79	WELLER ESTHER	DA	U	56		SSX HOLLINGTON	STEMPS?	16
55	WELLER ESTHER	ML	W	67	BLIND	SSX ROBERTSBRIDGE	BARRACKS	179
45	WELLER FREDERIC	SO	U	12		SSX ASHBURNHAM	YEW TREE	167
45	WELLER HARRIETT	WI	M	30		SSX ASHBURNHAM	YEW TREE	167
31	WELLER HENRY	LG	U	28	AG.LAB	SSX NORTHIAM	ADAMS LANE	236
59	WELLER JAMES	HD	M	25	RAILWAY LAB	WARDBENTON HILL	RAILWAY HUT	136
44	WELLER JAMES	HD	M	26	SHEPHERD	SSX HOLLINGTON	YEW TREE	167
70	WELLER JAMES	HD	M	63	CARPENTER	SSX RYE	SCHOOL HOUSE	15
45	WELLER JEREMIAH	HD	M	30	AG.LAB	SSX BEXHILL	YEW TREE	167
63	WELLER JERRY	SO	U	8		SSX HOLLINGTON	LAMBS COTTAGE	14
31	WELLER JESSE	LG	U	24	AG.LAB	SSX NORTHIAM	REEVES	236
63	WELLER JOHN	SO	U	25	CARPENTER	SSX BATTLE	LAMBS COTTAGE	14
59	WELLER MARY	DA	U	4		DOR STROTING??	RAILWAY HUT	136
63	WELLER MARY	DA	U	17		SSX HOLLINGTON	LAMBS COTTAGE	14
63	WELLER MOSES	SO	U	12		SSX HOLLINGTON	LAMBS COTTAGE	14
44	WELLER PHILLIS	WI	M	26		SSX CROWHURST	YEW TREE	167
45	WELLER RACHEL	DA	U	6		SSX HOLLINGTON	YEW TREE	167
41	WELLER SARAH	/	W	71		SSX BREDE	OCKHAM	221
45	WELLER SARAH	DA	U	2		SSX HOLLINGTON	YEW TREE	167
59	WELLER SARAH	WI	M	25	RAILWAY LAB	WARDBENTON HILL	RAILWAY HUT	136
70	WELLER SARAH	WI	M	59		SSX BRIGHTLING	SCHOOL HOUSE	15
4	WELLER SARAH ELIZABETH	WI	M	37		SSX UDIMORE	BEACON HOUSE	249
4	WELLER SPENCER DAVIS	HD	M	60	LANDED PROPRIETOR	SSX EWHURST	BEACON HOUSE	249
79	WELLER THOMAS	SO	U	57	AG.LAB	SSX GUESTLING	STEMPS?	16
44	WELLER WILLIAM	GS	U	1		SSX BEXHILL	NOT GIVEN	56
45	WELLER WILLIAM	SO	U	6M		SSX WESTFIELD	YEW TREE	167
63	WELLER WILLIAM	SO	U	15		SSX HOLLINGTON	LAMBS COTTAGE	14
16	WENHAM ELIZABETH	VR	/			UNKNOWN	NOT GIVEN	108
15	WENHAM EMILY	DA	U	17		SSX WESTFIELD	BLUMANS	163
15	WENHAM FANNY	DA	U	11		SSX WESTFIELD	BLUMANS	163
15	WENHAM JANE	DA	U	10		SSX WESTFIELD	BLUMANS	163
4	WENHAM JANE	WI	M	22		SSX ORE	WHEEL	162
4	WENHAM JOHN	HD	M	26	AG.LAB	SSX WESTFIELD	WHEEL	162
15	WENHAM JOHN	HD	M	62	AG.LAB	SSX BREDE	BLUMANS	163
16	WENHAM MARY A	/	6		SCHOLAR NURSE CHILD	SSX HELLINGLY	NOT GIVEN	108
15	WENHAM PHILADELPHIA	DA	U	15		SSX WESTFIELD	BLUMANS	163
15	WENHAM PHILADELPHIA	WI	M	52		SSX WESTFIELD	BLUMANS	163
61	WENHAM SARAH	HD	W	70	ANNUITANT	SSX HOOE	NOT GIVEN	95
77	WENHAM SARAH ANN	SV	U	22	HOUSE MAID	SSX WESTFIELD	STEMPS? LODGE	16
54	WENHAM WILLIAM	LG	W	68	AG.LAB	SSX WESTHAM	LITTLE COMMON	57
43	WENHAM WILLIAM	SV	U	23		SSX WESTFIELD	IRELAND	167
31	WEST ANN	DA	U	12		SSX WESTFIELD	KENT STREET	165
15	WEST CHARLOTTE	DA	U	3		SSX WESTFIELD	PARKERS	153
15	WEST CHARLOTTE	WI	M	25		SSX WESTFIELD	PARKERS	153
31	WEST EDWARD	SO	U	2M		SSX WESTFIELD	KENT STREET	165
31	WEST EDWIN	SO	U	20		SSX WESTFIELD	KENT STREET	165
15	WEST GEORGE	HD	M	30	AG.LAB	SSX MARESFIELD	PARKERS	153
31	WEST HARRIETT	DA	U	18		SSX WESTFIELD	KENT STREET	165
15	WEST HENRY	SO	U	1		SSX WESTFIELD	PARKERS	153
31	WEST JANE	DA	U	9		SSX WESTFIELD	KENT STREET	165
31	WEST JOHN	SO	U	16		SSX WESTFIELD	KENT STREET	165
31	WEST MATILDA	DA	U	2		SSX WINCHELSEA	KENT STREET	165
31	WEST MERCY	WI	M	41		SSX WESTFIELD	KENT STREET	165
31	WEST RICHARD	HD	M	43	AG.LAB	SSX WESTFIELD	KENT STREET	165
31	WEST RICHARD	SO	U	5		SSX WESTFIELD	KENT STREET	165
31	WEST ROBERT	SO	U	7		SSX WESTFIELD	KENT STREET	165
23	WESTON ALBERT	HD	M	35	RETIRED FARMER	SSX SEDLESCOMBE	SEDLESCOMBE STREET	189
23	WESTON ALBERT WELFARE	SO	U	8	SCHOLAR	SSX SEDLESCOMBE	SEDLESCOMBE STREET	189
22	WESTON ELIZA	DA	U	42		SSX BEXHILL	REDLEYS	174
22	WESTON ELIZABETH	HD	W	68	FARMER	SSX BATTLE	REDLEYS	174
83	WESTON EMILY	WI	M	27		SSX CROWHURST	NOT GIVEN (LITTLE COMMON)	47
8	WESTON HARRIET	DA	U	36		SSX SEDLESCOMBE	SEDLESCOMBE STREET	202
23	WESTON HENRY PLANTAGENET	SO	U	7	SCHOLAR	SSX SEDLESCOMBE	SEDLESCOMBE STREET	189
83	WESTON JAMES	HD	M	31	BLACKSMITH EMP 1	SSX BEXHILL	NOT GIVEN (LITTLE COMMON)	47
3	WESTON JAMES	LG	U	21	BRICKMAKER	OXF WOODSTOKE	FORWARD LANE	128
87	WESTON JOHN	LG	U	8	SCHOLAR	SSX BECKLEY	STAPLE CROSS	244
22	WESTON JOHN	SO	U	24		SSX BEXHILL	REDLEYS	175
23	WESTON MARY	WI	M	38		SSX BATTLE	SEDLESCOMBE STREET	189
8	WESTON ROBERT	HD	M	69	FARMER 150 AC EMP 9	SSX SEDLESCOMBE	SEDLESCOMBE STREET	203
8	WESTON SARAH	WI	M	72		SSX BREDE	SEDLESCOMBE STREET	202
35	WESTON THOMAS	GS	U	7	SCHOLAR	SSX PENHURST	CROWHAM	176
22	WESTON THOMAS	SO	U	41	FARMER	SSX BEXHILL	REDLEYS	175

22	WESTON WALTER	SO U	40			SSX BEXHILL	REDLEYS	175
80	WHATSON CAROLINE	DA U	19			SSX WESTFIELD	MOUN SION	182
80	WHATSON EDWIN	SO U	17			SSX WESTFIELD	MOUN SION	182
80	WHATSON MARTHA	WI M	57			SSX EWHURST	MOUN SION	182
80	WHATSON STEPHEN	HD M	55	MILLER & RETAILER OF BEER	SSX EWHURST	MOUN SION	182
58	WHATSON STEPHEN	VR U	22	AG.LAB		SSX WESTHAM	BARRACKS	180
22	WHEELER GEORGE	LG U	NK40	RAIL LAB		UNKNOWN	RAILWAY HUT	8
26	WHEELER GEORGE	SV U	17	PAGE		HAM FAWLEY	CATSFIELD PLACE CHURCH HSE	110
59	WHISMARK? ANN	SV U	16	HOUSE SERVANT		SSX CATSFIELD	NOT GIVEN	113
58	WHITBREAD ELLEN	SV U	23	HOUSEKEEPER		SRY BOROUGH ST.JOHN	HOLLINGTON LODGE	12
58	WHITBREAD JANE	VR U	14	SEAMSTRESS		SSX SALEHURST	HOLLINGTON LODGE	13
58	WHITBREAD MARY	SV U	20	HOUSEMAID		SSX SALEHURST	HOLLINGTON LODGE	13
6	WHITE ANN	DA U	12	SCHOLAR		SSX BEXHILL	ROSE COTTAGE - SIDLEY	65
6	WHITE DANIEL	HD M	38	BAKER/MILLER/FARMER 50AC 8	SSX UNKNOWN	ROSE COTTAGE - SIDLEY	65
6	WHITE ELIZA	DA U	7	SCHOLAR		SSX BEXHILL	ROSE COTTAGE - SIDLEY	65
23	WHITE ELIZA	WI M	23			NOR DICKLEBURGH	NOT GIVEN	131
23	WHITE GEORGE	HD M	42	GROCER & DRAPER		SRY	NOT GIVEN	131
7	WHITE HANNAH	WI M	23			SSX BEXHILL	NOT GIVEN	52
7	WHITE JAMES	HD M	27	AG.LAB		SSX BATTLE	NOT GIVEN	52
81	WHITE JOHN	HD W	60	BONE GATHERER		MDX FELTHAM	NOT GIVEN (LITTLE COMMON)	47
2	WHITE JOHN	LG U	26	RAIL LAB		HAM ALTON	RAILWAY HUT	4
6	WHITE JOSIAH	SO U	2			SSX BEXHILL	ROSE COTTAGE - SIDLEY	65
23	WHITE LYDIA	DA U	7			SSX CROWHURST	NOT GIVEN	131
6	WHITE MARIA	DA U	8M			SSX BEXHILL	ROSE COTTAGE - SIDLEY	65
6	WHITE MARY	DA U	10	SCHOLAR		SSX BEXHILL	ROSE COTTAGE - SIDLEY	65
6	WHITE MARY	WI M	37?			SSX BURWASH	ROSE COTTAGE - SIDLEY	65
62	WHITE SAMUEL	LG U	24	RAILWAY LAB		GLS STONEHOUSE	RAILWAY HUT	136
6	WHITE THOMAS	SO U	5	SCHOLAR		SSX BEXHILL	ROSE COTTAGE - SIDLEY	65
23	WHITE THOMAS	SO U	7			SSX CROWHURST	NOT GIVEN	131
21	WHITEMAN REBACCA	WI M	35			SSX SEDLESCOMBE	CRIPPS	252
21	WHITEMAN THOMAS	HD M	39	AG.LAB		SSX EWHURST	CRIPPS	252
4	WHITING ELIZA	HD U	28	SCHOOLMISTRESS		SSX HASTINGS	STREAM HOUSE	172
55	WHITING ELLEN	GD U	18			SSX BEXHILL	NOT GIVEN	112
1	WHITING REUBIN	SV U	38	BLACKSMITH		SSX CATSFIELD	CATSFIELD GREEN	119
55	WHITING RICHARD	HD W	85	AG.LAB		SSX CATSFIELD	NOT GIVEN	112
64	WHITING TOBEY	LG W	76	RAILWAY LAB		BRK BUCKLAND	RAILWAY HUT	137
11	WHYBORN ALFRED	HD M	25	AG.LAB		SSX BEXHILL	NOT GIVEN	90
11	WHYBORN CHARLOTTE	WI M	20			SSX BEXHILL	NOT GIVEN	90
11	WHYBORN EMILY	DA U	1			SSX BEXHILL	NOT GIVEN	90
14	WHYBORN FRANCES	SV W	60			KEN SANDHURST	SEDLESCOMBE STREET	202
28	WHYBORN JOHN	SV U	25	FARM SERVANT		SSX BEXHILL	WHITE HOUSE	92
2	WHYBORN KESIAH	DA U	16			SSX BEXHILL	BELL HILL	24
37	WHYBORN SARAH	WI M	23			SSX BURWASH	NOT GIVEN	93
37	WHYBORN THOMAS	HD M	33	AG.LAB		SSX LEWES	NOT GIVEN	93
2	WHYBORN THOMAS	HD W	54	AG.LAB		SSX HASTINGS	BELL HILL	24
55	WHYBORNE EDWIN	SO U	20	AG.LAB		SSX BEXHILL	ALM'S HOUSE SIDLEY	82
1	WHYBORNE FANNY	SV U	17	HOUSE SERVANT		SSX BEXHILL	INGREHAMS FARM - SIDLEY	75
71	WHYBORNE HENRY	SV U	18	AG.LAB		SSX BEXHILL	WOODS FARM SIDLEY	85
55	WHYBORNE MARIA	HD W	50	PAUPER AG.LAB'S WIFE		SSX BEXHILL	ALM'S HOUSE SIDLEY	82
35	WHYBURN ANN	WI M	32			SSX SALEHURST	SCHOOL HOUSE	253
89	WHYBURN ELIZABETH	MO W	87	PARISH RELIEF		SSX EWHURST	HOLLOW WALLS	244
66	WHYBURN ELLEN	SV U	22	SERVANT		SSX EWHURST	STAPLE CROSS	241
35	WHYBURN EMILY	DA U	11	SCHOLAR		SSX SALEHURST	SCHOOL HOUSE	253
35	WHYBURN HANNAH	DA U	2M			SSX SALEHURST	SCHOOL HOUSE	253
35	WHYBURN HARRIOT	DA U	5	SCHOLAR		SSX SALEHURST	SCHOOL HOUSE	253
35	WHYBURN HENRY	HD M	29	BRICKLAYER'S LAB		SSX SEDLESCOMBE	SCHOOL HOUSE	253
89	WHYBURN PHILADELPHIA	HD W	44	PARISH RELIEF		SSX SEDLESCOMBE	HOLLOW WALLS	244
35	WHYBURN THOMAS	SO U	8	SCHOLAR		SSX SALEHURST	SCHOOL HOUSE	253
89	WHYBURN THOMAS	SO U	15	AG.LAB		SSX EWHURST	HOLLOW WALLS	244
89	WHYBURN WILLIAM	SO U	14			SSX EWHURST	HOLLOW WALLS	244
23	WILLARD ELIZABETH	SV U	20	SERVANT		SSX SEDLESCOMBE	LORDINE	235
24	WILLARD MARY	SV U	26			SSX SALEHURST	ROCKS	175
19	WILLARD MARY	VR U	40			SSX EAST ASHLING	NOT GIVEN	53
56	WILLCOX SARAH MARIAH	HD U	37	SCHOOLMISTRESS		SOM BATH	NOT GIVEN	95
13	WILLIAMS FRANK	LG W	82	AG.LAB		SSX EWHURST	COLLIERS GREEN	234
63	WILLIAMS FREDERICK	LG U	24	BRICKMAKER		SSX BRIGHTON	BAULKHAM GREEN	196
60	WILLIAMS? JAMES	LG U	40	RAILWAY LAB		SSX HANDCROSS	RAILWAY HUT	136
15	WILLINGHAM MARY A	WI M	32			COR GWENNAP*	IN THE LIBERTY	39
15	WILLINGHAM THOMAS W	HD M	32	COAST GUARD		YORK HOLMPTON	IN THE LIBERTY	39
25	WILMARSH CHARLOTTE	WI M	21			SSX CATSFIELD	CATSFIELD STREAM	122
25	WILMARSH JOHN	HD M	26	AG.LAB		SSX CATSFIELD	CATSFIELD STREAM	122
52	WILSON CAROLINE	WI M	33			DEV PLYMOUTH	1 MARINE COTTAGES	29
10	WILSON CHARLES	LG U	25	RAILWAY LAB		HRT WATERFORD	FORWARD LANE	129
15	WILSON FANNY	/ U	2M			SSX HASTINGS	NOT GIVEN	90
52	WILSON WILLIAM	HD M	31	COAST GUARD		DEV PLYMOUTH	1 MARINE COTTAGES	29
27	WINBORN AARON	HD M	58	AG.LAB		SSX BEXHILL	NOT GIVEN	54
56	WINBORN ABEL	HD M	62	AG.LAB		SSX BEXHILL	NOT GIVEN	58
74	WINBORN AGNES	WI M	28			SSX BEXHILL	NOT GIVEN (LITTLE COMMON)	46
74	WINBORN ARTHUR	HD M	29	AG.LAB		SSX BEXHILL	NOT GIVEN (LITTLE COMMON)	46
1	WINBORN ELIZA	WI M	41			SSX CATSFIELD	CATSFIELD GREEN	119
54	WINBORN ELIZABETH	WI M	25			SSX BATTLE	2 STONE HOUSE	44
56	WINBORN ELIZABETH	WI M	55			SSX CROWHURST	NOT GIVEN	58
26	WINBORN GEORGE	LG W	78	AG.LAB		SSX BEXHILL	SIDLEY	69
37	WINBORN GEORGE	SV U	31	AG.LAB		SSX BEXHILL	BEXHILL STREET	28
27	WINBORN JAMES	SO U	20	AG.LAB		SSX BEXHILL	NOT GIVEN	54
54	WINBORN JOHN	HD M	25	AG.LAB		SSX BEXHILL	2 STONE HOUSE	44

	Name	Rel	Age	Occupation	County	Birthplace	Residence	No
1	WINBORN JOHN	HD M	41	VICTUALLER	SSX	CATSFIELD	CATSFIELD GREEN	119
60	WINBORN MARGARET E	DL U	12	SCHOLAR	SSX	BEXHILL	BIRCHINGTON	45
27	WINBORN MARY	WI M	55		SSX	HOOE	NOT GIVEN	54
63	WINBORN MARY ANN	WI M	33		SSX	BEXHILL	NOT GIVEN	58
74	WINBORN SARAH	DA U	10M		SSX	BEXHILL	NOT GIVEN (LITTLE COMMON)	46
60	WINBORN SOPHIA	DL U	10	SCHOLAR	SSX	BEXHILL	BIRCHINGTON	45
63	WINBORN STEPHEN	HD M	33	AG.LAB	SSX	BEXHILL	NOT GIVEN	58
74	WINBORN THOMAS	SO U	3		SSX	BEXHILL	NOT GIVEN (LITTLE COMMON)	46
1	WINBORN THOMAS	SO U	15		SSX	CATSFIELD	CATSFIELD GREEN	119
60	WINBORN THOMAS A	SL U	7	SCHOLAR	SSX	BEXHILL	BIRCHINGTON	45
15	WINBORN WILLIAM	SV U	20	WAGGONER	SSX	BEXHILL	CATSFIELD PLACE FARM	108
61	WINBORNE ANN	MO W	67		SSX	HOOE	SIDLEY GREEN	83
46	WINBORNE ELIZA	DA U	17		SSX	BEXHILL	SIDLEY GREEN	81
46	WINBORNE GEORGE	SO U	6		SSX	BEXHILL	SIDLEY GREEN	81
46	WINBORNE HANNAH	DA U	11		SSX	BEXHILL	SIDLEY GREEN	81
47	WINBORNE JAMES	HD M	74	FARMER 36 ACRES	SSX	BEXHILL	SIDLEY GREEN	81
47	WINBORNE JAMES	SO U	32	FARMER'S SON EMP AT HOME	SSX	BEXHILL	SIDLEY GREEN	81
47	WINBORNE MARY	WI M	70		SSX	BATTLE	SIDLEY GREEN	81
46	WINBORNE RICHARD	SO U	24	AG.LAB	SSX	BEXHILL	SIDLEY GREEN	81
46	WINBORNE SARAH	HD W	49	AG.LAB'S WIFE	SSX	EASTBOURNE	SIDLEY GREEN	81
24	WINCHESTER FRANCES	SV U	19	COOK	SSX	ASHBURNHAM	CATSFIELD RECTORY	109
30	WINHAM ARTHUR	SO U	3		SSX	BEXHILL	LITTLE COMMON	55
30	WINHAM ELLEN	DA U	1		SSX	BEXHILL	LITTLE COMMON	55
30	WINHAM EMMA	DA U	11		SSX	BEXHILL	LITTLE COMMON	55
30	WINHAM JAMES	HD M	31	BLACKSMITH	SSX	BEXHILL	LITTLE COMMON	55
30	WINHAM JANE	WI M	31		SSX	HASTINGS	LITTLE COMMON	55
63	WINTERMAN THOMAS	LG U	20	RAILWAY LAB		COLCHESTER	RAILWAY HUT	137
35	WISDEN JOSEPH	HD U	21	RAILWAY PORTER	SSX	BRIGHTON	BEXHILL STREET	27
27	WISE GEORGE	HD M	55	AG.LAB	SSX	SEDLESCOMBE	BRICKWALL	190
27	WISE GEORGE	SO U	24	SAWYER	SSX	SEDLESCOMBE	BRICKWALL	190
27	WISE HENRY	SO U	22	BRICKLAYER'S LAB	SSX	SEDLESCOMBE	BRICKWALL	190
27	WISE HERBERT	SO U	11	SCHOLAR	SSX	SEDLESCOMBE	BRICKWALL	190
27	WISE JANE	DA U	15		SSX	SEDLESCOMBE	BRICKWALL	190
27	WISE ROLAND	SO U	9	SCHOLAR	SSX	SEDLESCOMBE	BRICKWALL	190
27	WISE SARAH	WI M	49		SSX	BREDE	BRICKWALL	190
18	WISE THOMAS	LG W	37	CARPENTER	KEN	FRITTENDEN	SEDLESCOMBE STREET	203
27	WISE THOMAS	SO U	18	AG.LAB	SSX	SEDLESCOMBE	BRICKWALL	190
27	WISE WILLIAM	SO U	13	SCHOLAR	SSX	SEDLESCOMBE	BRICKWALL	190
63	WITMARSH JOHN	HD M	54	AG.LAB	SSX	NINFIELD	NOT GIVEN	113
63	WITMARSH JUDITH	WI M	55		SSX	BEXHILL	NOT GIVEN	113
26	WITMARSH MARTHA	DA U	11M		SSX	CATSFIELD	CATSFIELD STREAM	123
63	WITMARSH MARTHA J	SO U	19	AG.LAB	SSX	CATSFIELD	NOT GIVEN	113
26	WITMARSH MIHAYLEY	DA U	4		SSX	CATSFIELD	CATSFIELD STREAM	123
26	WITMARSH SARAH	WI M	30		KEN	APPLEDORE	CATSFIELD STREAM	122
63	WITMARSH TRATTON T	SO U	13	AG.LAB	SSX	CATSFIELD	NOT GIVEN	113
26	WITMARSH WILLOWBY	HD M	28	AG.LAB	SSX	CATSFIELD	CATSFIELD STREAM	122
10	WOOD ALBERT	SO U	9	SCHOLAR	SSX	CROWHURST	ADAMS FARM	143
10	WOOD ANN	DA U	4		SSX	CROWHURST	ADAMS FARM	143
52	WOOD CHARLES	SV M	40	BAILIFF LOOKER OF LAND	SSX	LINDFIELD	PAGES COTTAGE	44
65	WOOD CHRISTOPHER	SO U	15		SSX	WESTFIELD	ONION HILL	180
28	WOOD FRANCES	DA U	7		SSX	BEXHILL	WHITE HOUSE	92
28	WOOD FRANCIS	WI M	34		SSX	CROWHURST	WHITE HOUSE	92
19	WOOD GEORGE	LG U	25	RAILWAY LAB	HAM	HAVANT	CROWHURST VILLAGE	130
65	WOOD HANNAH	WI M	46		SSX	HASTINGS	ONION HILL	180
28	WOOD HARRIET	DA U	9		SSX	CROWHURST	WHITE HOUSE	92
65	WOOD HENRY	SO U	9		SSX	EWHURST	ONION HILL	180
27	WOOD JAMES	LG M	31	AG.LAB	SSX	BEXHILL	NOT GIVEN	54
63	WOOD JAMES	LG U	19	RAILWAY LAB	HAM		RAILWAY HUT	137
62	WOOD JAMES	LG U	29	RAILWAY LAB	SSX		RAILWAY HUT	136
65	WOOD JAMES	SO U	7		SSX	WESTFIELD	ONION HILL	181
52	WOOD JANE	/ M	37	BAILIFF'S WIFE	SSX	DENTON	PAGES COTTAGE	44
27	WOOD JANE	LG M	23		SSX	BEXHILL	NOT GIVEN	54
10	WOOD JANE	WI M	34		SSX	SEDLESCOMBE	ADAMS FARM	143
8	WOOD JOHN	HD M	52	FARMER 93 AC EMP 2	SSX	HAILSHAM	GOTHAM	52
8	WOOD JOHN	SO U	12	SCHOLAR	SSX	BEXHILL	GOTHAM	52
28	WOOD LOUISA	DA U	11		SSX	CROWHURST	WHITE HOUSE	92
35	WOOD MARY	HD W	76?	ANNUITANT	SSX	CATSFIELD	SIDLEY	71
8	WOOD MARY	WI M	38		SSX	CATSFIELD	GOTHAM	52
65	WOOD MARY A	DA U	11		SSX	GUESTLING	ONION HILL	180
10	WOOD RICHARD	HD M	39	FARMER 80AC EMP 2MEN	SSX	CROWHURST	ADAMS FARM	143
28	WOOD SARAH	DA U	4		SSX	BEXHILL	WHITE HOUSE	92
61	WOOD SARAH	HK M	39		SSX	BATTLE	RAILWAY HUT	136
10	WOOD THOMAS	HD M	35	FARMER 180 AC EMP 3	SSX	CROWHURST	WHITE HOUSE	92
28	WOOD THOMAS	SO U	2		SSX	BEXHILL	WHITE HOUSE	92
10	WOOD THOMAS	SO U	2		SSX	CROWHURST	ADAMS FARM	143
65	WOOD WILLIAM	HD M	49	AG.LAB	SSX	WESTFIELD	ONION HILL	180
10	WOOD WILLIAM	SO U	6	SCHOLAR	SSX	CROWHURST	ADAMS FARM	143
28	WOOD WILLIAM	SO U	14		SSX	CROWHURST	WHITE HOUSE	92
42	WOOD WILLIAM	SS U	25	AG.LAB	SSX	BEXHILL	SIDLEY	81
9	WOODEN ANN	SV U	14		SSX	CATSFIELD	WIDOWS	173
67	WOODEN BENJAMIN	SO U	2		SSX	CATSFIELD	NOT GIVEN	114
67	WOODEN ELIZA	WI M	38		SSX	BEXHILL	NOT GIVEN	113
67	WOODEN ELIZABETH	DA U	11		SSX	CATSFIELD	NOT GIVEN	113
67	WOODEN FILLY	DA U	9		SSX	CATSFIELD	NOT GIVEN	113
67	WOODEN HARRIETT	DA U	1M		SSX	CATSFIELD	NOT GIVEN	114
67	WOODEN JAMES	HD M	45	AG.LAB	SSX	CATSFIELD	NOT GIVEN	113

	Name	Rel	MS	Age	Occupation	County	Parish	Location	No
67	WOODEN JANE	DA	U	4		SSX	CATSFIELD	NOT GIVEN	114
67	WOODEN SARAH	DA	U	6		SSX	CATSFIELD	NOT GIVEN	114
66	WOODEN THOMAS	HD	U	46	AG.LAB	SSX	CATSFIELD	NOT GIVEN	113
67	WOODEN WILLIAM	SO	U	8		SSX	CATSFIELD	NOT GIVEN	113
39	WOODEN? JOHN	SL	U	8	SCHOLAR	SSX	CATSFIELD	NOT GIVEN	111
39	WOODEN? MICHAEL	SL	U	7	SCHOLAR	SSX	CATSFIELD	NOT GIVEN	111
39	WOODEN? SARAH	ML	W	79	PARISH RELIEF - PAUPER	SSX	PENHURST	NOT GIVEN	111
14	WOODRUFF CHARLOTTE	DA	U	1M		SSX	BEXHILL	IN THE LIBERTY	39
14	WOODRUFF GEORGE	SO	U	3		SSX	BEXHILL	IN THE LIBERTY	39
14	WOODRUFF HENRY	SO	U	6		SSX	BEXHILL	IN THE LIBERTY	39
14	WOODRUFF MARY	WI	M	32		KEN	SANDWICH	IN THE LIBERTY	39
14	WOODRUFF MARY A	DA	U	7		SSX	BEXHILL	IN THE LIBERTY	39
14	WOODRUFF MORRIS	HD	M	33	COAST GUARD	KEN	SANDWICH	IN THE LIBERTY	39
17	WOOLGAR DANIEL	SV	U	18	BLACKSMITH JM	SSX	HEIGHTON	SEDLESCOMBE STREET	188
116	WOOLGAR GAINEY	GD	U	18	SERVANT	SSX	BEXHILL	NOT GIVEN	102
72	WORSLEY ELIZABETH	WI	M	42		SSX	EWHURST	EWHURST GREEN	226
72	WORSLEY JAMES	HD	M	44	AG.LAB	SSX	EWHURST	EWHURST GREEN	226
72	WORSLEY JAMES	SO	U	18	AG.LAB	SSX	EWHURST	EWHURST GREEN	226
72	WORSLEY MARY	DA	U	20		SSX	EWHURST	EWHURST GREEN	226
72	WORSLEY SABINA	DA	U	9	SCHOLAR	SSX	EWHURST	EWHURST GREEN	225
72	WORSLEY SARAH	DA	U	13	SCHOLAR	SSX	EWHURST	EWHURST GREEN	226
26	WRATTEN STEPHEN	LG	U	74	AG.LAB	SSX	WARTLING	SIDLEY	78
33	WREN* FRANK	SO	U	18		SSX	CATSFIELD	BROOMHAM HOUSE	124
33	WREN* HENRY	SO	U	22		SSX	CATSFIELD	BROOMHAM HOUSE	124
33	WREN* HERBERT	SO	U	21		SSX	CATSFIELD	BROOMHAM HOUSE	124
33	WREN* JAMES	HD	M	51	FARMER 200 AC	SSX	CATSFIELD	BROOMHAM HOUSE	124
33	WREN* JAMES	SO	U	26		SSX	CATSFIELD	BROOMHAM HOUSE	124
33	WREN* MARY	WI	M	54		SSX	CATSFIELD	BROOMHAM HOUSE	124
33	WREN* MARY ELIZABETH	DA	U	17		SSX	CATSFIELD	BROOMHAM HOUSE	124
72	WRENN ANN	DA	U	16	DOMESTIC DUTIES	SSX	CATSFIELD	WATERMILL HOUSE	114
49	WRENN ANN MARIA	DA	U	1		SSX	HASTINGS	RAILWAY HUT	135
72	WRENN BENJAMIN	SO	U	8	SCHOLAR	SSX	CATSFIELD	WATERMILL HOUSE	114
72	WRENN CHARLES	SO	U	9	SCHOLAR	SSX	CATSFIELD	WATERMILL HOUSE	114
72	WRENN ELIZABETH J	DA	U	15	SCHOLAR	SSX	CATSFIELD	WATERMILL HOUSE	114
72	WRENN EMILY	DA	U	5	SCHOLAR	SSX	CATSFIELD	WATERMILL HOUSE	114
72	WRENN FREDERICK	HD	M	47	MILLER	SSX	CATSFIELD	WATERMILL HOUSE	114
72	WRENN FREDERICK	SO	U	11	SCHOLAR	SSX	CATSFIELD	WATERMILL HOUSE	114
49	WRENN GEORGE	SO	U	9		SSX	FOREST ROW	RAILWAY HUT	135
72	WRENN HANNAH	WI	M	43	DOMESTIC DUTIES	SSX	WESTFIELD	WATERMILL HOUSE	114
49	WRENN JAMES	SO	U	4		SSX	HARTFIELD	RAILWAY HUT	135
49	WRENN JANE	DA	U	7		SSX	FOREST ROW	RAILWAY HUT	135
49	WRENN JANE	WI	M	30		SSX	WITHYHAM	RAILWAY HUT	135
72	WRENN LOUIZA	DA	U	2		SSX	CATSFIELD	WATERMILL HOUSE	114
49	WRENN THOMAS	HD	M	30	RAILWAY LAB	SSX	EAST GRINSTEAD	RAILWAY HUT	135
75	WRIGHT BENJAMIN	SO	U	14	AG.LAB	SSX	BEXHILL	SPANKERS (LITTLE COMMON)	47
28	WRIGHT GEORGE	SV	U	18	HOUSE SERVANT	SSX	BEXHILL	WHEAT SHEAF INN	54
75	WRIGHT JOHN	HD	M	65	AG.LAB	SSX	ASHBURNHAM	SPANKERS (LITTLE COMMON)	47
75	WRIGHT SARAH	WI	M	61		SSX	DALLINGTON	SPANKERS (LITTLE COMMON)	47
23	WYBORN CHARLES	SV	U	26	AG.LAB	SSX	BEXHILL	GLINE FARM SIDLEY	78
14	YARROLD HANNAH	VR	U	16		MDX	BETHNEL GREEN	BELL HILL	25
70	YORK ALICE	NC	U	7	SCHOLAR	SSX	EWHURST	EWHURST GREEN	225
46	YORK EDWARD	NP	U	11		SSX	EWHURST	NOT GIVEN	238
46	YORK GEORGE	NP	U	6		SSX	EWHURST	NOT GIVEN	238
15	YORK JOHN	GF	W	79	BRICKLAYER	SSX	DALLINGTON	COLLIERS GREEN	234
51	YORK MARY	VR	U	26?	DRESSMAKER	SSX	SALEHURST	NOT GIVEN	112
2	YOUNG ANN	DA	U	21		SSX	BEXHILL	CLINCH GREEN HOUSE	51
2	YOUNG ELIZABETH	GD	U	13		SSX	BEXHILL	CLINCH GREEN HOUSE	51
2	YOUNG ISAAC	HD	W	59	FARMER 56 AC EMP 2	SSX	BEXHILL	CLINCH GREEN HOUSE	51
2	YOUNG JAMES	SO	U	17		SSX	BEXHILL	CLINCH GREEN HOUSE	51
13	YOUNG LUCY	VR	U	25	DRESSMAKER	SSX	BEXHILL	PICKNELL GREEN	52
13	YOUNG MARGARET	VR	U	1		SSX	BEXHILL	PICKNELL GREEN	52
41	YOUNG ROBERT	LG	U	19	RAILWAY LAB	DOR	BUKAM	RAILWAY HUT	134
22	YOUNG WILLIAM	/	W	63	TIMBER SAWYER	SSX	BUXTED	NOT GIVEN	54

IN THE VILLAGE	SEDLESCOMBE	211	OWLS COTTAGE.	WESTFIELD	177
INGREHAMS FARM SIDLEY	BEXHILL	75	PADDLESTONS	WESTFIELD	152
INMANS	WESTFIELD	177-178/180	PADGHAM	EWHURST	216
IRELAND	WESTFIELD	167	PADGHAM FARM	EWHURST	215-216
IRON LATCH	HOLLINGTON	9	PAGES COTTAGE	BEXHILL	44
KENT STREET	WESTFIELD	165-166	PAGES LODGE	BEXHILL	43
KEWHURST	BEXHILL	44	PARK COTTAGE	CATSFIELD	120
KEWHURST COTTAGE	BEXHILL	44	PARK GATE	CATSFIELD	120
KIDDS	WESTFIELD	173	PARK HOUSE	CATSFIELD	120-121
KITES NEST	BEXHILL	51	PARKERS	WESTFIELD	153
KNIGHTS	WESTFIELD	151	PARSONAGE	HOLLINGTON	9
LAMBS COTTAGE	HOLLINGTON	14	PEAR TREE	WESTFIELD	181
LAND MARES? SIDLEY	BEXHILL	68	PEAR TREES	BEXHILL	52
LANES END	BEXHILL	30	PEBSHAM FARM SIDLEY	BEXHILL	78
LANKHURST	WESTFIELD	155	PICKNELL GREEN	BEXHILL	52
LANKHURST COT	WESTFIELD	155	PIG HILL	WESTFIELD	166
LEWS	WESTFIELD	156	PIGLANDS	HOLLINGTON	7
LITTLE COMMON	BEXHILL	45-47/55/57	PINNIERS (LITTLE COMMON)	BEXHILL	45
LITTLE WILTING	HOLLINGTON	4-5	PIXES HOUSE	EWHURST	240
LITTLE WORSHAM SIDLEY	BEXHILL	78-79	PLACE	WESTFIELD	161
LODGE	WESTFIELD	176/179	PLATNIX	WESTFIELD	173
LONG LEES	EWHURST	219	PLOUGH INN	CROWHURST	142
LORDINE	EWHURST	235	PLOUGH INN	WESTFIELD	155
LORDINE FARM	EWHURST	235	POND HOUSE (LITTLE COMMON)	BEXHILL	47
LOW COTTAGE	WESTFIELD	153	POPPING HOLE LANE	SEDLESCOMBE	206-207
LOWER BARNHORN	BEXHILL	37	PORTER'S LODGE	CATSFIELD	121
LOWER FISHPOND	WESTFIELD	153	POTMANS	CATSFIELD	114
LUNSFORD LANE SIDLEY	BEXHILL	70	POWDER MILL LANE	CATSFIELD	110
LUNSFORDS CROSS HOUSE SIDLEY	BEXHILL	70	POWDERMILLS	CROWHURST	128
MABBS	SEDLESCOMBE	191	POWDERMILLS	SEDLESCOMBE	201
MADDAMS	EWHURST	220	PRAWLES	EWHURST	220
MARCHANTS	EWHURST	237-238	PRAWLES FARM	EWHURST	221
MARINE COTTAGES 1-4	BEXHILL	29-30	PRESTON COTTAGE SIDLEY	BEXHILL	81
MARLPIT COTTAGE	WESTFIELD	151	PRESTON FARM SIDLEY	BEXHILL	81
MARLPITS	CATSFIELD	122	PRESTON SIDLEY	BEXHILL	80
MARTELLO TOWER 46-47	BEXHILL	31	PRIMROSE COTTAGE	WESTFIELD	163
MARTELLO TOWER 48	BEXHILL	42	PUMP HOUSE	HOLLINGTON	13-14
MARTELLO TOWER 49	BEXHILL	41-42	QUEENS HEAD	BEXHILL	32
MARTELLO TOWER 50-53	BEXHILL	40-41	QUEENS HEAD	SEDLESCOMBE	189
MARTELLO TOWER 54	BEXHILL	38-39	RAILWAY COTTAGE	BEXHILL	30
MARTELLO TOWER 55	BEXHILL	38	RAILWAY GATE HOUSE	BEXHILL	41
MARTINS COTTAGE	WESTFIELD	178	RAILWAY HUT	CROWHURST	129/130/131
MAYFIELDS HOUSE	HOLLINGTON	6-7	RAILWAY HUT	CROWHURST	133-137/146
MAYFIELDS RAILWAY HUT	HOLLINGTON	6	RAILWAY HUT	HOLLINGTON	4/5/6/7-8
MILES'S	EWHURST	250	RAILWAY STATION	BEXHILL	30
MILL	WESTFIELD	177	RANSOM'S COTTAGE	CROWHURST	145
MILL COTTAGE	WESTFIELD	177	RANSOM'S HOUSE	CROWHURST	145
MILL COTTAGE - SIDLEY	BEXHILL	66	RANSOMS	WESTFIELD	178
MILL HOUSE SIDLEY	BEXHILL	66	RECTORY	SEDLESCOMBE	205
MILL PLATT	EWHURST	228	RECTORY HOUSE	EWHURST	224
MILLERS COTTAGE	BEXHILL	37	RED COTTAGE	WESTFIELD	181
MILWARDS	HOLLINGTON	9-10	REDLEYS	WESTFIELD	174/175
MOAT	WESTFIELD	167	REEVES	EWHURST	236-237
MOOR FARM	WESTFIELD	155	RENS	EWHURST	219-220
MOORS FARM	CROWHURST	146-147	RIAL? OAK	CROWHURST	144
MOUN SION	WESTFIELD	182	RIST WOOD SIDLEY	BEXHILL	76-77
MOUNT EPHRAIM	WESTFIELD	164	RIVER HALL	WESTFIELD	163
MOUNT IDOL - SIDLEY	BEXHILL	66	ROADSIDE CAMP	BEXHILL	60
MOUNT PLEASANT	SEDLESCOMBE	197	ROCK HOUSE BANK	BEXHILL	38
MOUNT PLEASANT	WESTFIELD	166/181	ROCKS	WESTFIELD	175
MOUNT PLEASANT SIDLEY	BEXHILL	68	ROCKS FARM	EWHURST	217
NASHES	CROWHURST	144-145	ROSE COTTAGE	BEXHILL	101
NATIONAL SCHOOL	CROWHURST	137	ROSE COTTAGE - SIDLEY	BEXHILL	65
NEAR FOOTLAND	SEDLESCOMBE	206	ROSE PLATT COTTAGE SIDLEY	BEXHILL	80
NEAR THE CHURCH	SEDLESCOMBE	205/	ROSE VILLA	WESTFIELD	153
NEW BARN FARM	CATSFIELD	106	SAM PIT COTTAGE	WESTFIELD	154
NEW COTTAGE	HOLLINGTON	14	SAMSONS SIDLEY	BEXHILL	69
NEW ENGLAND	WESTFIELD	164-165	SANDERS	WESTFIELD	174
NEW INN SIDLEY	BEXHILL	76	SCHOOL HOUSE	EWHURST	253
NEWHAVEN FARM	EWHURST	237	SCHOOL HOUSE	HOLLINGTON	15
OAK COTTAGE	WESTFIELD	152	SCHOOL HOUSE	WESTFIELD	162
OAKLANDS	WESTFIELD	174	SEDLESCOMBE STREET	SEDLESCOMBE	186-187/188-189/19?
OCKHAM	EWHURST	221			197/201-205/211
ODIAM	EWHURST	219			
ODIAM FARM	EWHURST	218/219	SEMPSTED FARM	EWHURST	235-236/240
ODIAM GATE	EWHURST	218	SEVEN OAKS	WESTFIELD	156
OFFICER'S COTTAGE	BEXHILL	39	SHOP HOUSE	HOLLINGTON	18
OLD CORNER	HOLLINGTON	10	SHOP HOUSES	CATSFIELD	124
OLD HOUSE	WESTFIELD	175	SHOREHAM	EWHURST	221-222
ONION HILL	WESTFIELD	180-181	SHORT WOOD HOUSE SIDLEY	BEXHILL	68
			SIDLEY	BEXHILL	64-71/75-85/89-90

EAST SUSSEX CENSUS - 1851 INDEX
Compiled by C.June Barnes

Volume 1 HO107 1634 folios 212-408 ISBN 1 870264 00 2
Parishes of Rye, East Guldeford, Iden, Broomhill and Playden; 5757 entries, with
full details (no addresses), plus supplement of Streets and Addresses index.
Price £3.30 collected, or £3.55 by post.

Volume 2 HO107 1634 folios 409-660 (end) ISBN 1 860264 01 0
Parishes of Peasmarsh, Beckley, Northiam, Brede, Udimore, Icklesham and
Winchelsea; 6529 entries, full details (no addresses), with streets &
addresses index included in book.   Includes descriptions of enumeration
districts.
Price - £2.95 collected or £3.27 by post.

Volume 3 HO107 1635 folios 1-232 ISBN 1 870264 02 9
Parishes of Guestling, Pett, Fairlight, Ore and All Saints, Hastings; 7005
entries including addresses; streets/addresses index included; descriptions of
enumeration districts also given.
Price - £3.30 collected or £3.61 by post.

Volume 4 HO107 1635 folios 233-476 ISBN 1 870264 03 7
Parishes of St.Clement and St.Mary in the Castle, Hastings.   Full details as
Volume 3. 8377 entries.
Price - £3.60 collected or £3.61 by post.

Volume 5 HO107 1635 folios 477-653 (end) ISBN 1 870264 04 5
Parishes Hastings - St. Michaels, St. Andrews, Holy Trinity, St.Mary in the
Castle outbounds; St.Leonards - St. Mary Magdalen, St.Leonards and St. Mary
Bulverhythe.   5767 entries, full details as Volumes 3 onwards.

To order these books please send cheque made payable to C.J. Barnes to -

Mrs. C. June Barnes,
50 St.Helens Parks Road,
Hastings.
East Sussex TN34 2DN

or phone (0424) 420065 to arrange collection.   If you wish to receive details
of future volumes please send a S.A.E. with your order.

- * -

NEXT IN THE SERIES

Volume 7

HO107 1636 folios 256-524 (end)
7537 full entries

PARISHES COVERED

Whatlington; Mountfield;
Battle
Brightling; Dallington; Penhurst
Ashburnham

- * -